A Choice of Inheritance

A Choice of Inheritance

Self and Community from
Edmund Burke to Robert Frost

David Bromwich

HARVARD UNIVERSITY PRESS
CAMBRIDGE, MASSACHUSETTS
LONDON, ENGLAND
1989

This book is printed on acid-free paper, and its binding materials
have been chosen for strength and durability.

Library of Congress Cataloging-in-Publication Data
Bromwich, David, 1951–
    A choice of inheritance : self and community from Edmund Burke to Robert Frost /
David Bromwich.
        p.   cm.
    Bibliography: p.
    Includes index.
    ISBN 0-674-12775-7 (alk. paper)
    1. English literature—History and criticism.   2. American
    literature—History and criticism.   3. Self in literature.
    4. Community in literature.   I. Title.
PR99.B73   1989   88-30411
820'.9—dc19   CIP

To George Kateb

Preface

THE ESSAYS that make up this book were written for various occasions over the last ten years. All but two of them have been published in journals or magazines, and they are reprinted here with few changes. "The Invention of Literature" and "Burke, Wordsworth, and the Defense of History" were written specially for the book, in order to give a wider meaning to certain concerns which the other essays share. It may be as well to say at the start what those concerns are.

My title adapts a phrase from the *Reflections on the Revolution in France*. It implies that something more than a memory binds the past with the present; and that the connection does not exist for us unless we choose it ourselves. I chose a diversity of subjects in the first place, and have felt it worthwhile to bring them together now, because I thought I could see versions of a single argument in the work of several authors from the end of the eighteenth century to the beginning of the twentieth. A motive for great writing throughout this period has been a tension, which is felt to be unresolvable, between the claims of social obligation and of personal autonomy. That these had to be experienced as rival claims was the discovery of Burke and Wordsworth. Our lives are lived today and our choices are made in a culture where any settlement of the contest for either side is bound to be provisional. There is nothing to approve or regret in such a situation; it is the way things are; and in a time like ours, it is what great writing lives on.

The word "literature" is more natural in English than "great writing," and I will use it from now on, but with a meaning that had better be explained. In the eighteenth century the field of letters properly included not only poems, novels, and plays but also works of moral philosophy, metaphysics, lectures, sermons, histories, tracts, and criticism. This sense of things appears to be coming back into general use; anyway, it is the sense that I am adopting here. Literature, thus conceived, is at home in a secular and democratic culture. Both in England and in America, that culture had its beginnings in the separation of books from official doctrine, from an enforced consensus, from the patronage of ladies and gentlemen and the supervision of academies. It leveled the institution with the individual, the great subjects of art with the humble.

Scholars of romanticism a generation ago talked about the psychology of the sublime. My own perspective has tended to be closer to that of moral philosophy. Under one description or another, I am usually writing about the necessary relationship among people in a community, by which a named person like the author is brought into contact with an unnamed person like the reader. This sense of relationship has its own bondage, and its own freedom. The argument I make for aesthetic autonomy is exactly as strong as the argument for personal autonomy; and, like the authors considered here, I write on different sides of the question at different times. With an argument that does have more than two sides, it is no use making a claim for thorough consistency—only for an accurate discernment of the size of the subject, and a right placement of occasional details. To treat a literary work as if it shared certain properties of a person seems to me a useful error, and I much prefer it to treating the work as plant-like, or machine-like, or as if it had the quality only of inhuman chance and accident.

If a political emphasis touches many of these essays, the reasons go back to the source of the point of view I have just described. Critics like Hazlitt, Shelley, and Leigh Hunt, whose thinking has shaped mine, were interpreters of the eloquent utterance at a moment of crisis—the sort of work or passage which makes us feel that, for the writer at that moment, everything depended on saying something truly and well. On their view literature was representative in a social and an aesthetic sense. It would remain so for as long as the writer moved us, said what no one else was saying, and had effects as unpredictable in other readers as in ourselves.

Yet, when thinking about romantic and modern authors, I have often been conscious of a mood of public-mindedness (whether real or affected) elsewhere in recent criticism, which expresses itself in a general distrust of literature. Moods can be persuasive without ever being embodied in an argument: this one, if thoroughly heeded, would again place books under the control of institutions. Accompanying the same tendency are hints of nostalgia for a republican ideology of art—a wish, I mean, to reduce to a practice the theory that individualism in the arts has gone too far. Modern decadence (in the conservative argument) or privatization (in the radical argument) can only be stopped by a return of faith in public scrutiny. The latter venture is to be guided, depending on one's preference, either by an elite or a popular vanguard.

The first three chapters in this book are anti-nostalgic. They suggest that we may be false to our actual beliefs in celebrating the public-mindedness of the eighteenth century; just as we are false to our own experience in deploring the individualism of the nineteenth. In either case we make a shallow mistake about the period in question. There is a strong continuity between the Enlightenment's discovery that history is made rather than given, that human nature is a story we tell about ourselves, and the most personal and idiosyncratic productions of modernism.

Some books survive however the reasons for reading them may change. In an essay "On Egotism," Hazlitt asked why that happened, and concluded: "Whatever interests, is interesting. I know of no way of estimating the real value of objects in all their bearings and consequences, but I can tell at once their intellectual value by the degree of passion or sentiment the very idea and mention of them excites in the mind." So, if one says that literature survives because of its truth to life, this does not imply fidelity to a set of facts, or adherence to a timeless standard of propriety. Rather it points to the consistency with which readers, for a long time, and with peculiar intensity, have admired a given work.

My sense of the nature of a canon follows from Hazlitt's understanding of interest. A canonical work is one that any participant in a culture feels obliged to come to know. In our time the canon has begun to be identified, in particular, with the drift of the university curriculum. Livelier, and not long past, moments of democratic culture showed a more unpredictable play of opinion between the canon and the curriculum. But taking the idea at its current value, some of the writers I discuss are canonical (Wordsworth, Keats, Emerson, Arnold), others have a reputation that is mainly popular (Kipling, Frost), while still others are neither canonical nor popular but warmly appreciated within a small circle (Cobbett, Edward Thomas). The last is a desirable sort of fame, from an author's point of view, because it draws the best readers. The universities, however, and the culture in general now leave a narrow margin between deepest obscurity and an ultra-legitimate respectability.

Whether and how a work is canonical is an adventitious matter. That is to say, it cannot be profitably discussed apart from one's personal estimate of the work in question. "What interests, is interesting": either the book holds or it fails to hold one's interest. Most of the recent debates in this area seem to me therefore to have started from wrong assumptions. Housed in a think tank, the new academician talks as if the future of civility itself could be decided by the reading of some books rather than others. Housed in a university, the new revolutionist talks as if genuine dissent were largely a matter of the successful displacement of some books by others. That these postures have become transparent suggests that the very word "canon" may soon be ready for retirement. With it will go unlamented a fund of sonorous nonsense concerning *the politics of interpretation*—for, to many who read and write, the politics of politics has an interest of its own.

As for the books we single out and come back to, something does depend on them. It does not matter greatly which ones we select (there are more to choose from than we can possibly know well); but a fair number should come from older, and other, ways of life than ours; and the list will be useless if it changes continually. Arrangements of this sort follow from a necessity merely of convenience. But it may be an important convenience. For, ultimately, "we" comes down to "one" and then to "oneself." A common knowledge of books exists for the good of keeping up a conversation among otherwise distinct readers.

Accordingly, these essays sometimes pass from interpretation to an account of the influence of books on those who care about them. I do not believe there is a right method for studying such things. To interpret an author is to construct a narrative about part of the world: one makes the effort from a wish to know whether others, who share one's interest, will also share certain impressions and be convinced by the pieces of texts and events that have been drawn into coherence. By contrast, the view that literature "creates its own world" is shared today by many connoisseurs, while the view that criticism exists to detect, or expose, or upset the contents of that world is shared by many anti-aesthetic theorists. The effect of these views is, in the first case, to exalt literature to a position of superior knowledge, and, in the second, to raise theory to an eminence from which literature itself may be known and regulated. The final two chapters in this book give reasons for concluding that neither standpoint is tenable.

Criticism has no professional knowledge to offer. I have written nevertheless from a hope that its findings may go some way to supply the human need for heroes. Who mine are will emerge in the pages that follow, emphatically enough. But a definition may still be asked for. Heroes are people who seem to know what others guess about the conditions of life; who give a strength to individual thought that is inseparable from social practices; who bring, with knowledge, belief, and with belief the hope of change or recovery. I ought to stress, since the point is often lost sight of, that one aims to honor the writing and not the writer. The person who bears the heroic name may be useful to know about, but only as a clue.

In revising, I have let stand certain repetitions of emphasis and argument, the result anyway of prejudices which were bound to emerge. With chapters that were first presented as public lectures, I have tried here to remove all merely local allusions. My rule about notes has been to identify in the text, where possible, the particular source that I was working with, and to supply a reference for every quotation of more than two sentences. The aim was to keep such interruptions to a decent minimum.

D.B.

Contents

I was not, like his Grace of Bedford, swaddled, and rocked, and dandled into a legislator; *"Nitor in adversum"* is the motto for a man like me. I possessed not one of the qualities, nor cultivated one of the arts, that recommend men to the favour and protection of the great. I was not made for a minion or a tool. As little did I follow the trade of winning the hearts, by imposing on the understandings, of the people. At every step of my progress in life, (for in every step was I traversed and opposed,) and at every turnpike I met, I was obliged to show my passport, and again and again to prove my sole title to the honour of being useful to my country, by a proof that I was not wholly unacquainted with its laws, and the whole system of its interests both abroad and at home. Otherwise, no rank, no toleration even, for me.

—Burke, "A Letter to a Noble Lord"

It is true, I admired the man; but what chiefly attached me to him, was his being, as he had been long ago designated, "the child and champion of the Revolution." Of this character he could not divest himself, even though he wished it. He was nothing, he could be nothing, but what he owed to himself and to his triumphs over those who claimed mankind as their inheritance by a divine right. . . . There were two other feelings that influenced me on this subject; a love of glory, when it did not interfere with other things, and the wish to see personal merit prevail over external rank and circumstance. I felt pride (not envy) to think that there was one reputation in modern times equal to the ancients, and at seeing one man greater than the throne he sat upon.

—Hazlitt, *The Life of Napoleon Buonaparte*

I

The Invention of Literature

LITERATURE IS A POWERFUL ABSTRACTION that did not always exist. It came to prominence about the same time as Man, and could be used in contrast either with books generally, or with books whose particular worth lay in their utility. In the same way, Man could be distinguished from the mere aggregate of men and women, or more strongly distinguished from the creatures with whom he shared only certain traits. The dominant sense of these two words was not necessarily "humanistic."

> For Hunger, or for Love, *They* bite or tear,
> Whilst wretched Man is still in Arms for Fear:
> For Fear he arms, and is of Arms afraid;
> From Fear to Fear successively betray'd.

Lord Rochester, when he wrote his "Satire against Mankind," would have seen books as an implicit part of his subject. Just as the decent habits of Man reshaped, but did not remove, a host of unameliorated instincts, so the manners of Literature grew partly separable from debates, panegyrics, instructions, all the persuasive or disciplined uses of words. On this analogy literary language and human nature are both answerable to brute sense. Yet Rochester only meant to challenge a trust in the efficacy of reason. The questions asked by a comparable skeptic today are likely to have a much wider scope. Anyone now who speaks of the universal, *man,* will be regarded doubtfully or at least ironically.

Has the same begun to be true of *literature?* I think it has; but it should be possible to give an account of how that has happened without ending in a resentment of literature; as, equally, one might give an account of the decline of man without therefore ending in anti-humanism. If the two accounts often do wind up in similar ways, the causes may be traced to an illiberal tradition of European modernism, which flourished between the wars for political reasons, and which, with the successful forgetting of those reasons, was still going strong in American translation as late as the 1980s. But that is the subject of another story, part of which is told in Chapter 15. I want here to give a partial survey of the fortunes of the literary ideal—literature, that is to say, in a special and nearly sublime sense it carried from 1790 to 1940 or so. My assumptions are that the belief in literature which we have lost was only ours to lose for about ten generations; and that the value it implied is best understood as a historical invention rather than a timeless discovery. Probably a different ideal will soon take the place of literature, and give a new name to public scenes of nondidactic instruction. Since there is no evidence that suggests the result will be an improvement on literature, I will not recite the later parts of the history gloatingly as others have done.

In the beginning literature was just books. Hume's *Treatise of Human Nature,* a founding text of modern philosophy, was in its time above all a work of literary ambition. When it "fell *dead-born from the press,*" the effect was temporarily to divert into other channels the talent in question. William Robertson's *History of Scotland,* in which Dr. John-son never took the interest Boswell hoped he would ("Sir, I love Rob-ertson, and I won't talk of his book"), was equally a candidate for the general fame of letters: hence the importance of getting it praised by the celebrated lexicographer and editor of Shakespeare. So, too, with Lord Kames's *Elements of Criticism;* with the *Letters* of Junius; with Beat-tie's *Essay on Truth*—there is no commonsense rule to order such a list, and no right method of restricting it. The *Elements, Letters,* and *Essay* once belonged all alike to literature, which Johnson's dictionary makes synonymous with "learning; skill in letters." A change in the word appeared gradually as a reader's knowledge of books like these (the virtue proper to an *homme de lettres*) was supplanted by the ability to cherish a better-defined set of books through reading them in a certain way. Among the nineteenth century's early tests of that ability were *The Sorrows of Young Werther* (read as a portrait rather than an author's confession) and *Paradise Lost* (read for its poetry and not its religious doctrine).

Thus the heroic age of literature comes after a special refinement of the common understanding of letters. Its first heroes are of the same stamp as the authors themselves: characters who, while they belong in fact to a particular social setting, belong in imagination to a solitary life. As for the reader, he was called upon to witness such characters in the process of being formed and reformed by their own ideas and sentiments. The works of the new school (Rousseau, Schiller, Godwin, Wordsworth, Stendhal) served as an incitement to people who could imagine becoming the heroes of their own lives. Of course, the authors of histories had already begun to teach the good of an affinity one might share with the persons and habits of another time. There was, they implied, in any portrait of an earlier period which one came to care for, both a deep intimation of identity and a peculiarly satisfying sense of distance. Romantic literature, of which autobiography is a defining genre, transfers the same attitude of ironic attachment to moments in an individual life.

Like the survivals of a remote period, the persistence of some aspect of a self can be looked at as if from afar. This analogy between ways of regarding an inward and an outward history may seem to derive largely from new habits of reading. But it has a psychological source as well. In an essay of 1868 entitled "Aesthetic Poetry," Walter Pater thought he could see a single motive for the emergent ideas of personal and historical recovery.

> In handling a subject of Greek legend, anything in the way of an actual revival must always be impossible. Such vain antiquarianism is a waste of the poet's power. The composite experience of all ages is part of each one of us; to deduct from that experience, to obliterate any part of it, to come face to face with the people of a past age, as if the Middle Age, the Renaissance, the eighteenth century had not been, is as impossible as to become a little child, or enter again into the womb and be born. But though it is not possible to repress a single phase of that humanity, which because we live and move and have our being in the life of humanity, makes us what we are, it is possible to isolate such a phase, to throw it into relief, to be divided against ourselves in zeal for it; as we may hark back to some choice space of our own individual life.[1]

On this view the conscious irony of the late historian, concerned with the intelligibility of a chosen revival, helps to explain the aesthetic attitude toward what is starting to be called literature. Both moods come from a sense of being "divided against ourselves in zeal" for something altogether personal. That is why a modern book of the early 1800s, whether peopled by real or imaginary characters, prefers to be read as a direct influence on the reader's thought and not an abstract monument. By the mere power of attention, it exhibits a single phase of humanity. In doing so it suggests an aspect of our lives under which art is no longer sunk in nature.

The first work of romantic theory to defend this way of reading is Schiller's *On Naive and Sentimental Poetry.* Writing in 1795, Schiller holds a definition of man as a self-legislating being: his ambitions for poetry fall in with his hopes for the widening of individual freedom and the amelioration of social life through reason. The essay aligns the naive with an early civilization and the sentimental with a late one; the naive, again, with nature and the sentimental with an "ideal" that follows from the mediation of nature by art. The second term appears, so far, to be the lower of two points in a decline. Yet Schiller also associates the naive with the *conditioned* and the sentimental with the *unconditioned;* the naive with mere existence and the sentimental with its modification by will; and, ultimately, the naive with the beautiful and the sentimental with the sublime. So the sentimental poet, though a lesser figure than the naive, is for Schiller the poet proper; for the same reason, he is a hero of invention who carries a good deal of weight in literature. From the sequence of definitions, one can infer that the sentimental marks the later standpoint that is necessary to create a historical perspective. It follows that the sentimental knows the naive as the latter cannot know itself. This conclusion, framed as a general thesis about literature, would become so central to criticism that it is worth recalling how Schiller arrived at it.

On Naive and Sentimental Poetry takes as a preliminary axiom that "Every true genius must be naive or it is not genius." And Schiller finds his model for this kind of naturalness in the ancients: *"They are what we were; they are what we should once again become.* We were nature just as they, and our culture, by means of reason and freedom, should lead us back to nature."[2] In arguing that only refined faculties can lead us back to the primary instincts that once were ours, Schiller makes plain the grounds of his leading paradox: that we are at once less capable than our naive exemplars, and more complexly gifted. We must strive to attain what they could be simply by virtue of being themselves. The naive thus comes to represent both the lost childhood of culture and an ideal discipline that still lies in the future: "We see in irrational nature only a happier sister who remained in our mother's house, out of which we impetuously fled abroad in the arrogance of our freedom."[3] Evidently, the prodigal son who does come back has a self-knowledge that is denied to all who have stayed at home. But there is yet a further paradox in Schiller's argument.

Aware, as he is, that the very presence of will (in the sentimental poet) betrays a need foreign to the person who is at one with his actions (as the naive poet must be), Schiller goes on to propose a dialectical relationship between the two modes of imagining.

> To the naive poet nature has granted the favor of functioning always as an undivided unity, to be at every instant an independent and complete whole, and to represent mankind, in all its significance, in actuality. Upon the sentimental poet she has conferred the power, or rather impressed a lively impulse, to restore out of himself that unity that has been disrupted by abstraction, to complete the humanity within himself and from a limited condition to pass over into an infinite one.[4]

If the naive poet can reveal, because he is part of, the nature that the sentimental poet can only wish to rejoin, still it is by the latter aim that we know a human consciousness. Granted that sentimental imitations of the naive, like the idyll or pastoral, can serve as a healing influence "only for the sick in spirit"; yet, if an aesthetic therapy is to have any chance of success, it must be followed out in all the effects of the disease. For what Schiller means by *completing the humanity* of an imaginative soul is not being healthy but becoming so.

There remains a final elaboration of the argument, in which the naive and sentimental are defined not as phases in the development of historical perspective or of self-consciousness, but rather as characteristic names for a natural antithesis in psychology. Whatever the other uses of this suggestion, in the present context it only explains away the force of the original contrast. If one assumes that the types are equally true for all places and times, then they turn into a romantic metaphor of symbiosis—one that, for practical criticism anyway, will be helpful mainly in picking up stray virtues associated with a classical ideal of balance. In fact, it was Schiller's move from the first, naturalistic understanding of his terms to the second, dialectical one that allowed for the invention of literature. Literature became the means by which an imagining of absent power could lead to self-recognition, even in a being whose powers were themselves limited and secondary. As for the author, he is a genius of recovery, who, for the sake of overcoming himself, is compelled to be self-conscious in his writing (as he cannot be in his life). To frame the matter less optimistically, a disease of consciousness is asked to cure itself by writing. But the only cure that writing can suggest is to think again.

It is fitting that the great attack on romanticism in the next generation, Carlyle's early essay "Characteristics," should have come as a challenge alike to literature and the very idea of consciousness. One says "early" of course, in deference to the pattern of his career, for the essay was published in 1831. But Carlyle was born in 1795, the same year as Keats:[5] putting it that way suggests how far this essay may have been the memorial of a generation he saw himself as already having outlived.

"Characteristics" presumes a terminology that Carlyle had lately worked out in "Signs of the Times" (1829), concerning a division between the "Mechanical" and the "Dynamical" nature of man. That distinction, as he sees it, cuts across science and art. The Mechanical is what the utilitarians have studied adequately; it stands for the outward life which divides man from himself. But to the Dynamical alone belongs imaginative power, whether in art or in science; and Carlyle identifies it with what is "free" and "unexpected," or unconditioned. About the inward life, which he wants to return us to, Carlyle's leading thought seems to be that *whatever has power cannot be known.* Above all, it cannot know itself. He will accordingly take such a phrase as "the dark forces of the mind" and use it in every variation that ingenuity offers, because the conjunction of darkness and force expresses what he believes to be a deep truth of our nature. The choice, however, of darkness as a metaphor for unconscious genius goes beyond any emphasis of Carlyle's predecessors. It points to the motives that will lead him eventually to exalt the brutal over the intellectual nature, and to identify tyranny with genius.

When Carlyle wrote "Characteristics," he had only come part of that journey. Indeed, what is striking about the essay is the extent to which it borrows the form of Schiller's argument for the sake of reversing the conclusion. We are asked from the first to consider all self-consciousness as a mark of disease: "The healthy know not of their health, but only the sick: this is the Physician's Aphorism; and applicable in a far wider sense than he gives it. We may say, it holds no less in moral, intellectual, political, than in merely corporeal therapeutics; that wherever, or in what shape soever powers of the sort which can be named *vital* are at work, herein lies the test of their working right or working wrong."[6] It is part of the essay's decorum that the physician's aphorism should stand for a while abstracted from the subject of consciousness. Instead, Carlyle affects a preoccupation with what he calls "Dietetic Philosophy": "Of our Thinking, we might say, it is but the mere upper surface that we shape into articulate Thoughts;—underneath the region of argument and conscious discourse, lies the region of meditation; here, in its quiet mysterious depths, dwells what vital force is in us; here, if aught is to be created, and not merely manufactured and communicated, must the work go on. Manufacture is intelligible, but trivial; Creation is great, and cannot be understood."[7] But Carlyle dwells not so much on the health of creation as on the disease that accompanies the want of it. A few years later, to remedy the same defect of invention, he will announce the dogma of sheer work. For the time being, however, he turns for encouragement to a more general analysis of the disease and its cure. The analysis is performed at a single stroke, by shifting the burden of genius from the individual to the race.

It is a startling transition. In the following passage Carlyle appeals to an unconscious sense of duty which holds, he says, in "the Body Politic" as much as in "the animal body": "This Idea, be it of devotion to a man or class of men, to a creed, to an institution, or even, as in more ancient times, to a piece of land, is ever a true Loyalty; has in it something of a religious, paramount, quite infinite character; it is properly the Soul of the State, its Life; mysterious as other forms of Life, and like these working secretly, and in a depth beyond that of consciousness."[8] That sentence brings out, more sharply than any other, a hidden motive for writing the essay. For Carlyle's questioning of all conscious activity was also meant as an attack on every social scheme of improvement; and this, in turn, is connected with his literary program. He wants to detach the genius of romanticism from the links that still bind it to the Enlightenment. When, therefore, he writes "The Self-consciousness is the symptom merely; nay, it is also the attempt towards cure," he is saying with cruel sarcasm what a romantic poet or critic would have believed with a conscious irony. The Immortality Ode, the Dejection Ode, Hazlitt's essays "On the Feeling of Immortality in Youth" and "Whether Genius Is Conscious of Its Powers?" all refer to the lesson that Carlyle's summary sentence makes oddly incredible. They hold off a relapse of the disease by a glimpse into the past, and by a creation of temporary order from whatever gift the past has given. It is understood that one may need several such returns in a lifetime, and also that any renewal is made only by thought itself and its medium, writing.

By contrast, the solution Carlyle looks for will operate once and for all, and will apply inclusively to the whole genius of the race. We can make something lasting for ourselves, he thinks, only if we annihilate all consciousness, and subsist instead in the silence of mere process: "The beginning of Inquiry is Disease: all Science, if we consider well, as it must have originated in the feeling of something being wrong, so it is and continues to be but Division, Dismemberment, and partial healing of the wrong. Thus, as was of old written, the Tree of Knowledge springs from a root of evil, and bears fruits of good and evil. Had Adam remained in Paradise, there had been no Anatomy and no Metaphysics."[9] We are still so much followers of the Enlightenment that it is difficult even to grasp quite what he is saying here. The twin virtues of silence and ignorance are to replace self-consciousness; and out of the resulting double negation Carlyle offers a new definition of man: "Our being is made up of Light and Darkness, the Light resting on the Darkness." The light of thought has ceased to be necessary except, perhaps, as a balancing metaphor, to keep up a romantic fiction of equipoise.

Like other metaphors that do the work of argument, Carlyle's darkness-and-silence can seem imprecise. Yet he is speaking not of what genius happens not to know, but of what it can choose not to know; and in showing this, both the metaphor and its reiteration serve his purpose well. A question may persist of the following sort: "How can an ignorant being know enough to choose to be ignorant?" But Carlyle in his final diagnosis seems to reckon with this:

Unconsciousness belongs to pure unmixed life; Consciousness to a diseased mixture of life and death: Unconsciousness is the sign of creation; Consciousness, at best, that of manufacture. So deep, in this existence of ours, is the significance of Mystery. Well might the Ancients make Silence a god; for it is the element of all godhood, infinitude, or transcendental greatness; at once the source and the ocean wherein all such begins and ends. In the same sense, too, have Poets sung "Hymns to the Night"; as if Night were nobler than Day; as if Day were but a small motley-colored veil spread transiently over the infinite bosom of Night, and did but deform and hide from us its purely transparent eternal deeps. So likewise have they spoken and sung as if Silence were the grand epitome and complete sum-total of all Harmony; and Death, what mortals call Death, properly the beginning of Life.[10]

He is meeting the question fairly; but his answer proves too much. The silent Ancients could not have praised silence in the manner Carlyle recommends, any more than the naive poet can *describe* the life from which he springs. These naturals are compelled to present rather than ever to represent that which they are. But it is wrong to stop dismissively at this fault of logic. For the ends he meant to serve, after all, Carlyle has produced a very satisfactory piece of mythmaking.

Schiller and Carlyle stand for two sides of a dialogue that goes on throughout the nineteenth century. They represent the meliorist of imagination and the skeptic. It is noteworthy that the meliorist, in every subsequent version as well, turns to a skepticism of his own with respect to a given founding ideal (the naive, or nature, or the self), while the skeptic has to appeal from general doubts to a particular myth of unconsciousness (an untraceable power in language or knowledge or material life).[11] Yet from both sides, poetry goes on being seen as exemplary rather than casual in its relations with human life. This seems a constant fact of romantic thinking about literature. The apparent effect may be a grave assurance of solidarity:

> What we have loved,
> Others will love, and we will teach them how;

or a return to the tokens of personal will that can be found only in certain ceremonies:

> Shall I at least set my lands in order?

Writers as different as Wordsworth and Eliot agree, in moments like these, that poetry has an inventive rather than a derivative knowledge, and that literature itself mediates the passage from old to new practices.

But Schiller's initial understanding of the naive, as an unqualified good, and Carlyle's rhapsody on the hymns of darkness and silence also exhibit two ways in which speculation on writing may grow indifferent to literature. The first exalts a particular phase of spontaneous existence, to the discovery of which literature is merely a pretext. The second looks upon writing, as well as speech, for testimony concerning the primary life of duty and action. It is false to think that literary theory or criticism will touch these extremes only at certain aberrant moments. Since the invention of literature, the idea that the theory of poetry is the theory of life has carried conviction only in a narrow defile between these rival versions of general distrust. Even in the 1810s and 1820s, when an aesthetic point of view was likeliest to appeal to many readers, it failed to achieve the coherence that might have been expected. The reasons for this are plain if one looks at the careers of Francis Jeffrey and William Hazlitt: critics who tried to pursue, the first in an institutional and the second in a personal way, some implications of a Humean idea of the critic as a qualified judge.

Hume had begun by imagining a culture divided between two worlds, which he calls the learned and the conversable. The learned, broadly speaking, concerns itself with the mind and nature, with what would later come to be called science, for in learned pursuits there seems to be a dispassionate relation between the student and the subject of research. The people working in this line are pictured as solitary: they commune chiefly with their own thoughts; and it is assumed that most of them will be men. The conversable world, on the other hand, is involved with society, social affections, and the judgments proper to social existence. It is sustained by mutual civility—the regular communication of thoughts and feelings, the softening of manners by commerce with other manners—and its inhabitants for the most part are women. Thus Hume, in his early writings, appears to have conceived of the learned world as a retreat in which pure knowledge flourishes. It is as it were a sealed chamber, beyond which occasional sojourns are allowed in a living room presided over by conversable women, whose company (Hume thinks) will give profitable relief to the heroes of the mind.

And yet in his later writings he gives up that conception altogether. The discussions of the learned and conversable worlds are now felt to be civilizing only so far as they are somehow reciprocally influential. One can feel here that the idea of a discourse peculiar to science has at last been reduced to a thing barren of interest. Or, if it interests at all, it does so only as a medium for the "monkish virtues" which Hume aims to discredit. Worthwhile knowledge is always in some measure sociable; it includes an idea of the listener who can give a reply; and this is a good that conversation alone can bring, whether to the authors of books or the adepts of lonely research. Discoveries may, of course, happen and talk may go on, even while the two worlds exist separately. But a culture takes its practical shape when the two start to matter to each other. [12]

This was the tenor of Hume's thinking when he wrote "Of the Standard of Taste." The judge there is described as someone who knows that taste is a kind of knowledge which conversation has brought into being. He, or she, is accordingly a person in whom certain habits of assigning value to an object have become second nature. There will always be a ready objection to such a definition of judgment: namely, that the particular choices by which it vindicates itself are apt to be more capricious than the very dignity of consensus has implied. One needs to recall in this regard Hume's confidence that a taste for Bunyan (rather than, say, Addison) would be cited by people long after his age as an epitome of transparent error. And yet his false prediction in no way upsets his general argument. He was saying that in questions about taste, coherence of judgment is both desirable and attainable within a culture. I use the anachronistic word "culture" to suggest what Hume was thinking of rather than the more accurate "society"— but at the cost of making a circular statement, since on his view there is never a culture without some such coherence.

Now a critic like Jeffrey, however imperfectly, was doing the work that Hume prescribed. He was doing it as much when he tried to remove Wordsworth from the map of English poetry as when, many years later in a private letter to Dickens, he confessed that "my heart [was] purified by those tears" that came from reading the death of Paul Dombey, and assured the author that he had "blessed and loved you for making me shed them." [13] Jeffrey was in fact an advocate and later a judge: professions, on the Humean argument, not at all incongruous for a critic. Under his direction the *Edinburgh Review* affected to judge new books by the canons of genuine fame rather than party prejudice; and in these matters even the affectation of a disinterested judgment is significant. If, nevertheless, a suspicion of mediocrity still clings to the *Edinburgh* translation of Hume, it is because that journal claimed a kind of authority which made its failures thoroughly visible. Hazlitt is Jeffrey's antithesis in this as in other respects. He saw himself as a steady, if ironic, advocate of original work no matter how odd, though he stopped short of offering material proofs of his delicacy. Maybe it is more convenient than true to think of either of these critics as the representative of a conscious tradition. But they do call to mind two distinct emphases within the work of public criticism. For many years after they wrote—indeed, for most of a century—these types were responsive to each other; and for as long as they were, a writer who pursued the theory of poetry in Schiller's way could be made conversable in Hume's way.

Jeffrey was a literary academician in an age before literary academies.

He claims to speak adequately for a body of opinion that already exists, but that has been waiting for someone like him to supply its correct formulation. In his school of taste, genius means among other things a *dangerous* idiosyncrasy. What he looks for instead, to express the feelings of a community that knows itself well enough, is pragmatic talent with a decent leavening of rhetorical skill. By contrast, Hazlitt begins from a supposition that the works of the present day can be sorted out chiefly by their uniqueness (as if that were a part of their excellence). In gaining credence for his views, he appeals only to himself, or rather to his experience as a reader. Public opinion, he trusts, will take care of itself, and thus correct the estimate of any author he has failed to treat with candor. To Jeffrey's review of *The Spirit of the Age,* which had called it brilliant but, in effect, too much an affair of genius, Hazlitt replied in one of his rare effusions of verse:

> The rock I'm told on which I split
> Is bad economy of wit—
> An affectation to be thought
> That which I am and yet am not,
> Deep, brilliant, new, and all the rest:
> Help, help, thou great economist
> Of what thou ne'er thyself possest.

Still in the same vein, "The Damned Author's Address to his Reviewers" ends with a salute to the editor whom Hazlitt elsewhere called "a Scotchman without one particle of hypocrisy, of cant, of servility, or selfishness in his composition":

> Teach me, great J————y, to be dull!

What is curious about the development of English criticism in the nineteenth century is how both types persist, warily respectful of each other's claims, but each without a hope of ever interesting the reader who could take the other for a guide. With Hazlitt, in any division of this sort, belong Coleridge and, of a slightly younger group, Leigh Hunt and John Hamilton Reynolds; in the middle Victorian generations, Hallam, Ruskin, and Morris in England, and Emerson, Thoreau, and Margaret Fuller in America; and at the end of the century, Pater, Wilde, Yeats, and Lionel Johnson. Among Jeffrey's successors are John Morley, Edmund Gosse, George Saintsbury, and the earnest critics of smaller pretensions whose way of life John Gross described vividly in *The Rise and Fall of the Man of Letters.*

In this confused company, Matthew Arnold appears as the first sponsor of a reconciliation between public opinion and personal judgment in aesthetics. Nobody could have succeeded here, least of all an aesthete with a bad conscience: that is why Arnold's "touchstones" (with their fancied utility and real idiosyncrasy) are untranslatable, in just the manner he had hoped methodically to overcome. Better compromises were achieved with less fuss by intellectuals like Walter Bagehot and Leslie Stephen, whom we no longer read as part of the same story because it is hard to think of them mainly as critics. Whatever one makes of these late nineteenth-century arguments, social consensus and originality in the arts do not naturally move in the same direction; but the weight of their drive against each other was probably good for criticism, as long as the attacks could be kept up. That some larger good will ever be served by a resolution of the contest, in favor either of "the public" or a "fit audience" alone, is a fantasy in which the academic conformist and the aesthetic connoisseur have always agreed.

Literature, in the argument I have been sketching, never aimed at becoming a special discipline of humanity. Nevertheless it was in time specialized by the terms of the discourse it had generated: at first, by the sense of historical irony with which an aesthetic idea of culture had to be tempered; and later, by the susceptibility of the idea itself to disenchantment, with the consequent transfer of interest from art to action and from the individual to the race. At the same time, literature was coming to be defined from outside more contingently than any theorist had expected, by the several publics an author would have to know in the length of a career. Hardly anyone did in the short run create the taste by which his work was truly to be judged. That is another way of saying no single intelligent audience came together for the reception of many books. From the point of view of the early romantics, such failure was often experienced as a personal catastrophe; even if, as they would have allowed, a limited failure may leave the mind less prostrate than an unresisting success. It is true that the ambitions once cherished for the writer as a center of forces got a fresh start in America in the 1840s and 1850s. But Emerson and his readers belonged to a society in which the belief that social distinctions were vanishing had already taken a strong hold. For the author here thinking about his likely or possible audience, a difference in numbers did not necessarily point to a difference in kind.

The idea (which is also a faith) that books have the power to free "imprisoned thoughts, far back in the brain of man," and that the poets therefore are "liberating gods," survives quite late in American writing peculiarly. It accounts for the mood in which Stevens can say of a chosen book:

> It reminded him how he had needed
> A place to go to in his own direction.

The book that has grown personal to a reader is now a metaphor for any native place that may be shared with others. But the place itself is hardly more than a direction, a drift of things. One might of course describe this late version of aesthetic individuality as a kind of propaganda for literature. Once, however, it became possible to say with Stevens that the theory of poetry is the theory of life, how could literature help being propaganda for itself?

Such moods of self-confidence are in fact an anomalous survival. If two distinct elements were necessary to the invention of literature—an argument about the consciousness of writers, and an argument about the circumstances of readers—the division of labor in criticism never quite allowed these to meet in one thinker. Indeed, the story of English literature in the nineteenth century is largely a story of their failure to meet. By the middle Victorian generations, to work for a popular audience means to be unadventurous in ideas; and yet, as Orwell pointed out in his essay on Dickens, this is now looked on simply as a necessary condition of fame. Chesterton was responding to the same situation when he said of the only great writer of the nineties: "Mr. Kipling is by divine caprice and natural genius an unconventional poet; but what he desires more than anything else to be is a conventional poet." About this time the debate between the aestheticism of Schiller and the anti-aestheticism of Carlyle turns into an argument about high and low in matters of culture generally. Something similar happens also to the debate between Hazlitt and Jeffrey about the good of personal taste and the worth of consensus. Every available position has begun to narrow emphatically, so that the ambivalence, for example, of the early romantics concerning their audience as well as the scope of their own ambitions, has ceased to be a live option even among poets. One can get a fair idea of the change by the extreme stances of Tolstoy and Yeats in writings a few years before and a few years after the turn of the century.

Defending an aesthetic point of view, Yeats now takes it for granted that the method proper to his work will be artificial (to the point of being esoteric). Defending a moral point of view, Tolstoy takes it for granted that the sentiments proper to his work will be natural (to the point of being commonplace). Neither argument would have been mounted with anything like this reductiveness even a generation before. Tolstoy, if one recasts his argument in Schiller's original terms, is interested in the naive of "temperament": a steady ideal of social being which, for Tolstoy, need not be a thing of the past. As an opposite term, Schiller had proposed the naive of "surprise": the flash of sublime simplicity, in a soul so refined that such things could not be expected from it. Schiller thought that only a break in an utterance could make us conceive of an earlier, unbroken, wholly characteristic mode of natural feeling; surprise and temperament were, at least in this way, always related. But Tolstoy in *What Is Art?* accepts the category of the naive without any such elaboration. He simply associates genuine art with temperament, and meretricious art with surprise.

So he makes a point of dismissing all that is *striking* or *interesting*— originality on his view being never much more than novelty. The new may be superior to the perverse, or to the preeningly artificial, but only to the degree that it makes an accurate representation. Tolstoy adds dryly that accuracy of this sort has always been common enough in anecdote or history: it is not to be cherished in itself. For the mark of genuine art is that it teaches love of God, and union among human beings. One recalls that Schiller, looking for a naive good deed, had told of the storyteller who describes a wretch expiring of poverty, and so causes his own son to steal his purse for the sake of the fictional sufferer. It was a deliberate irony that this high-minded parable could be a subject of art only for the sentimental poet. Yet the same example fits Tolstoy's idea of a naive Christian art which carries a timeless value. Such art repairs the split between imagination and morality that has been created by aesthetic self-consciousness.

"Every work of art," for Tolstoy, "causes the receiver to enter into a certain kind of relationship both with him who produced, or is producing, the art, and with all those who, simultaneously, previously, or subsequently, receive the same artistic impression."[14] From a modern perspective, this seems to be a definition of the stock response: in denying the individuality of the creator, it also denies the separateness of each member of the audience from the others. Yet, as Tolstoy argues, an appeal to readers or spectators, under the aspect of their differentness, can only lead to mannerism in the artist, and to idle affectation in those whom he persuades to take the work seriously. The leading thought of *What Is Art?* is that the very identity which unites author and reader may also unite reader and reader: "A real work of art destroys, in the consciousness of the receiver, the separation between himself and the artist—not that alone, but also between himself and all whose minds receive this work of art. In this freeing of our personality from its separation and isolation, in this uniting of it with others, lies the chief characteristic and the great attractive force of art." [15] In this way and no other, Tolstoy concludes, we may pass from an inscrutable art with various aims and achieve at last a transparent art with unified aims.

Yeats is the modern writer who sought, most consistently, to restore poetry to a thorough self-possesion:

> The rhetorician would deceive his neighbours,
> The sentimentalist himself; while art
> Is but a vision of reality.

That sentence appears in "Ego Dominus Tuus," the poem he gives as a foreword to *Per Amica Silentia Lunae;* and the lines are echoed later in the prose of the same work: "We make out of the quarrel with others, rhetoric, but of the quarrel with ourselves, poetry." Both formulas are meant to be weighed strongly against an emphasis both exclude: that the subject of art is union with others and the love of God. But Yeats himself was frank enough about the reasons for the exclusion—"All my thoughts have been drowned by an undisciplined sympathy." The suggestion is that a disciplined sympathy will touch only one's individual fate, without any thought or feeling which merely "comes to mind because another man has thought or felt something different." Instead of an attachment to others, poetry now projects "the other self, the anti-self or the antithethical self," which under whatever name "comes but to those who are no longer deceived, whose passion is reality." Being deceived is here pretty closely identified with having motives apart from self-reflection—from which a low kind of art will degenerately follow, as rhetoric follows poetry. Poetry, on the other hand, belongs to a reality known by oneself, as a passion may be known.

Such asceticism even in Yeats is frequently at odds with other impulses. He still believes for example that poetry is a recognition of nature ("the heart's discovery of itself"), and that this is only possible to a late consciousness already separated from nature. But for him the recognition does not have to dwell on aspects of the moral world—the good of mankind, or the practice of treating one's fellow men and women as ends. Rather poetry aspires to a self-knowledge that is achieved for its own sake and resists translation; except as a poet's life may be translated by his work, or a poet's work by his life. Curiously, therefore, it is Tolstoy rather than Yeats who most preserves the affective range of the early aesthetic ideal: above all, the concern with the aggregate wills of people living at a certain time, and with an idea of conduct which they share. Yet in order to preserve these, he has been compelled to detach the ideal from whatever discipline may be unique to poetry. With this last specialization of aesthetic and moral thought, the confidence of the high age of literature was already nearing its end.

Tendentious histories usually close with a sort of jeremiad. But the golden age in question here was rather short for that. For a certain period, literature was the honorific term that described a well-understood class of objects. Its adequacy to the task is less plain now than it was in 1917 when Yeats wrote his epigrams, or even fifty years later, when the academies had more or less caught up with Yeats. Some causes of the change are sufficiently clear without our having to suppose that the production of suitable objects has dropped off very steeply. In art as in science, discovery easily passes into refinement, and refinement into sophistication, among those who talk habitually of things that were once unfamiliar. At present, the whole field of humane letters is in the process of being redescribed in the jargon of the nonempirical social sciences. Shadows of an older language keep up a fugitive half-life anyway. Hence the obscure allusions to "the body" in recent criticism, by earnest persons who are struggling not to say the intolerable word "soul." But theology will not complete the work that anthropology leaves unfinished. Without the aid of either, it remains worth asking what a poem does that a political oration, or a newspaper report of some natural or human catastrophe, does not ever do. Here the best answers are likely to come in parables.

Robert Frost in "The Wood-Pile" tells of walking in a swamp on a gray day, when his mind was on nothing, or when, from sheer want of purpose, he was coming close to a thought of self-annihilation. He is in a place "Too much alike to mark or name a place by"; and, for himself, "I was just far from home." He passes a bird who knows enough to hide from him; and then, he sees a pile of wood: "It was a cord of maple, cut and split / And piled—and measured, four by four by eight." Carefully stacked, but sunk some way into the ground and almost dragging free of the props that held it, this survival from a human will now past recovery seems to summon the traveler beyond his thoughts and fears.

> I thought that only
> Someone who lived in turning to fresh tasks
> Could so forget his handiwork on which
> He spent himself, the labor of his ax,
> And leave it there far from a useful fireplace
> To warm the frozen swamp as best it could
> With the slow smokeless burning of decay.

The wood-pile is the work of someone's art, in the sense that it is a thing made for a reason, which stands apart from natural things. Its purpose has in the course of time become inscrutable to the passerby. Yet for this person without a destination, it brings a thought of a less aimless journey for himself.

What the wood-pile does by accident for its discoverer, the work of art does by design for its reader or witness. It brings a thought of purpose, even of energy without purpose. It, too, at least to our later sight, has always sunk some way into the conditions that formed it, and what remains is only a shape, or a sense that something *has* been shaped. That is the kind of meaning it cares for, from reader to reader, or from witness to witness. Thus its appearance is for us an incitement to attention. But such a work, if I have the parable right, means to tell us very little about the maker's inward humanity. We learn almost nothing about this poem's narrator, except what he reads in the landscape; and nothing much of the wood-pile, except the useless care its maker took.

A critic who greatly admired "The Wood-Pile," Edward Thomas, wrote the following sentences before he had seen the poem:

Men understand now the impossibility of speaking aloud all that is within them, and if they do not speak it, they cannot write as they speak. The most they can do is to write as they would speak in a less solitary world. A man cannot say all that is in his heart to a woman or another man. The waters are too deep between us. We have not the confidence in what is within us, nor in our voices. Any man talking to the deaf or in darkness will leave unsaid things which he could say were he not compelled to shout, or were it light; or perhaps he will venture once—even twice—and a silence or a foolish noise prohibits him. But the silence of solitude is kindly; it allows a man to speak as if there were another in the world like himself; and in very truth, out of the multitudes, in the course of years, one or two may come, or many, who can enter that solitude and converse with him, inspired by him to confidence and articulation.[16]

It is always for this solitude, Thomas implies, that literature comes to be written.

The result matters on the page, as it cannot always do aloud, or in professional colloquy; because on the page it carries a trace of effort, and there alone "it must acknowledge the spiritual forces which have made it."[17] In a time eager for moral certainty, the work of art is often held answerable, more than other works of uncertain utility, for the failures of a general life which it can influence only by chance. To defend it honorably, one need not go back to an idea of aesthetic autonomy, of which the more skeptical romantics were free from the start. A poem or story or painting has a place among the conditions of life, and for its creation other conditions were necessary. But among the objects of interest, we incline to use it differently from the rest. Concerning a poem which has survived a generation or more, we know in advance that we cannot say whose view it may have opened on fresh tasks, maybe for the first time, or again when the way seemed closed. With a great work it is too early to say for sure. This questioning of ends marks no tentativeness as to the size of the claim in question. A vision of reality is usually saying that it is a vision. At the same time, it obliges us to wonder how we can wish for more than that. It means to give an image of life, with the permanence proper to such an image, for the benefit of those with imagination.

2

Reflections on the Word Genius

THIS CHAPTER WILL TRY TO SAY what can still be said for the idea of genius, but to do that one needs to define the word carefully, since from long disuse its outlines have grown indistinct. My procedure will be simple. I begin by illustrating two different emphases the word was made to bear in eighteenth-century discussions of art and knowledge—or, as it was then called, science. Following the broader of these emphases into the nineteenth century, I trace the work of genius as a continuous enterprise in thinkers of three successive generations: a poet; his disciple, a philosopher of morals and science; and a reader of the philosopher who became a leading scientist in the next age. This is a story that has been told in parts, but, pursuing the maxim of shallow analysis, I enforce the necessary distinctions to make it feel like a whole. The range of subjects involved points to some such treatment in any case, and the relationships I describe all belong to a larger story that will be generally familiar: the displacement of the idea of nature by an idea of history. Since the interest of the topic may seem remote, I want to start by saying what it has to do with matters of present concern.

If we think of the artist, the philosopher, and the scientist together as engaged in interpretation, we can see that they share a common fate. Let us define an interpreter as a persuasive observer whose theory of a family of objects may acquire the authority of fact. What if he succeeds? The new kind of fact he has helped to create then becomes a datum against which the next group of interpreters can test their knowledge, until eventually the fact gives way. Once that happens it is renamed the bad or partial theory of an earlier time, and the interpreter joins the company of those who gave way to him for equally sound reasons. A series of such transitions yields our most available conception of intellectual advance. Here advance does seem the right word rather than progress, to guard against any suggestion that the change must have been for the better, and to make a recognition that anyway there is no turning back. We have had representations of this process from several points of view. Kuhn's studies of the psychology of research show how resourcefully scientists are able to defend their practice against an unforeseen challenge, with every tactic from resistance to redefinition of the object of research.[1] Stanley Fish's "interpretive communities," which assure their own stability by accommodating new readings, and Michel Foucault's *epistemes,* which give "the conditions in which [man] can sustain a discourse about things that is recognized to be true," are attempts to describe the groups and conditions in which the same process is at work outside science.[2] I will comment briefly on the last two of these writers.

Fish is concerned with academic critics of literature in the English-speaking world. His subject is the durability of a profession through its adjustment of a large body of assumptions which are always changing and always in force. Or, to put it another way: how the revolutionary literary science of 1945 becomes the normal science of 1960 and the exploded superstition of 1975, and yet the study of literature goes on. His typical demonstration may take us from a pre–New Critical reading of a poem, to a New Critical reading, to a structuralist or poststructuralist reading. These changes look important now and therefore seem to point a moral: the interpreter must cooperate with a mostly visible consensus in order to be heard when he seeks to modify it. There remains a question whether these changes will turn out to look important by comparison with others that took place over a comparable interval. One thinks, for example, of the mutation in the habits of thought and feeling that separates Milton's poetry from Dryden's. Again, to take a case of divergent readings of a particular text, one needs more help in moving from Johnson to Blake on the subject of *Paradise Lost* than in moving from the tame New Critical interpreter to the shocking poststructuralist. Fish, in short, deals with community on a modest scale, and with professionals whose relation to an understood consensus is constant and intimate. There seem to be writers who differ from these, in degree only but in important degree. His analysis is of course infinitely extensible to them, but it is not clear that it could pick out much beyond the accommodations that made them intelligible.

The culture Foucault writes about is not limited to a profession. It is, as he describes it, a finely organized network of power and knowledge, in which our possible choices of action and our minutest efforts of observation or self-description are in place when we arrive on the scene. At any moment Foucault selects to represent a culture, it is already a total system. Its conditions are not determined by anyone or anything in particular; they are inscribed without being inscribed *by;* they exhibit a form of life by virtue of their transparence. Such conditions, Foucault appears to believe, are best figured as metaphors, and he can write accordingly about social discipline as modeled on an entity like the panopticon. The texts that chiefly interest him are in fact textbooks of control which say more than they know, and say it by means of some commanding metaphor. The result is an account of the unacknowledgeable laws that shape our history. While Foucault tells us that one *episteme* is replaced by another, he cannot ever convincingly show what this looks like; and the reason, I believe, is that on his view the movement cannot in principle be traced in a single mind.

Now it seems to me that large and consequential changes do sometimes come about as a result of what happened in the mind of one thinker. And genius, I will be arguing, was a good name for this sort of thinker. The word dominated nineteenth-century discussions of interpretation and community, and it is only beginning to pass from view. This seems to me an accidental and not a necessary loss. It does not follow from a rejection of the idea that great works evolve by laws of their own, apart from human purposes. Nor is it a natural corollary of skepticism about the metaphysics of presence. For a long time, critics attached to neither of these ideals used the word to mean a poet or philosopher or scientist who, in a question of great importance, led his audience to change one perspective for another, and did so in a way that made them more conscious of his invention than of his accommodation with others in his field. The change, these critics often implied, was accomplished by the same means as the remoldings of opinion that we all engage in from day to day, but its effect was more visibly to alter an existing state of things. The sense of genius I mean to explore is thus closely related to Carlyle's idea of heroism and Emerson's of the representative man; but to show its value I have to return first to certain suggestions of the etymology.

As far back as the word can be traced, a "genius" was a tutelary deity or demon, so that by a routine transfer of meaning one could speak of the genius of a place, or for that matter of an entire race or community, as well as of the genius for a certain kind of enterprise. Edward Young's *Conjectures on Original Composition* (1759) affords the first modern association of genius with individual power, or with what we have come to call originality. The aim of Young's argument is to deprecate all imitation, but his mode is prayer against those who do tempt us to imitate: "For by the bounty of nature," he writes, "we are as strong as our predecessors"—meaning, in other words, "Nature, grant us to be as strong"—and he adds that "we stand on higher ground" than they, for "as to the *first,* were *they* more than men? Or are *we* less?"[3] The answer is that we are not less so long as we retain a faith in genius as directly inspired by nature. Young's man of genius can bear no stimulus or motive for his work; any commerce with tradition, like conscious thought itself, stands in the way of discovery; we are all in this sense the familiars of genius at birth and fading ever after: "Born *Originals,* how comes it to pass that we die *Copies?*" The aphorism, with its sad extravagance, is a fair enough deduction from Young's earlier assertion that "genius is from heaven, learning from man."[4] It is notable that Johnson, though aware of this latest turn in the use of the word, excluded from his *Dictionary* any mention of genius in Young's sense.

He would have seen it correctly as tending to remove the individual mind from history; his own preferred words in the *Lives of the Poets* are "original" and "invention." The uses he does allow stop with the peculiar bias to be found in someone "of large general powers, accidentally determined to some particular direction."[5] The *Dictionary's* best illustration comes from Pope in the *Essay on Criticism:* "One science only will one genius fit, / So vast is art, so narrow human wit." One notices here that "science" as knowledge of any sort, and "art" as the field of exercise for human skill, are also kept to their older senses. Johnson's was an Enlightenment concern lest art set up pretensions beyond the knowledge of a community; and where Young believed that "a *genius* differs from a *good understanding,* as a magician from a good architect," Johnson would have cared only for the difference between the original and the competent architect. These share the common end of providing a habitation for mortals. Thus, though we may sympathize with Young's daring, it is Johnson's motives after all that feel closer to ours. He regards invention as a thing apart, done by the artist alone, but from the tacit contributions of earlier inventors and for the sake of later appreciators.

In William Duff's *Essay on Original Genius* (1767), the word moves a step away from the sharp contrast with talent that one finds in Young, and a step closer to Johnson's emphasis on its steady relation to competence. The proximity of dates between Young's essay and Duff's is in fact misleading: Young was born forty-nine years earlier, lived with the great secondary monuments of neoclassicism all around him, and could easily suppose that an ideal of imitation had established itself for decades to come. Duff, looking back, could see that nothing like this had occurred—by the time he wrote, the consensus had already been shaken by the new poetry of Thomson and Collins. Partly for this reason, his argument for genius is less absolute than Young's, and his protest against tradition less desperate. It is true that he writes sometimes in Young's style of a "perfectly original" genius, and like Young he cultivates the miraculous belief that "a Poet of original Genius has very little occasion for the weak aid of Literature: he is self-taught. He comes into the world as it were completely accomplished."[6] Yet his admiration for Longinus, his decision to follow him in making oratory a central rather than a marginal case of genius, and his recognition of memory as a necessary faculty to the orator all stop him from affirming that genius may choose to repel tradition. It is rather the good fortune of the earliest poets that they had none to repel. Poets, however, are not Duff's sole concern, and he writes unexpectedly of the genius of philosophical science as being gifted with "accuracy of imagination."[7] I am not aware that the two words *accuracy* and *imagination* were ever before joined in this way. It is the first hint of a convergence between the ideas of genius in science and in art, and it was taken up almost in concert by several writers in the early decades of the nineteenth century.

The most intelligent of those who devoted whole essays to the topic are Hazlitt and Shelley. In Hazlitt's essay "On Genius and Common Sense," accuracy and imagination have not quite become synonyms, but he thinks it pointless to worry much about the distinction. Indeed, the difference between genius and common sense is mainly a difference between great and small occasions for the use of the mind: Hazlitt defines genius as "some strong quality in the mind, answering to and bringing out some new and striking quality in nature";[8] common sense—which he renames "tacit reason"—is not the antithesis of genius but its near ally. On this view the acquisitions of genius pass naturally into the keeping of common sense. A more vivid way of expressing it, with a more familiar pair of opposites, is that the imagination of one age becomes the understanding of the next. As for tradition, genius must be a collaborator in it, whether happily or not— happily at any rate in the work of Milton, of whom Hazlitt says in another place that "his learning had the effect of intuition." That phrase catches very well Shelley's sense of the effect that all poetry has. And by poetry he meant genius, to judge by the character of his illustrations: not only Shakespeare, Milton, and Dante, but the writings of Lord Bacon and the legal institutions of ancient Rome. When he calls poets "the unacknowledged legislators of the world," or again "mirrors of the gigantic shadows which futurity casts upon the present," the moral is not that they are the true though unheralded politicians of the present day, but that we will be acting out their readings of life in our daily lives in the future, even if their names are forgotten. We inherit their learning as intuition.

Shelley believed that the highest part of genius, and what makes it a kind of prophecy, is its divination of a human truth before the sense of it has become common. We may look on the result if we like as a discovery about the nature of things, but we experience it as a modification of our idea of nature in time; it matters to us for the encouragement it gives to connect our habitual self-image with our knowledge of the past. We can do this, according to Shelley, only through the understanding of metaphor. "Their language," he says of poets— and since he means something more than poets he evidently refers to language in the widest sense—"Their language is vitally metaphorical; that is, it marks the before unapprehended relations of things and perpetuates their apprehension, until the words which represent them become, through time, signs for portions or classes of thoughts instead of pictures of integral thoughts; and then if no new poets should arise to create afresh the associations which have been thus disorganized, language will be dead to all the nobler purposes of human intercourse."[9] However we may describe Shelley's intellectual loyalties in general, his thinking about metaphor is nominalist, historical, and pragmatic; and since in this it anticipates what seem to me the most adequate recent accounts of metaphor,[10] I want to comment on several implications of the passage. Shelley writes of a faculty by which we bring together observation and interpretation in a single act: the word *marks* in the context has to mean "endows with significance" as well as "points out." Yet the special significance we choose to assign comes not from apprehending things in themselves but the relations of things to each other. Further, if, as Shelley tells us, the relation does not matter until it is marked and carries no force unless it is perpetuated, it follows that discovery and justification are inseparable elements for the survival of a metaphor, far apart as they may be in time. Finally, there is nothing mysterious in the movement Shelley observes from living metaphors which are "pictures of integral thoughts" to dead metaphors which are "signs for portions of classes of thoughts." I take him to mean that a living metaphor is understood without analysis, as a consequence and then a cause of the way we look at nature. Once we do grow conscious of using it figuratively, so that we say to ourselves, "This is a metaphor. How illuminating it is, within its limits of course," then the metaphor is already dead.

To come to some commonplace illustrations, one might say that Foucault's network of power and knowledge is living and therefore perceptible to us as metaphor only in an official sense: nobody but a pedant would place the network on one side, power and knowledge on the other, and remark how curiously vehicle and tenor were combined. On the other hand, consider the older and related expression "climate of opinion." This is now almost dead, the casualty perhaps of a re-meshing of opinions within the network, which has not allowed the atmosphere to settle for long. "Currents of thought" died some years ago because we could no longer, even for academic purposes, imagine our relation to the past as that of a stream to its source. None of these phrases is good enough to be poetry by Shelley's standards, but I resist exposing them by contrast with examples from poetry because it seems to me that they bring out the larger distinction he has in view. When a metaphor is dead, we can go around in back of it and see what made it tick. But while it is living we cannot in a sense even see it; we are too busy seeing with it. Because there are rival theorists who regard with suspicion either metaphor-as-such or its routine incorporation in the life of a culture,[11] it needs to be added that Shelley saw the inventions of genius through metaphor as a means of freeing rather than enslaving man.

Let me turn now to the three persons I mentioned at the start. The poet and scientist are Wordsworth and Darwin, and for them the metaphor in question was nature. They received this as a figure about the physical universe designed by God. Their great work was to turn it into a figure about a universe without design and yet intelligible in relation to human history. It is from reflection on the long succession of inheritances leading up to them that both Wordsworth and Darwin discover the only order they believe can be got and the only one they are willing to demand. This gives the general ground of argument; but one has to work hard against some old prejudices about Darwin, as well as some up-to-date ones about Wordsworth; so I warn in advance that I am not concerned with the explicit meanings they assign to nature. What matters more is the heroic effort of abstraction by which they looked at a thing with eyes no poet or naturalist had looked with before, and saw in it the slow processes that had gone to its formation, and nothing but those processes, and still were moved and interested by what they saw. Both of them derive from history itself a sufficient reassurance about the value of the story they have to tell. They look back far into the past and suppose that if one can look back far enough the origin ceases to be of much concern. I think that is why in reading them one finds an intense reverence for the past, together with a wish, which they cannot justify in the old language, to retain as many signs of it as the present can hold. Each is in a position to see for the first time that the history he reconstructs is everything there is. Others, of course, would not find a value in the story without a revelation somewhere, and one reason neither Wordsworth nor Darwin attacked the existing faiths directly was that they sympathized with those others. But their aim was to win a new dignity for man without such helps, and I will try here to suggest the perspective from which the effort began. In drawing an analogy between their ways of reading nature, I will seek assistance along the way from William Whewell's *Philosophy of the Inductive Sciences.* Whewell was early a disciple of Wordsworth, to whom he dedicated his *Elements of Morality,* and later an influence on Darwin's thinking at Cambridge. There is a good deal of coherence between his writing about morals and about science, and his importance in this connection has not been much noticed. [12]

Most readers of Wordsworth's 1802 Preface to the *Lyrical Ballads* can recall at least four main arguments: first, that poetry comes from "the real language of men in a state of vivid sensation"; second, that rustic life and rural occupations are especially well suited to poetry "because in that condition the passions of men are incorporated with the beautiful and permanent forms of nature"; third, that the poetic diction of the eighteenth century is absurdly artificial and ought to be scrapped; and fourth, that without a poet no community is fully human, for he is the representative instance of a man speaking to men.

Now the second and third of these points are occasional and adventitious. The attack on poetic diction is a clever polemic against an old idiom in favor of a new one, and the association of sincere speech with country places only shows that Wordsworth himself had found it there. By contrast, the first point, concerning the poet's attentiveness to the natural eloquence of the passions of men, may be said to define Wordsworth's understanding of his vocation. Yet the strength of his case depends on what we make of the fourth point, the answer to the question "What is a Poet?" I rehearse these details because the most celebrated commentator on the Preface, Coleridge, scored a great tactical success by treating the first three points as an attempt at a single argument which failed. The fourth he ignored altogether, and I believe the omission is significant. The passage, of about 2,000 words, describing the character of a poet, was added only in 1802, and it called the poet someone "nothing differing in kind from other men, but only in degree." By identifying the poet's genius with his incorporation in a community, Wordsworth was rejecting Coleridge's faith in "the creative, and self-sufficing power of absolute *Genius*"—a faith which he held at every period of his life, and which Wordsworth echoed convincingly when he was trying to sound like Coleridge. But Coleridge would have been troubled by the 1802 revision of the Preface for another reason as well. It compared the poet to the "Man of Science" in terms favorable to both, and proposed for them a common ambition.

For the poet, Wordsworth says, knowledge is pleasure, and the same is true of the chemist, the mathematician, and even the anatomist, "however painful may be the objects with which his knowledge is connected." The one restriction on the poet which is not shared by the scientist (to adopt the convenient though slightly anachronistic name) is the necessity of producing pleasure in his reader. But here Wordsworth is pointing to the accidental circumstance that the poet writes in a language every reader may be presumed to know; the scientist, too, produces pleasure in those who can read his language, and nothing in the nature of the language itself prevents his audience from becoming eventually as large as the poet's. Of the communication of pleasure by an interpreter of nature to his reader, Wordsworth observes that "it is a homage paid to the native and naked dignity of man, to the grand elementary principle of pleasure, by which he knows, and feels, and lives, and moves. We have no sympathy but what is propagated by pleasure." [13] His suggestion that these words apply to the scientist no less than the poet was unexpected. And the force of the argument has seldom been registered in modern, usually Coleridgean, discussions of what the Preface is saying. The very motto "knowledge is pleasure" was a play on Bacon's "knowledge is power." Our habitual thinking about culture inclines us to reserve pleasure for the poet alone and power for the scientist. But Wordsworth was here granting pleasure also to the scientist. His readers could be trusted to see the corollary, which was implicit anyway in every word he wrote: power belonged also to the poet. That is why the sentences I just quoted feel as much like a description of power as of pleasure.

It was in the light of this comparison between poet and scientist that Wordsworth understood his own claim near the end of the Preface, that poetry is "in its nature well adapted to interest mankind permanently, and likewise important in the multiplicity and quality of its moral relations." Quality had to do with the intensity both of the poet's pleasure and his power, and "in its nature" referred to the likely durability of men's interest in sharing such feelings. A question that arises at this point is, How did Wordsworth come into possession of his idea of the scientist, about whom his profoundest earlier sentiment appears to have been "We murder to dissect"? The answer is that he got it from Sir Humphrey Davy's 1802 introductory lecture on general chemistry at the Royal Institution. I owe this discovery to Roger Sharrock, from whose account I will borrow the passages I quote from Davy.[14] But it may be noted in passing that Wordsworth's probable motive for reading the lecture was not any prior interest in science but rather Davy's interest in poetry: he had been an enthusiastic early convert to the *Lyrical Ballads,* and Wordsworth liked to hear people's reasons for admiring him because he was sure they would be edifying. Davy, in fact, describes the task of the scientist in a language that recalls the first version of the Preface: "Natural history examines the beings and substances of the external world, chiefly in their permanent and unchanging forms: whereas chemistry, by studying them in the laws of their alteration, developes and explains their active powers, and the particular exertions of those powers." Again, he argues that the chemist must "interrogate nature with power, not simply as a scholar, passive and seeking only to understand her operations, but rather as a master, active with his own instruments." The study of nature therefore, under any aspect whatever, "must always be more or less connected with the love of the beautiful and sublime." And he goes on to affirm, very remarkably from Wordsworth's point of view, that science "may become a source of consolation and of happiness in those moments of solitude when the common actions and passions of the world are considered with indifference. It may destroy diseases of the imagination, owing to too deep a sensibility; and it may attach the affections to objects, permanent, important, and intimately related to the interests of the human species." The effect of this on Wordsworth, as Sharrock demonstrates, was immediate and proved to be lasting. It led him to think of the poet and the scientist simply as knowers in conversation with nature. And in the dream of the stone and the shell, which he was writing for *The Prelude* about the same time, it led him to picture them as allied in the pleasure and power of their knowing, to the brink of the catastrophe in which knowledge may end.

Here is the final form Wordsworth gave to the comparison, at the close of the 1802 passage I have been describing:

> The Man of science seeks truth as a remote and unknown benefactor; he cherishes and loves it in his solitude: the Poet, singing a song in which all human beings join with him, rejoices in the presence of truth as our visible friend and hourly companion. Poetry is the breath and finer spirit of all knowledge; it is the impassioned expression which is in the countenance of all Science. . . . If the labours of Men of science should ever create any material revolution, direct or indirect, in our condition, and in the impressions which we habitually receive, the Poet will sleep then no more than at present; he will be ready to follow the steps of the Man of science, not only in those general indirect effects, but he will be at his side, carrying sensation into the midst of the objects of the science itself.[15]

Thus poetry only seems more congenial than science to our idea of nature: the difference is a matter of how long it takes for each to invest objects with new sensations. The poet's discovery carries conviction at once—or so Wordsworth believed (and Davy's conversion may have made him optimistic). We are apt to regard it as "a necessary part of our existence, our natural and unalienable inheritance." The scientist's discovery is more remote in the sense that it takes more time for us to learn why it matters. Yet there may come a period, Wordsworth concedes, when these positions are altered or even reversed. He appears to have learned from Davy that chemistry, or geology, or anatomy was replacing physics as the scene of revolutionary changes in knowledge; and together these gave him a clearer picture than physics ever could of the role that human interests play in scientific discovery. Still, the argument of the 1802 Preface would be merely an appealing interlude in Wordsworth's thought if all it came to were the temporary granting of a reprieve to science.

My contention is that it tells us something important about the way he read his poetry. More particularly, it shows what kind of answer he would have made to the usual question of readers: "What are your poems good for?" To frame a reply at all goes against the tradition of nineteenth-century aesthetics which descends from Coleridge. And yet Wordsworth himself did not find the question contemptible, least of all in the Preface, where he was at pains to assure his readers that he *wrote with a purpose.* In the long passage quoted above, he speaks of "the impressions which we habitually receive," and as a short summary of his purpose I think he would have allowed that he was writing about the way nature forms a boundary condition of our habits. If this is correct, he never enforces the firm distinction he is sometimes credited with maintaining, either between nature and habit or between nature and convention. Habit, for him, is the residue of all our past thoughts, feelings, and actions to the extent that they still influence us in the present. It therefore merges with nature by insensible gradations— habit being the index of nature in a person, as history is the index of nature in a community. There is a reading of the Preface which holds that it definitively separated nature from convention after a century during which convention had crept in by stealth.[16] But this comes from laying a great deal of stress on Wordsworth's analysis of poetic diction, and even there he has in mind grotesque deformations of convention and not convention as such. It seems to me in any case that one cannot reconcile a view of nature-as-revelation with the whole moral tendency of his work from *The Borderers* on. Wordsworth writes about Solitary Man as distinct from man in a community. Solitary Man, who has broken utterly with the habits of common life, is shown as aspiring to a divinity which is really demonic. And that divinity he sometimes calls nature. Man in a community lives by habit, though he is modified in time by a lengthening past and in space by his moral relations with others. His way of life he too calls nature, with the conviction that it remains stable in keeping with efforts of the will, instead of being fixed forever.

To judge by the 1802 Preface, Wordsworth believed that the interest of his poetry had nothing to do with being redeemed by nature from habit or convention. It had much more to do with the impulses by which we may move from the shallow impressions of the moment to the deeper impressions of a past: this is the contrast that underlies, for example, the phantasmagorical descriptions of London in *The Prelude*. The contrast of shallowness with depth, however, is less important to him than that of opacity with meaning, and he characteristically translates the first pair into the second. He writes, that is, about the process of association—what we would now call interpretation—through which an object we began by regarding blankly enters into relation with us and strengthens our sense of certain feelings that link us with each other. I have kept that statement as close as possible to Wordsworth's own language, but one way of getting closer is to quote from his poetry. The best illustration I can think of is the opening of "Michael." The objects that yield the point of entry into the story are presented as opaque. Yet Wordsworth informs us that the story, by giving them a meaning, will bind its readers to him, and that his motive in writing is to leave behind a successor who will resume the work of interpreting such objects.

> If from the public way you turn your steps
> Up the tumultuous brook of Green-head Ghyll,
> You will suppose that with an upright path
> Your feet must struggle; in such bold ascent
> The pastoral mountains front you, face to face.
> But, courage! for around that boisterous brook
> The mountains have all opened out themselves,
> And made a hidden valley of their own.
> No habitation can be seen; but they
> Who journey thither find themselves alone
> With a few sheep, with rocks and stones, and kites
> That overhead are sailing in the sky.
> It is in truth an utter solitude;
> Nor should I have made mention of this Dell
> But for one object which you might pass by,
> Might see and notice not. Beside the brook
> Appears a straggling heap of unhewn stones!
> And to that simple object appertains
> A story—unenriched with strange events,
> Yet not unfit, I deem, for the fireside,
> Or for the summer shade. It was the first
> Of those domestic tales that spake to me
> Of Shepherds, dwellers in the valleys, men
> Whom I already loved;—not verily
> For their own sakes, but for the fields and hills
> Where was their occupation and abode.

And hence this Tale, while I was yet a Boy
Careless of books, yet having felt the power
Of Nature, by the gentle agency
Of natural objects, led me on to feel
For passions that were not my own, and think
(At random and imperfectly indeed)
On man, the heart of man, and human life.
Therefore, although it be a history,
Homely and rude, I will relate the same
For the delight of a few natural hearts;
And, with yet fonder feeling, for the sake
Of youthful Poets, who among these hills
Will be my second self when I am gone. [17]

Wordsworth says that he had felt the power of nature, but he defines nature by reference to the natural objects associated with this tale: the subject of the complicated sentence about what led him on to feel for passions not his own and think on human life is, in fact, "this Tale"; if instead we read the subject as "Nature," we go along with a faith he wishes for the moment to affirm, that nature came before books. What the passage asserts grammatically is something rather different: that nature is a name for a history not yet told. We are placed in a rural landscape whose features are undistinguishable—a hill and a brook, with a few sheep, and rocks, and stones, and kites. Somewhere in this is "a straggling heap of unhewn stones," an illegible landmark with nothing to make the uninducted traveler pick it out as a monument. Yet before he can repeat "It is in truth an utter solitude," there will be a story about it. An old shepherd Michael lived here, with his wife and their son; and the son laid the first stones of a sheepfold as a pledge of faith when he left home to assist his family by other work; later he slackened in duty, was lost in the great city where he disgraced himself, and sought refuge overseas. The half-built sheepfold nevertheless remained for Michael a mark of the strength of love: "Among the rocks / He went, and still looked up to sun and cloud, / And listened to the wind; and, as before, / Performed all kinds of labour for his sheep," and endured to an extreme old age. That straggling heap of unhewn stones finally interests us because it tells of the affections that humanize a solitude. We learn to read it from the poet whose knowledge is pleasure, and having learned we may become his "second self." The phrase in its context is not esoteric. It refers to the way a community may be enlarged by the knowledge of an object which they associate with common feelings.

It is a most ordinary tale, as Wordsworth thought the ballads should be, but this opening is one of the new things he brought into poetry. The once-upon-a-time comes in the fortieth line—"Upon the forest-side in Grasmere Vale / There dwelt a Shepherd, Michael was his name"—so that in retrospect, the introductory passage sounds like a challenge. What it questions is our belief that nature can ever be read for what it is without an interpreter who says, "And to that simple object appertains / A story." The poet, as Wordsworth understands his work, is not someone who remarks the fitness between a sentiment and a landscape, as in an older kind of loco-descriptive poem, or who knows in advance the proper range of sympathies for a character of a certain type, as in an older kind of pastoral. Rather, to adopt for a last time the language of the preface, the poet is "the rock of defense for human nature; an upholder and preserver, carrying everywhere with him relationship and love." By extending the objects that define our relations to each other, and thus by bringing to mind "absent things as if they were present," the poet can change our idea of human life.

The reason Wordsworth speaks of defense rather than change is that he conceives of it as a radical return to something in our nature that was already there. But it was only there in the same sense that a pile of stones in a natural solitude was a monument waiting to be read. The obstruction we have to pass at the start of the poem, like many comparable passages in Wordsworth, exists to show us that we do not know nature except by conversion. There are, on the one hand, objects that have acquired a sense from our concern—often *sense* is Words-worth's own word for all that we gain by coaxing an object into testimony. On the other hand, there are objects that somehow resist our effort, and these he commonly associates with repetition or mere being. This does not imply a distinction between two kinds of object but between two kinds of attention we give to an object, and evidently Wordsworth's ambition is to keep both of them always in view. He sees that we move in any case from the latter to the former, and he does not care for the efficiency of those who arrive without a halt. He seems to regard the patience for looking at something steadily as an irreducible moral virtue.

I will return to the last point when I come to Darwin. But I have to observe here that "Michael" is a poem about filial duty, that we have a more general poem from Wordsworth on this subject, the "Ode to Duty," and that an idea of duty came to play a curious part in Whewell's thinking about morals. He writes of "the constant and interminable moral culture of the affections" as a duty which "may suffer interruptions and reverses"; this can happen because the power even of an ideal like duty is modified by our success or failure in carrying it into action. "The moral progress of our affections is *interrupted* by every malicious act. . . . Our moral progress is *reversed* when such malice, or such coldness of heart, becomes habitual."[18] Whewell wants to reason about morals in a Kantian way—he draws a sharp contrast, for example, between principles and "transient and casual *Feelings,* which may be inconsistent with themselves." But the very idea of interruptions in our moral progress is non-Kantian.[19] On this account a malicious or benevolent act joins our moral being, as action affects habit and habitual feelings become a tributary to thought. The force of the argument is close to that of the "Ode to Duty" itself, where duty is addressed as "stern daughter of the voice of God" who "dost preserve the stars from wrong"; and yet to follow her command we must have felt "the weight of chance-desires" and "long for a repose that ever is the same." The half-realized personal sentiment of *longing,* Wordsworth is saying here, may be as necessary a motive to action as any moral imperative. This marks a substantial revision of Kant's usual distinction between an impersonal duty and mere sentiment.[20] The larger scheme of Whewell's *Elements of Morality,* in which duties operate in the service of principles but are themselves built up by habit, is also of course Wordsworthian: "So feeling comes in aid / Of feeling, and diversity of strength / Attends us, if but once we have been strong." The concern of both writers is that "the culture of the affections" should have a place for the act done rightly without reflection. Of Whewell in particular, J. B. Schneewind observes that his "concern is always with ordering the moral knowledge we already have";[21] but in practice this means what it did for Wordsworth, that the history of a person in a community becomes the leading fact about morals.

Whewell believed that his thinking about morals and science held to a single pattern, and with a very little work one can see that it does. He represents the knowledge we can achieve in either area as emerging not from a direct confrontation with nature but rather from an interpretation of a story. The result can still have the character of fact because the book of nature has been with us a long time, and in order to carry weight any revision must have preserved some part of its inheritance. I am condensing Whewell's exposition here, but I want to stress that the metaphor is his, for it explains much of his interest in terminology. Any technical term should reflect the theory accepted in its field, and if the theory is mostly new the term may be wholly so. Otherwise it should preserve as far as possible a sense of the older theories which the present one has absorbed; in this way the best terms bring to mind the connection between still usable thoughts of the past and the present state of thinking. Whewell distinguishes scientists and philosophers from other men only on the ground that "most men are unconscious of this perpetual habit of reading the language of the external world, and translating as they read."[22] Again, he says of our ideas—in a figure I borrowed earlier to explain Shelley's conception of metaphor—that we do not see them, we see through them. This way of thinking is so customary with Whewell that in phrases here and there he can speak casually of "the texture of our knowledge." And in support of his assertion that we can never tell facts from inferences or interpretations of facts, he quotes the "philosophical poet" who described "all the world / Of eye and ear, both what they half create / And what perceive." When Darwin called "the process of scientific thought . . . identical with everyday thought, only with more care," he was looking back to Whewell as Whewell did to Wordsworth.

Two main features of the argument of Whewell's *Philosophy of the Inductive Sciences* are what he names the "colligation of facts" and the "consilience of inductions." The colligation of facts implies the tying them into a bundle for the sake of explaining the world more convincingly. Because Whewell supposes that "the distinction of Fact and Theory is only relative"—that "a true Theory is a fact, and a Fact is a familiar theory"—it is no part of his ambition that the facts should be seen to belong together necessarily. On the contrary, when he writes, "The pearls once strung, they seem to form a chain by their nature," the emphasis is on "seem" as much as "nature." Hypotheses may therefore be useful "when they involve a certain portion of incompleteness, and even of errour," since they "bind together facts which without them are loose and detached."[23] The reason this sounds like a century-early proposal of the web of belief is the high rank it gives to coherence as a mark of a good hypothesis. But it is worth looking more closely at "consilience." This, as Whewell tells us, occurs when "inductions from classes of acts altogether different have *jumped together*," the last two words being a plain translation of the Latin *con-salire*. The idea would have interested Darwin, since it can be shown to support his method. He took in facts from widely disparate fields and combined them with an adventurous confidence. At the same time he was determined to remain answerable to the doctrine *natura non facit saltum* (nature makes no jumps).[24] On this point he was firmly materialist in his bias, and it is here that Whewell's idealism comes to his defense. If the mind's interpretations jump together by consilience—and on Whewellian grounds there is no way to distinguish interpretations from facts—one cannot in principle object to a theory that crosses over gaps in nature. The story may be justified by the results even if these come from separate sciences where the record stands still.

By many intellectual historians, Whewell's influence has been discussed as a burden to be overcome in Darwin's attack on the argument from design.[25] This seems to me a comparatively minor point. Whewell's version of the argument is in fact borrowed from the teleological sections of the *Critique of Judgment,* which Collingwood summarized as follows: "The thing in itself which underlies the phenomena of nature has the character of mind: so that what we know in our practical or moral experience is of the same kind as what we think, but cannot know, in our theoretical experience as students of natural science."[26] So Whewell remarks, for example, that our understanding of bodies as subject to disease includes an idea of final cause, or of things not attaining their proper end. One can trace the consequences in parts of the *History,* as when he affirms that *"species have a real existence in nature, and a transmutation from one to another does not exist."*[27] Yet the nominalist emphasis of both the *History* and *Philosophy* is always working against such a definition. "The Names of things are governed by their use." If one believes this, it follows that "a Natural Group is . . . not precisely limited; it is given in position, though not circumscribed"; so that a species is "determined not by what it strictly excludes, but by what it eminently includes."[28] A structure of argument that Whewell partly took over from Kant, in science as he did in morals, encouraged him to make a strong stand on design and thus to suppose that after all there was one right reading of nature. But his own sense of interpretation had already moved him far in the opposite direction, and for a scientist like Darwin, with theological needs less pronounced than Whewell's, the point was that there were only readings.

What does a Darwinian interpretation look like? The answer, I think, is clear only by contrast with an earlier procedure, and the analogy at the start of Paley's *Natural Theology* is worth giving in the words Darwin knew by heart. "In crossing a heath, suppose I pitched my foot against a *stone,* and were asked how the stone came to be there: I might possibly answer, that, for anything I knew to the contrary, it had lain there for ever; nor would it perhaps be very easy to show the absurdity of this answer. But suppose I had found a *watch* upon the ground, and it should be inquired how the watch happened to be in that place, I should hardly think of the answer which I had given before." [29] Paley goes on through the catechism of the elements, glass and metal, and then the parts, spring, chain, and box, until he arrives at the conclusion: if a contrivance, then a contriver. The hidden premise which makes this a tautology is that we know in advance that the watch exists in order to tell time. Concerning a found object in nature, the most we know is that it exists in order to live. If one imagines Darwin pitching his foot against the watch, his first questions will possibly be how far its hinge resembles that of other molluscs, and whether its shininess attracts or repels predators.

Paleyan explanations are good for things that exhaust our interest when they reveal the intention of their designer. Darwinian interpretations, on the other hand, are good for things about which we constantly reform our interest as we learn their relations with other things. To exhibit Darwin's own movement from the assertion of this view to its illustration, the best passage I can give comes from the chapter "Difficulties on Theory" in *The Origin of Species.*

> He who believes in separate and innumerable acts of creation will say, that in these cases it has pleased the Creator to cause a being of one type to take the place of one of another type; but this seems to me only restating the fact in dignified language. He who believes in the struggle for existence and in the principle of natural selection, will acknowledge that every organic being is constantly endeavouring to increase in numbers; and that if any one being vary ever so little, either in habits or structure, and thus gain an advantage over some other inhabitant of the country, it will seize on the place of that inhabitant, however different it may be from its own place. Hence it will cause him no surprise that there should be geese and frigate-birds with webbed feet, either living on the dry land or most rarely alighting on the water; that there should be long-toed cornkrakes, living in meadows instead of in swamps; that there should be woodpeckers where not a tree grows; that there should be diving thrushes, and petrels with the habits of auks. [30]

Darwin is attacking a later sophistication of a familiar argument, the theory that the unaccountable species are God's afterthought within the laws of nature, or what Dewey called "design on the installment plan."

But though the controversy over renewable special creation helps to account for the range of Darwin's examples, the passage exhibits a more general tendency of his conduct of argument. He almost never fixes on a solitary object as a master clue to the right reading of itself. It is for this reason that a lay reader today cannot remember *The Origin of Species* as a whole, whereas the parts of the *Natural Theology* are memorable in themselves and add up to the whole. The habits of storytelling one associates with the *Origin,* however, were fairly settled by the time Darwin wrote *The Voyage of the Beagle.* He recalls there how interested he was to find the fossils of large quadrupeds, the Megatherium, Megalonyx, and Scelidotherium, embedded in the stratified gravel and reddish mud at Punta Alta, in a region lacking the rich vegetation such creatures were supposed to have required. With them he found shells of a kind still existing in a bay only twenty feet from the fossil bed at high water. An easy conjecture was that the vegetation was once less sparse—but that left the shells unexplained. Now, having reached this turn, design would counsel that the vegetation must indeed have been rich to support large quadrupeds. Either, therefore, the two sets of remains belong to discrete categories of evidence, or what look like shells are something else. Darwin's procedure instead was to collect facts about Africa, North America, and other places where large quadrupeds still did exist amid sparse vegetation, or were absent in spite of rich vegetation. He thus demonstrated what he felt convinced of from the first, that the region might once have been as it now was, and yet have supported the creatures whose remains he found.

Researches like these fall short of the passage I quoted from "Difficulties on Theory." But they make it plain that the "colligation of facts" was Darwin's common practice, and they account for his response to those who set up any *kind* of fact as a limit to interpretation. He made a note to himself in a copy of Chambers's *Vestiges of Creation,* "Never use the word higher and lower." But I think one can see a similar response in a more personal confrontation with a scientist whose opinions he often valued. We know that Darwin once found a "large worn tropical volute shell" in a gravel pit near his home, and that Adam Sedgwick remarked that "if really embedded there, it would be the greatest misfortune to geology, as it would overthrow all that we know about the superficial deposits of the midland counties."[31] The reaction surprised Darwin. His interest in history followed from his belief that thinking about one sort of object did not naturally stop at a certain point. In saying this I have to differentiate my view from that of Darwin's literary admirers, who sometimes associate his narrative method with the free play of the mind and a quest for diverse opinions.[32] These are excellent aims, but, as the author of a persuasive interpretation, it was not Darwin's role to encourage opinions against himself, and I cannot see that he did. Only in one respect is he concerned to open the future to those who may succeed him. He gives attention to objects whose use is as yet inconceivable, and he cannot help exemplifying the value of such attention. As with Wordsworth, it seems to me difficult to do more than connect this with a virtue like patience. One watches an object closely, even when it does not fit an available story, because one trusts that it will matter. The practice is not a wager or a sound investment but the pursuit of a calling.

In the age of Wordsworth and Darwin genius became a practical ideal. It suggested the farthest reach of an interpreter who attached his readers by unforeseen links to the world they already thought complete. This was what Wordsworth meant when he called the poet the rock of defense for human nature; and it was what Darwin meant when he said it was possible for man to be *nested* in his environment. Yet the sense of interpretation and history that Wordsworth and Darwin shared was gradually lost in the work of later poets and scientists. An obvious cause is that poetry and science in any case had long been moving in opposite directions: poetry toward an aesthetic language-without-truth, science toward an objective truth-without-language. But the change was larger than that. Knowledge, practice, and representation were all being dispatched to separate areas of study. Ruskin's summary of these divisions in *The Eagle's Nest* (1872) is idiosyncratic, but it shows that the tendency was well advanced by then and could be taken for granted even by a defender of genius. "The knowledge of things, whether Ideal or Substantial" is Ruskin's version of science; "the modification of Substantial things by our Substantial Power" is art; and "the modification of Ideal things by our Ideal Power" is literature, which contains all the fine arts under the aspect of interpretation.[33] About this time and in keeping with these divisions, the word *genius* itself was growing specialized again. I will conclude by noting its appearance in two very different texts.

Francis Galton's *Hereditary Genius: An Inquiry into Its Laws and Con-*

sequences (1869) is a hard-factual work of eugenic sociology. If one takes Social Darwinism broadly, as implying any belief that the discovery of natural selection points a moral for social policy, then the movement of which Galton was a pioneer may be seen as a humane refinement of Social Darwinism. The eugenic moral is that the forward edge of a species ought to be cultivated as suggesting the ideal type for each member of the species.[34] Among the past geniuses whose laws of formation Galton wants to codify, we find statesmen, commanders, literary men, poets, and divines. Thus far we are within the family of the Carlylean hero. But Galton also includes senior classics of Cambridge, wrestlers of the North Country, judges of England between 1660 and 1865, and oarsmen. In the more prosaic statistical chapters one may learn that Byron "did not show genius when at Harrow"; that Condorcet "was deficient in brilliancy. His principal faculty was in combining and organizing"; and that "it is not easy to classify the rowers, especially as many of the men have rarely, if ever, pulled in skiff matches, but formed part of crews in pair-oared, four-oared, or six-oared matches." But from the mass of well-sifted information Galton derives this hope: "If we could raise the average standard of our race only one grade, what vast changes would be produced! The number of men of natural gifts equal to those of the eminent men of the present day, would be necessarily increased more than tenfold, as will be seen by the fourth column of the table, p. 34, because there would be 2,423 of them in each million instead of only 233."[35] Galton thinks of natural gifts as steadily improvable, and of great works as a reasonable expectation of heredity, with no relation to circumstance. This way of thinking was the euthanasia of genius.

My last quotation is a postmortem from Samuel Butler, who in an early work had tried to link Wordsworthian memory and Darwinian evolution by means of a strong definition of habit. The effort was a failure; yet what Butler found remarkable was that nobody wanted it to succeed; and in *The Way of All Flesh,* writing as the narrator Mr. Overton, he meditated briefly on the fate of a word. He begins by recalling Christina Pontifex's lament that "as for genius—hoity-toity, indeed,—why, a genius should turn intellectual summersaults as soon as it is born"; and he observes that she was plainly disappointed in her own children.

"My children are none of them geniuses, Mr. Overton," she said to me at breakfast one morning. "They have fair abilities, and, thanks to [their father's] tuition, they are forward for their years, but they have nothing like genius; genius is a thing apart from this, is it not?"

Of course I said it was "a thing quite apart from this," but if my thoughts had been laid bare, they would have appeared as "Give me my coffee immediately, ma'am, and don't talk nonsense." I have no idea what genius is, but so far as I can form any conception about it, I should say it was a stupid word which cannot be too soon abandoned to scientific and literary *claqueurs*.[36]

It remains only to set Butler's opinion in context by remarking what a curious reversal the word has undergone until it almost arrives at its origin. With Galton's oarsmen and judges we were back at Pope's "One science only will one genius fit." But Mrs. Pontifex takes us all the way back to Edward Young. Genius has again become a natural power arising mysteriously from a creative principle to which few have access. It is associated with pure subjects like music and mathematics. The intellectual summersaults are prodigious, and we respect them as a thing apart from us.

3

Burke, Wordsworth, and the Defense of History

In the writings of Burke, one feature of Enlightenment thinking is pressed to an extreme, so that it becomes an obstacle to the very idea of enlightenment. Let me begin with a general sketch of the idea that Burke hoped to make difficult.

Philosophes such as Voltaire, in common with Hume, Kant, and other eighteenth-century moralists, supposed that there was a real subject of knowledge called human nature, and that knowledge of that subject could be achieved from a historical and anthropological point of view. They likewise supposed that the improvement of mankind was in prospect. The results, it followed, of historical and anthropological inquiry would naturally disclose the likely direction for the improvement to take. In sum, conclusions from the past, and from other societies, pointed out the way to the cultivation of man's nature in a given society in the future. This view of knowledge assigned a large and even exalted role to the philosophical inquirer himself. It was his disinterested exploration of the laws and patterns of life that suggested a way for the voluntary modification of those laws and patterns, or *change*. A tacit assumption was that human life could, in fact, change radically, and still remain human. Reform was understood to consist chiefly in the eradication of prejudice: the displacement of local custom and habit by a more than local refinement or serenity of mind. Indeed, the motive for thinking about human nature had been to make our virtues, and our consciousness of ourselves, universal. The further back in history we look, the more deeply do we find men plunged in the obscurity of prejudice, ignorance, and fear. To alleviate this condition by thought is to move from barbarism to civilization.

Like the thinkers mentioned above, Burke adopts the premise that history is an adequate weapon of criticism. However, he does so in order to question the practicability of just those large-scale reforms which had been relied upon as a clear effect of historical research. History—and, so far, he agrees with the *philosophes*—is the repository of all the existing evidence of our nature, the record of how our moral and cognitive life came to be what it is. Yet history, Burke sees, may also challenge the notion that, by the exercise of theoretical reason, we can actually perfect human nature. How after all does the rational theorist argue? Dig down, he says, beneath the tangled growth of adventitious prejudice, and the truth of our nature will be disclosed. It is there for the theorist that our essential nature resides. It is on that foundation that we have to build, if human life is to receive improvement, and if we are to be freed from aimless suffering. Burke's reply comes in two parts. He observes, first, that history and reason do not afford this sort of reliable joint testimony; their verdicts do not necessarily coincide in this way. Reason may tell us which of our practices are the consequence of mere prejudice and, as such, are impediments to reform. By contrast, all that history can show is the existence of certain prejudices—habits of mind that foster practices, and that protect us from always having to question our practices. A prejudice may of course lead to bigotry (which gives the word its pejorative modern sense), but it is itself merely a disposition of judgment (the kind that "renders a man's virtue his habit"). The historical and anthropological record discovers an immense variety of social arrangements. As to whether, or how far, a particular arrangement is right—either good for survival as such, or good for the survival of what is best in a society—that is something history alone can never answer. Thus to give historical evidence for the directive of reason is to assume the very thing that was to be proved.

Burke has a second way of raising his doubts, which almost amounts to a second challenge. In the usual Enlightenment metaphor about nature and circumstance, prejudice appears as a circumstantial entity—it is added on, supplementary, and to be done away with when we please. Burke says that this metaphor itself is the contribution of reason, at a certain moment of human development, and that nothing about the nature of history can justify taking it seriously. Given the limitations of our research into the past, as also of our self-knowledge, it is false to suppose that we can see beyond the layers of prejudice that confront us. Neither history nor any other study can tell what human nature would be like without those layers. Beneath prejudice, more prejudice. It is easy to imagine how doubts of this sort could lead to skeptical conclusions; and Hume exemplifies one of them in his *Natural History of Religion:* if the revelations of divinity become more improbable the closer we get to their source, then such revelations are likely to be false, as a general rule. One can certainly imagine a similar argument applied to nature and the prejudices that constitute it. But Burke, having argued to this point in the Enlightenment manner, now offers an unexpectedly consistent defense of nature. All those habits, customs, and local superstitions you complain of (he says to the party of improvers), just *are* human nature. They are what we are. The thought of eradicating them is therefore something like a thought of self-destruction for the species.

It had long been a habit of moralists to treat prejudice on some analogy with mere imposed belief. The practice survives in the therapies of taste worked out by Hume in his essay "Of the Standard of Taste" and by Kant in the *Critique of Judgment.* Both aim to clear the mind of all irrelevant previous opinions and inclinations. The removal of prejudice will, on this view, be the predictable effect of reform at all times, but especially in an age of reform like the Enlightenment. Burke seems to suggest on the contrary that our prejudices, like certain deep and not imposed beliefs, may have an almost ineradicable character. Plans for the whole-length reconstruction of human life can only follow from a rational counter-prejudice, which will not itself be more credible than, say, the suppositions of religious faith or dogma. Burke thinks it probable that many of our smaller-scale beliefs, to which we apply the name of prejudice, have been brought into our lives all along by a process resembling natural selection.[1] If that is so, he can make his case *a fortiori* that the way for reason to assist our nature is by gradual reform.

Concerning the truth or falseness of this or that belief, Burke has his opinions. He says, for example, that superstition is the religion of feeble minds. But even in a judgment like this, it is plain that questions about the truth of a prejudice hold no interest for him: they are the sort of thing that interests "philosophers" (a term of opprobrium, for Burke, almost as much as "metaphysicians"). Even a prejudice that is only a truth for weak minds may help toward the survival of some human design. And the worth of that survival is a consideration apart from the truth of the prejudice.

If, then, the Enlightenment has cherished a hope that the part of us in bondage to custom will some day vanish, as a thing of no use except to retard our progress, Burke is able in the current language of the Enlightenment to insist that such a liberation cannot sanely be hoped for. From his discovery that the past humanizes—that history shows only a bondage to custom under various descriptions—he infers that amelioration by degrees is all our condition may allow. To the extent that we aim at something more grand, we are pretty sure to make ourselves monstrous. Still, it does rest with us to say what we shall aim for; and the reason is that we make our own history. We can, in short, as Burke suggests in a remarkable phrase, choose our speculations rather than our nature. But it is the latter alone that belongs to us, and rightly "becomes us" as the sort of beings that we are.

All this train of speculation is original with Burke.

Subtle as the argument is, it may seem to come to little more, practically speaking, than a justification of inherited social arrangements. Yet Burke's stress on human volition is not conservative, in any common understanding of that word. He says again and again that the choice is ours to make; that the history of which we are composed will be written only by ourselves. For a believer in nature, this seems as curious a paradox as anything to be found in Hume. And in Burke's own thinking it goes with a far from rigid idea of authority. He concedes, it is true, every imaginable power to a community over individuals; and yet, the definition of a given community is always left in suspense. He seems to think that the operability of any such definition is a matter of persuasion and implicit consent. One can easily fail to see this, for Burke writes mainly about communities which he feels to be threatened; and he sympathizes with a community for the sake of its traditions, as distinct from the schemes of displacement contemplated by its enemies. Thus, in France, the community is the *ancien régime,* and the enemies are constitutional theorists, men of letters, the Jacobins and the mob. In India, the community is the system of folkways and loyalties that had matured long before England dreamed of an empire, and the enemies are the commercial proxies for imperial rule, the men of the East India Company.

Because it has often been argued that a tradition, for Burke, centers on a fixed religious establishment and the idea of an unalterable human nature, I need to say what becomes of these things in my account of his thinking. He will want of course to defend both; but the sort of defense he will have to offer is tactical: not, that is, a matter either of dogmatic assertion or of inherited metaphysics. It must suffice for him to say that human nature (though it has no laws) affords a continuous and coherent subject for political reflection; that it does so from the gradual accretion of practices which have become habitual; and that nature is, accordingly, a strong figure of speech, marking the depth of our identity with certain ways of acting, and the permanence of our attachment to certain associated sentiments which we prefer not to surrender.[2] As for religion, it evidently has a high place, perhaps the highest of all, among those very sentiments. Yet it is pertinent that Burke describes himself in a letter as being "attached to Christianity at large; much from conviction; more from affection"; and that, in a passage of the *Reflections on the Revolution in France,* he defends the social function of monks as follows: "Suppose them no otherwise employed than by singing in the choir. They are as usefully employed as those who neither sing nor say. *As usefully even as those who sing upon the stage*" (emphasis added). To pass from the monastary to the theater implies no declension, either as to dignity or utility, but rather an appeal from a sure to a still surer authority.[3] Besides, it would be odd for Burke, once he had challenged the Enlightenment's faith in scientific laws and in truths that regulate our nature, to want to put in their place other laws and truths of exactly the same scope.

For he had set himself against not only the authority of any *detached* science—where society, conceived as a contract, was "a partnership in all science; a partnership in all art"—but against the notion that social existence could ever be regulated by a theory, system, or dogma. He had challenged the view that society was upheld by anything less contingent than shared beliefs and practices and the sense of a community. But he had claimed as a point of stability (only it may be more than a point) the whole history of social practices and of the prejudices that foster them: a history shaped by chosen and inherited loyalties, by works of art and by forms of government. These arguments can sound modest, or else casual and chaotic. They mean to be as much so as our experience itself. Burke aims to defend the possibility of our being attached to a continuous true story of human actions. But this implies the necessity of our realizing, even as we change or retell its episodes, that all moral knowledge derives from a sense of ourselves as actors in that story.

History, then, is something we have to strive to retain. It can be lost; and it follows that there is a certain frailty in what we took to be its substantial fabric. To this intimation about history Burke adds a similar suggestion concerning human nature. Though we say that human nature rightly is, and ought only to be composed of, such or such qualities, they also can be lost. Apart from the ordinary gradual shifts of circumstance, human nature can come to an end in a moment of historical catastrophe. And if our nature is once lost, it will do no good to say that the new thing is Monster, that it bears nothing but the name of human nature. As Burke observes at the end of "Thoughts on French Affairs": "If a great change is to be made in human affairs, the minds of men will be fitted to it, the general opinions and feelings will draw that way. Every fear, every hope will forward it; and then they who persist in opposing this mighty current in human affairs, will appear rather to resist the decrees of Providence itself, than the mere designs of men."[4] Given the character of his fears and the conditional quality of his defense, one can see why Burke was tempted to make religious faith appear as the groundwork of his other beliefs. Such faith would give a substantial meaning to history and human nature. Yet, though he wants to have religion on his side, Burke does not argue like a man who believed its claims. That is why for example, speaking of the confiscators of church lands, he can say "they have learnt to talk against monks with the spirit of a monk."[5] Religious institutions stand among many others that help us to sustain a connection between a given present and a chosen past. But, as we have noticed, for Burke the theater outranks the church as a school of moral sentiments. The striking fact about history, too, remains how far it is shaped by acts of the imagination. However qualified by faith or doctrine, such acts are not finally guided by either faith or doctrine.

Doubtless this view of Burke still makes him out to be a conservative of some kind. But the terms he offers for the possession of the past bring anxiety rather than consolation; and they allow a wide field of invention for political actors in the present. His sense of the little any defense of history can accomplish is discernible in other eighteenth-century writers (Hume again, for one). But no one else carries the theme with anything like his force. Burke's interpreter to the nineteenth century, for this whole side of his thinking, was, I will be arguing, Wordsworth. In a larger survey of his influence, such a claim would have to be balanced against that of Scott, whose novels offer a myth of personal sacrifice on behalf of a moral community. The relevant fact about the anti-individualist Scott, as about the individualist Wordsworth, is that any community he can imagine has its authority not from faith or contract, or from formalized consent, but simply from memory and practices. But the present chapter is confined to a part of Wordsworth's achievement; and to prepare for that one needs to recall a few moments of Burke's career.

Burke's first full-scale political work is called a defense, almost: *A Vindication of Natural Society.* Yet the title means the reverse of what it says. Here, as in Swift's essay on abolishing Christianity, the author who speaks the text is a character at some distance from the real author. Burke, like Swift, by casting a book in this form, at once exemplifies and attacks the plausibility of a certain style of speculation. He himself no more wants to vindicate natural society than Swift wanted to abolish Christianity. Rather, ideally imitating and exaggerating, his argument mocks a pattern of Enlightenment reasonableness. The same logic by which it has been shown that religion is natural rather than revealed might also be taken to show that society is natural rather than artificial: this is what the *Vindication* sets out to prove. And it does so merely by the logic of impersonation. We come to feel that the two arguments are as like each other as the characters who would advance them.

Throughout this pamphlet the word "natural" and its implied opposite, "artificial," work against their usual meanings. Natural society, as Burke construes it, is in fact devised wholly by theory, from the exercise of reason; on the other hand, artificial society is built up gradually by the experience of human practices. The former implies a consistent plan of social regulation cleared of prejudices, superstitions, local and inveterate customs. The latter implies a system of social adaptation from a knowledge of the past and present; and, with it, the need to conciliate old manners, even in the process of reforming morality. Burkean society is of course artificial society. And his premise here—that, from the force of habit, everything we call artificial becomes natural *to us*—will be affirmed explicitly in a late work, the *Appeal from the New to the Old Whigs.* He there lays it down as an axiom of politics that "Art is man's nature."

And yet, any whole-length parody like the *Vindication* is liable to convey, even to the reader who knows its machinery well, a persistently eerie sense of unfamiliarity. Let us grant that the pretended author stands for an actual enemy of the real author. It is as if, having done the pretended author the homage of speaking in his voice, the real author were then obliged, against his own design, to seem to give his enemy the same importance that the enemy gives himself. The reader will listen patiently to the shallow apology for progress, refinement, methodical perfection, all made ridiculous in this light. Meanwhile Burke, since he is writing it, appears to be listening too. Bad as the theory is, the momentum of the parody seems to show that one *could* think about society like that if one chose; and if enough others were persuaded, society would have to be altered accordingly, with whatever effects of mayhem.

As a first essay in politics, it is a decidedly odd performance. Burke is imagining how far the thing he hates might come out a success from the consequences of persuasion. But his imagining takes him further than he could have expected. After all, in his way of thinking about the mind, it is persuasion that really decides what nature is: we can envision any practice, so long as it follows from a voluntary reform of our self-image. But the manner of the presentation makes the experiment psychologically troubling as well, in a way that sorts oddly with the well-behaved rhetorical flatness of the writing. For Burke is imagining *himself* as one of the persuaders—as the advocate of a reductive, revolutionary principle of thought. His sense of how much, for Britain, may depend upon his choice will be taken up later in some of his most personal writings. As, here, when he mentions the deaths of millions of people, he can dandyishly put them out of mind as a side effect of obsolete thinking, so in the "Letter to a Noble Lord," when he imagines the Duke of Bedford cut up along dotted lines into rump and brisket, he will skirt round the horrors of the shambles with a bland allusion to a new fact: "His Grace's landed possessions are irresistibly inviting to an *agrarian* experiment." There, he only affects the Jacobin use of a Lord; in the *Vindication,* he only pretends to be Bolingbroke; but full in his mind is the question, What if I chose to be the thing I feign? His satire is of that uneasy kind that turns against the party it means to protect; or anyway, readily entertains the thought of what it would be like to turn against them.

In 1770, a decade after the *Vindication,* Burke's *Thoughts on the Present Discontents* clinched his reputation as an observer of politics. It was written in the middle of the controversy over Wilkes, and it contains the following nonpopulist statement of republican prudence: "The people have no interest in disorder. When they do wrong, it is their error, and not their crime."[6] What can this observation be supposed to say about human nature in general? The first sentence does not quite assert that the people have an interest in order. One might even read a Hobbesian moral into the two sentences together: those who wield power, like those who suffer it, need some limitation upon the "restless desire" that produces disorder; but only the prudent organization of political life will bring that. Burke would then be urging a tolerant remedy for natural errors. Yet there is also a suggestion that such organization is difficult to attain; that, once achieved, it starts to earn respect from the mere fact of duration; and that, becoming a part of what the people have an interest in, it will grow obscurely attached to their self-interest. By contrast, a mob of complacent lords can always destroy an existing order rapidly through negligence or vain projections.

Burke, in a letter to French Laurence of July 1796, claimed as "my monument" his long prosecution of British commercial rule under Warren Hastings in India. Even at the end of the *Reflections,* he describes himself to his correspondent as "one who snatches from his share in the endeavours which are used by good men to discredit opulent oppression the hours he has employed in your affairs; and who in doing so persuades himself that he has not departed from his usual office." These two sides of his later career have seemed to many readers hard to reconcile: on the one hand, the relentless hunting down of the private interests of Britain's imperial elite; on the other hand, the defense of the French aristocracy against the revolution. I think there is a clue about how they fit together in an acute remark by H. N. Brailsford: "Of Burke one must ask not so much What did he believe? as Whom did he pity?"[7] He pitied the Indian people because they were remote, undefended, and in mortal peril from an empire's greed. He pitied the Queen of France because there was only one of her, one for all time, against the numberless array of tormentors who filled up all the mind of the present. One can feel that Burke is defending the coherence of these choices when he writes in the *Reflections* that he loves liberty, and that liberty like any other idea is nothing when abstracted from circumstances, "stripped of every relation." A liberty Burke can care for will proceed from our natural interest in great things. But things become great for us, as he had argued in his *Enquiry into the Sublime and Beautiful,* only by taking a strong hold of the mind, from association with its permanent ideas of pleasure and pain.

So, according to Burke, the artificial dominance of such powers as we invent, affirm, and take to represent us is part of our imagining of ourselves, which we cannot do without. Why not? Because in the absence of those powers, there would be nothing to ground man's nature on: no "natural law" in the old sense, for example, to rely on against the ideas of those who have an interest in disorder. All the inherited observances and small arts by which a society is built up exhaust its store of *natural* possessions. To dispense with them in every circumstance is to strip ourselves of every relation. This explains, I think, Burke's admonition to his correspondent in the *Reflections:* "You began ill, because you began by despising everything that belonged to you." We show ourselves the character of everything that belongs to us only through the exercise of taste: the faculty by which manners are organized into morals. In his comments on the fall of the Queen, Burke seems to say as well that such a demonstration will work most vividly when it has to face a moment of sudden privation, defeat, or rupture. "In events like these," he observes, "our passions instruct our reason; because when kings are hurled from their thrones by the Supreme Director of this great drama, and become the objects of insult to the base, and of pity to the good, we behold such disasters in the moral, as we should behold a miracle in the physical order of things. We are alarmed into reflection."[8] By "miracle" Burke evidently means the visible token of disaster, an event that gives a sublime shock. His suggestion is that without the recovery enforced by taste—which includes my knowledge, for instance, that "some tears might be drawn from me, if such a spectacle were exhibited on the stage"—nothing will restore the mind to its proper order after so sudden a halt. We then remain alarmed but without reflection.

In his own life Burke was absorbed, one can truly say obsessed, with the idea of bequeathing an estate to a successor in the next generation, and to an illimitable posterity thereafter. Every such estate must some time be new; and in this case Burke would himself have been the founder: it was his deepest grief that his son, Richard, dying young, left him without an heir. The *Reflections* were written before that happened, but he says in a revealing sentence there: "People will not look forward to posterity, who never look backward to their ancestors"; and again: "The power of perpetuating our property in our families is one of the most valuable and interesting circumstances belonging to it, and that which tends the most to the perpetuation of society itself."[9] There is a sound imaginative reason why a backward look should so uniquely sanction the concern for posterity. For the idea of oneself in the present, as recalled by someone in the future, is already an imaginative idea of a past. In the same gesture by which we honor people and things that have survived in memory, we make a possible place for the survival of something of ourselves. Now, what Burke sees about the Jacobins is that they, too, have come to understand this: hence their wish to destroy both the dead and the remembering living, each for the sake of assuring that the other will be impotent.

A horror of the thoughtless iconoclasm of revolution—the obliteration of all records, all monuments, all art without a plain use—starts from the early pages of the *Reflections,* where the author himself is afraid of being disinterred: "Do these theorists mean to imitate some of their predecessors who dragged the bodies of our ancient sovereigns out of the quiet of their tombs?" The same image appears more strikingly in the "Letter to a Noble Lord": "They unplumb the dead for bullets to assassinate the living." The last sentence has an unexpected power from its double reference: to the literal depredations of the Jacobin tomb-robbers, who were, in fact, digging up coffins to melt them down for bullets; and to their moral usurpation of the past, their slander against the authority of the noble dead. It is in condemning this inversion of nature by speculation—both intellectual and economic speculation—that Burke can allude to his own party in the phrase I mentioned earlier: they are those who have "chosen our nature rather than our speculations, our breasts rather than our inventions." [10]

Recall, however, that nature is known to us by prejudice above all. It is worth noticing what a very anti-Rousseauist claim this is—as if there were nothing intuitive, nothing natural, even about nature itself. Burke's implicit argument seems to be conventionalist and Humean; yet it supports an effort of political more than social description. If we suppose as Hume did, that obligation springs from convention, then justice too may spring from convention. Justice, of course, "belongs" less properly to strangers than to those for whom we bear an intimate affection. But its source in convention may suggest an insight into the good of bringing justice to strangers. Hume thought that sympathy, itself merely a condition of approving or disapproving actions, might counterfeit, and so be functionally the same as, general benevolence. [11] Burke says in his different but parallel idiom: "Prejudice renders a man's virtue his habit." To justify the conventions by which we act, and to teach them some day to others, we have to come to know ourselves through the history that is our nature.

Among principled opponents of Burkean historicism, the question most liberals at one time and most radicals today would ask is, Who writes the history? If the perspective is just anyone's, then anyone may include the losers, the oppressed and the inarticulate, whom, though we do not know them well, we certainly know to have existed: if the past belongs in part to them, its history ought to be in part their history; yet this is a choice for which Burke seems to have made no allowance. If, on the contrary, history means the perspective of the winners, then Burke's thinking is exposed as nothing more exalted than an ethic of success, a very rough and ready pragmatism with a high gloss of sentiment.

This objection is not quite anticipated in Burke's writings. One cannot, that is to say, find a single passage in which he forestalls it. And yet it does not dispose of his argument. The truth is that Burke's reverence for the past, so far as his writings exhibit it, is not merely a superstitious reverence (though it may have elements of superstition). In his way of thinking, historically sanctioned practices are to be cherished for something apart from themselves. The value they represent, and in the name of which he defends them, is *order.* To grant even this much weakens the objection that it is all a question of whose perspective. For Burke, any history, any set of inherited practices (that of the village culture in India, for example, which Warren Hastings and his "Jacobins" of the East India Company were destroying) will very likely be acceptable, so long as it has issued in order.[12] This, as distinct from pastness or power or success, is his final point of reference. But he makes one restriction on the understanding of order itself. An order of the sort familiar in Europe is appreciable only to the extent that it permits modification through the work performed by men of talent like Burke. There is a different restriction to which, in turn, men like him must submit, composing as they do the active and reason-giving part of society. They must consent to be admitted to an establishment in suitably small numbers.

Inertia, and a class solely desirable because of its inertia, are also necessary components of a Burkean social order. But a society which was completely immobile, such as those which in his time were called oriental despotisms, would not qualify as a social order at all. Inertia can be inherited and no one need labor much to obtain it. Its genuinely civic counterpart is docility, which, by contrast, is cultivated with a purpose in view, by all who assent to the legitimacy of their rulers. Only the latter of these dispositions is a virtue in itself. The opposite of both is *energy:* a possible virtue that, when cut off from right prejudice or "untaught feelings," can be turned to vicious ends. In the "Letter to a Member of the National Assembly," this analysis becomes the ground of Burke's attack on the French revolutionaries:

They who always labor can have no true judgment. You never give yourselves time to cool. You can never survey, from its proper point of sight, the work you have finished, before you decree its final execution. You can never plan the future by the past. You never go into the country, soberly and dispassionately to observe the effect of your measures on their objects. You cannot feel distinctly how far the people are rendered better and improved, or more miserable and depraved, by what you have done. You cannot see with your own eyes the sufferings and afflictions you cause.[13]

Revolutionary energy in these years could still plead the necessity of using its resources against the imposition of arbitrary power. To this, however, Burke offers a clear answer, even if seldom a direct one. He says—often in the impeachment of Hastings, but occasionally elsewhere too—that *there never was an arbitrary power.* The times when such a power held sway are unrecorded and unthinkable; they are the waste intervals in the life of a society; and to their supposed lessons neither political thought nor moral judgment can ever address itself.

Still, how can one know when one sees the kind of order that Burke approves? By what traits does one pick it out from others with which it shares a manifest structure of subordination and a climate of general tranquillity? At this point, it must be allowed, Burke simply loses patience and turns us back to the keeping of a common sense of things. We do know when we see it, he says, because order is a sufficiently rare achievement; and a peaceable social order, which actually permits of an increasing degree of liberty and toleration, is now for him a visible achievement in "Europe"—an allegorical entity that seems to have been Burke's invention, and that for him meant something very like what "the West" means for us. It was because he could regard the American colonies as an extension of this European order that he defended their right to representation. For he discerned in the American protests nothing like a revolutionary motive. Rather, they pointed out the reasonable means—if England could grasp their significance—toward a reform of the empire generally. It was because he thought the French Revolution had no relation at all to the European order that Burke opposed it from the start, came to speak of the Jacobin ideology as "armed doctrine," and hoped to see the revolutionaries wiped out forever.

It will now be plain that Burke's historicism can be interpreted in at least two ways; and though I am partial to one, this seems the right place to summarize both: the reactionary argument which I want to reject; and the defensive argument which I want to put in its place. On the first view, Burke writes as he does because he has inherited an intuition—having been properly tutored to inherit it—of an eternal order of things which it is his duty to transmit to others. If anyone declines to receive his teaching, the cause must be a perverse failure of knowledge and self-knowledge alike. On the second view, Burke supposes that he himself has helped to make the order he admires. That order is daily advancing, but it may be overturned by the combined acts of human beings like himself, and like the unknown readers for whom he writes. But if this interpretation is accurate, then the rebels whom Burke deplores are, in his own eyes, candidates for success as plausible as himself. They too aim to build up an order by linking their choices each to each.

One effect of seeing Burke like this is to make his defense of an establishment more a matter of active resistance, less a matter of intellectual police-work, than it can ever be for historians who picture him as a master rhetorician of orthodoxy. His predicament appears at once ancient (as old as republican eloquence) and yet curiously modern (as new as the impracticability of an alliance of church and state). When nothing supports a sense of the past other than the reiterated words and repeated actions of people like Burke; when the very definition of human nature depends on the victory of such people, and their victory is not engraved in all our hearts—then for the first time, a general defense of history can take on an air of heroic defiance. That was certainly the shape in which Burke appeared to Wordsworth, long before the memory of his eloquence was invoked in Book VII of *The Prelude*. For Wordsworth Burke's writing, and not just his presence as a figure of oratory, stood for a power of choice, of individual agency, and of hope.

What may first have drawn Wordsworth to explore Burkean habits of feeling is that they give an unexampled moral authority to an idea of place. It is a part of his legacy that has not been much appreciated. And yet Burke's understanding, for instance, of "subordination" presumes that there can be no permanent or worthy political order where there is no durable relationship among the existing places in a society. *Place* in this conception has to be interpreted both geographically and socially. One grows alert to the latter sense when in the *Reflections* Burke writes: "After I had read over the list of the persons and descriptions elected into the *Tiers Etat,* nothing which they afterwards did could appear astonishing." What did he find there? A list, he says, of "practitioners in the law": "There were distinguished exceptions; but the general composition was of obscure provincial advocates, of stewards of petty local jurisdictions, country attornies, notaries, and the whole train of the ministers of municipal litigation, the fomentors and conductors of the petty war of village vexation. From the moment I read the list I saw distinctly, and very nearly as it has happened, all that was to follow."[14] But it is not only that men must know their place. They ought also to come from a certain place, and to be always conscious of that fact as a source of loyalties and obligations: this, Burke argues, is the one continuous link between self-definition and social identity. The weight of his protest against the recombination of districts, which the new establishment had dictated in France, centers on the danger of a policy that would systematically destroy that link. The "French builders" are accused of adopting the same policy as all bad improvers of estates, "clearing away as mere rubbish whatever they found." But at the bottom of "this geometrical basis of theirs," Burke finds a worse offense:

> These pretended citizens treat France exactly like a country of conquest. Acting as conquerors, they have imitated the policy of the harshest of that harsh race. The policy of such barbarous victors, who contemn a subdued people, and insult their feelings, has ever been, as much as in them lay, to destroy all vestiges of the ancient country, in religion, in polity, in laws, and in manners; to confound all territorial limits; to produce a general poverty; to put up their properties to auction; to crush their princes, nobles, and pontiffs; to lay low every thing which had lifted its head above the level, or which could serve to combine or rally, in their distresses, the disbanded people, under the standard of old opinion. They have made France free in the manner in which those sincere friends to the rights of mankind, the Romans, freed Greece, Macedon, and other nations.[15]

This is as close as Burke ever gets, in the counter-revolutionary language of his French writings, to the anti-imperialist language of his Indian writings. But plainly the two registers are much the same; it is reflection on place that has made them so.

Even at moments like this, it is possible to associate Burke (in his use of historical commonplaces) with the line of Scottish Enlightenment thinkers who favored the expansion of British commerce for the sake of a liberal civilization. But in the long run, Burke will disappoint those who seek an alliance between civic virtue and the progress of a commercial society.[16] He was in every phase of his life an advocate of reform, not progress (being, perhaps, a believer in civility more than civilization). And reform, unlike progress, must be carried out with a steady view to preserve the places that exist. The genuine Burkean nightmare is not a loss of profitable markets, or of the energy of enlightened persons who can exploit such markets, but rather the passing from sight of old places consecrated by use and custom. As early as the *Thoughts on the Present Discontents,* he reflects upon a tendency to disorder in "degenerated establishments," where old office-holders are quickly replaced by a new set of men: "A species of men to whom a state of order would become a sentence of obscurity are nourished into a dangerous magnitude by the heat of intestine disturbances; and it is no wonder that, by a sort of sinister piety, they cherish, in their turn, the disorders which are the parents of all their consequence." [17] When Burke comes to write of those who can be trusted to oppose such sinister piety, he will employ a metaphor like "the well-placed sympathies of the human breast." Feelings of this sort are impossible to separate from the well-placed memories of a town or village.

Thus, in the third of his *Letters on a Regicide Peace,* addressing the leaders who temporarily stopped the war with France, he declares: "That day was, I fear, the fatal term of *local* patriotism. On that day, I fear, there was an end of that narrow scheme of relations called our country, with all its pride, its prejudices, and its partial affections. All the little quiet rivulets, that watered an humble, a contracted, but not an unfruitful field, are to be lost in the waste expanse, and boundless, barren ocean of the homicide philanthropy of France." [18] But it is an important feature of Burke's last writings, and a fact very easy to miss, that he keeps his harshest scorn for those, in France or England, who affect a temperate impartiality. Such men-without-place, we are warned in "Remarks on the Policy of the Allies," "can serve no cause, for this plain reason,—they have no cause at heart. They can, at best, work only as mere mercenaries. They have not been guilty of great crimes; but it is only because they have not energy of mind to rise to any height of wickedness. They are not hawks or kites: they are only miserable fowls whose flight is not above their dunghill or hen-roost. But they tremble before the authors of these horrors." [19] Attachments of any sort, whether to an inherited morality or to a theory of universal rights, are alike anyway in being attachments. That certain of them are *wrong* can become, at times, a secondary matter for Burke, as he follows out the dramatic motive of the contest that absorbs him.

If the foregoing passages are in earnest, then to be a thorough ideologist is to be touched by piety (albeit a "sinister piety"). By contrast, the lowly persons who stood to the side of the great debate of the 1790s, and who failed to see that a battle for the soul of man was in agitation, are the epitome of a life without belief. The Jacobins, Burke felt, at least acted from intelligible passions, no matter how evil the result. But their half-apologists among the French in exile, who pretended that England might deal sympathetically with aristocrats as well as revolutionaries, lacked even the humanity of love and hate. Men of no place, they had broken free of every rooted sentiment, and therefore lived without any principle of action at all. For persons of this stamp, a given settlement is always only provisional, and their own country seems perpetually a borderland between two others.

Wordsworth wrote *The Borderers* in 1797–1799, not long after Burke's "Remarks on the Policy of the Allies"; and the play is about what it means to live in a place without authority or sovereignty: a border-region where, by its very nature, no one ever knows for long what spot of ground is his. The band of men whom Wordsworth shows in the play are, of course, hardly the sort of abject minds Burke had characterized as placeless. In their way indeed they are active, energetic, adventurous—men who would be great, except that their objects are not sufficiently great. Still, like other borderers, they have grown so used to an inverted order that questions of right and wrong are now for them almost enigmatic. Any evil that they do is contingent and defensible in their own eyes. How far, if that is so, *all* disputed claims of justice have to be argued, thought about, and felt again as if for the first time, with results at war with the common feelings of humanity, is the question Wordsworth means for us to ask.

In the background of the play are the baronial wars which occupied the region between England and Scotland about the time of Henry III. Concerning the public right and wrong of these events, Wordsworth seems to have held a republican view, namely, that Henry had rescued the people from the usurping claims of the barons. But the story takes place before that liberating act of monarchial power; it deals with the hazards of individual power in a society without law. More particularly, it is the tragedy of two members of a single border band: Rivers, about whom the first thing we are told is that in the last crusade he "despised alike / Mahommedan and Christian"; and Mortimer, the leader, in whom Rivers discerns another soul "self-stationed" and participating in "no common life."[20] Thus Mortimer, as Rivers pictures him, has

just the virtues that Rivers once claimed for himself, though from a
Burkean perspective they are scarcely virtues. Mortimer despises both
contending parties in the border wars; and for this he earns the praise
he gets from Rivers early in the play:

> Happy are we,
> Who live in these disputed tracts, that own
> No law but what each man makes for himself;
> Here justice has indeed a field of triumph.   (II.i.595-598)

Yet Rivers has at heart not justice, as any law would interpret it, but
one act of wild justice, the murder of a blind old man who hates the
borderers. It is pertinent that the man, Herbert, should say of them,
in a reversal of their own language, that they "prey alike on two dis-
tracted countries, / Traitor to both."

The Borderers tells about a plan for murder, even more than the action itself, but my concern here is only with an aspect of its violence.
What *sort* of crime did Wordsworth think he was describing? Apparently, it has much to do with how the killing of sentiments must
precede the killing of people. Rivers lays a trap to convince Mortimer
that in fact Herbert is not, as he had supposed, the father of the
woman he loves. Herbert long ago snatched her from her real mother,
and has now struck a filthy bargain with the worst of the barons and
sold her into slavery for life. This is a lie, but a well-told lie: it persuades Mortimer to take Herbert alone to a desolate place and there
desert him. As we are later shown, Rivers himself had once been
tricked in the same way by a gang of men aboard ship. In the belief
that their captain's wickedness justified any revenge, he led a mutiny
and left the captain to perish alone on a desert island, "A man by men
cast off." This makes a strong parallel between the characters of Mortimer and Rivers, and there are further parallels of which neither can
be conscious. But the point about the crime which they share is that
it is directed against all society. That "plot, / A hideous plot, against
the soul of man," of which Mortimer repents at the close of the play,
alludes to the break with human kind which both men carry out, once
they have discredited every possible moral community. As they harden
themselves, each gains confidence by thinking about the existence of
the other. The reflection each finds in the other, Wordsworth implies,
may serve them instead of the place that they have always lacked.
Wordsworth is almost explicit on this point in an early note to the
play: the motive of Rivers's crime, he says, is traceable to nothing but

an "original pride." Yet pride is a sociable feeling. It involves both a confirmation of knowledge about oneself and a sense that such knowledge is open to someone else's view.[21]

Still in the same note, Wordsworth remarks that "in a course of criminal conduct every fresh step that we make appears a justification of the one that preceded it; it seems to bring back again the moment of liberty and choice; it banishes the idea of repentance and seems to set remorse at defiance. Every time we plan a fresh accumulation of our guilt we have restored to us something like that original state of mind, that perturbed pleasure, which first made the crime attractive."[22] This is a Burkean observation about the psychology of revolutionaries; indeed, the sense of it so pervades his work that one is hard pressed to give a short passage: his remark, in the *Regicide Peace,* that the only Jacobin fraternity is "the brotherhood of Cain and Abel" may suggest how closely he associates murder, revolution, and the doubling on each other of men who have wandered from their place. It is a repellent thought, about a repellent subject. Wordsworth himself supposed that to inquire much further here would be to assault the right orientation of our sentiments. That, he says in the note, is why most people harbor "a kind of superstition which makes us shudder when we find moral sentiments to which we attach a sacred importance applied to vicious purposes." Within the play he must be referring to the sentiment of pity, especially the pity one feels for a person whose sufferings typify a system of abuses. By a wrong reorientation of pity, his story runs some risk of doing actual harm to its audience. But while acknowledging the good of the taboo on certain subjects, as a defense against actions both wicked and uncommon, Wordsworth says that his aim in *The Borderers* has been "to shake this prejudice," since he was "persuaded that in doing so I was well employed." Anyway it is not the public at large but the isolated individual, like Mortimer or Rivers, when he has cut himself off from morality, who will exhibit pity in a monstrous shape.

Wordsworth's ending shows as careful a respect for poetic justice as one would predict from compunctions like these. Mortimer, certainly, is seen to understand the wrong that he has done. But to live in exile thereafter, as he declares that he will do, "by mere intensity of thought, / A thing by pain and thought compelled to live," is to prolong the very way of life the crime itself demanded. It is a life of separate being which carries the risk of thinking compulsively, always "shaking" one prejudice too many: not, in a certain light, greatly different from the youthful stance of a poet like Wordsworth himself. A happier alternative may exist, of course, even for such a poet, and Wordsworth speaks of it in his sonnets on liberty, with a high feeling for "the talk / Man holds with week-day man in the hourly walk / Of the mind's business." But there are likewise times when daily life affords no example of such activity. Then even the kindliest of men, alone, may find "a transition in my soul," and, rising up against everything that once belonged to him, may feel that he has suddenly "traveled into things to come."

In a fragment never incorporated in *The Borderers,* Wordsworth wrote lines for a woman to say as comfort to a pilgrim wanderer (who may be an early version of Mortimer):

> there is a power
> Even in the common offices of love
> And friendly ministration, to revive
> Nature within thee, bid thee smile again
> With those that smile, weep with them that weep.[23]

It is very like Miranda in *The Tempest,* who says "O, I have suffered / With those that I saw suffer"—a sentiment echoed less innocently by Wordsworth in *The Excursion,* where we are told of the Wanderer: "He could *afford* to suffer / With those whom he saw suffer." More immediately in Wordsworth's career, however, the same lines look forward to "Michael" and to a consolation the poet there will offer to his hero:

> There is a comfort in the strength of love;
> 'Twill make a thing endurable which else
> Would overset the brain, or break the heart.

The endurance given to Michael comes, just as it does for Mortimer, from an act of repetition and imitation, but in his case it remembers rather than nullifies a former way of life. Individual power, "original pride," have no part in the tribute Michael pays to nature, among time-honored practices and almost monumental objects.

"Michael" as a whole I believe was written as a deliberate counterpart to *The Borderers.* It seeks to exhibit a coherence of the individual will with nature, common affections, and the ordinary powers that now no longer have to be discouraged. Yet it shows these things fitting together as if their doing so at all were a matter of controversy. As for Wordsworth's own confidence about such goods in their new setting, it relates to two elements of Michael's situation: his right to perpetuate a certain inheritance as a freeholder;[24] and his independence of commerce, that is, of any distant moral or economic interest that could abstract him from his place.

Yet in extending the argument here, one encounters a difficulty. For Wordsworth's moral concerns of the late 1790s cannot easily be squared with the usual reading of his poetry and politics, according to which he began as a radical in both spheres and then gradually retreated. To credit that account we have to suppose him a political radical in 1792–1795, when in fact his poetry was conventional; and still the same in 1795–1798, when his poetry was avant-garde but a specific politics had become hard to extract from his writing. By common consent anyway, he was some sort of agrarian Tory by the time he published *The Excursion* in 1814. But recent commentators like James Chandler, Michael Friedman, and Nicholas Roe have exposed the fallacy of these periods;[25] and I agree with Chandler in particular that Wordsworth was a Burkean thinker already by the late 1790s, when he wrote the two poems I want to speak of now. "Michael" and "The Brothers" interest me, in part, because they were the ballads Wordsworth pointed out to Charles James Fox, in the hope of demonstrating that "men who do not wear fine clothes can feel deeply." Most likely, he had a political aim in showing these poems to Fox. They would prove that England still held a strong traditional community—but of a sort not compatible with the ideology of commerce. This too, rather than a complaint about the reading public, was surely what he meant by a famous sentence of the Preface to *Lyrical Ballads,* which linked "the increasing accumulation of men in cities" with the application to the human mind of "gross and violent stimulants."

Wordsworth in *The Prelude* tells of the "daring sympathies with power" that he shared during the revolution. We have seen him in *The Borderers* touch on something of the experience which that phrase conceals. Yet how he came to speak of the defense of human nature and human history—ideas that, in his writing as in Burke's, tend to become tropes for each other—cannot be explained with equal justice to his political and poetic development. He himself eventually gave up trying to explain. His own attempt in *The Prelude* is superior to that of his critics, but the sequence it proposes is implausible, and so is the ideal, gradually evolving, identity it asks us to credit. What, then, are we to imagine in its place? I suggest the following: a poet and citizen in whom the revolutionary planner (the adept of conversions of the soul) and the pious communitarian (whose principle of deference to a neighbor is, *I love the father in you*) for a long time cohabit and share a single name.[26] When they finally do separate out, this happens in reaction not only to a sense of self-betrayal, but to the memory as well of having betrayed others. Nor is it probable that the area of betrayal was personal, or sexual, as much as it was political. Wordsworth later said that during his residence in France he had been in the heat of politics there. For a long time before and after 1794, he was a republican who never in theory discountenanced the killing of public enemies. If, as seems to me likely, *The Borderers* is a more exacting allegory of his mental life at that time than *The Prelude* or *The Excursion,* one may surmise that the play served him as a delayed apology. He came to think that by an acceptance of "natural society," and a wrong reeducation of his feelings, he was guilty of having pursued an abstract loyalty to the point of inhumanity.

Mere errors of thought, however, do not make a man condemn himself in this way, though Wordsworth in *The Prelude* wants to persuade us that they do. We must therefore suppose an action—and an action consistent with the evidence of complicity and omission in *The Borderers,* as well as with the known activities of the Committee of Public Safety (which in its heyday Wordsworth always admired in theory). He had himself, perhaps, let fall a chance word that could convict a man in a revolutionary tribunal; or allowed such a word to pass, when someone else had spoken it; and then seen the fatal practical effects of his act of theoretical solidarity. That would fit the intense wish for solitude and even exile which is strong at the end of "The Brothers" and throughout "Tintern Abbey." Again, in the latter poem, his wish in seclusion to discover "thoughts of more deep seclusion" appears less a consequence of having found a chastened and transcendental self, than of feeling that he has grown unworthy of human company. Only his sister is allowed on the scene now. With her tacit loyalty and early knowledge of his life, she alone can be trusted to find him guiltless. In this, his luck proves at least superior to that of Leonard in "The Brothers" and Luke in "Michael," and their prototype Mortimer: all deserters who are themselves deserted, men "by men cast off." But as we shall see, the connection among these works—their Burkean distrust of the placeless soul whom history cannot include—is far more complete than even the hard-earned consolation of "Tintern Abbey" wants to admit.

"The Brothers" and "Michael" seem to have been written by Wordsworth as acts of expiation. In the first poem one of two brothers, Leonard, who has spent most of his life at sea, returns to a mountain village to track down the sickly one, James, whom he left at home and whom he had aimed to support. He learns that he is too late, but learns it slowly and falteringly, because he has forgotten how to read the natural language of uninscribed monuments (including the stones in a graveyard without epitaphs). In the second poem, of which Chapter 2 gave a short account, it is significant that Michael has held his family together by the cottage economy of clipping and spinning wool. When his son Luke goes bad, Michael is left to tend his way of life alone. Both poems honor the adequate readers of social and natural traces which may become personal memories: to the extent that the poet is in either of these poems, he is there to learn how to read from someone native. At the same time, both are declarations of a fresh piety toward an aggregate social body that Wordsworth till then had thought of only in the way of the pamphleteer. They offer vivid representations of exile to show that the exiles themselves—Luke, who falls from a virtuous life and seeks a refuge beyond the seas; and the still-living brother Leonard, who will die with only the sea for a home—are rightly understood as persons removed from society, important as warnings but not as objects of compassion.

There are two lessons here, one national and one personal. England, because of the system of commerce just then emerging, was in the process of creating multitudes of lost or wandering souls on the pattern of Luke and Leonard. Wordsworth aimed in poems like these to restore faith in a kind of experience that was passing from English life. The experience itself E. P. Thompson has called, in a happy phrase, "moral economy," and that is as good a name as we shall find.[27] It suggests why the reader of these poems soon comes to feel that "The Brothers" is really about the homely dead brother, James, and his now illegible way of life; just as "Michael" is about the character of that name and not the son who connects him with the world at large. Both, too, have at their center a hardly traceable vestige of the older life: in "The Brothers," the burial place of the brother who died young; in "Michael," the half-built sheepfold that recalls the broken covenant between father and son. The failure to notice the significance of this object in "The Brothers" prompts the dismissal of the errant brother to a lifelong term of wandering. By contrast, the success in "Michael" allows us to feel that the poem ends, not with a catastrophe after all, but an answered prayer for continuity. Yet it works out in this way, in spite of an actual death, only because Wordsworth has listened to the tale told by shepherds; so that his final hope depends on his having found in the reader another poet, who "Will be my second self when I am gone."

The ambition of "Michael" is to show how a faith in human nature is strengthened by habit, and by the mere carrying on of observances from a more than personal past. We are told near the start that all the impressions of "Those fields, those hills" among which Michael lived,

> had laid
> Strong hold on his affections, were to him
> A pleasurable feeling of blind love,
> The pleasure which there is in life itself.

The word, "pleasure," which will be vital to Wordsworth in the Preface, seems particularly elusive here, as does the notion of a "blind love." What is plain in this Wordsworthian hypothesis is that we evolve an affinity to the habits by which we know our life as ours. Thus, we come to identify ourselves with just such habits, until they seem to us the very tokens of our nature. Yet nature as Wordsworth employs the idea likewise resists analysis. It has the quality of instinct, but a kind of instinct we can reflect upon, even if its causes are forever closed to us. Burke would, I think, have appreciated the lines quoted above, from an analogy between "blind love" and his own phrase, "untaught feelings." Nevertheless, Wordsworth here adds something original to the Burkean understanding of habit and sentiment. It is the idea of pleasure as a renewable motive for feeling and reflection; a pleasure, also, which no longer composes one half of pleasure and pain, but is rather a name for the benefit we draw from the almost-instinct that is nature.

There remains a certain ambivalence in Wordsworth's attitude toward all these related goods: habit, nature, pleasure, and the return of old feelings. It is the kind of ambivalence that Burke always tried to contain, and that Wordsworth is great for his powerlessness to contain. Yet habit, of all these terms, brings the difference most to light; and then one sees that it is a difference of vocation as much as temperament. Burke frequently raises doubts like Wordsworth's concerning a good he chooses to inculcate: one need only think of the grand, rolling, oppressive descriptions that sponsor an inert nobility in the *Reflections;* or the sentence in the "Letter to a Noble Lord" which weighs the

Duke of Bedford's title against Burke's merit, and which runs in full: "I have strained every nerve to keep the Duke of Bedford in that situation, which alone makes him my superior." However, the work of a moralist, as Burke saw it, was to induce a directive from experience— at least when that was consistent with what he had seen with his own eyes, and what he had felt with his own hands. At times, he would consent to deal in the mere recollection of precepts. Whereas it was the whole task of a poet like Wordsworth to acknowledge, and even to dramatize, the career of a personal will. In that perspective of course, moral precepts, including those he had taken as his own, could always seem an intervention from elsewhere.

This is to make the argument depend for much of its force on hidden intuitions. But one can just as easily translate it into a difference of public views about taste. For Burke, the work of taste appears as a kind of *resumption*—a restoration, as in the passage on the "miracle" of the Queen's fall, of an accustomed former continuity of moral sentiments. Wordsworth, too, plainly wants to associate the use of taste with moral choice. But he often seems to suggest—among other places in the "Essay, Supplementary to the Preface" of 1815—that any genuine verdict of taste is a *usurpation.* In the light of such an act, when it is once accomplished, every previous continuity will have to be described again. The reward of doing so can hardly be "a pleasurable feeling of blind love." Once, then, we have dissociated imaginative power and habitual pleasure, what do we make of a life like Michael's? The question is odd; yet it was often in Wordsworth's mind, and poignantly so in the "Ode to Duty":

> Me this unchartered freedom tires;
> I feel the weight of chance-desires:
> My hopes no more must change their name,
> I long for a repose that ever is the same.

The poet himself speaks here as Luke might speak if he could wish to return to Michael's state. But Wordsworth sometimes explores both sides of a complex feeling about habit by the movement of a single metaphor. Compare, for example, "A pleasurable feeling of blind love, / The pleasure which there is in life itself," with what seems at first an antithetical figure of speech in the Immortality Ode. There, shades of the prison-house close round the growing boy, and he is warned:

> Full soon thy Soul shall have her earthly freight,
> And custom lie upon thee with a weight
> Heavy as frost, and deep almost as life!

It is as if the weight of custom could sink the soul so deep that it would reach down to "life itself"—thence to bring us back a knowledge that is somehow not unlike pleasure. In the argument, pleasure, being composed merely of habit, is a shroud that darkens vision: blind love has given way to blind endurance. But there is no escaping the strangely affirmative note in "deep almost as life." A Burkean reading is available, up to a point: we must be buried so deep, and feel the weight of custom lie so full upon us, before we can think truly of the bonds that link us to the whole moral system of life. Gone, however, is any sense that the nature we touch in this way is something with which we would choose to burden ourselves (if somehow we could choose).

In "Michael," all the last part is unmoralized; and Luke is dispatched in a few lines, as if Wordsworth here wanted to believe that he had always been offstage:

> Meantime Luke began
> To slacken in his duty; and, at length,
> He in the dissolute city gave himself
> To evil courses; ignominy and shame
> Fell on him, so that he was driven at last
> To seek a hiding place beyond the seas.

If the story were the tragedy of Michael and Luke, this ought to be the end. But it is rather, as the title simply announces, the pastoral of Michael alone. The anticlimax does, therefore, point a moral. In the final short stretch of the poem, Michael will find "a comfort in the strength of love"; but he does it by recurring to the worn tracks of his customary existence, the same life as before amid "those fields, those hills." We are meant to see this return not as a declaration of community—there is hardly a word about his wife or neighbors—but rather as something like a repetition of the pleasurable feeling of blind love. Only now, since it requires no human object to fix upon, it has become an effect capable of operating without a cause. To put it another way, Luke has been turned into all the associations by which Michael's usual life is governed. In place of the sense of loss we have the half-built sheepfold; and, instead of any lamentation, this "pastoral." We are made to feel that Michael's observances, from a habit that is now second nature, are all he has ever needed to affirm the strength of love. One might say in a less Wordsworthian idiom that the mere sentiment of social coherence is alone a certain help to personal endurance. In fact, its power may be so great as to serve in the absence of any actual renewal of the experience on which the sentiment was founded.

This conversion of a social to a personal good is something that Wordsworth invented. He takes what began as a common sentiment and uses it to strengthen only the power of solitary experience. For this movement of his mind, there now exist a pair of unpleasant but serviceable adjectives, "internalizing" and "monumentalizing." But the two words describe aspects of a single process: the monument is an outward memento of a life that has to be felt with a special force inwardly, and has so to be felt because it has ceased to be lived. Granted, it is a cold self-trust that seems to be opened up by Michael's return to a familiar place, and to the limitless self-sustenance he derives from the knowledge of that place. One can imagine such a principle of recovery working against the social affections. Yet the poem is moving, if one does find it moving, as a direct apology for the sort of community which seemed real to Wordsworth, once the prospect of revolution had withdrawn and his own life had been contained within well-marked borders. Unless one keeps in view the social changes that turned him to such a response, the poem will appear to be both elegiac and pastoral in an altogether restrictive sense.

I have to add here a word about property, and the place it holds in the conversion that I describe. Michael, before the poem begins, had "been bound / In surety for his brother's son," who came to misfortune, so that Michael was called upon to discharge the forfeit: a penalty amounting to nearly "half his substance." The following lines bring a resonance to the word *hope* which it will carry ever after in Wordsworth's poetry. It denotes a solid expectation—which here has been cut off—of some day bequeathing land to a descendant:

> This unlooked-for claim,
> At the first hearing, for a moment took
> More hope out of his life than he supposed
> That any old man ever could have lost.

Hope is treated as a quantifiable stuff: one knows, or at any rate can guess, just how much of it is in one's grasp. Michael then explains the predicament to his wife; seventy years of toil will have been without compensation if his family goes without the enlarged property he has worked to provide: "if these fields of ours / Should pass into a stranger's hand, I think / That I could not lie quiet in my grave." He sees the risk of sending out Luke so young—"I wish indeed that I / Were younger," because he could more safely trust himself to perform the hard task ahead. "But," he adds, "this hope is a good hope."

Later, when seeking a way to bind Luke to him and his place, he elects to tell a story (much as Wordsworth himself tells a story to the reader): "I will relate to thee some little part / Of our two histories; 'twill do thee good / When thou art from me." To keep a history alive, for as long as Luke is away, he himself "will begin again / With many tasks that were resigned to thee; / Up to the heights, and in among the storms, / Will I without thee go again, and do / All works which I was wont to do alone, / Before I knew thy face." When we are shown Michael again, after Luke's flight and disgrace, we do see him performing just the same routines he mentioned, for the sake of "the land, his small inheritance." Thus, the narrowing, to a therapy of self-recovery, of a work and a life originally meant for more than one, goes with the curtailment of a claim of actual property. Michael's isolation would in a poem by anyone else feel like a punishment; but here the guilt belongs to Luke and the other life that corrupted him. The poem defends Michael's right to constitute himself on his remaining land as a community of one.

So the story of "Michael" internalizes, in a single life, the idea of a tradition; even as it monumentalizes, for an unnamed audience, a personal idea of memory. This was a difficult accomplishment. The whole of Wordsworth's ambition for more than a decade after was to carry its meaning home to the readers he thought his poems would find. Usually, he performs this work with the help of two implicit equations. Hope is a figure for individual property. Local attachments in general, however, are the index of a wider moral consciousness, which may issue in "natural piety." For Michael, the hope of a living posterity is bound up with the idea of his name being carried forward, in the patrimonial fields. More largely, his piety will come to be shared only if the poet communicates a certain sense of things to his readers, who themselves will constitute a place of natural piety. It is because the struggle is always for so vivid a gain or loss that Wordsworth's poetry comes back continually to a favorite plot: a long-unchallenged loyalty, broken by a sudden betrayal, and renewed under the aspect of time-honored practices.

That betrayal is the great revolutionary sin Burke's *Regicide Peace* had presented as a discovery of moral science. After all, from the perspective of a faithful earlier self, betrayal may seem a kind of twisted loyalty—*warm* emulation gone monstrously wrong. Yet this, says Burke, is what comes of the severing of relations in time that the modern revolutionary always aims to effect. One is left thereby in a world without parents, without children—only a self facing a self. When, at last, such reflection has charmed away every idea of tradition or continuity, then speculation (in the etymological sense of mirroring) has taken the place of nature. Yet the story that Burke had framed as special to the political character of a revolutionary, Wordsworth projects as a story true for an individual thinker in all the moral relations of life. Indeed, he can often spot a betrayal where, to the untutored eye, only an accidental change of life happens to separate two characters. A key to the morality of "The Brothers," for example, is that the vicar of that story, who presides over the old village and its memories, at first treats the returning Leonard as a *tourist*. But in this the vicar agrees with Wordsworth: the mariner, by once alienating himself from home, has innocently but irreparably lost all the virtue of the place. His going to sea for that matter bears some of the blame for his brother's death. After Leonard's first departure, James was subject at night to fits of sleepwalking, when he would grasp vainly for his brother; and the suggestion is somehow left that his fall from a mountain summit occurred in a similar daze.

Clearly the moral of such a story, if carried to a practical extreme, would stop at a profession of faith in inertia. Wordsworth, any time after 1796, was seldom far from that. He was prevented from sounding complacent only by the force of his personal myth. With every worldly impulse contributing to drive men from their homes, Wordsworth sees that a sustained attachment can have the quality of an almost unselfish conquest. Not steady attachment however, but the strengthened attachment of a return, is the plot he commonly chooses. This must somehow be vouched for by a second self who testifies that the hero has not changed from what he was. Or rather, the second self does see the change, but still knows the original self from which the change began, and can bear unchallengeable witness to the continuity that binds together its moments of identity. But the second self in Words-

worth's greatest poetry—I exclude certain set pieces of *The Prelude*—
cannot be summed up as "an aspect of the poet himself." It must instead be the reader, or a Friend, or Dorothy: she, perhaps, most of all.
"Tintern Abbey" almost fails to control a suspicion that without her,
he might "suffer his genial spirits to decay." That is to say (for the
words are a euphemism), he would feel himself rightly cut off from
human kind. Rivers, near the end of *The Borderers,* offering a motive
for the terrible deception he has carried out, says only: "Know then
that I was urged, / (For other impulse let it pass) was driven, / To seek
for sympathy, because I saw / In you a mirror of my youthful self." The
tenor is the same as that of the speech assigned to Wordsworth himself
at the end of "Tintern Abbey."

The chief question about that poem ought not to concern Wordsworth's identity as a poet. For his crisis there has a moral as well as an
aesthetic character. He is a man so overtaken by fear that he lapses into
complete stillness, feels thankful that he need not move a muscle ever
again, and passes on to an ignorant other the whole record and responsibility of his life. This, again, Wordsworth has to say euphemistically:
"thy mind / Shall be a mansion for all lovely forms, / Thy memory be
as a dwelling-place / For all sweet sounds and harmonies." But the
sense of the words is entirely self-protective. Through her intervention
the forms and memories of his own life are purged of the guilt that
haunted them as long as their mansion was *his* mind. In this poem
about a successful return, "after many wanderings, many years / Of
absence," a consoling self-recognition is thus achieved by proxy. But
what has been repressed is the memory of something that those wanderings contained. It is the knowledge of his complicity in an act of
terror that now prompts Wordsworth to describe himself, in a rather
shadowy phrase, as "more like a man / Flying from something that he
dreads, than one / Who sought the thing he loved."

His "sense sublime" here corresponds to physical immobility and
seems close to a wish for death. It is also spoken of as "that blessed
mood, / In which the burthen of the mystery, / In which the heavy
and the weary weight / Of all this unintelligible world / Is lightened,"
so that, "Almost suspended, we are laid asleep / In body." De Quincey
echoed these lines, perversely it would seem, in his essay on the murder in *Macbeth.* But he had the right clue: possibly he had heard
enough to read the phrases as the direct allegory of a Parisian assassination of thirty years before. Wordsworth anyway gives a similar res-

onance to Mortimer's words, after his first acceptance of killing in *The Borderers:*

> Deep, deep and vast, vast beyond human thought,
> Yet calm—I could believe that there was here
> The only quiet heart on earth.—In terror,
> Remembered terror, there is love and peace.
>
> (III.v.1466–69, 1797 version)

The weird lines are a sort of tryout for "Tintern Abbey," and one has to remember that hardly a year separates the two. The presence of a second self, a good one like Dorothy, not a bad one like Rivers, makes it possible for the remembered terror and the peace to subsist as if in different persons. In such a condition the person addressed can, from the ordinary action of sympathy, help to repair diseases of the imagination which the poet has brought upon himself.[28]

My comments on these works of 1797–1800 have been selective, but a generalization may still be worthwhile. Some of Wordsworth's great poems of the nineties are an attempt to reconstruct a humanity which the poet fears he has lost in a heartless agreement to do good on behalf of humanity. He accordingly turns against something he has come to know in himself, the sentiment Burke described as a "sinister piety." But the act of reformation that he would complete for others has to begin at home: its ways are not yet appropriate to an entire nation. Wordsworth, who is otherwise as lost as Mortimer or Luke or Leonard, sees that to exist again he must be recognized to exist. That can be assured by the true historian who is embodied first in a dear friend and then in the reader. But the absolution he asks from Dorothy, above all, is in keeping with the severity of his unforgiving memory. Well-placed sympathies shared by someone else do seem the alternative to a terror confined to oneself alone.

If, at this extreme of imaginative action, Wordsworth seems to have *lived* the Burkean myth of revolutionary disenchantment, he did not have to do so consciously. It just happened that his own experience and Burke's analysis tallied at every point where a practical test could matter. This may account as well for a curious quality in his story—the quality that can make it seem representative. It survives every attack on the self-interest or the self-deception of the hero, because the former ideal which he now rejects is neither benevolence nor self-knowledge. It is rather an ideal of detachment from society, and of speculative freedom. Returning from the wreck of those high things, the hero tells us to cherish, more than we easily can, the attachments we live with anyway as a matter of routine. We credit his private testimony, however, with a peculiar weight, since in back of it stands Burke's meditation on a great public event. And perhaps also we credit Burke's prophecy more than we otherwise would because it produced in the next generation a confirming instance like this. But there is an irony in the working out of their stance, of which Wordsworth is often aware, as Burke, with his steady pragmatic motive, appears to be less often aware. The defense of nature, Wordsworth shows, is another name for the defense of history. But the latter is itself a product of speculation—even if (as he may want to say) of deeper, longer-lasting or longer-tried, speculation than the thing it fights against. It follows that nature is another name for a *common* speculation which responds to hopes and not only to projections. This thought, however, would not become a guide to Wordsworth's public reflection on politics until a decade later, with *The Convention of Cintra*.

In the early summer of 1808, Napoleon's armies and his government in Spain were met by a general revolt of the Spanish people. By August, a British expeditionary force under General Wellesley had landed in Portugal, and the French were repulsed on both sides. The convention helped to save them, and the British agreed to it in a spirit of short-sighted expediency, against the hope of Spanish national independence. It is fair to say that at this moment, in Wordsworth's conception of Europe, Spain appeared as the second self of England. Quite early in the essay, he asserts: "There are promptings of wisdom from the penetralia of human nature, which a people can hear, though the wisest of their practical Statesmen be deaf towards them"; as a consequence of the English sympathy with Spain, he adds, "We were intellectualized also in proportion." Wordsworth then goes on:

> We looked backward upon the records of the human race with pride, and, instead of being afraid, we delighted to look forward into futurity. It was imagined that this new-born spirit of resistance, rising from the most sacred feelings of the human heart, would diffuse itself through many countries; and not merely for the distant future, but for the present, hopes were entertained as bold as they were disinterested and generous.[29]

Here Wordsworth, speaking as England, with Spain in the role of the betrayed and venerable elder, is able to cast himself as Dorothy (from "Tintern Abbey"), or as the humane republican soldier Beaupuy (from *The Prelude*). The result can be felt as his most eloquent statement of a republican creed. The surface echoes of Burke are, it happens, far more crowded in this essay than anywhere else in Wordsworth's writing.[30] One can hear them in passages of eulogy—as when he says that the English have thought of the "past greatness" of the Spanish people "not as the undermined foundation of a magnificent building, but as the root of a majestic tree recovered from a long disease, and beginning again to flourish with promise of wider branches and a deeper shade than it had boasted in the fullness of its strength." But there is something of the same effect even in passages of reprehension. He recalls, for example, how "taught by the reverses of the French revolution, we looked upon these dispositions [the stirrings of the Spanish people for independence] as more human—more social—and therefore as wiser, and of better omen, than if they had stood forth the zealots of abstract principles, drawn out of the laboratory of unfeeling philosophists." The casual parallel in "more human—more social" comes straight from Burke.

One feels, however, that Wordsworth is not quite true to himself when he borrows so thoroughly from an earlier style of defense. It is all the more interesting therefore to see what happens when the imitation stops. Near the end of the *Convention*, he offers his own view of the way human nature cooperates with political independence. The language here is that of the sonnets on liberty; and it gives support to David Erdman's interpretation of the sonnets.[31] Erdman says that Wordsworth in the early 1800s believed a mood of freedom, engendered by the fight against Napoleon, would irresistibly animate England when at last the continental wars were over. The fight against tyranny abroad would end in an accession of liberty at home. This seems to be a common thought with disenchanted revolutionaries, and perhaps especially among the English. Orwell in "The Lion and the Unicorn" cherished a similar hope for England during the Second World War: the resistance to Fascism would lead to a socialist revolution among the resisters; indeed, such a movement offered the only prospect of fighting the war itself with success. In the anomalous history of Wordsworth's own thinking, the alliance of Spanish independence and English liberty implied a deep vindication for an idea of the self, which he had come close to renouncing before on Burkean grounds. The crucial passage seems to me this:

> Not by bread alone is the life of Man sustained; not by raiment alone is he warmed;—but by the genial and vernal inmate of the breast, which at once pushes forth and cherishes; by self-support and self-sufficing endeavours; by anticipations, apprehensions, and active remembrances; by elasticity under insult, and firm resistance to injury; by joy, and by love; by pride which his imagination gathers in from afar; by patience, because life wants not promises; by admiration; by gratitude which— debasing him not when his fellow-being is its object—habitually expands itself, for his elevation, in complacency towards his Creator.[32]

The end of the sentence modulates a little, as Burke himself occasionally did, into an earlier language of natural law. But what is revealing is the stress Wordsworth lays upon the continuity of future, present, and past: "anticipations, apprehensions, and active remembrances"; as if our lives made sense only when held together in this individual way.

The thought in this passage seems to me non-Burkean, above all in the primary importance that it assigns to the autonomy of the self. Thus in the clause which gives the elements of a human community, one notices that "self-support and self-sufficing endeavours" come first. The expansions that yield sympathy, gratitude, and so on, are later or secondary developments. Here the germ of all the social affections is no longer what it was for Burke, "the little platoon we belong to in society," but rather the duties that we lay upon ourselves. And here, though doubtless it would have dismayed Wordsworth to think so, he writes as the disciple of Rousseau and Kant rather than Burke. The pressures of duty and of inclination he now feels to be antithetical, and for once he does not think of using "sentiment" as a mediating term. In fact, the liberty required by the self is so demanding as to exclude for a time all sense of other persons as an aggregate. A premonition of the same feeling occurs in a line already quoted from the "Ode to Duty":

> I feel the weight of chance-desires.

Written four years earlier, that poem knows more than it means to say about liberty. "Chance-desires" in any ordinary figure of speech would have to be of an almost flimsy lightness. But Wordsworth's point is that liberty must be felt as listlessness, and so as a burden of tremendous weight, before we can wish to balance against it the weight of duty. Liberty and obligation are in any case strongly connected because both work in the irreducible medium of personal experience.

It is true that when, in another passage of the *Convention,* Wordsworth organizes the scheme of all social relations as concentric circles, with the self at the core and humanity at the outermost rim, he can still seem to write as a follower of Burke. Yet, for Wordsworth, the self gives the original impulse to the other sympathies, rather than merely enhancing them from the dearness of the associations it brings. For him, the identity of the inmost circle is given to itself by itself. His definition of duty is thus inextricable from the definition of a freedom that has risen above inclinations. Burke would have professed not to understand any such way of thinking: his version of duty follows only from constraint; and when he says "more human—more social," he measures the ideal docility that there is in the very conjunction of these ideas. This last difference from Burke means that Wordsworth can never quite dedicate himself to other-regarding practices. Such practices, though they may sometimes confirm self-support, do not ever precede it. But we can go much further here. Wordsworth's belief in the authority of the self is so far antipaternalist that the experience it favors can come from anywhere—from the lives of men who feel deeply and do not wear fine clothes, as much as from the luminous sphere inhabited by the Queen of France.

Burke wrote in the third of his *Letters on a Regicide Peace:*

> Men are rarely without some sympathy in the sufferings of others; but in the immense and diversified mass of human misery, which may be pitied, but cannot be relieved, in the gross, the mind must make a choice. Our sympathy is always more forcibly attracted towards the misfortunes of certain persons, and in certain descriptions: and this sympathetic attraction discovers, beyond a possibility of mistake, our mental affinities and elective affections.[33]

Something of this principle must hold true if we come to value the self against the background of humanity, about which great works are written to show us the proper order of our sympathies, and great traditions are then formed from those works. But Wordsworth replied in "Rob Roy's Grave":

> Said generous Rob, "What need of books?
> Burn all the statutes and their shelves:

> They stir us up against our kind;
> And worse, against ourselves."

That it is worse to turn against oneself than against one's kind is, from a Burkean perspective, as wild a paradox as that the relations of the self engage us before those of the community. Nevertheless, it begins to answer the question I asked in first moving from Burke to Wordsworth—the question why in a poem like "Michael," the social catastrophe can end up seeming only a whispered parenthesis.

The truth is that for the Wordsworthian hero there can never be a time when his nature was not as he now realizes it to be. Before and after Luke come all the things that Michael knows, and feels, and does, because he is the man he is, in the place he inhabits. The property that he might have passed on to Luke is actually reclaimed through the memories he passes on to himself. There is a strength, to return to the poem's own word, in this imagination of life, which makes it a far from settled ally of political reaction, even as it repels any thought of progress in nature. Emotionally, that is Wordsworth's great discovery. Had Burke written the story himself, he would have been content to end with the ordinary and restrictive lesson: "Nothing will ever be the same again." It is a note that poetry is apt to strike as often as philosophy. But Wordsworth the poet, and not Burke the moralist, seems farthest here from every literary conclusion. In this respect the difference between these founders of English romanticism is not so much a matter of belief as of untaught feeling. Wordsworth alone, it must be added, has the final courage of Burke's convictions. He affirms that if we have chosen our nature strongly enough, it cannot be lost in any revolution however astonishing, for it will come back in the very texture of our speculations.

4

William Cobbett, Reformer

ANY ENGLISH HISTORIAN rash enough to talk about the causes of an event will tell you that three things produced the Reform Bill of 1832: a series of working-class protests, some spontaneous and some closely planned, with the fear of a more general uprising to follow; the growing influence of the early Utilitarians, who offered specific proposals for reform; and William Cobbett. Of these causes the last is the most interesting as well as the easiest to credit. Starting in 1802, and after 1810 with an extraordinary single-mindedness of attack, he wrote and published his own newspaper, the *Political Register,* which had for its constant theme the radical reorganization of society. An entirely new parliament, responsible to every class in society, would be the first step in such a change, but the first step only. From 1816 on, to square his policy with his practice, Cobbett sold the paper also in a smaller and cheaper version, printing the comment without the news, so that any common laborer could afford to buy it. This edition was nicknamed by his enemies "two-penny trash," and characteristically he took over the name and made the most of it. He had, it was sometimes supposed, a special interest in the plight of the farm laborer, for he himself had practiced the "cottage economy" of a farmer and knew what the land might yield if the government did not plunder harvests annually with tithes, taxes, and a price fixed by the emerging class of capitalists. But it would be wrong to think of Cobbett as an agitator among one sector of the working class. With the postwar discontent that climaxed in the Peterloo Massacre of 1819, and that erupted at intervals for more than a decade after, he became, as much as any man in history, a tribune of the people, a voice so trusted that when he spoke out they seemed to be hearing themselves.

Cobbett must be one of the hardest great writers to think about. He published a score of books, apart from his millions of words for the *Political Register;* but the diverseness of his subjects and the unpredictable course of his opinions together form an imposing obstacle. So there have been good portraits of him—Hazlitt's essay in *Table-Talk,* Chesterton's *William Cobbett*—but until now only one good full-scale biography, by G. D. H. Cole. George Spater's *William Cobbett: The Poor Man's Friend* nearly makes a second.[1] It provides a more detailed record than Cole's and, if less exciting as a story and less confident in its workmanship of prose, is at any rate clear, sympathetic, and conscientious throughout. Cole wrote as a Guild Socialist, more interested in the way Cobbett might seem to look forward to Marx and William Morris than in the way he actually cast his sidelong glances at Paine and Robert Owen. That had its disadvantages: Cobbett was in truth no more a socialist (because he cared about equality) than he was a conservative (because he cared about the national debt). On the other hand, the animus of Cole's book, which made it seem partly a tract for the times in the 1920s, succeeded in giving it a distinct character. Spater's biography has no such character, and the reason is that Mr. Spater is not quite a political man; indeed, insofar as one can say this about any author's dealings with a subject as massively provoking as Cobbett, he seems to be altogether without crotchets; he tries hard to be fair all around, and for Cobbett's life and times the effort is hopeless. One feels nevertheless that his book was written out of love, and its warmth of dedication carries a reader through two large volumes without complaint. *The Poor Man's Friend* includes, as Cole's biography could not, a scrupulous account of Cobbett's family life, which has the effect of making its hero less legendary without once introducing a note of the undignified or the ignoble. It is also generous with quotations, and I will be using some of them here.

The force with which Cobbett kept up for three decades his one-man challenge to the government of a great country has no explanation in the range of normal human endurance; but Cobbett even as a physical presence was outside the normal range, as sketches and paintings of him show. The tall figure (tending to portliness), the lion's head, both contribute to the impression of a *substantial* ferocity—his person, like his periods, had a girth that defied cavil. One incident from his life makes the point better than any description. He had agreed to speak to a meeting, at an inn in Lewes, Sussex, during the agitations of 1822. For him this would have been a negligible entry in a busy schedule, and he went only because someone had warned him against it. As soon as Cobbett's health was proposed, a murmur rose up from the audience (which became gradually intelligible as a counter-proposal), one man stood on a table and read aloud some offensive remarks from the *Political Register,* and a motion was made for evicting Cobbett from the premises, to the approving cheers (as Cobbett himself describes them) of "six or eight of the dark, dirty, half-whiskered tax eaters from Brighton." Cobbett, who knew better than to start a contest of shouting, gave his answer in another way. "I rose, that they might see the man that they had to put out." They saw; and he gave his speech without interruption. The government, too, for three decades made its counter-proposals and motions for evicting him, with as little success as the tax eaters from Brighton.

He was born in 1763, the son of a tavern-keeper, and grew up in Surrey. His apprenticeship to a London solicitor, and later his army service in North America, have nothing in them to discourage anyone's prediction of a safe career as an officer, or as a prosperous farmer. It was not before the second decade of the nineteenth century, for that matter, that anyone could have guessed he aspired to be something more than a prosperous writer. But the events of his early life made Cobbett feel, only half voluntarily, the calling of a reformer. While in the army he had watched his superior officers for signs of superiority, as hopeful of guidance as any tavern-keeper's son. He could not help noticing how they diverted to themselves money that rightly belonged to the common soldiers under them, and being Cobbett he could not help keeping records of what he knew. Back in England, he inquired more closely into the regimental books: the evidence seemed unambiguous, and he brought charges against four officers of the regiment. His petition to the Secretary of War was granted and a court-martial convened on March 24, 1792, but Cobbett failed to appear in court and so the charges were dropped. He had, as it turned out, been traduced by the government. A few days before the hearings were to begin, he had discovered that some of the evidence he needed was now unavailable to him, some had been tampered with, a large number of witnesses had been bribed and others silenced. Instead of going ahead to certain defeat in a rigged case, he fled to France. He intended a stay in Paris, with the woman he had met in America and married in England, but, hearing of the arrest of the King and Queen and the massacre of the Swiss Guard, he had to reverse direction once more. In August 1792, five months after their arrival in France, the couple sailed from Le Havre. The next eight years Cobbett spent in America, as a pamphleteer against the party of Jefferson, whom he never lost a chance of denouncing as Jacobins.

He wrote now under the pen name Peter Porcupine, and earned the gratitude of the Federalists, without their pay or personal favor. Washington said of his work, "It is not a bad thing"; and with every allowance for Washington's habit of understatement, this was the most that could be said by any American; for Cobbett made a point above all of being a loyal Englishman, and more than once implied that the American Revolution was as much to be regretted as the French. In 1797 a libel action was brought against him by Dr. Benjamin Rush (whose treatment of yellow fever he had called a recipe for certain death). When the case finally reached court in December 1799, the judge presiding was a close friend of Governor Thomas McKean of Pennsylvania, whom Cobbett had reviled in stronger terms even than Rush; and the jury's verdict, obedient to elaborate instructions from the judge, was against Cobbett for damages amounting to $5000. He chose this moment to depart again for England, where he made the apparently easy transition from Federalist to Tory. His politics, however, in these first years of his return, were misleading to everyone including himself.

Cobbett would tolerate the English government under Pitt and his successors only so long as he felt that he himself was a potent influence on its actions. He still sought an end to the shoring up of old alliances by the awarding of places and pensions—the same enhancement of "the sons and daughters of corruption" which he had found in the army—and at first the Tories seemed to him less irremediably mercenary than their rivals. This illusion was sustained by the war against Napoleon, whose staunchest advocates, Lord Grenville and William Windham, he regarded as men of good will. Then too, Windham was a rhetorician in the grand style: the disciple of Burke, he had called the French Revolution "the second fall of man," and in 1800 Cobbett was still capable of enjoying that sort of talk. But with the Treaty of Amiens, in 1802, Cobbett ceased to look on Napoleon as an object of national concern. His loss of interest in the enemy whose existence alone justified the policies of the government marks the real beginning of his political education. When Windham took over as Secretary for

War and Colonies in the Ministry of All-the-Talents, he naturally expected Cobbett to fall into line: after all, he was a patron of the *Political Register,* and Cobbett was on record as considering at least *this* talent to be genuine. But he misjudged his man; Cobbett retained complete independence. And when he saw the new ministry at once concealing and widening the abuses of its predecessors, he grew more virulent than ever. In July 1809 he wrote a savage article denouncing the manner in which the government had suppressed a mutiny among the local militia at Ely. German troops had been brought in, and the guilty men had been sentenced to receive five hundred lashes each. It was not the severity of the sentence but the presence of foreign mercenaries that offended Cobbett's sense of honor and indeed of patriotism. His article was a passing thing and might easily have been allowed to drop from sight; but the government was very sure of its power. Cobbett therefore found himself charged with seditious libel, and eventually sentenced to two years in Newgate with a fine of one thousand pounds. This time there was no escape.

During his stay in prison the *Political Register* kept appearing. The reversal strengthened Cobbett's mind by giving him a personal humiliation to brood on—and "the System" as he called it, or sometimes just "the Thing," came to seem worse than corrupt. It was monstrous; a devourer of its own children, whether in prisons or in graves; a thing, simply, to be rid of. This was the tone in which he would speak of it almost to his death in 1835. But his imprisonment taught Cobbett a degree of wariness, and several years later, in 1817, when he received a polite suggestion from Lord Sidmouth that he stop publishing the *Political Register* and devote himself full time to his proper work as a farmer, he understood it as an immediate threat to his liberty and arranged another voyage to America rather than endure another prosecution. Still the newspaper appeared, only a little the poorer for being some weeks behind the pace of events in England. And the William Cobbett who returned to England in 1819 was the writer Hazlitt could describe as "a kind of *fourth estate* in the politics of the country." That phrase as Hazlitt used it was precise in a way that is seldom recognized; for while in America Cobbett had written the words that would serve as his credo for the years to come:

> Society ought not to exist, if not for the benefit of the whole. It is and must be against the law of nature, if it exist for the benefit of the

few. . . . I say, then, distinctly that a society, in which the common labourer, with common health and strength and with economy and sobriety and industry and good morals and good manners, cannot secure a sufficiency of food and raiment, is a society which ought not to exist; a society contrary to the law of nature; a society whose compact is dissolved.[2]

From a reporter of occasional disappointments, he had become a prophet: "Such a system must come to an end, and the end must be dreadful." But no law of historical development would assure that end; no already existing agency would bring it about. The fate of the common laborer depended on his coming to see himself not as a victim of circumstances but as a designated casualty, in a system which fostered the single basic injustice of denying the benefit of the whole.

To help people see this, Cobbett throughout the 1820s collected facts. He rode about the countryside and *looked*—where other reformers brought their charts to plan, he brought his eyes to witness. He noticed that farm laborers were being kept at a level of bare subsistence, and sometimes below; and yet, the fields were rich with an annual crop of rye, wheat, barley. He calculated how much it would take to feed all the laborers who worked the land, and found they could feed themselves, and many more, with the food they produced. He asked how then it happened that they were starving. The answer was that the prices and distribution of goods were determined not by the productive members of society but by "the whole tribe of tax eaters," by the "nabobs, negro-drivers, generals, admirals, governors, commissaries, contractors, pensioners, sinecurists, commissioners, loan-jobbers, lottery dealers, bankers, stock-jobbers; not to mention the long and *black list* in gowns and three-tailed wigs." The country had gone into debt to speculators and plunderers, those who made money from nothing but the need of others for money. The national debt had been built up to finance the war against Napoleon, and the economy had never recovered from that plunge. But Cobbett always kept a finger pointed at those who grew rich from the forty-year-long depression. For the new names attached to old houses, signifying the displacement of the smaller gentry by a class as yet nameless, were another prominent feature of the countryside. The sight of consecrated places being deprived of their history shocked him more than anything else, and he described the rapacity of the new owners, visible in the condition of their estates, as eagerly as he recounted stories of their personal cruelty.

What was happening to the country estates was happening also to the laborers, and according to Cobbett from much the same cause. Those with the luck to possess ready funds when the nation wanted to borrow had been rewarded not for labor performed or even for capital ventured but for the simple willingness to make others poor, and they were the class that had to be removed before England could be healthy again. Beside this insight and his ability to bring it home everywhere, Cobbett's choice of groups such as Quakers or Jews to condemn as typical money-lenders seems a local and occasional tactic. But it must be added that his readiness to exploit an existing prejudice is not an accidental part of his genius. He needed, especially for his comic effects, the kind of compression that the rhetoricians call synecdoche. If I look for twenty ships to come into port, why should I not say that I scan the horizon for twenty *sails?* And if the ships are loaded with precious cargo, which embody the profits a merchant has realized by cheating me through a middle-man financier, it is only a step further to say: "There come the twenty *Quaker Tubs.*"

That the land itself was fertile; that the people who tilled it were shut out from a wealth by all rights theirs; that a class of corrupt idlers could be named, sought out, and deprived of their power: this was half of Cobbett's message. The rest had to emerge from his patient investigations into the past. His antagonists here were the Malthusian school of political economists, with their argument that misery was a necessary curb against the rapid increase of the population. The argument had its direct uses, of course, in contesting such policies as the "Speenhamland" system of paying laborers out of the poor rates, to keep wages just at the level of subsistence no matter how prices rose or fell. But this whole line of reasoning started from the assumption that the population had in fact been increasing in the past several decades. Again, Cobbett looked at the countryside, and saw a puzzling disproportion between the size of the older buildings and the number of persons they sheltered in the 1820s. In the Valley of the Avon alone, there were thirty-one churches, many of them extraordinarily spacious, with seating-room sufficient to hold several times the present number of worshipers. Since other evidence informed him that the people of the region had not declined in faith, he concluded that they had declined in numbers.

This kind of argument from observation Cobbett set against Malthus's geometrical and arithmetical progressions, and he never wearied of taunting all those who excogitated schemes for the emigration of laborers from the countryside, for the supposed well-being of an over-crowded England. The most influential of Malthus's disciples were Scottish, so Cobbett nicknamed them *feelosofers;* they went about hatching schemes, so he called them *vagabonds.* The first nickname was a routine piece of derision. The second was a profound stroke of poetic justice: where this generation of social scientists charged the common laborer with shiftlessness, Cobbett was replying that there was hardly a more stable being on earth; and he made his reply *tell* by portraying the Malthusians as what they were, nomads who scoured the country-side in the hope of some day conducting a successful forced migration. It is as characteristic of Cobbett's intellectual vices as of his demagogic virtues that he should have used the two names indifferently.

The depth at which Cobbett entered into his conversation with those who were either poor or becoming poor may be seen particularly in the history of his relations with the Luddite protestors. In 1816 he published a *Letter to the Luddites,* expressing sympathy with their cause but regretting the tactics of the frame-breakers, as an irrational resist-ance to the universal benefits promised from the machines for knitting and weaving. In the next few years he came to see that more was at stake than a question of mechanical progress, a "matter in the ab-stract." The cottage industries of individual artisans were being broken up by the life of the factory: workers whose labor had once been mixed with daily affairs in a community now found that their lives, and often their very families, were divided. Cobbett was willing to show in pub-lic how his understanding of the Luddites' motives had altered his estimate of their conduct. He announced that in many instances, "the mechanic inventions, pushed to the extent that they have been, have been productive of great calamity to this country, and that they will be productive of still greater calamity." He made, that is, a deduction from the evidence, similar in spirit to E. P. Thompson's more than a century later in *The Making of the English Working Class:* "The gap in status between a 'servant', a hired wage-laborer subject to the orders and discipline of the master, and an artisan, who might 'come and go' as he pleased, was wide enough for men to shed blood rather than allow themselves to be pushed from one side to the other." In most cases the factory's product was demonstrably inferior to the artisan's, and Cobbett, happy to appeal to self-interest when he could, cited this as a still plainer reason for refusing to buy any cloth that had been mass-produced.

Like the owners of country estates whom he had never heard of, the factory owners were new men, and Cobbett hated them. He was less hostile to members of the established gentry who gave a steady charity to their poor neighbors; but these too he felt free to criticize, when their benevolence served to enforce class distinctions through an interested paternalism. He warned very emphatically against the cant about "the deserving poor": "Amongst the labouring people, the first thing you have to look after is, *common honesty, speaking the truth* and *refraining from thieving;* and to secure these, the labourer must have *his belly full* and be *free from fear;* and this belly full must come to him from out of his wages, and not from benevolence of any description."[3] In his emphasis on work Cobbett anticipates an equally thoroughgoing prophet of the next age, Thomas Carlyle. The difference between them may seem only a difference of rhetoric; and yet it has broad consequences for their politics. Chesterton took stock of this when he remarked that Carlyle was deeply acceptable to the emerging men of power, even when he seemed to pray against their success, whereas Cobbett from the whole temper of his work was somehow out of bounds.

> [Carlyle] meant by the profit-and-loss philosophy a small and mean philosophy that could not face a small loss even for the sake of a great profit; he never contradicted the whole trend of the age as Cobbett did. On the contrary, Carlyle called the capitalist by a romantic name, where Cobbett would have called him by a shockingly realistic name. Carlyle called the capitalist a captain of industry; a very sad scrap of Victorian sentimentalism. That romantic evasion misses the whole point; the point which Cobbett kept steadily in sight all his life. Militarism would be much less respectable and respected if the captain of a line regiment had pocketed the rent of every acre that he fought for in Flanders. Capitalism would be much more respectable and respected if all the masterbuilders climbed to the tops of towers and fell off; if there were as many capitalists knocked on the head by bricks as there were captains killed at the front by bullets.[4]

But another great difference separates these two social critics. Cobbett, by his manner as well as his audience, was a genuinely popular writer.

Repeat yourself many times in a few pages and you will not yet sound like Cobbett. Nevertheless, sheer repetition is one secret of his style. He understood how a truth returning grips the mind with double force; how it comes back to haunt the reader who may have been struck by an impression, but who needed an echo of it to settle well in his memory; to store it there, and use it later as an incitement to the sleeping mind, and a fixed mark to the awakened conscience. Anaphora is the usual device for giving point to such repetitions, and my last sentence illustrates its structure; but it is a formal illustration only: it has none of Cobbett's naturalness, and is spoiled at the end by a trick of balance and antithesis—the sort of conscious grace he excluded as wrong for the purposes of demotic speech. Italics and nicknames are among the other more obvious weapons in his arsenal, which the foregoing quotations have displayed liberally. But the nicknames can go a long way: after a certain point in his life, London became to Cobbett simply "the Wen"; the dilapidated village of Old Sarum, which could send members to parliament without the inconveniences of voting, became not just a *rotten borough* but "the Accursed Hill"; and for some time Cobbett, who hated potatoes as a substitute forced on the poor for good English bread, took to calling them "the root of extreme unction."

A phrase like that brings to mind the range of his persuasive effects, and how much they owe to a humor verging on the burlesque. Almost never, so far as I can recall, does he choose to appear as an ironist. Yet he sometimes mimics irony, by a deliberately misplaced affectation of a neutral tone; as when, during his second American visit, he describes the Scottish peddler who walked up the steps to his house, entered without saying a word, and threw his knapsack on the parlor table, "which I, with reciprocal taciturnity, took hold of and tossed out of the window, which, being a free country, was standing wide open, as it were, on purpose to admit of the ejectment. It was not till after this that the Scotchman spoke, which he did in a manner that would certainly have procured him the honour of following the pack, if he had not, upon due notice given, taken the more circuitous route by the door."[5] The passage and many others like it were made possible by Cobbett's experience on another hot afternoon, in his eleventh year, when he purchased a book with the curious title *A Tale of a Tub,* sat down under a haystack, and read with small comprehension but a wholly unfamiliar pleasure, until the sun went down. From that moment he dated his resolve to be a writer; and it is true that Swift is the only writer with whom he can be even remotely compared. Like Swift, in all of his prose Cobbett *connects:* this profession with that practice; this expensive and useless achievement, with that forgotten reason for attempting it; what this man suffered, with the escape that man could have contrived in his place. Nor are Cobbett and Swift so opposite in temperament as at first appears. The resemblance comes out in Swift's treatment of his servants, and Cobbett's treatment of his family. Both valued the morally sound but restrictive act of generosity over the careless warmth of a personal kindness. Both were principled, benevolent, but unsentimental to the point almost of callousness; glad to be known as rule-makers of an unappeasable rigor, so long as it was added that their rules were just.

Cobbett's gift for connecting professions with practices is essentially a political gift. One might show the way it works in countless passages; but the finest is his account of a visit to Dover. He had come there, he says, to see a picturesque seaport, but could not help noticing, as he looked at the Southern Cliff, the fortifications built a few years before and now falling into disrepair. These were Pitt's answer to the popular fear his government had stirred up—the fear of an invasion by Napoleon. Now, twenty years later, Cobbett scouts the terrain,

> line upon line, trench upon trench, cavern upon cavern, bomb-proof upon bomb-proof. . . . The question every man of sense asks, is [here Cobbett turns to the ghost of Pitt and addresses him directly], What reason had you to suppose that *the French would ever come to this hill* to attack it, while the rest of the country was so much more easy to assail? . . . Just as if the Frenchmen would come to this hill! Just as if they would not go (if they came at all) and land in Romney Marsh, or on Pevensey level, or any where else, rather than come to this hill; rather than come to crawl up SHAKESPEARE'S cliff.[6]

The motive for so profligate an expenditure on so foolish a project can only be that the rulers of England had determined to prevent the landing "not of Frenchmen, but of French principles." The making of those fortifications was an enormous distraction for English laborers, and evidently a successful one. Cobbett's reasoning so far is a *tour de force,* and the normally acute political writer would stop here, satisfied to have seen through a devious plan. Cobbett, however, is never content merely to expose a limited evil. His work is not done until his readers have seen past it and been moved to action. In this instance he shows the way by pointing out that from Dover, you have an excellent view of the French coast; you can see, across the channel, not only the chalk-cliffs of Calais but the cornfields nearby; and they make a chastening picture: the French farmers are bringing in a harvest with no tithes to pay out, because the French have had a revolution.

The account of Dover comes from *Rural Rides* (1830), the only book that adequately represents the sort of writing Cobbett did in the *Political Register*. But as a reasoner about political facts, he can be matched by others, who work with a shorter fuse but comparable detonations. Where Cobbett has no peer is in absorbing such episodes into a personal drama. Thus, in one of his rides, he mentions a fit of bad temper which made him speak rudely to his son Richard. As he started to reflect on his own unreasonableness, "just at this time, my eyes met his, in which I saw *great surprise;* and, feeling the just rebuke, feeling heartily ashamed of myself, I instantly changed my tone and manner." He had eaten very little that day; hunger may, he thinks, have shortened his temper; but it occurs to him to ask whether the little he got was not more than the common laborer expects to eat every day of his life. His calculations show that he and his son had actually eaten "more, and much more, than the average of labourers, their wives and children, have to eat in a whole day, and that the labourer has to *work* on too!"[7] No lesson is indicated; Cobbett goes on to something else. But the reader is left with something to reflect on. In such passages, one learns what it means to have a moral imagination.

This was Cobbett's leading trait. Yet he had also, what in others can seem incompatible with it, a well-developed sense of opportunity. He was always fond of ad hoc gimmicks, a large case in point being his custody of the bones of Tom Paine. Cobbett in his early years had denounced Paine, but in 1817 and 1818, back in America, he took the trouble to read him, and discovered a congenial writer on economic questions. The problem was that his youthful attacks were still remembered. Rather than dismiss the entire matter Cobbett chose to canonize Paine—and implicitly by doing so to absolve his earlier self. So he took Paine's bones to England, without having considered what he would do with them once ashore. A resting place sufficiently conspicuous, a climactic moment for installing them, could not be found, and he had to let the grand event of *Cobbett's return to England with Paine's bones* trail off inconsequently. The unhappy business seemed to Chesterton a serious act of atonement and therefore a touchstone of Cobbett's best qualities, but Hazlitt was more shrewd: "The fact is, he *ratted* from his own project. He found the thing not so ripe as he had expected. His heart failed him: his enthusiasm fled, and he made his retraction."

Still there is a distinction, pretty firm in the minds of most people, between opportunity-seeking and opportunism, and Cobbett is always on the near side. Even with the French Revolution, what happened to him between 1792 and 1819 does not warrant a charge of inconsistency. He feared and deplored the violence of the Jacobins, and, believing England to be the home of liberty, he trusted his own country to reform itself without violence. This was a faith easily cherished from a distance, and it was strong in Cobbett throughout the 1790s, when he lived in America. He began to record his doubts almost as soon as the name Peter Porcupine began to seem inappropriate for a patriot no longer in exile; and by 1810 he thought the violence of the Revolution was something to be measured beside the gains it had realized. All along, Cobbett could regard himself in good faith as struggling for a single cause. Reform had been his aim from the first; only its probable agency shifted with time. The distresses of the country, as it appeared by the 1820s, could expect no remedy but from those who felt them constantly: "The mass of the people do not now live; they crawl about, and die by inches." But in his last years Cobbett had come even further than that sentence can show; its "they" still belongs to the surveyor who stands apart from his subject. Cobbett would not pretend to share the people's sufferings, but in every possible context, wherever to do so would not imply a false claim, he preferred to say "we." He even speaks (truly) of "our low birth." It is the most generous and yet the most self-conscious *we* that a political writer has ever used, and its effect is to create a community.

5

Keats's Politics

TO THE PAST THREE GENERATIONS of Keats's scholars and critics, a title like mine has implied a shallow misreading of a great poet. Plainly, for them, what Keats did in his poetry was to cultivate (or celebrate or explore) something called "sensibility" (or "the creative imagination" or "epistemological doubt"), something that modified our nature without itself being shaped by our circumstances. To interpret Keats in this way left the reader with a clear choice from the start: it was Keats *or* politics. If you chose politics, you would deplore Keats's poems as evasive or merely aesthetic, and show that his interest in certain sensations presupposed an indifference to the sufferings of mankind. If you chose Keats, you would admire his superiority to the pleasures and pains that come from social misery, and identify his genius with a conscious refusal to be irritated by the daily effects of power in the world. On the latter view, history comes down to literary history. But that may seem a small enough sacrifice, when the cost of restoring poetry to its circumstances is the demotion of a poet as original as Keats.

Both of these views depend on a rather narrow understanding of history, and an impoverished conception of poetry. I cannot see that Keats's poems, or even his letters, if one reads in them widely and inquisitively, afford much cause for either sort of privation. In the following remarks, however, I will stop short of suggesting a political interpretation that his poems and letters might support. My only aim is to make permanently incredible the choice between Keats and politics, and by doing so to make the views I have described even more unsatisfying than they already seem. This calls for quoting some pas-

sages from his poems, with some passages of convincing political testimony; placing them in conjunction, and showing that the results are
interesting; imagining their disjunction, and showing that the results
would be less interesting. The passages I will give are not obscure,
and some of them used to be well known. The excuse for quoting them
at length is that they are no longer remembered, or, what amounts to
the same thing, that we have forgotten how to read them.

A first step in displacing any standard reading is to remind ourselves
that it was invented at a certain time. In this case the political reading
of Keats, which deplores his escape from the pressures of his time and
place, is the invention of thirties Marxism. It can be traced back to a
conviction that economic realities are the determinant of all other realities; that social criticism from earlier periods is valuable to the degree that it begins to realize this truth; and that great writing may
inadvertently become a weapon of criticism, since it cannot help bearing witness to its material origins. John Strachey's *The Coming Struggle
for Power* gave life to these assumptions in a memorable chapter on
literature: its moral was the gradual, though unconscious, progress of
romantic and modern authors, from an experiment with individual
freedoms to a recognition of their bondage in the kingdom of necessity.
In Strachey's account a dedication to "pure art," such as Keats was
supposed to have cherished, was immediately suspect as a withdrawal
from actual conditions. It could be defended, therefore, only with
grave reservations, as an unhappy gesture of defiance.[1] A subtle version
of this account survives in E. P. Thompson's pages on Keats in *William
Morris: Romantic to Revolutionary*,[2] and cruder versions have continued
to appear up to the present moment. We ought to credit them only in
proportion as we credit the habits of thought from which they derive.

The consensus which dandyism proposed and communism ratified,
concerning the necessary limitations of aesthetic poetry, had itself been
preceded by a remarkably instructive lack of consensus. As late as
1921, a political reader could feel it was plausible to eulogize *Isabella*
in the following terms: "Keats achieved the very curious feat of writing
one poem of which it may be said that if Karl Marx can be imagined
as writing a poem instead of a treatise on Capital, he would have
written Isabella." The sentence comes from George Bernard Shaw's
contribution to a memorial volume on Keats;[3] and Shaw goes on to
cite the stanzas describing Isabella's brothers, which I will look at
more closely later; for now, it is important simply to see that Shaw
could make this judgment without any sense of paradox. "Every-

thing," he says, "that the Bolshevik stigmatizes when he uses the epithet 'bourgeois' is expressed forcibly, completely, and beautifully in those three stanzas, written half a century before the huge tide of middle-class commercial optimism and complacency began to ebb." Indeed, Shaw prefers Keats's epithet "ledger-men" to Marx's "bourgeois" on the ground that it is better and less euphuistic English.

Here then is a critic with political concerns, not condemning Keats for his evasion of politics, but calling attention to the implicit power of his analysis. The aesthetic reading of Keats gained its plausibility, and came as it now does to exclude politics, when Shaw's sort of generosity ceased to be a live option among critics. This change we owe to the tightening disciplines of ideological analysis on one side and anti-ideological interpretation on the other. But it would be wrong to think of the aesthetic reading chiefly as a counter-statement from the New Criticism of the thirties. Dandyism apart, it had a steady following among the later Victorians, and was refined to something like its present shape in the generation before Shaw's by readers whose sense of politics and literature alike was more innocent and more exclusive than his. Gerard Manley Hopkins wrote, for example, in a letter to Coventry Patmore:

> It is impossible not to feel with weariness how his verse is at every turn abandoning itself to an unmanly and enervating luxury. It appears that he said something like "O for a life of impressions instead of thoughts." It was, I suppose, the life he tried to lead. The impressions are not likely to have been all innocent and they soon ceased in death. His contemporaries, as Wordsworth, Byron, Shelley, and even Leigh Hunt, right or wrong, still concerned themselves with great causes, as liberty and religion; but he lived in mythology and fairyland the life of a dreamer. Nevertheless I feel and see in him the beginnings of something opposite to this, of an interest in higher things and of powerful and active thought.[4]

I take Hopkins's bias to stand for that of many subsequent commentators. But notice that the charge of an unconcern with great causes is here combined with an older charge, that of an indulgence in unmanly and enervating luxury. Now of this last criticism we can say exactly rather than approximately when it was invented. John Gibson Lockhart did it, in his attack on the Cockney School of Poetry.

Lockhart wrote with plain malice whereas Hopkins affects to be merely candid. But malice can be discerning, and what is curious about Lockhart, from a modern point of view, is that he found Keats at once enervatingly luxurious and transparently political. Or to vary the comparison again: like Shaw, he thought Keats's dedication to poetry far from escapist; unlike Shaw, he was repelled by its implications. "We had almost forgot to mention," he writes near the end of his review, "that Keats belongs to the Cockney School of Politics, as well as the Cockney School of Poetry. It is fit that he who holds Rimini to be the first poem, should believe the Examiner to be the first politician of the day."[5] So far, it may seem an opportunistic dismissal, with no firmer basis than Keats's association with Hunt. Yet Lockhart believed this association was a clue to something disturbing in Keats's poetry. "We admire consistency, even in folly. Hear how their bantling has already learned to lisp sedition." And he quotes the opening lines from Book III of *Endymion:*

> There are who lord it o'er their fellow-men
> With most prevailing tinsel: who unpen
> Their baaing vanities, to browse away
> The comfortable green and juicy hay
> From human pastures; or, O torturing fact!
> Who, through an idiot blink, will see unpack'd
> Fire-branded foxes to sear up and singe
> Our gold and ripe-ear'd hopes. With not one tinge
> Of sanctuary splendour, not a sight
> Able to face an owl's, they still are dight
> By the blear-eyed nations in empurpled vests,
> And crowns, and turbans. With unladen breasts,
> Save of blown self-applause, they proudly mount
> To their spirit's perch, their being's high account,
> Their tiptop nothings, their dull skies, their thrones—
> Amid the fierce intoxicating tones
> Of trumpets, shoutings, and belabour'd drums,
> And sudden cannon. Ah! how all this hums,
> In wakeful ears, like uproar passed and gone—
> Like thunder clouds that spake to Babylon,
> And set those old Chaldeans to their tasks. —
> Are then regalities all gilded masks?[6]

The invective is all in the service of a familiar progression, from mortal titles to immortal fame, or from a false to a true sublimity.

Still, Keats is detained by his invective for a long time. His motive is a protest against material oppressions, and oppressors whom he names: those who, though they cannot pen great words, are able to "unpen / Their baaing vanities" through the power of money, that "most prevailing tinsel"; those whose laden sacks of gold can make an artificial tally for "their being's high account," and conceal the emptiness of their "unladen breasts" by singeing the "gold and ripe-eared hopes" of all who have felt more keenly than they. The passage might be called seditious from its contempt for divine right; but that alone is too commonplace to have provoked Lockhart. He quotes the entire passage, the scorn for accumulated wealth as well as the scorn for "regalities," because he knows that together these sentiments become risky, though apart they are safely poetic. Keats, as Lockhart read him, was proposing an idea of genius independent of worldly honors, and he was observing that to take the idea seriously would require an abolition of the *medium* of worldly honors, the existing system of wealth and privilege.

One can reduce this claim to a plea for the career open to talents; Keats will then emerge as a liberal. But that word may have come to be too quickly understood and therefore too easily dismissed. It was, in fact, the word Keats himself used to describe his politics: when he expresses satisfaction at having given up the apothecary's trade and hopes, tentatively, that he can live without compromise by his writing, he says "My occupation is entirely literary; I will do so too [that is, keep it so]. I will write, on the liberal side of the question, for whoever will pay me. I have not yet known what it is to be diligent."[7] That is from a letter to Charles Brown, on September 22, 1819; the same day, he wrote to Dilke: "By the Examiner coming in your handwriting you must be in Town. They [the Examiner's reports of the protests after Peterloo] have put me into spirits: notwithstanding my aristocratic temper I cannot help being very much pleas'd with the present public proceedings. I hope sincerely I shall be able to put a Mite of help to the Liberal side of the Question before I die."[8] But several distinctions have to be made at this point. First, to be a liberal, even of the enlightened-Whiggish variety, took more courage and independent resolve in 1819 than it did in 1832. Second, for a young writer with only a foothold in the middle class, it involved a threat of sustained persecution, as it never could for established men of affairs like Francis Jeffrey or Lord Holland.

More important, when Keats used the word "liberal" he did not mean what the enlightened Whig meant. He had in view a liberal-mindedness like Robin Hood's, the pursuit of which implied a thorough reformation of sexual mores and economic arrangements. "Robin Hood," a fanciful and serious poem, was one of the shorter pieces by Keats well-appreciated in his circle of friends, partly because of its speculations about Robin's fate in 1818, under a tyranny more cunning than any he knew earlier. Could he live now, he "would swear, for all his oaks, / Fallen beneath the dockyard strokes, / Have rotted on the briny seas"—because, in short, use and value have become utterly divorced; as for Maid Marian, "She would weep that her wild bees / Sang not to her—strange! that honey / Can't be got without hard money." Recurring to the long passage from *Endymion,* one may conclude that honey suggests everything associated with "the juicy hay / From human pastures," and everything it may be turned into by the invisible hand of a society built on commerce. Hunt, who talked Byron into starting a magazine called the *Liberal,* used the honey-money rhyme with comparable effects in a verse epistle to Hazlitt; but he gives a more general sense of the reforms in question in his second sonnet "On Receiving a Crown of Ivy," where a final appeal is made to

> Love of things lasting, love of the tall woods,
> Love of love's self, and ardour for a state
> Of natural good befitting such desires,
> Towns without gain, and haunted solitudes.[9]

If one bears in mind Macaulay's description of a liberal society as "leaving capital to find its most lucrative course, commodities their fair price, industry and intelligence their natural reward, idleness and folly their natural punishment,"[10] one can see what a different thing the liberality of Keats was.

His was a position most of his contemporaries described as radical. Since it was fortified, however, by an unfaltering belief in progress, it did not warrant revolutionary allegiances. Keats felt a closer kinship with the politics of Leigh Hunt and his brother, John, than with powerful demagogues like Cobbett and Orator Hunt, even if he did enjoy taunting George Keats with the probable justice of Cobbett's attack on the new American settlements. The processes of social leveling, and of fitting morality to the uses of commerce, were uncongenial with any idea he could form of greatness; and in another letter to George, of October 14, 1818, speaking characteristically of the want of anything "manly or sterling in any part of the Government" at a time when "the motives of our worst men are interest and of our best vanity," he still reserved a worse fault for American society.

Dilke, whom you know to be a Godwin perfectibility man, pleases himself with the idea that America will be the country to take up the human intellect where England leaves off—I differ there with him greatly—A country like the United States whose greatest men are Franklins and Washingtons will never do that—They are great Men doubtless but how are they to be compared to those our country men Milton and the two Sidneys—The one is a philosophical Quaker full of mean and thrifty maxims the other sold the very Charger who had taken him through all his Battles—Those Americans are great but they are not sublime Man—the humanity of the United States can never reach the sublime.[11]

It cannot, I think Keats meant, because it began wrongly, by guarding the rights of a corporate body, and distrusting all the powers of individual men. Accordingly, in a sense that he explores elsewhere, it is destined to be a nation without genius.

Where Keats nevertheless agrees with both democrats and revolutionaries is in admitting the practical necessity of shock, as a means of bringing to consciousness a whole system of abuses. This can be done quickly by reducing the abstract to the personal: Cobbett called the new political economists *feelosofers;* and we have seen Keats's nickname, "ledger-men." But more oblique or metonymic figures may carry greater force, and the pertinent stanzas from *Isabella* show why.

> For them the Ceylon diver held his breath,
>   And went all naked to the hungry shark;
> For them his ears gush'd blood; for them in death
>   The seal on the cold ice with piteous bark
> Lay full of darts; for them alone did seethe
>   A thousand men in troubles wide and dark:
> Half-ignorant, they turn'd an easy wheel,
> That set sharp racks at work, to pinch and peel.   (113–120)

Without breaking the narrative for the sake of reprehension, the word "half-ignorant" suggests that these ledger-men were fully aware of what they did, and legally equipped to claim ignorance.

The stanza that follows gives the reiterated question "Why were they proud?" four times in seven lines, before its closing variation: "Why in the name of Glory were they proud?" Only after all this do we hear them actually named "ledger-men" and, for a further variation, "money-bags": "How could these money-bags see east and west?" This is conveniently poised between nickname and metonymy, and it does more polemical work than Marx's use of the same name, Money-bags, to explain Contradictions in the Formula of Capital. Asking the reader of *Capital* to imagine a typical investor, Marx pictures him thus: "Our friend, Moneybags, who as yet is only an embryo capitalist, must buy his commodities at their value, must sell them at their value, and yet at the end of the process must withdraw more value from circulation than he threw into it at starting."[12] It looks as if Shaw's compliment was less fanciful than we took it to be. For it is the contradiction described above that leads Marx to conclude, "Capital is dead labour, that vampire-like, only lives by sucking living labour, and lives the more, the more labour it sucks"—a metaphor that flatly states the relation of Isabella's brothers to Lorenzo, who on his final journey is called "their murdered man." Even before his death, he is a person whom they have already turned into a thing.

Marx's "friend Moneybags" does not convey the electric response that Keats's "these money-bags" does. Why? In part, it is a matter of the conventions of naming, and here Marx was perhaps following Dickens. At any rate Moneybags repels every effort of practical rage as thoroughly as Pecksniff or Bounderby: the name seems a total quantity or condition enveloping the helpless person who suffers it. But Keats's money-bags are different. They were once men, and if they no longer are, it is because they have chosen to be something more and something less. They are in the business of emptying other men of all their life but the husk. What remains is the human commodity, and they who realize the profit are money-bags. So, if we translate Keats's question into his own terms and ask, "Why were they money-bags," the answer is "For the same reason that Orgoglio is Orgoglio, or the Houyhnhnms are Houyhnhnms." They are the exact sum of what they make, know, and do. The name shocks by its power to restore a single perspective of literalness, and by its trick of arriving at this casually, with a passing allegory in a larger dramatic action. *Isabella* was a favorite of Keats's contemporaries, and most of them would have been disposed to pick out details like these almost incidentally. Yet they were prepared to interpret them as political statements, by their knowledge as readers of Spenser and Swift.

Given the beliefs I have sketched, one would expect Keats's full-scale attempt to write a political allegory, in *Hyperion,* to emerge as a fable of progress. Keats on the contrary seems to have imagined it as the story of a god untouchable by humanity. It would, he told Benjamin Haydon, in a letter of January 23, 1818, present his readers with a new sort of hero; where Endymion was "led on, like Buonaparte, by circumstance," Apollo "being a fore-seeing God will shape his actions like one."[13] But, as one reads *Hyperion,* it shows instead an ironic pattern of repetition, in which gods like men are unforeseeing and led on by the circumstances of power. Further, this seems to be a view encouraged by the very manner of presentation; as when, in the opening description of Saturn, the sceptre of power alone confers sight: "His old right hand lay nerveless, listless, dead, / Unsceptred; and his realmless eyes were closed." Nerveless, listless, dead, because unsceptred, and in consequence also blind: such is the logic that the syntactical choices and the line-ending together build up. Oceanus's great speech adds a suggestion that defeat may be implicit in the means by which power comes to know itself:

> Great Saturn, thou
> Hast sifted well the atom-universe;
> But for this reason, that thou are the King,
> And only blind from sheer supremacy,
> One avenue was shaded from thine eyes,
> Through which I wandered to eternal truth.
> And first, as thou wast not the first of powers,
> So art thou not the last.   (182–189)

These lines speak for Keats against the order that excluded him from political enfranchisement as well as poetic recognition; and one may feel that he admires the new gods at least to the extent that they help to overthrow it forever.

Yet an emotional ambivalence unsettles the poem throughout. Its perspective, as Tilottama Rajan observed in *Dark Interpreter,* is never quite decided between a naive and a sentimental treatment of myth; and in a dissertation on Keats's politics, Thomas Reed traced its difficulty there to a range of sympathies with which the poem surprises itself: it cares more for the Titans than its design had seemed to allow.[14] Again, I suspect a political motive was at work. Keats was writing wishfully and not accurately to Haydon when he said that after *Endymion* he had done with Buonaparte. In *Hyperion* one feels him still impressed by the grandeur of Napoleon's conquests, and full of speculations about the possible good of his defeat. He wanted to avoid the celebratory look of Hunt's masque *The Descent of Liberty,* written and published the year of Waterloo. But he borrowed several of its properties all the same. Prominent among these is the *Descent's* closing tableau, in which "Silence, listening as at dead of night, / Sits with her finger up, hushing Delight":[15] a figure that Keats reframed as the Naiad of his opening lines, who "'mid her reeds / Press'd her cold finger closer to her lips." Her gesture sets the stage not for a replacement of tyranny by liberty but for the succession of one order by another. Since even the gods will suffer a human fate, the Naiad would seem to be hushing pity rather than delight.

According to Hunt's fable, liberty needed only one thing for its achievement: the abolition of the slave trade. Napoleon could not serve as a hero of that quest, and indeed he may be supposed to round out the Vision of False Glory: "the Conqueror dressed in purple, in a haughty attitude, with a crown of laurel on his head, and holding in his hand a globe with the figure of Victory," behind him "several turbulent, weeping, and indignant shapes, representing the Passions, Misery, Widowhood, &c." By contrast, the Vision of Real Glory shows the conqueror's palaces and triumphal arches in the foreground, but with a background of rural fields and a sustaining pageant of "yeomanry or armed peasants crowned with laurel, each bearing a sheathed sword in one hand and a bunch of wheat in the other. These are followed by poets, painters, and musicians, carrying the emblems of their respective arts, but wearing an air of frankness, and treading with firm step." I recount the details to establish an available myth that Keats chose *not* to repeat. And yet he disliked Buonaparte; what, then, stood in his way? He identified himself with neither of Hunt's visions of glory because he shared the regret to which Hazlitt gave a voice in "Whether Genius Is Conscious of Its Powers?":

> While my friend Leigh Hunt was writing the *Descent of Liberty,* and strewing the march of the Allied Sovereigns with flowers, I sat by the waters of Babylon and hung my harp upon the willows. I knew all along there was but one alternative—the cause of kings or of mankind. This I foresaw, this I feared; the world see it now, when it is too late. Therefore I lamented, and would take no comfort when the Mighty fell, because we, all men, fell with him like lightning from heaven, to grovel in the grave of Liberty, in the stye of Legitimacy![16]

But Keats was capable of feeling this while regretting as well the need to adopt Napoleon or any great man at all as a hero of liberty. The Saturn of his poem, therefore, bears the double burden of representing the mighty who fell, and showing the deception by which we lament the cause of one king as if it were the cause of mankind.

Something is still missing from the portrait of Keats as a political man. He made his vow to contribute on the liberal side of the question, but he did it in letters only a month after the Peterloo massacre: his failure of explicit comment on the working men's actions of that summer and autumn has sometimes been taken to lay him open once more to Hopkins's objections. But what qualifies as explicit among other writers of the period? Read the *Examiner* for the summer and autumn of 1819, and you find that the massacre is in fact a turning point. Before that, Orator Hunt is a "coarse" character and his motives suspect; afterwards, he becomes a hero; there is a convergence between the middle-class radicals in London and the "outstanding" laborers in Manchester and elsewhere; several eyewitness reports from Peterloo are printed (for three or four issues running), and the paper even carries a personal letter from Hunt in prison. We know from Keats's allusion in the letter to Dilke that he was reading the paper steadily at this time. The main evidence of its effects on his thinking comes in an entry, dated September 18, 1819, from a long journal-letter to George which he wrote throughout the last two weeks of September. He wrote a great deal on that day particularly because he was fresh from a walk among the extraordinary crowd in the streets. The occasion was Orator Hunt's release from prison: having lately conducted his own defense and exposed the trumped-up charges, Hunt was cheered as he proceeded to a dinner given in his honor. And yet, the applause for him also implied a tacit mourning for the victims of four weeks earlier.

Keats leads up to this slowly; and as he does so, he reflects on the idea of progress, which has grown actual to him with the experiences of the day:

All civilized countries become gradually more enlighten'd and there should be a continual change for the better. Look at this Country at present and remember it when it was even thought impious to doubt the justice of a trial by Combat—From that time there has been a gradual change—Three great changes have been in progress. First for the better, next for the worse, and a third time for the better once more. The first was a gradual annihilation of the tyranny of the nobles, when kings found it in their interest to conciliate the common people, elevate them and be just to them. Just when baronial Power ceased and before standing armies were so dangerous, Taxes were few, kings were lifted by the people over the heads of their nobles, and those people held a rod over kings. The change for the worse in Europe was again this. The obligation of Kings to the Multitude began to be forgotten—Custom had made noblemen the humble servants of kings—Then kings turned to the Nobles as the adorners of their power, the slaves of it, and from the people as creatures continually endeavouring to check them. Then in every kingdom there was a long struggle of kings to destroy all popular privileges. The English were the only people in Europe who made a grand kick at this. They were slaves to Henry 8th but were freemen under William 3rd at the time the French were abject slaves under Lewis 14th. The example of England, and the liberal writers of France and England sowed the seed of opposition to this Tyranny—and it was swelling in the ground till it burst out in the French Revolution.— That has had an unlucky termination. It put a stop to the rapid progress of free sentiments in England; and gave our Court hopes of turning back to the despotism of the 16th century. They have made a handle of this event in every way to undermine our freedom. They spread a horrid superstition against all innovation and improvement—The present struggle in England of the people is to destroy this superstition. What has rous'd them to do it is their distresses—Perhaps on this account the present distresses of this nation are a fortunate thing—tho so horrid in their experience. You will see I mean that the French Revolution put a temporary stop to this third change, the change for the better—Now it is in progress again and I think in an effectual one. This is no contest between Whig and Tory—but between right and wrong. There is scarcely a grain of party spirit now in England—Right and Wrong considered by each abstractedly is the fashion.[17]

What is striking in this long and impassioned discussion is Keats's willingness to give his credo so familiar a shape.

From the polemical anti-Burkean use of innovation and improvement as near synonyms, to the suggestion that the wickedness of "superstition" may always be distinguished from the good of time-honored beliefs, Keats appears as a ready sympathizer with all the efforts of enlightenment: but a historical enlightenment, moved forward by accidents and partial efforts of the will, rather than a rational enlightenment like Godwin's. His refusal of party spirit sets him in a company with most of the *Examiner* writers, who believed in a translation of sectarian issues into questions of "right and wrong" for humanity. Finally, the word "distresses" belongs to the radical usage of the period: it is a strong, deliberately impersonal word, evoking a powerful abstraction; something between the pains of sensation and of thought, but demanding relief as part of the act of recognition. It may be noticed that Keats's three stages of political liberation oddly coincide with the three-stage progress through the mansion of many apartments which he had outlined in his May 3, 1818, letter to J. H.

Reynolds on the progress of poetry. That letter ended with a pause, the "dark passages" that Wordsworth's poetry explored; and this one stops in mid-process as well, after an "unlucky termination" but with a new movement now "in progress." One cannot understand the force of either letter without taking account of the parallel, for even Wordsworth's power to "think into the human heart" was evidence to Keats of a grand march of intellect, and, like the cause of the people, it "depended more upon the general and gregarious advance of intellect, than individual greatness of Mind." [18]

Let me return to the September 18 letter which I interrupted just before its praise for Carlisle, the bookseller of deist pamphlets; its description of his government tormentors as an anonymous "they"; and its picture of Keats among the others gathering for Hunt's procession. "After all they are afraid to prosecute: they are afraid of his defence: it would be published in all the papers all over the Empire: they shudder at this: the Trials would light a flame they could not extinguish. Do you not think this of great import? You will hear by the papers of the proceedings at Manchester and Hunt's triumphal entry into London. It would take me a whole day and a quire of paper to give you any thing like detail—I will merely mention that it is calculated that 30,000 people were in the streets waiting for him. The whole distance from the Angel Islington to the Crown and Anchor was lined with Multitudes." The number is probably a low estimate, but numbers hold little interest for those who have once walked in such a crowd. Four days after this entry, Keats spoke of becoming a political writer. The day after, he wrote "To Autumn." Great poems come out of a long arc of feeling, and not only a masterly engagement with a literary genre. But I can do no more here than suggest what an interpretation of "To Autumn" would feel like that took into account the things Keats was feeling in these September days. It is a poem about the ideal ending of a human season, a poem in the present tense that perfects a hidden surmise *as if*. It imagines a world where nature and circumstance would be the same thing, and where immortality would exist as the memory of humanity; so that death itself would be a passing into another process, like the echo of life. The pathos we feel in reading the poem is connected with our awareness that this is not our state now.

None of the foregoing comments aims to deny that Keats was the first aesthetic critic of his own poems. He, more than anyone else, created for English poetry the distinct moments of the seeing soul. My purpose has been to add to the usual idea a warning: that his inventions may grow less vivid, and our praise of them merely habitual, unless we hold in view a sense of exclusion that he knew continuously. But it seems to me as false to deny the reality of the freedom he associated with poetry, by calling it an escape or an evasion of social imperatives, as it is to assert the same freedom as a timeless value. It is enough that it won something for him and for readers like him, and we are wrong to weigh it against the freedoms he cared for but left others to win. Or rather, these things cannot be compared in a way unfavorable to his poetry, except on utilitarian grounds which no one who ever attacked Keats has been prepared to defend. His writing does what Adorno invites us to hope that art may do, in helping to keep alive "the memory of accumulated suffering."[19] It does so by its irresolute wanderings of fancy, its fortunate conquests of truth and beauty, and in intervals of another kind, by declaring its solidarity with the "fashion" of each man considering right and wrong abstractedly for himself. Thus its example of autonomy for itself is also an example for others. To his question in *Endymion,* "Are then regalities all gilded masks?" Keats had the confidence to reply: "No, there are thronèd seats unscalable / But by a patient wing."

6

The Genealogy of Disinterestedness

THIS CHAPTER WILL SKETCH part of a longer story about the invention of the literary object, and the sort of interest we are supposed to take in it. The main work was done, it seems to me, by Matthew Arnold in the 1850s and 1860s, and the most important revisions were offered in the next two generations, by Pater and Wilde. I therefore confine my account to these critics, with Hazlitt in the background. Other romantics would have served almost as well—Shelley in the "Defence," Wordsworth in the 1802 "Preface"—yet there are certain tendencies in romantic critical thought which Hazlitt represents more emphatically than anyone else, and I want to say at the start what I take these to be. He understood art as one human activity among others. It might be exalted above the rest simply for its survival, the recognition it earned in ages that conceived of the activity differently, and the knowledge it seemed to afford of what remained common to our nature. At the same time it might be criticized in the light of other concerns, since its power was both for good and for ill. To value *Coriolanus,* for the working class, or *The Merchant of Venice,* for the Jews, was perhaps to make too high a sacrifice. Whatever decision we arrive at in a given instance, Hazlitt always reminds us that the price is worth counting. This is his own way of giving value to what he admires.

Phrases like "a betrayal of genius" appear frequently in his criticism, without paradox, and with both words stressed. When he wrote of Wordsworth's betrayal, or Burke's, he had in mind their subtle understandings of the commerce by which eloquence passes into action, and action into eloquence: with these understandings as their weapons, they had begun in the service of one cause and ended as apologists for another. Both careers gave him a field for speculation on the vicissitudes of his interest in art. That interest after all, he concluded, was inseparable from his interest in the uses of art, and a language to explain either had better be as recalcitrant as possible about distinguishing human qualities from artistic ones. Hazlitt has, in fact, two vocabularies, one centered on words like "gusto," "character," and "fullness," and the other on words like "intensity," "self," and "bias." His early *Essay on the Principles of Human Action,* with its theory of the natural unselfishness of the mind, together with his steady preference for dramatic over lyric poetry, may seem to imply that these are discrete vocabularies, of praise and blame respectively. But in Hazlitt's criticism they exist in constant tension with each other, and the single term that unites them is "power." The sympathetic power that enabled Milton to create Satan is not distinct from the egotistical power that first urged him to find Satan in himself. And what holds for Milton holds no less for the next reader who discovers his poem; we cherish in reading and writing alike the energy of interpretation that they share. Hazlitt's definition of poetry is careful to telescope the two processes so completely that we cannot be sure which is being defined: "the natural impression of any object or event, by its vividness exciting an involuntary movement of imagination and passion, and producing, by sympathy, a certain modulation of the voice, or sounds, expressing it." Writing and reading have in common the work of the impression.

The relevance of all this to the concerns of Arnold, Pater, and Wilde will be plain without further comment, but I need to defend the practice of treating them as a group. In one way or another they were disciples of Keats, and from his letters they would have come to know both of Hazlitt's vocabularies: that of "sympathy" in the comments on Shakespeare and negative capability, that of "egotism" in the comments on Wordsworth and the egotistical sublime. The same debate, between Shakespeare and Wordsworth, sympathy and the self, drama and lyric, community and retreat, was carried on with the same fierceness in Keats's poetry; and without our later and academic constraint, "prose for the doctrine, poetry for the thrills," Arnold, Pater, and Wilde read deeply enough to find it there. Still it may be asked how far each of these critics encountered the debate through his reading of Hazlitt. My guess is founded on the external evidence of quotation and reference as well as the internal evidence of style and procedure. Pater, I think, read Hazlitt, borrowed from him freely, if narrowly, in matters of taste, but derived his own style from the less colloquial idioms of De Quincey and Lamb, and would have reckoned Hazlitt an important predecessor who was somehow not a decisive influence. Wilde read Hazlitt with great enthusiasm—especially the Shakespeare criticism and theater reviews—admired him above all for the speed of his epigrams, and would have rated him only below Keats. In contrast, Arnold seems to have read Hazlitt as attentively as Wilde did, but he covered his tracks far more thoroughly than Pater. This pattern is queer enough to require the sort of documentation I have tried to supply. It belongs to the troubled history of Arnold's debt to romanticism, of which D. G. James's *Matthew Arnold and the Decline of English Romanticism* gives a much fuller account. My reason for devoting more space to Arnold than to critics whom I read with greater pleasure is that his still seem to me the dominant assumptions in the teaching of literature, even among those who begin as rebels against them. Whether as an awkward ally (for those who want criticism to be centered on the play of interpretation) or as a chosen one (for those who want it to be centered on the work of guarding a permanent canon), he remains with us because he does endorse method, and it is in the nature of any academy that it should prefer institutional method to personal interest.

Hazlitt did not commonly resort to the noun *disinterestedness;* he was friendlier to the adjective it could generate to suit this or that occasion: a certain estimate of character or view of a question might be "disinterested." But the idea can often be detected where every form of the word is absent—as when he makes it a "test of the sense and candour of any one belonging to the opposite party, whether he allowed Burke to be a great man." One obstacle in the way of understanding what he meant is the modern confusion of *disinterested* with *uninterested.* The disinterested man is still looking at what he judges; the uninterested one has gone on to something else. Another confusion, also of recent origin but less easily recognized, comes from the overeducated reader, who in rescuing *disinterested* from its use as a careless synonym for *uninterested* displays his prize as a grave synonym for *impartial* or *detached.* This has the advantage of pedantry but is equally destructive of Hazlitt's meaning.

A disinterested investigator, a disinterested judge, a disinterested historian, need not be detached. He may be immersed in a question and, having started on one side, conclude his engagement on the opposite one—or even on the same. What is unimaginable is that he should remain strictly neutral (human nature being what it is) except when treating a question in which he is also *un*interested. The over-educated reader thus falls into an error comparable to that of the half-educated reader whom he wants to save. *Disinterestedness,* for the person who keeps to it, ought to mean only that his final judgment will be affected by nothing but what he sees, hears, and feels to be the merits of the case. He has no vested interest in what he undertakes to judge, and his thoughts will not be swayed by prejudice, by tormenting fears or habitual associations. Yet he *will* have felt stirrings within him even as he made his judgment. A biographer of Cromwell may end by approving of his protagonist, or by condemning him—may, in either case, feel reservations so strong that he wishes he had taken another subject to write about—and still be disinterested. But if *disinterested* is taken to mean "neutral," it follows that ten disinterested biographers should arrive at the same opinion of Cromwell. This, Hazlitt would have said, is a fair account neither of why we read books and think about lives, nor of how our knowledge advances.

In tracing this second confusion about disinterestedness I have already begun to paraphrase Arnold's definition of the word. "The Function of Criticism at the Present Time" asks the critic not only to hold himself free of vested interests, but to think about literature without taking sides. Disinterestedness, Arnold proposes, is what English culture needs more of, and perhaps thinking about the word will lead to acting on the principle. His touchstone of disinterestedness comes from Burke, predictably enough when we recall Hazlitt's "test." It is Burke's "return upon himself" that most appeals to Arnold: he illustrates it with the final turn of *Thoughts on French Affairs,* in which Burke considers that a new system of things may have entered the world, and reflects that if this is so the record of his protests will matter little to posterity. Arnold makes no allowance for the dark-beyond-dark irony many have felt in reading the passage; but he uses it very effectively, and it gives him a new sense of disinterestedness: it is now the characteristic virtue, not of the member of the opposite party who can still recognize Burke's greatness, but of the member of no party at all. Culture stands apart from a world of passions, and returns upon itself. We are well on the way to the complaint against a modern political columnist: "You are too resolute in your defense of X; try to be more disinterested."

Arnold in this essay does not speak of "objectivity" and "subjectivity." Yet these terms are on his mind: they had come into play in his "Preface" of 1853, with its contrast between "the calm, the cheerfulness, the disinterested objectivity" of the classics, and the modern "dialogue of the mind with itself." (To feel the redundancy of "disinterested objectivity" one may weigh it against interested subjectivity.) By 1864, when "The Function of Criticism" was first published, disinterestedness had won out over objectivity as the master-term. It had the right touch of mystery. When, however, Arnold condemns the romantics by saying that "they did not know enough," a further premise is introduced without warning. He means that they were not sufficiently disinterested in his new sense. But to Hazlitt this use of "know" would have been incomprehensible unless it were taken to mean "see, hear, and feel one's way into this or that situation." Doubtless it is a limitation not to go out of oneself; but for Hazlitt's sense of disinterestedness, the alternative was to imagine other selves; whereas for Arnold's it is to enter the condition of selflessness.

Thus the unlimited plurality of interests which Hazlitt used to link his ideal of disinterestedness with the superiority of drama to lyric, with the identity of the imagination in art and in action, and with "the prospect of some good to mankind" has come down to us through Arnold's essay as the negation of interests which forms the prerequisite of the critic, whose function is to assign the proper value to every item in our cultural inventory. The rest of Arnold's vocabulary has been less influential, and yet it is worth taking stock of for what it reveals about his general strategy. In full revolt against his own poetry, Arnold needed to avoid the romantic vocabulary of "impressions" (which was well suited to the particular occasions of poetry besides Arnold's). That is why he summed up seeing, hearing, feeling, and so forth, with the cover-sense, knowing. This in turn entailed his commitment to "the best ideas" rather than the keenest or profoundest or most far-ranging impressions. His criticism betrays no awareness of the growth of ideas from impressions—a piece of knowledge that had entered English criticism through Hume's *Treatise,* and through Hazlitt's persistence as a revisionist of Hume.

But Arnold wrote with a more immediate polemic in view. Where Ruskin called that art greatest which "includes the greatest ideas," he would reply by calling upon the critic to "make the best ideas prevail." Language has a short memory, and we may no longer see much significance in the move from "greatest" to "best." Yet for Arnold and Ruskin the distinction between these two sorts of ideas was vivid enough.

"Greatest" still carries overtones of Longinus, and of the Longinian elements in Johnson and Reynolds: a colloquial word for "lofty," it could only be applied to ideas that filled the mind with awe. "Best" belongs to the new vocabulary of the fair-minded Victorian intellectual, who has read the right books and taken the trouble to inform himself in matters outside his province. Arnold also has at heart—though he does not say so—a standard of decorum. The best ideas will prefer to consort with the least irregular subjects. Other subjects, Empedocles jumping into a pit for instance, they rightly scorn as unfit for poetry. The pretty good ideas we associate with the Empedocles of Arnold's poem—a thinker, but painful to contemplate—are also *wrong* because they fix us in an unhealthy attitude toward life. Arnold cautions us gently because he knows which are the best: if we settle for less, we forfeit our survival in the long run, and are seen even now to be fatally out of step.

One might justify Arnold's suppression of "Empedocles on Etna" on grounds very different from those he gives in his "Preface." It was a lofty conception that did not work out; and no failure should reach a second edition. But this Arnold refuses to say. Instead of the failure of genius he directs our attention to the failure of subject. Indeed, from the "Preface" on, his criticism sustains an extraordinary effort to foster a revival of the great subject. In this, it must be said, he worked alone, whatever one thinks of the result. His contemporaries, like Ruskin, had inherited from Hazlitt the conviction that no subject was intrinsically unpoetic: the sublime could be nourished in the most unarable soil, and make it yield plenty. The triviality of *thinking* about subject was one consequence. In the face of this Arnold insisted that genius of the highest sort naturally reflected on its aims in advance: the critic's job, as a specialist of the understanding, was to help the lesser genius do the same. That is the point of the relation he sketches in "The Function of Criticism" between the epoch of concentration (which instructs) and the epoch of expansion (which has learned its lesson). Evidently he did take this scheme seriously, or he would not have risked embarrassment with his remarks, full of a strange finesse, on the places where Shakespeare goes too far. *King Lear* is a leading example, "where the language is so artificial, so curiously tortured, and so difficult, that every speech has to be read two or three times before its meaning can be comprehended." One wonders how far he would apply the criticism to Gloucester's "But I shall see / The wingèd vengeance overtake such children," with Cornwall's reply: "See't shalt thou never." But Arnold exaggerates to help us share his excitement. Literature, he believes, would be better off if it recognized by explicit contract the link between the ends to be sought by genius and the right means of attaining them.

To the question, "How then do I go about writing the best sort of poetry?" Arnold makes a somewhat elusive response. But he does tell us that poetry is "a criticism of life under the conditions fixed for such criticism by the laws of poetic truth and poetic beauty," and we note the words "fixed" and "laws." An audience like Arnold's, familiar with the critical premises of romanticism, would have found this more startling than we do. In a casual phrase Arnold was declaring his intention to fight a rear-guard action against expression and "the mind of man," and he was identifying as the chief patron of his cause Sir Joshua Reynolds. The strangest fact about Arnold's criticism is that it was militant under *those* banners. For it was not only a return, it was a deliberately simplified return, to Reynolds's teachings. Reynolds's suspicion of fixed laws, in his Burkean eleventh discourse, and the many remarks subversive of acquired talents which he scattered throughout the *Discourses* (about one of which Blake could say "Here is a sentence which overthrows all his book"), drop out of the account. Essentially, Arnold deals in the caricature of Reynolds that we know from Blake's less generous comments. He accepts, that is, the romantic account as a fair one, and his own Reynolds is still the enemy of genius, the man hired to depress art—Reynolds, indeed, as he could only have appeared to a mind touched by the most academic and cautionary of his discourses, and by nothing else. Yet Arnold turns the romantic attack into an admiring paraphrase. He looks at the creature whom Blake and Hazlitt revile and instead of saying, "He is nothing like that; let me alter the lines," concludes equably: "Yes, your portrait is to the life; and it tells me just why I adore him."

Arnold followed Reynolds even where we might expect any nineteenth-century critic to part company with him, in his attachment to general nature and middle forms. Only the vagaries of translation prevent this from being immediately obvious: where Reynolds tells the student to draw his noses not too big and not too small, Arnold talks about calm pathos and noble simplicity. Again, Reynolds's distrust of "peculiarities" resurfaces as Arnold's impatience with "anomalies." Arnold needs the more difficult word because he hopes to occupy a wider terrain; under his supervision, the regulative program of a normal science will be extended to all of culture.

A member of the House of Commons said to me the other day: "That a thing is an anomaly, I consider to be no objection to it whatever." I venture to think he was wrong; that a thing is an anomaly *is* an objection to it, but absolutely and in the sphere of ideas: it is not necessarily, under such and such circumstances, or at such and such a moment, an objection to it in the sphere of politics and practice.[1]

Given this faith in the normative tendency of eighteenth-century thought—even where his source offers it as one tendency in a confusion of others—Arnold might have been relied on to cherish a high opinion of eighteenth-century poetry. But his judgments in that area make an extreme version of the standard romantic hatchet-job: Dryden and Pope, in the most celebrated of his dismissals, are "classics of our prose." Hazlitt had given the same judgment a more delicate shading, and by doing so made it seem better than a dismissal: "The question, whether Pope was a poet, has hardly yet been settled, and is hardly worth settling; for if he was not a great poet, he must have been a great prose-writer, that is, he was a great writer of some sort."[2]

Now, when Hazlitt writes in this way, he is using an Augustan sense of balance to question the permanent sufficiency of one element of Augustan practice. He does not define either poetry or greatness in such a way as to exclude the greatest writers whom the eighteenth century chose to call poets. Nevertheless, the reservations that he feels as strongly as Arnold when, mounted in the reader's saddle, he has to hear the rocking-horse antithesis and balance of the heroic couplet through a forced march of hundreds of lines, show where the elective affinities of the two critics intersect. Both, appealing to a judgment freed from sectarian bias, cannot help thinking that poetry was meant for other ends than this; and Arnold paraphrases Hazlitt once more in describing his own appeal as a quest "to see the object as in itself it really is." One of many essays in which Hazlitt speaks of a similar quest is "On Knowledge of the World."

> If any one has but the courage and honesty to look at an object as it is in itself, or divested of prejudice, fear, and favour, he will be sure to see it pretty right; as he who regards it through the refractions of opinion and fashion, will be sure to see it distorted and falsified, however the error may rebound to his own advantage.[3]

The slight verbal differences between this and Arnold's better-known formulation are signs of an overriding temperamental difference that would have marked out writers of the same age for perfect antipathy. For Hazlitt does not say "really." The omission, a result of unconscious tact, allows even his manner of statement to imply what he says more clearly elsewhere: that history changes the meaning of anything we regard as real. His introductory lecture on the Age of Elizabeth is particularly notable for such awareness, but one can feel it in almost any passage where he tries to explain the mind of another period. Arnold's deference to what is "really" there carries the weight of opposite beliefs. No word was a greater favorite with him, and its use argues a commitment, for which he did not hold himself answerable, to a full-scale metaphysic of realism. Arnold believed that art was an imitation of nature, and he governed his thinking with mirror metaphors far more strictly than Dryden, or Johnson, or Reynolds had done before him. Of the metaphors themselves he was conscious: they belong to a deliberate policy of fatiguing our patience with what stares us in the face, till we are no longer embarrassed by it. But how far the metaphors drove him backward—beyond the reductions of any neoclassicism that ever flourished in England—he appears not to have recognized. He was therefore able the more confidently to grant himself a corollary assumption without which most of his strictures on individual poets are unimaginable. It is, *that poets in every age have tried to succeed in the same way.* Their words may vary, but in each case the aim has been to reflect the same object, to solve the same problem, and for this task some are better suited than others.[4]

Only such an assumption can license Arnold's claim for the touchstone theory—the claim that by "using the poetry of the great classics as a sort of touchstone" we may correct the bias of a merely personal estimate. A change of vocabulary that in retrospect defines an entire age of poetry, or even a change of declared aims, fully visible when it occurred, becomes on this view an affair of the surface, dazzling but inessential. The critic does best to ignore it. So when Arnold wants to judge the achievement of Dryden and Pope against what poetry really is, he invokes timeless standards. These may amount to a criterion of dramatic truth drawn from Shakespeare's plays, or a criterion of lyric intensity drawn from the romantics: to qualify as timeless, the sample quotation that forms the touchstone need only be somehow isolable from its context. Yet Arnold's touchstones, like his respect for the grand style, are the curious produce of self-culture, and not of natural growth. Hence for all his admiration of the *Discourses,* he takes very few details from Reynolds and others whose programs for art were conceived in response to particular historical moments. But he has an excellent motive for refusing their aid. History, after all, is what Arnold's disinterestedness has to leave out of its reckoning, and to supply a style with its genealogy or a touchstone with its context would only give the game away.

From an eminence outside history, Arnold sifts all his reading for the best that is known and thought. His weakness is that the negative part of his criticism depends on his memory of period polemics, yet we are supposed to have advanced beyond such wrangling; while the endorsements can be defended only as personal taste, and Arnold's criticism makes no allowance whatever for the personal. In the end we may be baffled by the variety of his tactics.

Underlying Arnold's investigations of the spirit of romanticism is a single master-comparison, between Byron and Goethe. Goethe, he tells us in "The Function of Criticism," "knew life and the world, the poet's necessary subjects, much more comprehensively and thoroughly than Byron. He knew a great deal more of them, and he knew them much more as they really are." It may have needed Arnold to remind us that Byron saw too little of the world. Still, after this echo of Carlyle's "Close thy Byron; open thy Goethe," it is in every reader's power to recall how often, in his last years, Goethe was to be seen opening his Byron. Arnold's response to the objection, in his essay on Byron, is to retranslate, analyze, ponder and gently hover over Goethe's compliments until they seem only good-natured concessions to a man of possible talent writing in another language. But the question is not whether in this instance Arnold has produced an unhelpful invidious comparison—on the pattern of those which set Keats against Shelley, or Shelley against Byron, with Arnold moving in either direction—but whether he could ever admit to himself the instability of *any* classical ideal, as Goethe did in the *Conversations:* "I laid down the maxim of objective treatment in poetry, and would allow no other; but Schiller, who worked quite in the subjective way, deemed his own fashion the right one, and to defend himself against me, wrote the treatise upon *Naive and Sentimental Poetry.* He proved to me that I myself, against my will, was romantic." If Arnold had such an intuition, he killed it many times over.

One may connect Arnold's hopes for objectivity with his strict-constructionist interpretation of Reynolds on the grand style. Yet both ideas became plausible only with his invention of a disinterestedness that neither begins nor ends in self. In its final form, his theory sounds like this: the plainness and simplicity of Homer has fostered critics like Reynolds and Arnold, who alone can prepare the way for another Homer; and that can happen because they know Homer's secret, which is the ability not to look beyond the self but to live outside it. The masters of the grand style have done in their art what critics must now do in their commentaries.

Yet on this reading, Arnold draws the line between creation and criticism no more definitively than his successors, who are supposed to have eradicated all his teachings when they joined the two sorts of activity. It is only a difference of ideals. Arnold has an objective ideal, his successors have a personal one, for both artist and critic. The burden of proof is a good deal heavier for the objective critic. He must explain how, without anomaly, without the return of a new genius to a different "sole self," the history of art has ever shown *movement;* for when we see a change, we suppose a clash of separate wills, and not the absorption of ever-increasing constituencies in a permanent ritual of consent. Our most familiar habits of observation tell against Arnold, and many readers will want to stop here. Some sense of the incompatibility between culture, in Arnold's sense, and history, between his advocacy of great actions and his use of the touchstones for arbitration, between the timelessness of his claims and the multi-periodic eclecticism of his prejudices, will have been enough to decide them against his ideal. But I think these are insufficient grounds for rejecting Arnold, and if treated as decisive they leave the argument where it stood. For the suspicion lingers that Arnold was a fine practical critic, and that the selfless ideal of disinterestedness, always present to his mind, helped to make his discussions both of poetry and culture as exacting as they are.

As a reader I have found Arnold a memorable critic, and one whose judgments survive the rejection of his program. But what is worst in his criticism, it seems to me, was encouraged by what is most dubious in his program: his view of culture, far from being incidentally helpful, was systematically harmful to his practice. Hurried away by his scruples, he sometimes grants himself liberties which only the objective ideal could give a warrant for, and at such moments there seems to be for Arnold as intimate a connection between tactlessness and selflessness as there is for other critics between tact and the self. He admires Keats, for instance, and praises him for a Shakespearean exuberance, but he cannot conclude his estimate without looking at the letters, and he cannot look at the letters without finding that Keats said to Fanny Brawne, "My Creed is Love and you are its only tenet." Arnold comments:

A man who writes love-letters in this strain is probably predestined, one may observe, to misfortune in his love-affairs; but that is nothing. The complete enervation of the writer is the real point for remark. We have the tone, or rather the entire want of tone, the abandonment of all reticence and all dignity, of the merely sensuous man, of the man who "is passion's slave." Nay, we have them in such wise that one is tempted to speak even as *Blackwood* or the *Quarterly* were in the old days wont to speak; one is tempted to say that Keats's love-letter is the love-letter of a surgeon's apprentice. It has in its relaxed self-abandonment something underbred and ignoble, as of a youth ill brought up, without the training which teaches us that we must put some constraint upon our feelings and upon the expression of them. It is the sort of love-letter of a surgeon's apprentice which one might hear read out in a breach of promise case, or in the Divorce Court. The sensuous man speaks in it, and the sensuous man of a badly bred and badly trained sort.[5]

We need not excuse the judgment as typically Victorian: Bagehot, for one, was sufficiently able to avoid this tone in dealing with the still more provoking case of Shelley. Even within Arnold's period it presents something of an anomaly, and that is the trouble. For an objective ideal cannot—any more than the opposite ideal—prevent a critic from making such judgments and eventually suffering for them. What it can do, with the promise of judicial immunity, is encourage him to venture much farther in this direction than his social sense might otherwise allow. Yet any extreme instance is fully consistent with Arnold's usual practice and would receive from him the usual apology. On his premises, why should we take offense? Because disinterestedness has carried him too far into Keats's privacy? But he is a critic and so can judge, perhaps better than Keats, Fanny Brawne as in herself she really is. In his effort to regulate both art and its associated energies, which will not submit to regulation, Arnold ends up preferring the well-bred sensuous man to Keats: the former is at least superior to his own loathsome activities. By framing the matter like this, he echoes an old and, as it has proved, not a timeless charge against Keats, the charge of ingenuousness. He admits as allies the *Blackwood's* and *Quarterly* reviewers, and might have added Byron, who deplored "Johnny Keats's *p–ss a bed* poetry." It is strange to find Arnold in that company, but the names confirm an impression which, in other contexts, he made sure would resist analysis. He needs the ideal of objectivity as a guide to personal conduct no less than to literary performance, and under certain pressures it becomes indistinguishable from an aristocratic ideal of detachment.

Arnold thought detachment the proper attitude for the critic because he had persuaded himself that there were objective grounds for our interest in a thing. We received value from the thing itself, instead of half-creating it from our knowledge of the sorts of things we care about; so that calling a thing interesting was as bluntly descriptive an act as calling it magenta, rotten, prolix, or shaggy. This is the reverse of Hazlitt's saying that a thing is interesting when it interests *us*. Indeed, the whole range of Hazlitt's aphorisms on interest were framed as responses to an imaginary questioner like Arnold, who credits some version of realism as the common sense of mankind. Pater, replying to the same questioner, wrote in his Preface to *The Renaissance:* "'To see the object as in itself it really is,' has been justly said to be the aim of all true criticism whatever; and in aesthetic criticism the first step towards seeing one's object as it really is, is to know one's own impression as it really is."[6] Pater was right, though it cooled the enthusiasm of his disciples, to deny that this was in any way revolutionary: coming in 1873, it was rather a drastic restatement of temporarily forgotten lessons. He would have preferred, I think, simply to adopt the Hazlitt-Keats vocabulary, without argument or apology. But Arnold's intervention had made so direct a course impossible. Pater therefore brings the contest up to date, and acknowledges his opponent. At no point, however, does Arnold cause him much anxiety. His task—not a difficult one as he understands it—is to chart the full consequences of an empiricism that includes the mind in its idea of experience. This makes him "theoretical" in the sense that he advises his audience to reflect on a form of life they have long since adopted. As readers, as critics, they care for their impressions just as Hazlitt and Keats did; from this point of view, Arnold's objectivity is a detour only if we choose to follow it; let us take him, Pater says, for his motto about the free play of the mind, and for such impressions as he cannot help yielding us in spite of his doctrine.

Pater is a conscious inheritor of the skepticism of Hume. Without sorrow he accepts that everything the mind knows can only be itself, and not even itself as a unity. The same view of knowledge to which Arnold had denied existence—by writing as if the history of nominalism since Hobbes was a long, uninteresting mistake—Pater thus endorses as matter of fact. But where Hume had described his resolution of the object into impressions as a philosophy that could be believed but never lived, Pater shows us how to live it. By its argument we may still end in solipsism, but this need not be what Hume supposed it, "the most deplorable condition imaginable, inviron'd with the deepest darkness."[7] We can rather derive from our very environs a great consolation, when we realize that the shades are not all dark, that "each moment some colour is choicer than the rest."

A central assumption of Hazlitt's which Pater refines is that of the elective affinity between artist and subject, or between critic and artist. We create a second nature and choose, in Hazlitt's phrase about Rousseau, "another self" from the past or the present, by the work of such affinities. This "key to the understanding of the Greek spirit," as Pater names it, alone ensured the survival of the great Renaissance interpretations of the classics; and this

> Winckelmann possessed in his own nature, itself like a relic of classical antiquity, laid open by accident to our alien, modern atmosphere. To the criticism of that consummate Greek modelling he brought not only his culture but his temperament. We have seen how definite was the leading motive of that culture; how, like some central root-fibre, it maintained the well-rounded unity of his life through a thousand distractions. Interests not his, nor meant for him, never disturbed him. In morals, as in criticism, he followed the clue of instinct, of an unerring instinct.[8]

The "instinct" of affinity, which led Winckelmann to study this subject rather than any other, has no place in Arnold's thinking. Arnold would direct every student from the errant path of the individual mind to the grand highway of culture; and it is the normative character of the advice that Pater questions with his play on the word "error." Far as the study of Greece may have progressed since Winckelmann, Pater suggests that his instinct was unerring *to him*. When we read him we feel the rightness of the affinity, and that is another way of saying that we come to know the strength of Winckelmann's temperament. He was undeterred by "interests not his." Thus interest has replaced Arnold's disinterestedness as the groundwork of culture.

The "Conclusion" that follows Pater's chapter on Winckelmann seems to me a point-by-point rebuttal to Arnold. After resolving first the outer and then the inner life into their unstable elements, it argues that interest must begin in an attitude not of patient humility before a given object, but passionate apprehension of a chosen one. For our passions, whether we know them or not, work into every interest we can have. By saying so a last time, in four paragraphs at the close of his studies, Pater restores value to the personal and subjective impulses that animate even the effort to be disinterested.

Culture, as Pater explains it, is not the attainment of high ends by well-tested means, or the reward of having inculcated the best ideas, but something closer to what William James would later call the "total drift" of a mind's questings.

> Not the fruit of experience, but experience itself, is the end. A counted number of pulses only is given to us of a variegated, dramatic life. How may we see in them all that is to be seen in them by the finest senses? How shall we pass most swiftly from point to point, and be present always at the focus where the greatest number of vital forces unite in their purest energy?
>
> To burn always with this hard, gemlike flame, to maintain this ecstasy, is success in life. In a sense it might even be said that our failure is to form habits: for, after all, habit is relative to a stereotyped world, and meantime it is only the roughness of the eye that makes any two persons, things, situations seem alike.[9]

A comma in the second sentence hints at a tacit connection between what is "variegated" in our lives and what is "dramatic." Something is dramatic for Pater, then, in the degree that it is wide-ranging as well as intense—an extension of meaning that accords with Hazlitt's description of how the dramatic artist persuades us of his sympathy by "passing into successive minds." Each of us, when we can feel the mind as a convergence of "vital forces," aspires to be such an artist in life, to pass "swiftly from point to point." This sort of movement Pater does not connect with sympathy, but rather with "curiosity" (which usage assigns to pleasure and etymology to pain). His choice is justified constantly, if somewhat obliquely, by his references to the "strangeness" of the object we seek, its unfamiliarity to the self.

Yet Pater has lost much of the warmth his predecessors brought to their task, by his success in refining them. His flame has to be "hard and gemlike" because he has elected to view the mind's energy from the outside, as if it were a delicate found object. The mixed metaphor is not, however, presented to us as the rare fruit of an unnatural wisdom. On the contrary it expresses Pater's sense of the alliance between aestheticism and naturalism—a point he had made explicit in the last paragraph of the essay on Winckelmann: "Natural laws we shall never modify, embarrass us as they may; but there is still something in the nobler or less noble attitude with which we watch their fatal combinations." When we try to conceive of a gemlike flame, we see the mind's energy under pressure, being converted into something hard, and determined by the work of such laws. Thus determined, as we are even in our beginnings, and will continue to be in spite of every effort to break the "fatal combinations" that hold us, we cannot be expected to submit to a new and arbitrary law, of our own devising, which commands us to love what is fixed or objective. To do so would be merely to form habits, and thus to fail by adopting a less noble attitude. Pater's identification of habit with *Arnoldian* law is a splendid touch, for he knows that without some roughness of the eye, we could hardly live from one moment to the next; and without some means of abstracting a routine of behavior from the flux of sensations, we would be unequipped to perform the commonest actions. Habit, since it implies continuity, belongs to our appreciation of art as much as it does to our conduct of life. But Pater gives us his objection, "habit is relative to a stereotyped world," as a counterweight to Arnold's equation of habit with regularity, and regularity with grandeur.

After an elaborate metaphor which sets Pater's own historical moment near the end of the mind's winter, the "Conclusion" returns to its contest with Arnold.

> With this sense of the splendour of our experience and of its awful brevity, gathering all we are into one desperate effort to see and touch, we shall hardly have time to make theories about the things we see and touch. What we have to do is to be for ever curiously testing new opinions and courting new impressions, never acquiescing in a facile orthodoxy of Comte, or of Hegel, or of our own. Philosophical theories or ideas, as points of view, instruments of criticism, may help us to gather up what might otherwise pass unregarded by us. "Philosophy is the microscope of thought." The theory or idea or system which requires of us the sacrifice of any part of this experience, in consideration of some interest into which we cannot enter, or some abstract theory we have not identified with ourselves, or of what is only conventional, has no real claim upon us.[10]

The two sentences beginning with "What we have to do" closely echo the language in which Arnold himself attacked every facile orthodoxy but his own, and Pater salutes him to the extent that he served this negative function. Yet Arnold would also have been the leading example of a critic who made *a priori* theories "about the things we see and touch." He was in fact telling us which things we ought to see and touch, and that gave a bad name to theory. We can see how much broader a service he might have performed when we recall his remark, at the beginning of *Culture and Anarchy,* about the unhappy limitation of the English use of "curiosity" to imply eccentricity instead of diverseness. Arnold himself sought to bring curiosity—the word and the quality—into the constellation of the "flexible intelligence," and Pater now takes up the challenge with his suggestion that curiosity invites rather than repels the exercise of discrimination. His own extensions of curiosity, into a region of pleasant pain and continual testing, help Pater to execute two well-defined tasks: they satisfy Arnold's wish to make this the ruling virtue of the critic, and they oppose the tendency to set up theories that leave no room for its operation.

To the particular theory that literature ought always to benefit from the best ideas of the age, Pater replies that if our moments of sight and touch are fine enough, we shall hardly inquire whether they have support from the best ideas: the ideas will themselves be indistinguishable from the way we assimilate and reflect on our experience. Nothing compels us to separate the "ordinary self" of experience from the "best self" of culture, as Arnold did in *Culture and Anarchy.* Still, we may be attracted to professions of orthodoxy because we know our neighbors are watching. Without acquiescing in an explanatory system that deified Progress, or the Absolute Spirit, Arnold himself wrote largely to supply the need for some such orthodoxy. To this Pater evidently alludes, first in speaking of "a facile orthodoxy of Comte, or of Hegel, *or of our own,*" and again in denying the claim of theories which ask us to sacrifice any part of our experience "in consideration of *some interest into which we cannot enter.*" The essence of Arnold's orthodoxy is the vow to enter into no interest at all.

Pater's final paragraph shows, by anecdote and parable, what it must be like to possess a disinterestedness that pursues only interests we have found for ourselves, in conformity with no method that may attract us with promises of unimaginative gain.

> One of the most beautiful passages of Rousseau is that in the sixth book of the *Confessions,* where he describes the awakening in him of the literary sense. An undefinable taint of death had clung always about him, and now in early manhood he believed himself smitten by mortal disease. He asked himself how he might make as much as possible of the

interval that remained; and he was not biassed by anything in his previous life when he decided that it must be by intellectual excitement,
which he found just then in the clear, fresh writings of Voltaire. Well!
we are all *condamnés* as Victor Hugo says: we are all under sentence of
death but with a sort of indefinite reprieve. . . . Some spend this interval in listlessness, some in high passions, the wisest, at least among "the
children of this world," in art and song. For our one chance lies in
expanding that interval, in getting as many pulsations as possible into
the given time. Great passions may give us this quickened sense of life,
ecstasy and sorrow of love, the various forms of enthusiastic activity,
disinterested or otherwise, which come naturally to many of us. Only
be sure it is passion—that it does yield you this fruit of a quickened,
multiplied consciousness. [11]

Rousseau belongs here as the man of sensibility, beside Voltaire as
the man of reason. Yet Rousseau's way of feeling requires his last interval before death to be lived in accord with the principle of his life—
something not to be confused with the "previous biasses" of his life.
And he discovers to our surprise that for the moment he wants nothing
more than "the clear, fresh writings of Voltaire." This generous moment can be surprising for us only because it was impulsive in Rousseau. He acted, against his supposed *parti pris,* with as much disinterestedness as one could wish, and yet he did so from the point of
view of an interest all his own. Choosing from passion alone, he was
led—not out of himself, for Pater would have thought that impossible—but away from the routines of his self-culture. Pater's astonished and gleeful "Well!" expresses his satisfaction at how much this
episode of disinterestedness has told for his understanding of the idea.
We feel after hearing it that Pater identifies himself with Rousseau and
Arnold with Voltaire: the former for obvious reasons, the latter for his
praise of Voltaire's lucidity, plainness, and Homeric simplicity in the
lectures "On Translating Homer." As Rousseau was capable of a generosity denied to Voltaire, so too with their successors. Pater can therefore welcome "the various forms of enthusiastic activity, disinterested
or otherwise," without fear of being misunderstood. Disinterestedness
ought to be admired as one form of enthusiasm rather than used as a
weapon against all forms.

In this light Pater's warning, "only be sure it is passion," takes on
an especially poignant irony. An Arnoldian critic, more than others,
would need the reminder to "be sure," since the calm of mind Arnold
wished for could easily seem a freedom from all passion. In the hands

of T. S. Eliot for instance—Arnold's involuntary disciple in "Tradition and the Individual Talent"—it produced the hermetic distinction between experiential "feelings" and "a new art emotion." Pater here would have acknowledged that by common consent we recognize a difference between art and life, and between poetry and criticism; but he would have added that discussion of the boundaries has no interest for those who are still curiously testing; and the only effect of busying ourselves with such matters is to land us in some facile orthodoxy. As for Pater's idea of passion, I think it would have been much the same as Leigh Hunt's: "*Passio,* suffering in a good sense—ardent subjection of one's self to emotion." That makes it comprehensive enough for us to doubt the worth of any distinction between art- and life-emotions, or between passion as the motive of poetry and passion as the motive of criticism.

The essay "What Is Poetry?", in which Hunt supplies his definition, is also prophetic for its emphasis on the work of discrimination which both poet and critic perform. This late in his career (1844), with the sanction of Keats's odes and Hazlitt's criticism, Hunt refers us to an "impression" midway between Hazlitt's sensation ready to be greeted as an idea, and Pater's moment too fine to be violated. Again, his sense of poetry's appeal owes something to Hazlitt's "power," and at the same time looks forward to Pater's "quickened, multiplied consciousness." In him one may see the romantic poetics of expression just poised on the brink of aestheticism, but with its ancestry still visible: his later writings link Hazlitt's definition of poetry in "On Poetry in General" with Pater's definition of criticism in *The Renaissance.* Hunt, too, cares most for eloquence, not propriety, and would no more ask if a given instance was poetry or criticism than anyone after Wordsworth would ask if it was poetry or prose. He writes:

> Poetry is a passion, because it seeks the deepest impressions; and because it must undergo, in order to convey, them.
> It is a passion for truth, because without truth the impression would be false or defective.
> It is a passion for beauty, because its office is to exalt and refine by means of pleasure, and because beauty is nothing but the loveliest form of pleasure.
> It is a passion for power, because power is impression triumphant, whether over the poet, as desired by himself, or over the reader, as affected by the poet.[12]

Impression triumphant: the commonplace acquired new force once Pater had shown that to revive it was an act of defiance. The next generation knew that their freedom came from the recovery of an old idea and looked for the impression to gain ascendancy once more throughout literature. Arnold's revisions of the canon, however, together with his eulogistic term, "culture," had conquered readers who would have found either of these alone unnecessarily arbitrary; others, who dissented from Arnold's particular judgments, still honored the sense of his argument by addressing a culture beyond the claims of the self. Henry James seems to have profited from the rich confusion of this atmosphere—at any rate he is a sensitive register of all its elements. In "The Art of Fiction," where his critical sympathies are less Arnoldian than his prose, he affirms that "there is no impression of life, no manner of seeing it and feeling it, to which the plan of the novelist may not offer a place" only a paragraph after having noticed the unimpressionable boundaries for "the treatment of reality." Thus Pater's triumph turned out to be less secure than the history of romanticism seemed to predict it would be. This fact goes a long way to explain the tone of his followers, and why they retained, without the tiresome humility, something of the protectiveness of disciples. Somehow they are still an embattled minority, and the shock of saying so turns them into ironists. It makes their natural vehicle the aphorism, which can present as common wisdom what others denounce as violent paradox. In one celebrated example, Pater's sentence about knowing one's impression is twisted and teased until it rejects the Arnoldian sentiment it had tried to absorb, with an uncontroversial ease Wilde asks us to savor: "The highest Criticism, then, is more creative than creation, and the primary aim of the critic is to see the object as in itself it really is not."[13] Test it as we will, the aphorism replies by affirming nothing. It demonstrates only the question-begging futility of its opposite, that creation is more creative than criticism. "Really" is treated with cruel but expeditious justice, and tapped neatly into its grave among the systematically misleading expressions of faith in culture.

The dismissive style of such remarks gives a special éclat to "The Critic as Artist." In a more closely argued dialogue, "The Decay of Lying," Wilde's inversions are more thoroughgoing; having disposed of the object, he wonders what can be made of the sum of objects that we call nature: "For what is Nature? Nature is no great mother who has borne us. She is our creation. It is in our brain that she quickens into life. Things are because we see them, and what we see, and how we see it, depends on the Arts that have influenced us."[14] Only, he argues, when we look at a nature chosen by art, can we feel a presence that creates all nature for us. But the result can never have universal interest. Pater's most acute twentieth-century critic, Edward Thomas, described his nature as one atmosphere, touched by "a chilly unchanging light as of a northward gallery. It has not ease or warmth or music, but dignity, ceremony, and educated grace."[15] We may feel that Wilde's nature excludes still more, with its refusal of any outward exposure chilly or otherwise, its air thick with smoke, epigrams, and intentions that do not matter. In that air Wilde can say of Thomas Wainewright, an artist renowned equally for chalk portraits and strychnine jellies, "His crimes seem to have had an important effect upon his art. They gave a strong personality to his style, a quality that his early work certainly lacked." By such refinements of fancy, Wilde is able to advance Pater's argument with a home-felt confidence Pater lacked. He ends his reflections on Wainewright with the sentence, "There is no essential incongruity between crime and culture."[16]

The polemical motive is as strong here as in the aphorisms. Those who insist on the objectivity of culture are put on notice that *he* will not be governed by the fears that led them to cherish an ideal of detachment. He is ready to overturn Arnold's implicit laws of conduct as much as his codified laws of taste, and answers the criminal with the same reserve as the man whose taste he deplores—not "You are wrong, because unreal" but "All things considered, you are unacceptable." In some instances, as the case of Wainewright makes us see, all things may present a greater enigma than we like to believe. Up to this point, Wilde writes as Pater's advocate, though with a strategy Pater would have shrunk from—as the transcendentalist who was Fichte's advocate pointed to the weather outside and said, "Look! I'm snowing." But he goes beyond Pater in his objection to one consequence of Arnoldian criticism, its separation of critical justice from the possibility of personal growth. Against this view of the critic as a man who has reached a standstill, he protests with an entirely serious eloquence in "The Critic as Artist:"

> *Ernest.*   Well, I should say that a critic should above all things be fair.
> *Gilbert.*   Ah! not fair. A critic cannot be fair in the ordinary sense of the word. It is only about things that do not interest one that one can

give a really unbiassed opinion, which is no doubt the reason why an unbiassed opinion is always absolutely valueless. The man who sees both sides of a question, is a man who sees absolutely nothing at all. Art is a passion, and, in matters of art, Thought is inevitably coloured by emotion, and so is fluid rather than fixed, and, depending upon fine moods and exquisite moments, cannot be narrowed into the rigidity of a scientific formula or a theological dogma.[17]

"Fluid rather than fixed" quotes Hazlitt, "fine moods and exquisite moments" nearly quotes Pater, but the occasion for this flurry of allusions is Arnold's incessant quotation of himself. In "The Function of Criticism" alone, to take the example that would have been most available to Wilde, he borrows prominently from "On Translating Homer" for the statement on the object in itself, and from his attack on Bishop Colenso for some strictures on the relation between force and right. Wilde's point is the unhappiness most of us know when we fall into repetitions of this sort. But Arnold takes pride in them. It is the pride of owning an intelligence that does not change, in a life that has no epochs. "Through constant change," Wilde comments, "and through constant change alone, [the critic] will find his true unity. He will not consent to be the slave of his own opinions. For what is mind but motion in the intellectual sphere?"[18] In these sentences, however, Wilde radically understates his doctrine of the truth of masks. He was in love with reversal even more than with change, and that led finally to his deification of the mask itself, in a number of aphorisms unguarded by irony. "Those who do not love beauty more than truth never know the inmost shrine of art." "The only beautiful things . . . are the things that do not concern us." "What people call insincerity is simply a method by which we can multiply our personalities." Here sympathy has passed from the system of motives and actions to which Wilde can grant intelligible meaning. His mature practice is, as often as possible, to run together sympathy and duplicity as if they were the same thing, both equally desirable as a venture into new selves.

Any account of this change in the morality of art must return to the question of solipsism. Hazlitt and Keats, though they regarded themselves as intellectual allies of Hume, Burke, Wordsworth, and Hunt, and therefore maintained a preference for "realities" at the expense of "reality," did not see that this entailed any narrowing of experience. It meant rather that they could scarcely help taking everything they came to know and feel as personal to themselves. Pater and Wilde, on the contrary, treat solipsism as a shattering truth of the spirit. "Experience," writes Pater in the "Conclusion" to *The Renaissance*, "already reduced to a swarm of impressions, is ringed round for each one of us by that thick wall of personality through which no real voice has ever pierced on its way to us, or from us to that which we can only conjecture to be without." Had he been shown this sentence and asked for his opinion, Hazlitt would have expressed a very general assent, but then inquired into the choice of a word, a phrase, and a metaphor: the word, "reduced"; the phrase, "no real voice"; the metaphor, "that thick wall of personality." Why reduced?—unless we look back to some great original of experience, from which our impressions are the degenerate offspring. Why no real voice?—a complaint that grants reality to what lies outside us, when reality is precisely the thing to be proved. Why a *wall* of personality?—as if we were constantly guessing at a realm beyond our impressions, instead of identifying our impressions with everything that is the case for us. It seems from these choices that Pater was moved to describe the solipsist's condition in realistic language, and to afflict it with a realist yearning for certitude, before he could sally out against his antagonist in properly heroic style. Keats was less troubled: "I see, and sing, by my own eyes inspired." To rival so calm a sense that one's limitations are a gift, Pater's sentence would have to be rewritten as follows: "Experience, the impressions we are always receiving, with all their compositions and decompositions, we infuse at every moment with the colours of our own personality, so that we can never know a voice that has not first mingled with our own, and in a manner become ours as soon as we heard it."

The difference between this and what Pater actually wrote suggests that from common premises with the skeptical wing of the romantic movement, he derived a new conception of the mind. His vocabulary—and Wilde inherited it—builds up a picture of impressions as a finished lapidary set, easily damaged but, since they are hidden in the mind, secure from the more obvious sorts of assault. In reading both Pater and Wilde one notices how the adjectives of still-life predominate, *fine, delicate, exquisite* taking the place occupied for Hazlitt and Keats by *warm, vigorous, radiant*. How much this implies, for every detail in the practice both of writing and seeing, Hazlitt and Pater explained to their readers in two essays on style. Hazlitt's "On the Prose-Style of Poets" and Pater's "Style" deal, in each case, with a prose exemplar whom the critic sets above all others—Burke for Hazlitt, Flaubert for Pater—yet the apology for a master is conceived by each as an implicit apology for himself. The "he" referred to in Hazlitt's portrait is ambiguous, being sometimes "Edmund Burke," sometimes "any great and serious writer of prose," and sometimes "I, William Hazlitt (though I will not say so)."

> The principle which guides his pen is truth, not beauty—not pleasure, but power. He has no choice, no selection of subject to flatter the reader's idle taste, or assist his own fancy: he must take what comes, and make the most of it. He works the most striking effects out of the most unpromising materials, by the mere activity of his mind. He rises with the lofty, descends with the mean, luxuriates in beauty, gloats over deformity. It is all the same to him, so that he loses no particle of the exact, characteristic, extreme impression of the thing he writes about, and that he communicates this to the reader, after exhausting every possible mode of illustration, plain or abstracted, figurative or literal. Whatever stamps the original image more distinctly on the mind, is welcome. . . . In prose, the professed object is to impart conviction, and nothing can be admitted by way of ornament or relief, that does not add new force or clearness to the original conception. The two classes of ideas brought together by the orator or impassioned prose-writer, to wit, the general subject and the particular image, are so far incompatible, and the identity must be more strict, more marked, more determinate, to make them coalesce to any practical purpose. Every word should be a blow: every thought should instantly grapple with its fellow. There must be a weight, a precision, a conformity from association in the tropes and figures of animated prose to fit them to their place in the argument, and make them *tell*.[19]

As the last phrase indicates, Hazlitt's "impassioned prose-writer" is one sort of storyteller; Pater's is another sort, whose aim is to wander beautifully, and only at last to return.

> The blithe, crisp sentence, decisive as a child's expression of its needs, may alternate with the long-contending, victoriously intricate sentence; the sentence, born with the integrity of a single word, relieving the sort of sentence in which, if you look closely, you can see much contrivance, much adjustment, to bring a highly qualified matter into compass at one view. For the literary architecture, if it is to be rich and expressive, involves not only foresight of the end in the beginning, but also development or growth of design, in the process of execution, with many irregularities, surprises, and afterthoughts; the contingent as well as the necessary being subsumed under the unity of the whole. . . . With some strong and leading sense of the world, the tight hold of which secures true *composition* and not mere loose accretion, the literary artist, I suppose, goes on considerably, setting joint to joint, sustained by yet

restraining the productive ardour, retracing the negligences of his first sketch, repeating his steps only that he may give the reader a sense of secure and restful progress, readjusting mere assonances even, that they may soothe the reader, or at least not interrupt him on his way; and then, somewhere before the end comes, is burdened, inspired, with his conclusion, and betimes delivered of it, leaving off, not in weariness and because he finds *himself* at an end, but in all the freshness of volition. His work now structurally complete, with all the accumulating effects of secondary shades of meaning, he finishes the whole up to the just proportion of that ante-penultimate conclusion, and all becomes expressive.[20]

With Pater's "much contrivance, much adjustment" still in mind, one may note that this essay forms an exception even to the most fastidious meditations on style by ornate writers, from its eagerness to solicit the reader's interest in the half-coalesced materials of the workshop. The contrast with Hazlitt is the more stark because Hazlitt wants to avoid any suggestion that ornate writing suits the ends of prose: his pedagogy doubtless has in view the composition of a book like *The Spirit of the Age;* Pater's, the revision of an essay like "The Child in the House." In keeping with this contrast of temperament is a marked disparity of purpose between Hazlitt and Pater, when they tell us what uses the vivid impression ought to serve. Once felt, Hazlitt's impression works dynamically, from the inside out; it is communicated instantly, and "every word should be a blow." Pater's impression is decorative, and the indoor settings of Wilde's dialogues allude to this for all it is worth. Curators of the impression, Gilbert (in "The Critic as Artist") and Vivian (in "The Decay of Lying") follow Pater in describing found objects of the mind as from a distance, or through a pane of perfect glass; to Wilde as much as Pater, the chosen object of pleasure-pain must be treated as one specimen of a life from which he is estranged— though Pater's is the tragedy of unrealized contact, and Wilde's the comedy of switched identities. This is true even of the way they treat celebrated *critical* impressions: in "The Critic as Artist" Wilde exhibits Pater's description of the Mona Lisa with the hushed reverence of a connoisseur, like Mr. Gutman unwrapping his falcon. To measure the distance from Hazlitt and Keats, one need only compare, from that same description, a line like Pater's "and keeps their fallen day about her," with Keats's "While barred clouds bloom the soft-dying day." The sensuous and outward-working verbs have been stilled. Into Pater's imaginings the sense of process cannot enter, but only forms fully achieved and now to be prized, on which the present perfect tense ("She has been dead . . . and learned . . . and been . . . and trafficked . . . and all this has been to her") keeps lock and key.

Convinced that one could never go outside the self, Hazlitt and Keats found everything in themselves; seeking themselves in everything, Pater and Wilde conclude that the "thick wall of personality" is impenetrable. From some place outside the wall—a place to which they extend diplomatic recognition by quarreling with it—objects float up to them, one by one and half-remembered. But these are parts of a life others live, to which the new men must never give credence. They acknowledge the predominance of, and then build their retreat within, the world of natural laws. How far this was the world of Zola's novels has already emerged in Pater's sentiment of "the nobler or less noble attitude with which we watch their fatal combinations." The need to make a similar acknowledgment prompted Wilde to write the most earnest passage of "The Critic as Artist":

> By revealing to us the absolute mechanism of all action, and so freeing us from the self-imposed and trammelling burden of moral responsibility, the scientific principle of Heredity has become, as it were, the warrant for the contemplative life. It has shown us that we are never less free than when we try to act. It has hemmed us round with the nets of the hunter, and written upon the wall the prophecy of our doom. We may not watch it, for it is within us. We may not see it, save in a mirror that mirrors the soul. It is Nemesis without her mask. It is the last of the Fates, and the most terrible. It is the only one of the Gods whose real name we know.[21]

The mind's self-enclosure no longer counts as evidence that individual thought and feeling can make a fourth estate in society. That was the conclusion Hazlitt drew, but Wilde here tells us that his philosophical beliefs are useful to him because they fortify the inner life against all disturbance. What else has naturalism left him? Zola was after all a necessary ally against the more restrictive elements of Arnold's thought, and Wilde is compelled to take this consolation, even if it means severing the contemplative life from any thought of mankind. We may sympathize with the sense of history that brought him to this juncture, and honor him for wishing to reflect his own moment more adequately than Arnold had. But because he does admit the personal motives and conditions of his thinking; because his own polemic was a legacy from Pater; because, in expanding that legacy, he could only unbuild the Arnoldian dogmas, and return criticism to a point it had reached before Arnold launched his campaign against interest; because he did so in unhappy circumstances, when the idea of the self had ceased to be as generous as it was for the romantics: for these reasons he seems to me an unrewarding hero for us now.

I hope it will be plain that I read both Pater and Wilde as genuine successors of Johnson, Hazlitt, and the tradition of criticism I most admire, which extends in our time to Orwell and Empson. But their revolt against Arnold forced them to adopt restrictive attitudes of their own—their inner world too confirms and exalts special inhibitions—and it is striking that in all their criticism, though we still value Pater on Wordsworth, Lamb, and Coleridge, and Wilde on Browning, Meredith, and Kipling, there is no piece of sustained critical eloquence to match the great passages of Johnson and Hazlitt. This may seem part of the burden of the past: for the successors of critics like those, and of Ruskin after them, what remained to be done? But the simple answer makes too clean a sweep. A generation ahead are Shaw's Preface to *Androcles and the Lion,* his discussions of Ibsen, Wagner, Shakespeare, and the melodramas of the nineties, and with them the return of just those qualities, an unforced command and ready exuberance of wit, which after a time we cease even to look for when we read Pater and Wilde. Perhaps the highest cost of the Arnoldian reaction can be traced here, in the language of those who saw beyond it, into the past as well as the future, but who were driven in defiance of it to claim for the self the same office of discriminating vigilance and exclusion that Arnold assigned to culture.

7

Emerson and the
Ode to W. H. Channing

EMERSON WROTE SUCCESSFUL POEMS of at least three kinds. The most familiar is the Concord Poem, or sociable ramble. Here he is often charming, and much closer to the style of his time and place than he lets himself appear elsewhere, in either verse or prose. In a very different mode, the Wordsworthian elegy or meditation, he writes with enough ease to rival Bryant, but with a power of invention that makes us want to ignore all other claims and think of him as the first American poet. Finally, Emerson is himself a pioneer of the sort of poem he calls for in "Merlin," the shocker or far-fetcher, the prophetic blast that we hear as the "strokes of fate," and see as "Sparks of the supersolar blaze." These classifications turn out to be a hindrance in reading, however, because so few of the poems are willing to stay put and respect the boundaries. "Monadnoc" is a ramble that leaps into prophecy, and then tip-toes back; "Bacchus" is an elegy, modeled on the Immortality Ode, which opens up an apocalyptic prophecy of renewal; "The Snow-Storm" is a *Wordsworthian* ramble. The only point of beginning like this is to warn ourselves against inferring much about Emerson's poetry from the discussion of a single poem: with him, even more than with most poets, any conclusion drawn about his "characteristic" tone or strategy is pretty certainly going to be false. In the following remarks on the "Ode Inscribed to W. H. Channing," I assume only that it is an unsettling poem which we have not yet begun to make our peace with, and that Emerson would have placed it with "Uriel" as the most serious of his prophecies.

Here is the poem:

Though loath to grieve
The evil time's sole patriot,
I cannot leave
My honied thought
For the priest's cant,
Or statesman's rant.

If I refuse
My study for their politique,
Which at the best is trick,
The angry Muse
Puts confusion in my brain.

But who is he that prates
Of the culture of mankind,
Of better arts and life?
Go, blindworm, go,
Behold the famous States
Harrying Mexico
With rifle and with knife!

Or who, with accent bolder,
Dare praise the freedom-loving mountaineer?
I found by thee, O rushing Contoocook!
And in thy valleys, Agiochook!
The jackals of the negro-holder.

The God who made New Hampshire
Taunted the lofty land
With little men;—
Small bat and wren
House in the oak:—
If earth-fire cleave
The upheaved land, and bury the folk,
The southern crocodile would grieve.
Virtue palters; Right is hence;
Freedom praised, but hid;
Funeral eloquence
Rattles the coffin-lid.

What boots thy zeal,
O glowing friend,
That would indignant rend
The northland from the south?
Wherefore? to what good end?

Boston Bay and Bunker Hill
Would serve things still;
Things are of the snake.

The horseman serves the horse,
The neatherd serves the neat,
The merchant serves the purse,
The eater serves his meat;
'Tis the day of the chattel,
Web to weave, and corn to grind;
Things are in the saddle,
And ride mankind.

There are two laws discrete,
Not reconciled, —
Law for man, and law for thing;
The last builds town and fleet,
But it runs wild,
And doth the man unking.

'Tis fit the forest fall,
The steep be graded,
The mountain tunnelled,
The sand shaded,
The orchard planted,
The glebe tilled,
The prairie granted,
The steamer built.

Let man serve law for man;
Live for friendship, live for love,
For truth's and harmony's behoof;
The state may follow how it can,
As Olympus follows Jove.

Yet do not I implore
The wrinkled shopman to my sounding woods,
Nor bid the unwilling senator
Ask votes of thrushes in the solitudes.
Every one to his chosen work; —
Foolish hands may mix and mar;
Wise and sure the issues are.
Round they roll till dark is light,
Sex to sex, and even to odd; —
The over-god

Who marries Right to Might,
Who peoples, unpeoples,—
He who exterminates
Races by stronger races,
Black by white faces,—
Knows to bring honey
Out of the lion;
Grafts gentlest scion
On pirate and Turk.

The Cossack eats Poland,
Like stolen fruit;
Her last noble is ruined,
Her last poet mute:
Straight, into double band
The victors divide;
Half for freedom strike and stand;—
The astonished Muse finds thousands at her side.

We know enough about Concord in the 1840s to reconstruct the occasion of this poem. Through much of 1845 and 1846, Emerson was working against the odds to find strength in solitude, while Texas was annexed, the war of persuasion between the slave and free states grew heated, and America embarked on its imperial war against Mexico. Thoreau went to jail rather than pay taxes for the war, and Channing, in league with other neighbors or friends, sought to extract from Emerson some comparable gesture of public defiance. It would be wrong to view Channing and Emerson as natural allies. Channing was convinced that all progress must come from unified movements; he had objected to Emerson's thinking as early as the Divinity School *Address:* "You deny the Human Race. You stand, or rather seek to stand, a complete Adam. But you cannot do it." [1] In the background of the Ode we thus have three temperaments, each occupying a distinct position: Channing, the man of great public causes, who denounces the war on principle; Thoreau, the disciple of self-reliance, who resists the war as an invasion of his privacy; and Emerson, who so far has taken no public stand, though from time to time he confides in his journal.

Emerson's conduct during this crisis would have been a familiar story to anyone who knew him well. His pattern generally was to withhold himself from the fray until the last possible moment, when the force of a calamity became unendurable. Then, at the beckoning of others, he would make his statement. Once he had played the part, he would confess to a sense of having been besmirched, or somehow cheated of himself, in the course of making his eloquence serviceable to a cause. When, for example, President Van Buren's sham-treaty with the Cherokees first contracted for the exchange of all Cherokee lands and the transportation of the entire tribe beyond the Mississippi River, Emerson's friends prevailed on him to write an open letter of protest to Van Buren. It is an eloquent but also a curiously personal document, in which a long stream of interrogatives is suddenly closed tight: "A crime is projected that confounds our understandings by its magnitude—a crime that really deprives us as well as the Cherokees of a country." With this letter Emerson satisfied the cause while speaking not as the agent of a cause but as a private citizen. Yet after writing it, he says in his journal that on all such occasions, "my genius deserts me"—and he adds, "It is like dead cats around my neck."

We now come to a moment eight years later, with nothing changed in Emerson. Once again, the question he has to ask himself is, How, given my purity of self-reliance, can I ever ally myself with the common sentiments of men, and not feel besmirched by having consummated the alliance in public? The Ode shows us what it looks like when he tries to meet the question head-on. The poem is a very mixed success, in an area where Emerson's ideas seem to have ruled out any kind of success whatever; but it is an important poem to the American imagination, for reasons that have nothing to do with our search for masterpieces. To explain its importance we need to return to three of Emerson's favorite words: *commodity, spirit,* and *power.*

The Ode exhibits a cleavage that Emerson had often sought to deny or repair, between commodity and spirit; and it impresses us more strongly than ever with his tendency to mistake them for each other, especially when they were joined by the pivotal third term, *power.* We are conscious of power in our sovereignty over the realm of commodity and our liberty in the realm of spirit. As we discover in *Nature,* commodity has a very low place on the Emersonian scale of being, and spirit the highest place. Since, however, it is power that gives us access to both realms, the two can look dangerously alike. Because they can, and because we find the resemblance attractive, we risk forgetting our end in the infatuation with our means: we become sovereigns of commodity and call it spirit. The Ode, I think, exemplifies this confusion but does not surmount it; and my conclusion, which I will try to keep in sight as I proceed, is that there can be no convincing resolution of the quarrel between Emerson's scholarly interpreter, Henry Thoreau, and his national interpreter, Henry Ford. Both tell us what they mean, and in both cases the name of what they mean is Emerson.

The journal entries around the time of the Ode are haunted by the evils a nation can do, and adroit in baffling their impulse to condemn with a nervous suspicion of all motives. "Mr. Webster," writes Emerson, "told [us] how much the war cost, that was his protest, but voted the war, and sends his son to it. They calculated rightly on Mr. Webster. My friend Mr. Thoreau has gone to jail rather than pay his tax. On him they could not calculate. The Abolitionists denounce the war and give much time to it, but they pay the tax." Webster's position is wrong, and yet Thoreau's protest—with its incidental reward of allowing him to be seen as an incalculable—is too idiosyncratic to be repeated or bear consequences. On the other hand, the very brazenness of the American government testifies to its strength of will, which almost looks like *self*-will, and compels us to recognize its power, which part of us wants to admire. "These—rabble—at Washington are really better than the snivelling opposition. They have a sort of genius of a bold and manly cast, though Satanic."[2]

In another entry of roughly the same period, the calculability of the abolitionists has ceased to be a warrant for rejecting their cause, and we find Emerson oppressed by the weight of soul-sickening events. He admits to himself that his only reason for keeping silent is the still greater oppression that would come if he allowed his anger to settle on an easy target. "Really," he writes, "a scholar has too humble an opinion of the population, of their possibilities, of their future, to be entitled to go to war with them, as with equals. This prison is one step to suicide. He knows that nothing they can do will ever please him. Why should he poorly pound on some one string of discord, when all is jangle?"[3] These are the words of a man whose temperament will permit him neither to pursue his calling in spite of public events nor to join the crowd that tries to effect a change in them. From the jail, suicide is but a step away; but one feels that for Emerson, as he writes, total paralysis is but a step in the opposite direction: few passages in his journals have this one-tone grimness. And, after this, we find it impossible to believe that Emerson could credit, or long be happy with, his remark that "The annexation of Texas looks like one of those events which retard or retrograde the civilization of ages. But the

World Spirit is a good swimmer, and storms and waves cannot easily drown him. He snaps his fingers at laws."[4]

I have quoted these three entries out of sequence because, in their present order, they reproduce the movement of the Ode. We begin with the disagreeable summoning to public speech, the refusal to supply eloquence for the occasion, and the rather anxious speculation on the motives of others who do speak. There follows the survey of America's estate, with the admission that evil *is* abroad in the land, but an evil that has come to dominate nature itself, to the point where all action is equally useless and equally blameless. Finally, about-face; the World Spirit is a good swimmer. The end of the poem is made inevitable not by a master-stroke of dialectical cunning, or because Emerson has convinced even himself of its propriety. It has only the claim of necessity. There was nothing else for Emerson to do if he wanted to go on writing.

Emerson speaks the first two stanzas, and Channing—or whatever in Emerson is embarrassable by Channing—the next three. Emerson gets pretty much the rest of the poem, his mind ranging far and wide to produce new contradictions while his stomach labors hard to digest the old. At the outset Emerson wants only to defend the solitude a poet builds so that poetry will visit him; abridge your solitude at the urging of society, and the "angry Muse" puts confusion in your brain. This would seem to require no apology. But in the third, fourth, and fifth stanzas Channing quickly gets the better of it: "While you preen yourself with fine talk about culture, one of your hapless neighbors is being assaulted in a back-alley of the Republic." And the pollution of slavery covers everything: "I found by thee, O rushing Contoocook! / And in thy valleys, Agiochook! / The jackals of the negro-holder." We have expected a different climax—something more like, "I found by thee . . . / The flower that grows no other-where." Emerson loves these place-names; they belong to his New England, and mean as much to him as Monadnoc, or the troop of colonists in a famous opening line: "Bulkeley, Hunt, Willard, Homer, Meriam, Flint." The jackals are not here yet, but you can smell them in the air; the Fugitive Slave Law is on its way; and this is a betrayal of the intransigence that the very names were meant to convey. In the fifth stanza New Hampshire's men are seen as unworthy of the sublime landscape they inhabit: they are full of ambition, mean egotism, and complicity, and the land towers over them in gigantic scorn.

Yet, as this stanza continues, something strange is happening to the logic of the poem. A specific revulsion from those who would countenance slavery is generalized into universal disenchantment. The saber-rattling of the abolitionists is really just coffin-rattling; in such a time all eloquence becomes merely funereal. Channing's argument has touched an extreme at which it plays into Emerson's hands. The mode of much of the fifth stanza—beginning with "Small bat and wren / House in the Oak"—is close to Blakean satire, and we see that political remedies of the usual sort are out of the question. "Things are of the snake." Therefore, render unto Caesar what is Caesar's; and while you do it there will be plenty of time for debate.

The debate that occupies the rest of the poem ought to interest students of American politics as much as students of Emerson. *Service* has been on Emerson's mind from the start: whether or not to be pressed into service for a cause, whether to say his "I will not serve" to Channing or to the rabble in Washington. Now he observes that the right disposition of service has been inverted throughout nature: the horseman serves the horse, the eater serves his meat, "things are in the saddle, / And ride mankind." This happens because, of the "two laws discrete," "Law for man and law for thing," the second runs wild and "Doth the man unking." When I first read the Ode and came to the ninth stanza, I took it to be straight irony, a demonstration of how law for thing runs wild. But after all, *it is we that feel the irony.* What Emerson knew was that he needed two stanzas; one each, to demonstrate the proper functioning of law for thing and law for man. And law for thing includes: cutting down forests, building steamers, annexing new lands. Emerson is writing this poem to attack at the root the man-thing confusion that has tricked us into war. Yet the perfected man that he envisions has agreed neither to leave things alone nor to serve law for man. On the contrary, the march of technological optimism brings us back where we began, at the annexation of Texas, and determines it to have been legal in a more than political sense. We can see what the trouble is. Down this path a little way, things get in the saddle, and we are in Mexico with the rifle and the knife.

For "thing" let us temporarily substitute "commodity." Emerson writes in *Nature:*

> Under the general name of commodity, I rank all those advantages which our senses owe to nature. . . . [But] Nature, in its ministry to man, is not only the material but is also the process and the result. All the parts incessantly work into each other's hands for the profit of

man. . . . The useful arts are reproductions or new combinations by the wit of man, of the same natural benefactors. He no longer waits for favoring gales, but by means of steam, he realizes the fable of Aeolus's bag, and carries the two and thirty winds in the boiler of his boat.[5]

Commodity thus includes both the thing and what man does to the thing—which is understood as part of the thing itself, its final cause. In *Nature* as in the Ode, we can gauge Emerson's high spirits by the catalogue of things which he regards as a wonder requiring no comment. And yet the chapter in *Nature* closes with an admonition: "This mercenary benefit [conferred by nature with the help of man's skill] is one which has respect to a farther good. A man is fed, not that he may be fed, but that he may work." And if we are set to work on deeper tunnels and vaster prairies—what then? Work, after all, implies self-reliance only for a scholar.

The truth is that Emerson had a lover's quarrel with commodity, and liked to speak of its advancement in the language of manifest destiny. His journals portray it as an energy-giver to man, who may require coaxing to unleash his genius; and as the maker of harmony in those vicissitudes where man can hear only jangle. "By atoms, by trifles, by sots, Heaven operates. The needles are nothing, the magnetism is all." This is simple enough, as one instance of a monism that Emerson never leaves unqualified for long. (But the needles, I suspect, are the lives of individual men.) More amusing, and a good deal more puzzling, is the entry that runs: "Alcott should be made effective by being tapped by a good suction pump."[6] Here Alcott is to be understood as either inflated, or constipated, or both. The suction pump will make his genius serviceable. But something else is happening too. The machine is turning Alcott into a *thing*, and Emerson is expressing a certain satisfaction in the fact. It is fitting. The machine was made to do this to Alcott, and he needed to have this done to him. Which is in the saddle?

For "man" let us now substitute "spirit." Again, in the relevant chapter of *Nature,* we discover an admonition: "You cannot freely admire a noble landscape if laborers are digging in the field hard by." In the sight of bare commodity you do not participate in spirit. But what of a large mountain with a tunnel through it, when the laborers have gone away? If commodity may be assimilated to nature as the steamboat to Aeolus, the mountain-with-tunnel can plausibly become one of the hieroglyphs we read in identifying ourselves with spirit, and the power we feel in contemplating it is not to be wholly severed from the power the laborers spent in gouging it from rock. Perhaps when the scholar of nature does come to speak of spirit, he will see the lofty land taunting little men. But it is the same scholar who tells us that the land ought not to be left alone. Power occupies a landscape or nation as naturally as it fills a stanza. When, in a journal entry of 1846, Emerson transforms his distinction between our engine power over commodity and our contemplative power of spirit into an *ethical* distinction, between the politician who serves things and the poet who serves men, he gives us this:

> *Amalgam.* The absolutist is good and blessed, though he dies without sight of that paradise he journeys after; and he can forgive the earth-worms who remain immersed in matter and know not the felicities he seeks. But not so well the middle man who receives and assents to his theories and yet, by habit and talent formed to live in the existing order, builds and prospers among the worldly men, extending his affection and countenance all the time to the absolutists. Ah, thou evil, two-faced half-and-half! how can I forgive thee? Evil, evil hast thou done. Thou it is that confoundest all distinctions. If thou didst not receive the truth at all, thou couldst do the cause of virtue no harm. But now the men of selfishness say to the absolutist, Behold this man, he has all thy truth, yet lo! he is with us and ours,—Ah, thou damnable Half-and-Half! choose, I pray you, between God and the Whig Party, and do not longer strew sugar on this bottled spider.
>
> Yes; but Confucius. Confucius, glory of the nations, Confucius, sage of the Absolute East, was a middle man. He is the Washington of philosophy.[7]

The face Emerson had before him when he spoke of Half-and-Half must have been Webster's. But Webster turns into Confucius quite effortlessly, and Emerson thought of himself now and then as a sage of the Absolute East. To the sentence at the end of this passage one wants to add: yes, and America is the Washington of nations; and the Ode is in this sense a thoroughly American poem.

In the penultimate stanza the over-god appears, bringing the honeycomb from out of the lion but also doing rather bloodier work: it is he that peoples and unpeoples, exterminates races by stronger races. He is the subtlest of artificers and, like the gardener of *The Winter's Tale*, "Grafts gentlest scion / On pirate and Turk." But another allusion, at once more strange and less remote, is also at work in these lines. Emerson was returning, for the iron will and martial cadence, to Wordsworth's "Ode: 1815," which had addressed an unequivocal prayer to the God who

> guides the Pestilence—the cloud
> Of locusts travels on his breath;
> The region that in hope was ploughed
> His drought consumes, his mildew taints with death

—the God, that is, of victory in battle:

> But Thy most dreaded instrument
> In working out a pure intent,
> Is Man—arrayed for mutual slaughter,
> —Yea, Carnage is thy daughter.

Wordsworth later softened and qualified this terrible utterance; yet it belonged to the eccentric canon of poems that mattered greatly to Emerson; it makes an ambiguous legacy, which Emerson was too honest to deny and yet too canny to welcome by its original name. It is curious to reflect that his summons to the over-god observes all the forms of a war-whoop for the allied adventure against Napoleon, in the very depth of the winter of democracy in England.

Having given over the discreteness of laws to the keeping of the over-god, Emerson retreats once again to his solitude—this time, however, accompanied by an army of thousands who stand ready to fight for liberty *and* solitude. One of Emerson's best known early poems, "Each and All," ends with the line: "I yielded myself to the perfect whole." Here we would have to alter it to read: "Aided by the over-god, I caused nature to yield a perfect whole, to which all in turn must yield." Emerson was of course shocked by the Russian invasion of Poland; but in the poem it seems hardly worse than a boyish trespass; the atmosphere in which the over-god subsists has converted everything to its own terms, and worked an eerie change on the words we use for good and evil. The muse, we remember, grew angry when Emerson deserted her for a cause. Now she is astonished because the cause has joined her. With some assistance from both her and the over-god, Emerson has won his right to stand alone. But at what cost? In the final sentence of "Experience" he wrote: "the true romance which the world exists to realize will be the transformation of genius into practical power." Every reader on coming to this sentence at the end of that somber essay will have felt certain of one thing: Emerson could not have known exactly what he meant. And anyone who knows Em-

erson well may feel certain of another: he was not speaking meta-
phorically. The iron in the soul of the Channing Ode is that a part of
Emerson is in deep and unacknowledged sympathy with Channing's
enemies and his own.

Poetry like history has its afterthoughts, the return in an almost
penetrable disguise of an event too large to be easily recalled, and there
is a troubling resemblance between the Ode and a more recent political
poem, by another cunning respecter of "the angry Muse," Robert
Frost's "Provide, Provide." Frost's occasion is a strike by the charwomen at Harvard, in the early years of the New Deal. He professes
no sympathy for the strikers, and no shame or confusion about the
sympathy withheld. The Abishag of his poem washes the steps "with
pail and rag" after having fallen "from great and good," and we understand that no fall is without its cause. The poem affirms only that she
should have planned her future with greater craft.

> Better to go down dignified
> With boughten friendship at your side
> Than none at all. Provide, provide!

When we provision ourselves with boughten friendship, we turn a
spiritual good into a commodity; we know this, but are not less flat-
tered and not less consoled for knowing it. The poem is delivered, as
a kind of sermon, in the radically complacent tones of a Yankee minister, endeavoring at one stroke to confute every New England jeremiad that dared to lament the decline of a religion of faith into a habit
of work. "What's the difference?" says this new and imperious voice of
conscience. "If things are in the saddle, it is because we put them
there. And what more have we ever desired, than to catch a trace of
our own glory in the dazzle of theirs?" The Ode, "astonished" as it is,
energetic and imperfect, may appeal to us more searchingly than the
perfect freedom of satisfaction that we hear in Frost. But there can be
no doubt that both poets had drunk deep from the same source.

8

Literary Radicalism in America

LEFT-WING LITERARY PEOPLE talk more these days about criticism than about fiction or poetry or plays. The statement sounds too flat to be true, and it is fair to ask what "left-wing" signifies in the context. I am using it simply and I hope accurately to mean: people who in a better time would be doing political work. The criticism I have in mind is addressed to readers familiar with the current theoretical debates. It uses a political vocabulary ("undermining," "totalizing," "reification," "rupture," "bad faith"), yet it has no implications for practical politics. The aim is not to interpret texts but to change them, and there the enterprise stops. Action means action with respect to texts. On occasions when one can sense other interests at work, the effect is very curious. In a polemical exchange, for instance, between a Marxist critic and a poststructuralist, one may know what sort of event is being staged; but, as one listens to the presentations, and compares the eloquence on both sides with its apparent subject, one sees that criticism is not the point at all. They are really arguing about something else—a social question of some kind—though neither knows it yet. Skeptics like to reply that the underground quality of such encounters is a sign of a hopeless cultural moment.

But the debates I mentioned have a more immediate cause. The language now spoken in literary theory is a language of the avant-garde. There is nothing surprising in this: every marginal movement in culture leads a second life in the history of criticism. What has changed is that the avant-garde has taken up residence in the academy. To be more precise, it has come to be identified with literary study in the universities, which once seemed a natural home for the academic view of art. An academy in the older sense existed for the purpose of inculcating received ideas and judgments. Now, with that function suspended, the avant-garde seems to be in force everywhere. It has become universal, and at the same time it has migrated inward. Much of this was foreseen by those who observed the progress of modern painting. The most acute descriptions of our situation were written more than a decade ago by Harold Rosenberg, from a position sympathetic to the avant-garde but unhappy about the completeness of its acceptance. We have lately begun to get alternative descriptions from critics who speak for the homeless academy.

The *New Criterion* was launched in the early 1980s as a monthly journal of the arts. Its editor, Hilton Kramer, and the regular contributors who set the tone are nonuniversity academicians. They present themselves as lonely and embattled figures. If their style is heavy, that is because their task is heavy. They are trying to invent cultural conservatism in America. In keeping with this aim, they satirize the universities, where the avant-garde is known to have taken cover; and yet, the tone of the attack is itself borrowed from the militant avant-garde, in the days before its triumph and assimilation. It is a pamphleteering manner, sometimes direct, sometimes ironic, always hectoring.

In this, the journal betrays a certain nostalgia. Its very name makes a similar point, for it honors as a precursor T. S. Eliot—founder of the old *Criterion,* but an avant-garde poet and critic before he became a Classicist, Royalist, Anglo-Catholic, and editor. "Tradition," Eliot wrote, "cannot be inherited"—not, that is, passed on like a correct opinion. "What happens," he added, "when a new work of art is created is something that happens simultaneously to all the works of art which preceded it." To believe this is not to deny the need in every culture for authority and deference. It gives the critic authority, indeed, to create new values, and not only to guard the values already in place. But the conservative wants to perform the latter function above all. He is guided in his judgments by a sequence of implicit equations: taste = inherited opinions = rules = norms (= social norms). His idea of culture is that it can be understood, and once understood it can be kept running smoothly by a team of impartial custodians.

Why does this sound strange to an American? Our daily habits of feeling seem to tell against it, and I think one reason is that the principle of self-trust, which we grew up believing, favors those who shake tradition in some way. We are still Emerson's disciples more or less, and he is a possible, though difficult, ally for a radical, as he cannot even begin to be for a conservative. O. W. Firkins wrote about this aspect of Emerson's appeal:

> His hunger was not greedy precisely because it was insatiable. Of two travellers, one, refusing to stop at the half-way house, pushes on to the large town which is his destination: he may stand for the average radical. The other, for whom the large town is itself a half-way house, whose destination is on the verge of the continent, stops contentedly at the first good lodging place: he may stand for Emerson. Both differ sharply from the man who stays at home.[1]

Radicals are so little in evidence now that it is hard to know what an average radical would be. But when they reappear, in large enough numbers to think of travels like this, they will still be meeting Emersonian ideals along the way.

This chapter is about the nature of those ideals, and I take it for granted that they are what we have to work with. A revisionist, whether in politics or culture, can no more exclude them than a speaker can exclude the perfect tenses, for they point to habits we still renew unquestioningly. If this is correct, the sort of criticism now emerging from the university avant-garde, as well as from the homeless academy, is in fact irrelevant to the growth of a new literature. These represent merely the latest efforts of exclusion—armed on one side with conventional skepticism, and on the other with conventional faith. Both attitudes retain the purity of assertions at the level of "as if." With no living tradition behind them, and an infinite vista of improvement ahead, they are free to enjoy the scandal of mimic wars. But the consequential debates in our culture have always taken place somewhere else, and the rival parties have agreed that words are acts that change our lives.

American literature is mostly the story of an avant-garde that did not stay at home. Many of its heroes come from two periods: in the nineteenth century, the twenty years leading up to the Civil War; and in the twentieth, the interval between the world wars. No single impulse unites such books as *The Scarlet Letter* and *The Sun Also Rises,* or even *Leaves of Grass* and *The Bridge.* But in the background of all these books has been an intellectual movement that could act as an incitement to their authors, and that saw itself as preparing the way for genius. The sort of figure who dominated such a movement used to be called a literary radical. I will use the phrase here because, provisionally, it helps to define Emerson. What he did was to describe, with sufficient plainness and sufficient profoundness, a condition of personal independence. And that was enough.

The great practical effect of Emerson's teaching was that it gave an idea of originality to a generation that included Whitman, Dickinson, Melville, along with others who seem minor talents only in that company. He accomplished this in a society where a shapeless conformity of opinion appeared to have taken hold forever. Indeed, if one tried to imagine an America free of Emerson's influence, the strictures of *Democracy in America* would turn into an accurate prophecy. As it is, they have come out looking *a priori* and short-sighted. Tocqueville simply did not bank on anyone like Emerson occurring.

This account may concede too much to the "great man" theory of history (in which, however, I believe). From another perspective Emerson was only the accidental success among many comparable types of the 1840s and 1850s. Evert Augustus Duyckinck, for example, and Cornelius Mathews, along with the critics, patrons, and entrepreneurs who made the subject of Perry Miller's *The Raven and the Whale,* set themselves up as New York's rivals to Concord, in the search for a native literature. They believed that they were looking for a home-grown epic to surpass Sir Walter Scott. What they wanted to foster, it seems clear in retrospect, was a gigantic second-rate literature, a sort of continuous collaborative American sublime, a high, flat, reliable, democratic achievement. It was not their fault that they could find nothing in that line big enough to satisfy their expectations. But when, from within their precincts, *Moby-Dick* emerged, they were unequipped to appreciate it. The circumstance suggests that their ambition was essentially distinct from Emerson's. For the group around the first *Dial*—edited by Emerson and Margaret Fuller—formed an avant-garde in something like the modern sense. Other writers have noticed this, but the analogy has sometimes been called exotic, and I will try briefly to justify it.

An avant-garde differs from other societies for mutual promotion in only one way. It is willing to regard failure as a mark of election. It tells the artist, as Emerson told his young audience in "The American Scholar": "If the single man plant himself indomitably on his instincts, and there abide, the huge world will come round to him." This was a good translation of Wordsworth's injunction to "create the taste by which you are to be enjoyed" (grant *nothing* to the existing taste); and in the details of his practice, Emerson adopted the strategy of the Lake school in English poetry half a century before. He settled in a place unknown to letters, gathered significant neighbors around him, treated all his younger disciples as equals; and occasionally, instead of a Preface, he issued a Declaration. He is not quite a miracle, for he knew very well what he was doing. His glory was that he did it. The defect of many commentaries on Emerson—especially those written in the 1940s and 1950s, from an effort to interpret the "American Renaissance"—is that they regard him altogether as a special case. Often, this is a result of valuing him as an encourager while underrating him as a writer. I believe it is more interesting to think of him as a *beginning:* someone, like Rousseau, whom others have to return to before they can start for themselves.

In what follows I try to sketch a recurring pattern for our literature since Emerson. I borrow Matthew Arnold's idea of antithetical "epochs": the epoch of expansion, in which great works are created; and the epoch of concentration, in which critical thinking advances and the impetus is given for expansion in the next age. This pattern of course leaves out a good deal, and I use it in a non-Arnoldian spirit, with fairness intended only to a few. Beginning, then, with Emerson, we have had an age of concentration and expansion close together; a second age of concentration in the early years of our century, with the criticism of Randolph Bourne, Van Wyck Brooks, and Waldo Frank; a second age of expansion, including Hemingway, Faulkner, Stevens, Frost, Hart Crane, Marianne Moore, Allen Tate, and William Carlos Williams, among others. What we see around us now, on the other hand, is probably not far different from the way things looked in the 1880s. The ages of contraction (to add a third term to Arnold's pair)— the age before Emerson's, the Gilded Age, ours—coincide with periods of retrenchment in politics. That is why the names Van Buren, Harrison, Tyler, Polk, Hayes, Garfield, Cleveland, McKinley, Nixon, Ford, Carter, Reagan make such a homogeneous list.

A change for the better usually happens like this. A small number of writers get together, agree that their culture has lost vitality, and decide to blame everything on its habitual arrangements, which they hold in contempt. If their analysis succeeds in fostering a literature that is powerful, the analysis and the literature stand doubly vindicated. But the important moment for a literary radical comes earlier, when he discovers that his analysis is widely shared; and the effect of such moments is to give fresh life to other radicals, who seek political remedies. There is a sense—better understood by historians than by critics—in which an Emerson makes room for a William Lloyd Garrison. What began as a program of literary revisionism thus works its way into all the channels of reform. One can see this in Emerson's writing, even when his subject is formal and aesthetic, as in the following lines from "Merlin":

> Great is the art,
> Great be the manners, of the bard.
> He shall not his brain encumber
> With the coil of rhythm and number;
> But, leaving rule and pale forethought,
> He shall aye climb
> For his rhyme.
> "Pass in, pass in," the angels say,
> "In to the upper doors,
> Nor count compartments of the floors,
> But mount to paradise
> By the stairway of surprise."

It is, on a narrow view, technical advice to poets about their craft. But there seems to me a nominal rather than a practical difference between this and his "Note to the Reader" of the *Dial,* written for the first issue in collaboration with Margaret Fuller:

> [The] spirit of the time is felt by every individual with some difference,—to each one casting its light upon the objects nearest to his temper and habits of thought. . . . In all its movements, it is peaceable, and in the very lowest marked with a triumphant success. Of course, it rouses the opposition of all which it judges and condemns, but it is too confident in its tone to comprehend an objection, and so builds no outworks for possible defense against contingent enemies. It has the step of Fate, and goes on existing like an oak or a river, because it must.[2]

The step of Fate and the stairway of surprise, the house without compartments and the fortress without outworks, offer variations on a single trope with a single moral: the power of individuals is equal to the power of fate.

Emerson's admirers, who liked his cunning, still heard the same sermon no matter what the text. It taught that a poem of 1,350 lines could be written proclaiming "oneself." Or it made the state appear as a contingent enemy to the man who would not pay taxes for an evil war. Responses like these have the terrible simplicity Emerson asked for but distrusted. He was, in consequence, the cruelest satirist of his own followers: he called Brook Farm "a perpetual picnic, a French Revolution in small, an Age of Reason in a patty-pan." Yet his warnings were directed against sects rather than causes, and in his 1851 address on the Fugitive Slave Law he told a Concord audience that it was "a law which every one of you will break on the earliest occasion." I quote these familiar judgments to show that his saying, "Whenever a man comes, there comes revolution," was merely an adequate description of the way his thinking had mattered in his own life. But his most solid effect may be seen in the lives of others who would have been free minds anyway, but were made bolder by his example. Margaret Fuller can stand for these; and, from an Emersonian point of view, I believe she had the better of her famous exchange with Carlyle, where she took a chance in speaking high-mindedly.

Fuller's "I accept the universe" meant that the universe was hers, to make of what she would (and change how she could). She was announcing her intention not to quit the contest, while acknowledging the conditions in which she was obliged to work. Carlyle, it seems, took her to be showing a polite condescension to the universe; and his reply, "By Gad, she'd better," was aimed at the paltriness of the human conceit that we have any choice in the matter. But, of course, we do have a choice. We can decide to risk everything for what we believe in, and there may be vastly different grounds of defense for such a step, even in thinkers as congenial as Emerson and Carlyle. Emerson's appeal, when he urged disobedience to the Fugitive Slave Law, was to a conscience that ought not to comply with the dictates of social expediency, or even the ultimate injunctions of social order. Carlyle's appeal, when he backed the South in the Civil War, was to an ideal duty, with fighting representatives in the actual world, who were to be honored as an active principle of order and the preservers of the spirit of a race. This is the light in which his witty reply must be read, and in this light it is honest enough, yet coarse and contemptible.

For we know what acceptances he had in view. In case we have forgotten, Emerson brings them all together in one sentence of a journal entry: "Carlyle is no idealist in opinions, but a protectionist in political economy, aristocrat in politics, epicure in diet, goes for murder, money, punishment by death, slavery, and all the petty abominations, tempering them with epigrams."[3] Fuller knew most of this as well as Emerson. And yet, after a meeting not much tempered with epigrams, she found a use for Carlyle, as he could not for her, and published an appreciation in the *New York Tribune:*

> His works are true, to blame and praise him, the Siegfried of England, great and powerful, if not quite invulnerable, and of a might rather to destroy evil than to legislate for good. At all events, he seems to be what destiny intended, and represents fully a certain side; so we make no remonstrance as to his being and proceeding for himself, though we sometimes must for us.[4]

She speaks here on behalf of those who do want to legislate for good— "we sometimes must for us." She is determined nevertheless to build with such materials as the time affords, however intractable in appearance. We can use Carlyle for his hatred of the laissez-faire system, though, to arrive at something better, we need to think beyond his sense of "the duty to be intolerant."

The generosity of the verdict is Fuller's own, but it owes its confidence to Emerson's thought that genius is serviceable in spite of itself—that it cannot even be known, except as it assists the practical ends of those who admire it. He wrote in "The Over-Soul": "That which we are, we shall teach, not voluntarily but involuntarily. Thoughts come into our minds by avenues which we never left open, and thoughts go out of our minds through avenues which we never voluntarily opened. Character teaches over our head."[5] So, once we have seen past the words of a writer, or the acts of a leader, to the soul that produced them both, it turns out that we are looking at something in ourselves. Emerson has more than one name to describe what we recover then. But whatever he calls it, he is sure that it has the power to alter traditions and laws as well as customs and habits. He saw the extravagance of his claim, and warned: "I unsettle all things." The tendency of his writing is to break down the boundaries that separate literary invention from the conduct of life.

Since Emerson, the project of literary radicalism has never been isolable from an ambition to reform our social arrangements. At the same time, it has resisted any steady collaboration with the short-term plans of reformers. It starts as a general hope, touching those who sympathize with movements outside literature, yet it ends in a general bewilderment. The strength of our individualism in culture appears to have been paid for by the eclecticism, the impatient or capricious en-

ergy; and above all the discontinuity of our radicalism in politics. The
reason the balance works out this way is that, between cultural and
political radicalism, the former adds up to the stronger tradition.
Every American is born with a little of it. The pattern holds true to
such an extent that some people have a special name for left-wing
writers who think consistently about politics: they call them "Euro-
pean-style radicals." That label, if unfair, is at any rate intelligible,
and we would be better off if it were not. But sometimes, the only
way of changing an old story is to retell its happier episodes, in the
hope that their atmosphere will invigorate. I turn accordingly from
Emerson's group to their successors, the social critics whose work began in earnest about 1915.

In *America's Coming-of-Age*, Van Wyck Brooks argued that our official and popular cultures had taken opposite paths in the eighteenth
century and continued apart ever since, with results disabling for both.
He allegorized the split by adopting the names "lowbrow" (for a writer
like Franklin) and "highbrow" (for a writer like Edwards). The first
type was marked chiefly by the instincts of gregarious self-advance-
ment, the second chiefly by the duties of solitary speculation; and
according to Brooks, they had joined only once, almost freakishly, in
the writings of Whitman, whom he therefore called a "middlebrow."
These types are cartoons. Yet they belong recognizably to a life we still
know, where the literacy of our neighbors has nothing to do with their
conversability. Liberals call the result pluralism, and think it the very
stuff of democracy. Brooks, on the contrary, felt that while capitalism
thrived on such divisions, democracy grew weaker from them. Searching our tradition for a cause of the trouble, he came up with Emerson,
whose thinking assured that we would remain content with our discrete virtues: for the lowbrow a vulgar gusto, for the highbrow an
austere refinement. In short, the personal culture that Emerson invented had foreclosed the possibility of a common culture, even as it
made ideals a redundancy for self-reliant men of action:

> The social ideal of Emerson . . . is a sort of composite of the philoso-
> pher, the mystic, the skeptic, the poet, the writer and the man of the
> world. I wonder what passed through the mind of the American busi-
> ness man of Emerson's day when he heard all these phrases [of Emer-
> son's], phrases so unrelated to the springs of action within himself. Did
> he feel that his profound instincts had been touched and unified, did he
> see opening before him the line of a disinterested career, lighted up by
> a sudden dramatization of his own finest latent possibilities? Did he not

rather, with a degree of reason, say to himself: "These papers will serve very well to improve my mind. I shall read them when I have the time"? And did he not thereupon set to work accumulating all the more dollars in order that he might have the more time to cultivate his mind—in legal phrase—after the event?

Looked at from this side, Emerson has all the qualities of the typical baccalaureate sermon; and the baccalaureate sermon, as we know, beautiful as it often is, has never been found inconveniently inconsistent with the facts and requirements of business life.[6]

My argument thus far has been that Emerson is so expansive a friend of revolt as to be favorable to no particular party. Brooks, however, implies that this in effect makes him a valuable servant of the status quo, which in America is itself expansionist. I believe that his interpretation is wrong; but it was sufficiently provoked. It reminds us of Emerson's insistence, in a work like *The Conduct of Life,* that he be taken at once as a detached aphorist and a guide to worldly advancement—part of his appeal that Melville captured in *Pierre,* with its portrait of Plotinus Plinlimmon, the half-inspired enthusiast with an eye for the main chance. Yet Brooks, in a passage like this, was also reacting against the pragmatists, that is, against another school of Emerson's readers.

Brooks understood pragmatism as a decadent idealism that had betrayed genius in the name of practical power. He refers specifically to James and Dewey, but otherwise leaves the charge unexplained, and I can offer only a surmise about what he might have said. Emerson's own thinking had been an idealist answer to the materialism he supposed was becoming the dominant philosophy of the age. His purpose was to give us back the world of our ideas, and hence of our ideals and spiritual laws, as identical with the world of practice. He meant this scrupulously: all the disposable materials of nature and art, which he summed up as "commodity," were an outward realization of "Man thinking," a writing-it-large for the slow of wit. Now, James and Dewey saw themselves as fighting the same battle, a little further on. But idealism as they knew it was an exhausted orthodoxy of a thoroughly anti-empirical character. When, therefore, James taught his readers to care for the live option—when Dewey identified truth with warranted assertibility—they were seeking to make practical wisdom again coincide with the highest instincts of men and women. To act as if one's beliefs were part of a total drift that might some day carry everything with it, was to be *sound* on the only going definition of soundness. The life that these pragmatists wanted to encourage was not mainly or even largely "business life."

Yet Brooks's analysis did not depend, after all, on a questioning of motives. Rather, he took it as simply demonstrable that the alliance suggested by pragmatism—between new successes of any kind and the creation of new truths—left radicals on a lower moral ground than before, in their contest with the heroes of industry and commerce. All this remains implicit in Brooks's discussion. It became a conscious emphasis in the writings of Randolph Bourne, who had started as an admirer of the pragmatists. After Dewey lent his support to American participation in the war, Bourne published a record of his disenchantment, in an essay called "Twilight of Idols":

> To those of us who have taken Dewey's philosophy almost as our American religion, it never occurred that values could be subordinated to technique. We were instrumentalists, but we had our private utopias so clearly before our minds that the means fell always into place as contributory. And Dewey, of course, always meant his philosophy, when taken as a philosophy of life, to start with values. But there was always that unhappy ambiguity in his doctrine as to just how values were created, and it became easier and easier to assume that just any growth was justified and almost any activity valuable so long as it achieved ends. The American, in living out this philosophy, has habitually confused results with product, and has been content with getting somewhere without asking too closely whether it was the desirable place to get.[7]

Earlier I quoted Emerson's disclaimer, "I unsettle all things"; and it is worth recalling here that his next words were: "No facts are to me sacred; none are profane; I simply experiment, an endless seeker with no Past at my back." For Bourne, this had become the voice of American capitalism. It gave the master-clue to the workings of a state that was only healthy when at war.

On this analysis pragmatism, itself the offspring of idealism, was eventually converted to the uses of realism in the vulgar sense, which implies a hostility to all ideals. The hope before the war had been to fortify the individual in his plural relations with life, by representing his ability to shape it variously and inventively, from one situation to another. But a mistaking of product for results led the pragmatist (*we instrumentalists,* as Bourne puts it) to think well of those already employed in reshaping the world. This included the entrepreneurs of business and war. I do not want to enter into the merits of Bourne's view; but one thing about his argument is certainly attractive: it, too, is pragmatic. World War I was a disgraceful period in our intellectual life, and Bourne proposed to test radical ideas by the character they showed in surviving it. He had no stomach for truckling or compromise; in "The War and the Intellectuals" he wrote: "This realistic boast is so loud and sonorous that one wonders whether realism is always a stern and intelligent grappling with realities. May it not be a mere surrender to the actual, an abdication of the ideal through sheer fatigue from intellectual suspense?"[8] About the same time, Brooks was writing a polemic against literary critics who pleaded for realism of a well-behaved sort.

Such critics exist at all times, and often speak on behalf of the imperative of the actual, or some similar phrase. The phrase always means, "Show us what is good about our society (we are so lost in it that occasionally we forget)." In *Letters and Leadership,* Brooks's immediate target was an assertion by W. D. Howells that "the more smiling aspects of life" are "the more American," and a request of novelists that they be faithful to our "well-to-do actualities." This thought has lately been echoed by Joseph Epstein in a review of two novels in *Commentary,* which concludes: "of plain pessimism . . . we have had quite enough. Let, please, the sun shine in." Brooks replied in 1918: "Could one ask for a more essential declaration of artistic bankruptcy than that? For what does it amount to, this declaration? It identifies the reality of the artist's vision with what is accepted as reality in the world about him."[9] Artists, Brooks added, who do follow such advice "do not so much mature at all as externalize themselves in a world of externalities." One can expand this statement in a way that seems consistent with Brooks's intentions. An artist works from an internal life— thoughts, feelings, impressions—which he seeks to render external. There is no *thing* (at once diffuse and substantial) that the word "reality" helps to explain. There are only the available externalities. If we like some of them, we may call them actual; if we dislike others, we may call them pessimistic or less smiling. An artist is sometimes improved by a critic who shows how his work is careless or foppish. No artist has ever been improved by a critic who urges him to portray a certain kind of subject, or eliminate a certain mood.

The legacy of Emerson, Fuller, James, Dewey, Bourne, and Brooks is what we still have to build on. A sustained effort to reverse their style of cultural tolerance came in the 1930s and 1940s, from the Eliotic-

Trotskyist group around *Partisan Review*.[10] These were critics who pointed to a recent past, and said: "The great thing is already there." They wrote with equal assurance as skeptical observers of American culture and as monumental historians of the European avant-garde. By this double emphasis, their work appeared to offer a new conception of intellectual freedom. The Emersonian sermon against public opinion is simple though hard to act upon. It tells us to stand apart from our society. The Eliotic-Trotskyist sermon against mass culture was less simple, and perhaps less hard to act upon. It told us to stand apart from one element of our culture. What, exactly, did the suggestion amount to?—for anyone, I mean, but especially for an American? We have to come at this a long way around. In his 1939 essay "Avant-Garde and Kitsch," Clement Greenberg imagined a Russian peasant after a long day's toil, offered him a choice of pictures to look at—on the one hand a battle scene by Repin, on the other a cubist abstraction by Picasso—and supposed he would prefer the Repin, on the ground that it was familiar. Repin's picture affords a "wealth of self-evident meanings" by which the peasant "recognizes and sees things in the way in which he recognizes and sees things outside of pictures—there is no discontinuity between art and life, no need to accept a convention."[11] The notion of a familiarity that may be realized in the absence of any convention is of course very odd. Nevertheless, Greenberg, who in this may be taken to represent many others, made the following deductions from his reading of the hypothetical incident.

First, the taste for mass culture is instinctive in an industrial society. (The case of the peasant accidentally proves too much, by suggesting that it may be instinctive even in a state of nature.) Second, art alone has the task of modifying conventions; and the conventions themselves are defined formalistically: "the arts," as Greenberg said in another place, "have been hunted back to their mediums," and a work only exempts itself from mass culture by virtue of an emphatic concern with its medium. Third, in this situation—where art, if it is to be vital, is fated to be modernist, and the appeal of modernist works is confined to a few—the distance between the cultural and political avant-garde has widened irreparably.

The diagnosis turns on the assumption that avant-garde artists have the same superior indifference to mass culture as avant-garde critics, when in fact their attitude has more often been one of ambivalent fascination. But I suspect, for American readers, this weighs very little by comparison with a more local objection. Substitute a New England yeoman for the Russian peasant, and what happens to the fable? It is refuted by the miscellaneous power of his emblems and symbols. "In the political processions," Emerson observed, "Lowell goes in a loom, and Lynn in a shoe, and Salem in a ship." The arts do not disdain these things: "Some stars, lilies, leopards, a crescent, a lion, an eagle, or other figure which came into credit God knows how, on an old rag of bunting, blowing in the wind on a fort at the ends of the earth, shall make the blood tingle under the rudest or the most conventional exterior."[12] We can hardly know culture at all, except as just such a mixed entity.

So we easily stray across the boundaries that separate the exalted from the humble—categories that, with us, are always being revised for present purposes, and that a single sharp challenge may suffice to upset again. Nobody knew this better than Emerson, or kept it more constantly in mind. He sympathized with a new thought at the moment of its invention, and left others to plan its consolidation. In the arts he did without ideas of high and low. In religion, long before, he had moved from the doctrine of a visible church to that of a hidden personal divinity. His motive was a readiness to suffer inexpediences as the cost of fresh truths. Without something of the same sentiment, culture would cease to be a vivid abstraction, and would turn into the sum of its institutional conquests. But "The Invisible Avant-Garde," which John Ashbery christened in an essay of that title, has always sustained a belief that culture is not identical with cultivation. The belief continues because the visible church takes many forms—a congregation, a board of censors, and an academy being only the most persistent.

Their successors appear to be "the media." But, writing in 1968, Ashbery saw all of these as contingent enemies, and remembered the example of Jackson Pollock in the late 1940s:

> At that time I found the avant-garde very exciting, just as the young do today, but the difference was that in 1950 there was no sure proof of the existence of the avant-garde. To experiment was to have the feeling that one was poised on some outermost brink. In other words, if one wanted to depart, even moderately, from the norm, one was taking one's life—one's life as an artist—into one's hands. A painter like Pollock for instance was gambling everything on the fact that he *was* the greatest painter in America, for if he wasn't, he was nothing, and the drops would turn out to be random splashes from the brush of a careless housepainter. It must often have occurred to Pollock that there was just a

possibility that he wasn't an artist at all, that he had spent his life "toiling up the wrong road to art," as Flaubert said of Zola. But this very real possibility is paradoxically just what makes the tremendous excitement in his work. It is a gamble against terrific odds. Most reckless things are beautiful in some way, and recklessness is what makes experimental art beautiful, just as religions are beautiful because of the strong possibility that they are founded on nothing.[13]

The situation today, as Ashbery describes it, when the artist commonly finds himself "at the center of a cheering mob," is doubtless more enervating than in the heyday of the avant-garde, when an interval of decent neglect was still allowed. Yet the present mood is not less favorable to creation; it merely warrants a change of tactics, for the artist "must now bear in mind that *he,* not *it,* is the avant-garde." This I take to be what Emersonian critics from the first have been saying in other words.

I am aware that there is a strong and a weak version of my argument. In the strong version, we Americans are all potentially of the avant-garde. In the weak version, this turns out to be so because for us the avant-garde is only another name for radical individualism. I do not claim that political radicals ought to take satisfaction from the results as they stand. But it does seem possible to view them as a broken series of victories; they have too often been recounted as a single continuous defeat. The encouraging parts of the story, varied as they are, may seem to lack a moral about the uses of art. One reason is that art meant anything for Emerson—"beauty," "language," "discipline"—anything, that is, outside the world of commodity. He concluded every attempt to define it further with a pleasant but inscrutable compliment. And evidently, for an object with this range of meanings, we have to be content with a surmise as to its function. I have quoted some instances already, but saved the best for last. It comes from Kenneth Burke, whose career almost spans the period from Bourne's generation to mine, and who wrote more than fifty years ago in *Counter-Statement:* "An art may be of value purely through preventing a society from becoming too assertively, too hopelessly, itself."

9

A Simple Separate Person

WHEN WHITMAN DESCRIBED HIMSELF as a *kosmos,* he may have meant that he contained a good deal of prose. But apart from *Leaves of Grass,* the only writing he brought to a finish went into two books, *Specimen Days* and *Democratic Vistas.* The first of these is entirely composed of moments: the vigils that Whitman kept over the dying or the wounded during the Civil War; and his intervals of solitary repose in nature. Both kinds of moment show Whitman's absorbing concern with sanity—literally, with the cleanliness of the body and of the soul—and the same concern seems to have been a leading motive in his defense of American democracy. These works share a common premise with his poetry as well. They imagine a more-than-empirical character, the self, whose existence is prior to the soul's aspirations, and whose fate is untouchable by the reverses of daily life. This self Whitman thought of as the product of American society at a certain time, the years of the successful fight of the Union against the slave-holding interests. Personal independence to him was the natural accompaniment of the self's assurance of survival, through its union with others; and such assurance could not be had in all the possible circumstances of a society: it would be ruled out, for example, in a society moving toward a more rather than a less restricted franchise. But Whitman had given a social definition of self-trust which he felt that the war itself vindicated. It proved that all inherited goods began in custom but ended in enslavement. This was another way of saying that the individual self had an exception-making power to any claim urged by others, a tendency to resist impositions which derived from its very knowledge of the body. Thus the liberating recognition of American political life turned out to be the same as that of American personal experience. All of Whitman's prose explores what he called "personalism," its moments and prospects, and all of it exists to help readers in bearing out the prophecies of "Song of Myself."

How far a single purpose animates his works ought to emerge now more plainly than ever before, with the appearance of his *Notebooks and Unpublished Prose* in six volumes edited by Edward Grier, together with the Library of America edition of his *Complete Poetry and Prose*.[1] Whitman filled more notebooks than anyone suspected. Apart from the short stories written in early youth, a temperance novel, and the miscellaneous contents of the *Collect* and *November Boughs,* he kept jottings of his moods, friends, false starts and late honors, eulogies to himself and paraphrases of other people's eulogies. In these pages one may discover him teaching himself the learned pronunciation of "insouciance" (een-soo-se-áwns); contemplating a Banjo Poem and a *"Poem of Large Personality,"* of which he remarks in passing, "make this poem for women just as much as men"; compiling lists of the men and women he meets, but the men chiefly, and later the names of the Union soldiers he has talked to. There are also notes for various prefaces and at least two drafts of a last will and testament. Some of the most interesting entries try out versions of lines which one knows from their subsequent life in "Song of Myself." Such a detail as, "And a mouse is miracle enough to stagger sextillions of infidels," did not come all at once: it took Whitman some time to arrive at a number with the appropriate weight. But the most susceptibly erotic passages of the "Song" were still more so in draft:

> Fierce Wrestler! do you keep your heaviest grip for the last?
> Will you sting me most even at parting?
> Will you struggle even at the threshold with spasms more delicious than all before?
> Does it make you ache so to leave me?
> Do you wish to show that even what you did before was nothing to what you can do
> Or have you and all the rest combined to see how much I can endure?
> Pass as you will; take drops of my life if that is what you are after
> Only pass to some one else, for I can contain you no longer.
> I held more than I thought
> I did not think I was big enough for so much ecstasy
> Or that a touch could take it all out of me.[2]

A few entries like this are enough to justify the publication of the *Notebooks;* and the paragraphs that follow will quote many more. But alone, they give a false impression of the general quality of the material. For these two editions of Whitman suggest, both as to purpose and utility, opposite approaches to the experience of reading.

The *Notebooks* are only the latest of those massive and licensed editions in which every last scrap of an author (including in this case his games of animal—vegetable—mineral) is dutifully reproduced and annotated, everything but (though the omission may be accidental) his contests at tick-tack-toe. Presumably, if Whitman's hand could be detected in the noughts and crosses, these too would appear; along with the entry, occupying a whole page, which runs in full: "The Daylight? magazine? annual? monthly? quarterly"—one line of doodling, escorted into posterity by five lines of notes indicating the paper on which it was written and the date to which unfortunately it cannot be assigned. The typical page of these volumes is half empty, and what there is of print has been given over to notes of insertions and deletions, fourteen such notes to eight lines of print being a not uncommon proportion. By whom will it be used? The responsible scholar needs to look at the papers and microfilms anyway, while the interested reader cares for Whitman's words and not his subliterary *disjecta membra.* Of course, researchers exist who belong to a class between these two: word-counters and deletion-counters, the behaviorists of the writing process, for whom rough specimens of their subject will do. Their toil is harmless, though it ought not to be humored or paid for. And yet, the sheer size of this edition can only have been determined by a considerate projection of their needs.

By contrast with the *Notebooks,* the Library of America *Whitman* prints everything of prose as well as poetry that Whitman cared to see survive. It is meant for the study rather than the vault, and is agreeable to handle besides being pleasant to read. Since Whitman thought of his words as an almost physical extension of himself, one can imagine him ranking these merits high. Two features of the book also make it preferable to any combination of earlier editions: the inclusion of a complete text of the 1855 *Leaves of Grass;* and a section of "Supplementary Prose" with Whitman's pamphlet on the eighteenth presidency. In the latter document, as nowhere else in his writings, one sees with Whitman's eyes the look of the depraved men from whom Lincoln redeemed the nation. "WHENCE," he asks, "DO THESE NOMINATING DICTATORS OF AMERICA YEAR AFTER YEAR START OUT?" "From lawyers' offices," he replies, "secret lodges, back-yards, bed-houses, bar-rooms; from out of the custom-houses, marshals' offices, post-offices, and gambling-hells." In answer to the next question—"WHO ARE THEY PERSONALLY?"—he pictures the nominators of Fillmore and Buchanan according to their works:

> Slave-catchers, pushers of slavery, creatures of the President, creatures of would-be Presidents, spies, blowers, electioneers, body-snatchers, bawlers, bribers, compromisers, runaways, lobbyers, sponges, ruined sports, expelled gamblers, policy backers, monte-dealers, duelists, carriers of concealed weapons, blind men, deaf men, pimpled men, scarred inside with the vile disorder, gaudy outside with gold chains made from the people's money and harlot's money twisted together; crawling, serpentine men, the lousy combings and born freedom sellers of the earth.[3]

This is done in Cobbett's style, with as sure a sense as Cobbett's of the mutually strengthening effects of the allegorical cartoon and the simple name. But it is strange to realize that Whitman was here addressing the same audience he hoped would listen to "Song of Myself": an audience of the shockable, haters of the unclean deed and the unclean side.

After the assassination of Abraham Lincoln, he knew of their existence as a certainty, because the news brought evidence of their feelings. "As to the other Presidents," he writes in a notebook entry, "they have had their due in formal and respectful treatment, in life & death. But this one alone has touched the popular heart to its deepest. For this one alone, through every city, every country farm, the untouch'd meal, the heavy heart & moistened eye & the sob in private chambers." The image of Lincoln dying seems to be associated throughout Whitman's writings with a more abstract conception: that of the "sane and sacred death" of a person, in the presence of whose body the mourners become conscious of their sanity, and of their sacredness to each other. Social obligations like personal ones thus follow from a recognition of sacrifice. The master-image for this, in his prose and poetry alike, is the passage of breath from a father to a son.

Whitman, however, was apt to dwell on one detail of the scene. In the lecture he used to give about the death of Lincoln, he ended his dramatic account of the murder by observing how "the life blood from those veins, the best and sweetest of the land, drips slowly down, and death's ooze already begins its little bubbles on the lips." In the great poem "As I Ebb'd with the Ocean of Life," the observer is Whitman

himself, but the dead man has become his father, whose broken career
the poet must resume:

> Me and mine, loose windrows, little corpses,
> Froth, snowy white, and bubbles,
> (See, from my dead lips the ooze exuding at last,
> See, the prismatic colors glistening and rolling).

Here the passage from death to life is marked by a return of all aspirations to a material trace, the oozing of a spirit into the air. But for
Whitman the consciousness of such a moment exalts rather than de-
grades. It recalls the soul to the things it is composed of, and points
to their recoverability by others.

Our usual mistake about immortality, as Whitman sees it, is to
imagine our survival as the extension of a single entity. We can avoid
this, he thinks, by supposing that we continue in time only as an
author's words continue in the minds of his readers. They create a
benefit that is inconceivable to the benefactor. Our extension in space,
through our moral relations with others, implies continuity of another
sort. But to explain it, Whitman suggests that we can appeal only to
what we know of existence (physical existence). This side of Whitman's thinking seemed to D. H. Lawrence praiseworthy beyond all
the rest since it released us from the tiresome superiority of the soul.
"Whitman was the first heroic seer to seize the soul by the scruff of her
neck and plant her down among the potsherds. 'There!' he said to the
soul. 'Stay there!'"[4] The soul's coincidence with the body is announced
in a line of "Crossing Brooklyn Ferry" which captures all Whitman's
doctrine: "That I was I knew was of my body, and what I should be I
knew I should be of my body." This belief forms an implicit apology
for his verbal innovations as well. Grammar and habitual usage agree
in enforcing a firm, if conventional, division between verbs and nouns.
But in Whitman a redefinition of language, by which common verbs
are shaped into nouns, brings with it a redefinition of experience, by
which the human joins the divine. "Dazzling and tremendous, how
quick the sunrise would kill me, / If I could not now and always send
sunrise out of me." In any poetry but Whitman's this would be an
instance of bathos. "Earth of the vitreous pour of the full moon just
tinged with blue! / Earth of shine and dark mottling the tide of the
river!" Again, in any other poetry this would be merely an overcon-
spicuous metaphor. As one reads "Song of Myself," however, both ges-

tures seem accurate representations of the constant and radical connection of soul with body.

Paul Zweig in a recent and engaging biography, *Walt Whitman: The Making of the Poet*, allows his subject a more narrowly literary originality.[5] Whitman here is not what Lawrence called him, a great changer of the blood in the veins of men, but rather a man "genuinely at ease with the moralizing idiom of Victorian America." Whitman's adaptability, as Zweig understands it, enabled him to act subversively in another way; and on the last page of the book, Zweig asserts that Whitman "assaulted the institution of literature and language itself, and, in so doing, laid the groundwork for the anti-cultural ambition of much modernist writing. He is the ancestor . . . of all who have made of their writing an attack on the act of writing and on culture itself." Elsewhere, in a similar vein, Zweig is rather careless of nuance: he sums up Whitman's belief that the self responds to experience as a "fundamental belief in the malleability of human personality." Still the summary statement, when placed beside the earlier suggestion about Whitman's congeniality to Victorian moralism, does make an interpretation of his career. Zweig invites us to look at Whitman as a theatrical personality whose bold experiments in language were aimed at destroying culture for the sake of a religious ideal. How well does this tally with the things Whitman said or did?

In his personal deportment, he appears not to have sought much conformity with the practices of his time and place. The sexual emphasis of the "Children of Adam" and of the "Calamus" poems in particular was thoroughly remarked by his contemporaries; but he did not follow the prudential advice to change or suppress them, even when it came from Emerson. It is true that he shared in a popular opinion whenever he could, and always avoided insulting a popular favorite. There may be a conventional ease, too, in his respect for such idols of the day as Longfellow and Whittier. But was his respect much more than tolerance? Whitman pointed out the good they did; and in Longfellow's case it certainly had to do with culture, in any possible sense of the word. But he never pretended to compare it to his good. As for Whitman's general "attack on the act of writing," what evidence is there of this? He writes in his notebook, "Make no quotations, and no reference to any other writers." But that is less an attack on writing than an echo of every great writer's demand to be read for his inventions; in short, a faithful and literal rendering of Emerson's admonition: "Meek young men grow up in libraries, believing it their duty to accept the views which Cicero, which Locke, which Bacon have given; forgetful that Cicero, Locke, and Bacon were only young men in libraries when they wrote these books." Such an attitude may turn to iconoclasm in the end; yet Whitman habitually instructs himself in a manner that could never be used by an iconoclast of writing: "In future *Leaves of Grass. Be more severe* with the final revision of the poem. . . . Also *no ornaments,* especially no *ornamental adjectives,* unless they have come molten hot, and imperiously prove themselves. *No ornamental similes at all—not one: perfect transparent clearness* sanity and health are wanted—that is the *divine style.*"[6] Whitman's hope was that, in America, the dignity of social life would reach a height at which this style expressed nothing more than the experience of the "divine average."

Zweig paraphrases the divine average as "the mystery of the ordinary," but they are not the same thing. For Whitman's idea relates to a godlike self-sufficiency that may be achieved by each person from his contact with every other, and from the impalpable modifications of his experience by theirs. There is nothing mysterious about it; and more than a point about usage is at stake. Whitman preferred democracy to feudalism (the latter being his name for everything before America) *only* on the ground that it promoted this sort of contact. "We will not," he says in *Specimen Days,* "have great individuals or great leaders, but a great average bulk, unprecedentedly great." He naturally admired Carlyle as an unsettler of outworn customs, but saw that his effect was vitiated by the cult of the hero. Later in the same book, he puts down the fault to a physical indisposition, "dyspepsia," from which Carlyle did in fact suffer, and which has for Whitman the significance of a bodily lapse from sanity.

> For an undoubtedly candid and penetrating faculty such as [Carlyle's], the bearings he persistently ignored were marvellous. For instance, the promise, nay certainty of the democratic principle, to each and every State of the current world, not so much of helping it to perfect legislators and executives, but as the only effectual method for surely, however slowly, training people on a large scale toward voluntarily ruling and managing themselves (the ultimate aim of political and all other development)—to gradually reduce the fact of *governing* to its minimum.[7]

The personalism, however, which America uniquely fostered, began for Whitman as an imaginative premise. It would join the practice of democracy later, with the widening of the franchise in the thirteenth, fourteenth, and fifteenth amendments to the Constitution. In this sense the future proposed by "Song of Myself"—"I concentrate toward them that are nigh, I wait on the door-slab"—could not speak for itself without looking back at the war.

Specimen Days carries out the task of retrospect for the author alone. (One of its provisional titles was *Autochthons . . . Embryons.*) But to the extent that this, and indeed all of Whitman's writings, are judged as an estimate of America, they have to be read in the light of *Democratic Vistas.* From its opening allusion to the *Areopagitica,* the book concerns the possibility of realizing a "copious, sane, gigantic offspring" among the aggregate persons in a democracy, though till now that has been an achievement reserved for nations as a whole. No literature before America's—which still lay mostly in the future—had recognized the people as its subject. Even Whitman did not see the depth of the error, he admits, before he visited the Civil War hospitals, and saw the courage of the individuals who suffered the agony of a nation. Yet the suffering that isolates strength and, in consequence, gives a first self-image to individualism, is only half of democracy: "There is another half, which is adhesiveness or love, that fuses, ties and aggregates, making the races comrades, and fraternizing all." Following the declaration of these two principles, Whitman asks that we change our idea of culture to bring it into keeping with both. The attempt will be not to overthrow but to civilize culture, so that we take "for its spinal meaning the formation of a typical personality of character, eligible to the uses of the high average of men—and *not* restricted by conditions ineligible to the masses." Throughout the argument Whitman insists on two facts about democracy: that it is an affair of daily experience and not simply of elections; and that its future is threatened, but need not be ultimately darkened, by the coming of the machine. He warns his reader emphatically against the "depravity of the business classes" whose authority has been tightened by the rationalization of labor. The weapon that the people can still use to defend themselves comes from their own sense of "the average, the bodily, the concrete, the democratic, the popular." These last, Whitman hopes to have shown, are different aspects of a single thing.

It has never been clear what it would mean to read Whitman just for the poetry. Readers who think they are doing so, either are not getting the poetry, or they are getting something more. Because he writes from a crisis in the history of American democracy, it may seem odd that he should implicate those who can take its victories for granted. And yet, because it was a crisis that defined the character of America, far more than the Revolutionary War ever did, he still seems to speak to us intimately. "What thought you have of me now, I had as much of you—I laid in my stores in advance." The attitude in which readers today are likeliest to find him objectionable is not that of the sage but that of the sympathizer. He cannot, they feel, sympathize with the runaway slave without reducing him to a victim, and at this point his sympathy is exposed as pity. But such an objection misunderstands Whitman's purpose in the narrative episodes of "Song of Myself" and elsewhere. These are not exchanges of identity, followed by a judgment, but experiments in a possible identity, followed by a *Stand back!* Even so, the resistance to Whitman's sympathy betrays the extent of the accommodation to another of his ideals. His individualism has done so well that readers want to forestall, as a trespass against themselves, any word or gesture that wears a momentary look of adhesiveness.

Lawrence said that the compulsion to love was at the bottom of Whitman's troubles, and he gave the illustration of the Eskimo in the kayak. Let Whitman see him sitting there and at once he will become the Eskimo though he does not know what a kayak is. It is a true picture; and in fact Whitman is routinely capable of stranger extravagances. In a passage of the *Notebooks* which he rephrased, rather obliquely, for "Song of Myself," he stands in the way of the man who is about to take his own life: "O despairer! I tell you, you shall not go down, / Here is my arm, press your whole weight upon me, / With tremendous breath I force him to dilate." He does this while staying quite free of the assumption he is charged with making, that he supposes the objects of his sympathy to be virtuous or reformable by himself. He does assume that "the universal and fluid soul impounds within itself not only all the good characters and heroes but the distorted characters, murderers, thieves." Impoundment is a long way from sympathy as most people interpret it, just as the divine average was a long way from the mystery of the ordinary. The most moving thing about Whitman after all is that he teaches, instead of an absolution from sins, a sort of patience with deformities from which a human charity might begin. A plausible further charge, that even acts of charity infringe on the rights of others, he has met by anticipation in an anecdote:

"Tell them," said the agent to the interpreter, "that the poet-chief has come to shake hands with them, as brothers." A regular round of introductions and hearty hand-claspings, and "How's!" followed. "Tell them, Billy," continued the agent, "that the poet-chief says we are all really the same men and brethren together, at last, however different our places, and dress and language." An approving chorus of guttural "Ugh's!" came from all parts of the room, and W. W. retired, leaving an evidently captivating impression.[8]

He wrote the news story himself; but it is not recorded that any of the Sioux Indian chiefs afterward complained of this treatment by the poet-chief. As usual, he had laid in his stores in advance.

10

Kipling's Jest

TWO OF KIPLING'S STORIES, "Wireless" and "Dayspring Mishandled," have a special bearing on his poetry, for they treat the notion of unconscious genius with a drastic literalness. The heroes of both stories are writers innocent of the contents of their own minds. In "Wireless," a cockney pharmacist falls into a trance and writes out several ecstatic passages from "The Eve of St. Agnes"; or rather he composes them, laboriously, as if for the first time: he has never read the poem and his interests are confined to his trade. Yet he loves a woman like Fanny Brawne, and he is consumptive. We are left with the matter-of-fact suggestion that, all circumstances being favorable, a citizen of modern London became an accidental passenger on a journey he never booked. In "Dayspring Mishandled," a hack journalist writes for his amusement some verses of Chaucerian pastiche. The result proves useful many years later, when, having disguised his invention, he arranges for it to surface as a fragment of an undiscovered *Canterbury Tale,* with the aim of embarrassing a lifelong rival who has assumed a venerable place among Chaucerian scholars. Bits of the tale are quoted: they are captivating in themselves and, after the glosses have been added, irrefutable. The scholar is of course taken in, though the story ends ambiguously, with his folly still unexposed. It may be noticed that two separate processes are at work in these confusions of identity. The young man who seemed to be a second Keats really was one for a moment, whereas the hack could rise above himself only by feigning another writer's effects. But it is not clear that this difference counts for much with Kipling; and in any case the stories share a curious

premise. They ask us to think of inspiration as closely related to forgery.

Kipling himself believed that all his writing was done at the command of a personal Daemon—a conception that shifts the emphasis
slightly. We know so little of the Daemon's activity that it may operate
under any number of aliases without our guessing the identity that
unites them. Style, I think Kipling would have allowed, is the verbal
character of an individual, expressed in a marked but variable idiom.
But for him the individual is the most doubtful of these elements:
when poetry is doing its work rightly, we forget the poet and hear a
style talking to an audience. This concern with impersonality, as well
as the ideal of direct emotional power, suggests a connection between
his way of thinking and T. S. Eliot's; and if one reads more than a few
of Kipling's poems with this in mind, one sees that the resemblance
is deep and not at all capricious. Kipling had an imaginative as well
as a technical interest in certain experiments. It occurred to him, for
example, that an ironic contrast might be shaped in verse without
an ironic voice, by deploying the same tone for different families of
words.

> "This is the State above the Law.
>   The State exists for the State alone."
> [*This is a gland at the back of the jaw*
>   *And an answering lump by the collar-bone.*][1]

Those lines were written in 1918, by a poet still learning and still
widening his craft, about the time of "Sweeney Among the Nightin-
gales." Yet the affinity covers a range of instances; the most facile line
Eliot ever wrote was also a Kipling line, with an imaginable context
in the ballads:

> Not with a bang but a whimper,
>   Not with a shout but a simper,
> The gentle ladies of Lahore expired over tea.

In the same way Eliot's phrases often wish for a second and demotic
life whose name is Kipling.

Whatever mode he elected to work in, Kipling was obviously a
great writer of some kind. Many critics have been able to concede this
without giving up a general disdain for his achievement (which could
be brought in to serve estimates of better authors, as a lowest common

factor of genius). Here Eliot's is both a typical and an exceptional case, and it seems to me worth pausing over. In the 1941 Introduction to *A Choice of Kipling's Verse,* he called Kipling a unique writer of verse, putting much weight on "unique" and asserting that verse was a thing apart from poetry. The reason one can still feel the need for some such description is that Kipling remains an uneasy experience for the literate. The problem is not his politics. Nor is it the vulgarity of his social judgments: where these are important and have worn badly, we do not read him, but the trouble comes when we do read him with pleasure. He seems willing to succeed in a dozen separate manners and to associate himself with none of them particularly. By his very success, he puts an unaccustomed pressure on the modern ideal of originality, since in his work we glimpse the ideal under a foreign aspect. Kipling cherishes, as do his successors, a language that enters the world already distant and already valuable, even to the point of unannounced parody and quotation. But his long career shows that such qualities may be consistent with the demands of public speech. What he made of this knowledge is an embarrassment for others besides himself, above all for those modernists who took the opposite path, into an almost anonymous private speech.

Eliot came close to saying this in a 1919 review in the *Athenaeum,* where he spoke at length about poetry and its audiences. The article is less positive, but also less condescending, than the later one I have mentioned. It starts by declaring that Kipling's poetry is "in fact, the poetry of oratory; it is music just as the words of orator or preacher are music; they persuade, not by reason, but by emphatic sound." The judgment may be felt to suppress—to acknowledge and depreciate without ever stating—a major fact about Kipling, his familiarity with the moods of the music hall. When, elsewhere in the review, Eliot does allude to this, he seems partly to admire; as the author of *"Under the bam / Under the boo / Under the bamboo tree"* ought naturally to admire; but on the whole he mingles contempt and self-conscious fondness with a dandyish impeccability: "The eighteenth century was in part cynical and in part sentimental, but it never arrived at complete amalgamation of the two feelings. Whoever makes a study of the sentimentalism of the nineteenth century will not neglect the peculiar cynical sentiment of Mr. Kipling. In a poem like Mr. Kipling's 'The Ladies,' the fusion is triumphant."[2] Notice, in the second sentence, the transition from "sentimentalism" to "sentiment." The latter has an honorable history—"sentiments to which every bosom returns an echo." And the audience of the music hall, as Eliot came to believe, were right in caring for just such sentiments as one finds in Kipling's poems. Yet by treating the two words as synonyms, he gives the whole comment a pejorative sound.

Nothing was more important to Kipling's appeal than his mastery of common sentiments. His self-knowledge here leaves very little for a critic to expose; in "My Great and Only," a prose sketch about writing a song that pleased, he reports: "I clung to the Great Heart of the People—my people—four hundred 'when it's full, Sir.' I had not studied them for nothing." Some way in, the song begins to catch; a few verses more and it brings down the house: "Who shall tell" (reflects Kipling) "the springs that move masses? I had builded better than I knew. . . . They do not call for authors on these occasions, but I desired no need of public recognition. I was placidly happy." Eliot would consent to be overheard by such "masses," in return for the privilege of overhearing them, but to write *for* them was at once below his ambition and above it. In the review itself, however, a contrast between his own attitude and Kipling's is only implied, by his pairing of Kipling and Swinburne as poets who deal with ideas as their stock in trade. Against them stands a figure like Conrad—or, we may suppose, Eliot—who has no ideas but "a point of view, a world; it can hardly be defined, but it pervades his work and is unmistakable." This appears to exclude Kipling so firmly that one is puzzled to reconcile it with the review's closing thought:

> And yet, Mr. Kipling is very nearly a great writer. There is an unconsciousness about him which, while it is one of the reasons why he is not an artist, is a kind of salvation. . . . It is wrong, of course, of Mr. Kipling to address a large audience; but it is a better thing than to address a small one. The only [still] better thing is to address the hypothetical Intelligent Man who does not exist and who is the audience of the Artist.[3]

We are left without any satisfying rival to Kipling's kind of greatness. There may be something hypothetically better. But the phrase "who does not exist" and the mocking upper-case letters (very different from Kipling's "Great Heart of the People") cheat us of any hope that the possibility may be realized.

The weakest element in this review is the use it makes of Conrad. For, if one compares similar stories by Conrad and Kipling—"The Lagoon," say, with "At the End of the Passage"—it is plain that Conrad writes with a more impressively on-purpose air, but it does not follow that his is the higher dedication. Thus, where Eliot believed he was separating art from non-art, he seems actually to have been recording a preference as to the proper stance for an artist. He admires the sort of artist who has nobody to convince: the modern, because he is undecided among beliefs; the medieval, because he is bound to a total system of belief. If, in Kipling's defense, one notices that "The Lagoon" and "At the End of the Passage" are stories about empire and that "At the End of the Passage" is the better story, it may still be replied that Conrad would be shocked to see his story read as an expression of empire ideas, whereas Kipling doubtless would not be shocked. But this is only a restatement of the fact in different words; it means that Kipling always has a house to bring down. For him, each new audience occupies a position like that of the listener in "Wireless" or the scholar in "Dayspring Mishandled." The artist, in short, works to convince the audience; the audience, simply by being there, serves to authenticate the artist. To take part in such an exchange may betray a mercenary complacency. But in Kipling this continual testing of his effects seems to be another form of restlessness. He is a virtuoso of nerves, a master tactician of the not-yet-commonplace. His success remains perpetually in question because it upsets the usual distinction between poetry and rhetoric—divisions of the larger category of writing, which, in his period and ours, have carried conviction as moral opposites. Kipling's refusal to accept the distinction, his poetry's refusal to be embarrassed by it, make him an unwelcome second self of the modernist. This I think is what Eliot recognized but did not want to say.

In his autobiography, *Something of Myself,* Kipling offers the following remarks on style: "I made my own experiments in the weights, colours, perfumes, and attributes of words, either as read aloud so that they may hold the ear, or, scattered over the page, draw the eye. There is no line of my verse or prose which has not been mouthed till the tongue made all smooth."[4] The tone is unexpectedly Paterian. But then, why unexpectedly? With lines like "Dominion over palm and pine" or "On dune and headland sinks the fire," Kipling wrote with the disciples of Pater as much in view as the disciples of Cecil Rhodes. Meditation on "the weights, colours, perfumes, and attributes of words" may be felt in every syllable of "Recessional." As poet and as rhetorician, what Kipling seeks is authority: he takes the measure of words, for the sake of persuasions that will occur as if in his absence. This helps to explain his interest in the ballad tradition, with its careful anonymity and automatic claim to authority; and it seems pertinent that forgery was always at home in that tradition. Kipling's bad poems are ventriloquized copies of a style that never existed.

Looking for other poets to compare him with, one may arrive at a list of ballad writers and regional writers, the popular wing of the romantic movement and some newer energetic second-raters: Scott, Campbell, Tom Moore, Hood, Gilbert and perhaps Henley (for whom Kipling professed the highest admiration). However, searching his poems for their footsteps, one is brought back again and again to a different company: Swinburne, Browning, Emerson, and Byron. The style of the young Kipling—his ground-note, apart from occasional poems and poems written in dialect—is fairly close to this:

> O'er the marsh where the homesteads cower apart the
>   harried sunlight flies,
> Shifts and considers, wanes and recovers, scatters and
>   sickens and dies—
> An evil ember bedded in ash—a spark blown west by
>   the wind . . .
> We are surrendered to night and the sea—the gale and
>   the tide behind.

Without the anomalous word, "homesteads," it could be mistaken for the Swinburne of the *Poems and Ballads,* right down to the echoes of Shelley. The debt is confessed more openly elsewhere: "I stayed the sun at noon to tell / My way across the waste of it; / I read the storm before it fell / And made the better haste of it." This in turn can sink into burlesque, as when Kipling adapts a celebrated chorus from *Atalanta in Calydon,* and, to Swinburne's Volatile Metaphors ("Before the beginning of years / There came to the making of man / Time, with a gift of tears; / Grief, with a glass that ran"), he replies with Crystallized Facts: "Before the beginning of years / There came to the rule of the State / Men with a pair of shears, / Men with an estimate."

Yet it is hard to calculate the distance between parody and a kind of inadvertent homage which only begins as parody. "To the Unknown Goddess" certainly has for its pretext Swinburne's "Hymn to Proserpine":

> Have I met you and passed you already, unknowing,
>   unthinking, and blind?

> Shall I meet you next season at Simla, O sweetest and
>   best of your kind?
>
> Does the P. & O. bear you meward, or, clad in short
>   frocks in the West,
> Are you growing the charms that shall capture and
>   torture the heart in my breast?
>
> Will you stay in the Plains till September—my passion
>   as warm as the day?
> Will you bring me to book on the Mountains, or where
>   the thermantidotes play?

Even here, what Kipling takes with "meward" he gives back with properties more truly his than Swinburne's: the P. & O., the Plains, "passion as warm as the day." By the end of the poem, all one can say is that somehow it has become Kipling's own. The provocation of the ur-Hymn's last phrase, "death is a sleep," is charitably passed over, yet from the general atmosphere of mimicry Kipling invents a fresh mood of wakeful acceptance.

> Ah Goddess! child, spinster, or widow—as of old on Mars
>   Hill when they raised
> To the God that they knew not an altar—so I, a young
>   pagan, have praised
>
> The Goddess I know not nor worship; yet, if half that
>   men tell me be true,
> You will come in the future, and therefore the verses
>   are written to you.

The last couplet is a free man's pontification that happens to fit the requirements of the poem, answering Swinburne's regret of the lost goddess with a faith in the still-to-be-found.

A better managed influence, Browning, may be heard in a straight-Kipling poem, "One Viceroy Resigns," with a stunning completeness of effect.

> So here's your Empire. No more wine then? Good.
> We'll clear the Aides and khitmutgars away.
> (You'll know that fat old fellow with the knife—
> He keeps the Name Book, talks in English, too,
> And almost thinks himself the Government.)
> O Youth, Youth, Youth! Forgive me, you're so young.

One has to look closely at the end-stopped lines (a habit of prose work-manship Kipling held onto in verse), with the consequent lack of var-iation in the breathing pauses, before one feels sure it is only a case of somebody doing Browning. Yet there is a tone of sincere moral bluster that is native to both poets. It accounts for Kipling's decision to write "The Lesson"—the small change of several full-scale jeremiads on the Boer War—in a style of relaxed monologue that might be supposed to follow after "No more wine then?"

> Let us admit it fairly, as a business people should,
> We have had no end of a lesson: it will do us no end of good.

The gruff but well-contented harangue marks a common ground be-tween Bishop Blougram and the ordinary hanger-on of empire.

Kipling spoke with pride of two circumstances respecting the poems he published during the last years of the century: he gave them di-rectly to the *Times,* where they could help to shape public feeling; and he took pay for none of them. He thought of himself as a propagandist, that is, a propagator of morals. But the partisan whose loyalty to a cause is least in question may be granted a certain license—just as the best athlete of a team is allowed the most cutting sarcasms. Kipling makes very full use of his privilege in battle poems:

> A scrimmage in a Border Station—
>   A canter down some dark defile—
> Two thousand pounds of education
>   Drops to a ten-rupee jezail—
> The Crammer's boast, the Squadron's pride,
> Shot like a rabbit in a ride!
>
> No proposition Euclid wrote
>   No formulae the text-books know
> Will turn the bullet from your coat,
>   Or ward the tulwar's downward blow.
> Strike hard who cares—shoot straight who can—
> The odds are on the cheaper man.

The abrupt phrases are so consistent that the title, "Arithmetic on the Frontier," can add only a rather pedantic irony. In pace as well as de-tail, the Byronic *flânerie* of battle is done to perfection here; and Kip-ling's success, like Byron's, owes much to the play of exotic names ("jezail," "tulwar") and toneless terms ("proposition," "formulae") against the assurance of the public-school vernacular ("shot," "blow," "odds," "cheaper").

The freedom of such writing from sonorous insincerities may itself be displayed with a cheapening pride. In the same attitude under slightly different circumstances, Lionel Johnson, an early and sympathetic reviewer, was offended by the swagger of the unshockable man:

> Angry with foolish shamefacedness, [Mr. Kipling] adopts a foolish shamelessness. Rather than let his work win its way by the subtle power of its ideas, he prefers to force our attention by the studied abruptness of his phrases. It is characteristic of the times: General Booth and Mr. Stanley, the German Emperor and General Boulanger, have done much the same thing in practical affairs. But Mr. Kipling, in his profession, is a greater man than they in theirs.[5]

It is true that Kipling avoids ever presenting a situation in which a sense of shame might lead to wisdom; and what he calls wisdom is often merely a return to an instinctive antipathy. But for all that, his sympathies do not seem to me at all predictable. He saw General Booth once at Invercargill near Australia, having first caught a glimpse of him "walking backward in the dusk over the uneven wharf, his cloak blown upwards, tulip-fashion, over his grey head, while he beat a tambourine in the face of the singing, weeping, praying crowd who had come to see him off." When they met later on the P. & O., Kipling complained of the scene on the wharf, but found that Booth refused to share his feelings of delicacy: "Young feller, if I thought I could win *one* more soul to the Lord by walking on my head and playing the tambourine with my toes, I'd—I'd learn how." In recounting the incident Kipling says only that Booth "had the right of it"; but plainly he is glad to show the evidence that Booth was a great man. I believe the sensation of discoveries like these is inseparable from the appeal of Kipling's imperialism.

A man, in his profession, interests Kipling not for his ability to conquer other men, but for his wit in subduing things to a human scheme. The saying often at the back of Kipling's mind is Emerson's "Things are in the saddle / And ride mankind"—a phrase from the "Ode Inscribed to W. H. Channing," which evokes the condition Kipling is always fighting against. Indeed, the Channing ode appears to be the source of one of the strangest and most powerful of all his imperialist poems, the elegy for Joseph Chamberlain called "Things and the Man." Literally this poem is about South Africa and Chamberlain. Morally it is a lesson in the pursuit of empire by which spiritual laws may some day become facts.

> The peace of shocked Foundations flew
>   Before his ribald questionings.
> He broke the Oracles in two,
>   And bared the paltry wires and strings.
> He headed desert wanderings;
>   He led his soul, his cause, his clan
> A little from the ruck of Things.
>   *"Once on a time there was a Man."*

Now, who, on hearing the sixth and seventh lines out of context, would ever suppose that they were written by Kipling? They suggest an idea that seems in principle beyond his reach—that the mere noise of fame is a low thing; that the hero is someone who leads his people not to the top of a heap, but—"A little from the ruck of Things." The words have an Arnoldian sound, and I have looked for words like them in "The World and the Quietist" and other poems by Arnold, without success. Arnold of course writes of practical power deferentially while renouncing any claim to its gifts. But the difference between these poets has in fact very little to do with sensibility, and much to do with the kind of energies they are ready to encourage, whether in imagination or in practice. Kipling values something larger than the world but believes it can be known only by the world's equals. His attitude is usually conceived to be the less poetic one. The truth is that it is the less common one among those whom the world turns out as poets.

Johnson again, in a review of *Barrack-room Ballads,* picked out a false note of bravado in Kipling's emphasis on deeds.

This glorification of the Strong, the Virile, the Robust, the Vigorous, is fast becoming as great a nuisance and an affectation as were the True and the Beautiful years ago. It is so easy to bluster and to brag; so hard to remember that "they also serve who only stand and wait." Indeed, there seems to be no virtue which Mr. Kipling would not put under the head of valour; virtue, to him, is *virtus,* and all the good qualities of man are valorous. From that point of view, saints and sinners, soldiers and poets, men of science and men of art, if they excel in their chosen works, are all Strong Men.[6]

But one may as well turn this around; for Kipling has meant to be as tolerant as the "point of view" he implies; only the word *strength* is misleading. If he praises men of different kinds for being similarly strong, he means that they are diversely noble in their work. Yet he needs a way of saying that noble works make secret kin of all who perform them: strength is a fair, but inadequate, choice, just as other choices would be.

In this Kipling writes as a follower of Ruskin. Any craft or project, seriously pursued as a calling, has for him the quality of a moral good: he takes pleasure in the faith of the attempt even more than the use of the result, and writes to communicate his pleasure. It is characteristic that he should have produced, for "The Song of the Banjo," verses close in spirit to the elegy for Chamberlain. Thus in a setting of sheer frolic, with many *Tinka-tinka-tinka-tinka-tinks* and *Plunka-lunka-lunka-lunka-lunks,* one comes at last to the challenge:

> Let the organ moan her sorrow to the roof—
>   I have told the naked stars the Grief of Man!
> Let the trumpet snare the foeman to the proof—
>   I have known Defeat, and mocked it as we ran!
> My bray ye may not alter nor mistake
>   When I stand to jeer the fatted Soul of Things.

Such echoes of the great in the small are an offense against good taste (if good taste be allowed to decide on the great). They confirm a suspicion that still clings to the magic of Kipling's rhetoric, which has lifted poems of both sorts equally, with an undistinguishing touch. This thoughtless generosity he defended only once—"There are nine and sixty ways of constructing tribal lays, / And every single one of them is right!" But on reflection the words turn out to be more a rebuke than an apology.

It is in passing from the tribe to the civilization that Kipling may appear to fail unanswerably. "In his earliest time," Henry James observed in a letter, "I thought he perhaps contained the seeds of an English Balzac. But I have given that up in proportion as he has come down steadily from the simple in subject to the more simple—from the Anglo-Indians to the natives, from the natives to the Tommies, from the Tommies to the quadrupeds, from the quadrupeds to the fish, and from the fish to the engines and screws." Kipling's movement, however, was not solely in this direction, and not more so in his later than in his earlier years. Besides, a single motive guided him throughout. The transition, as he conceived it, between the tribe and the civilization, was a small and always imperceptible affair, hardly more than a formalism of the refined. On this subject particularly Kipling requires a patience that his whole manner seems to resist. The following poem will be found in the Definitive Edition under the simple title "Ode," with the attached explanation "1934: Melbourne Shrine of Remembrance." It appears to have been commissioned for a monument to the war dead of Australia.

> So long as memory, valour, and faith endure,
>   Let these stones witness, through the years to come
> How once there was a people fenced secure
>   Behind great waters girdling a far home.
>
> Their own and their land's youth ran side by side
>   Heedless and headlong as their unyoked seas—
> Lavish o'er all, and set in stubborn pride
>   Of judgment, nurtured by accepted peace.
>
> Thus, suddenly, war took them—seas and skies
>   Joined with the earth for slaughter. In a breath
> They, scoffing at all talk of sacrifice,
>   Gave themselves without idle words to death.
>
> Thronging as cities throng to watch a game
>   Or their own herds move southward with the year,
> Secretly, swiftly, from their ports they came,
> So that before half earth had heard their name
>   Half earth had learned to speak of them with fear;
>
> Because of certain men who strove to reach,
>   Through the red surf, the crest no man might hold,
> And gave their name for ever to a beach
>   Which shall outlive Troy's tale when Time is old;
>
> Because of horsemen, gathered apart and hid—
>   Merciless riders whom Megiddo sent forth
> When the outflanking hour struck, and bid
>   Then close and bar the drove-roads to the north;
>
> And those who, when men feared the last March flood
>   Of Western war had risen beyond recall,
> Stormed through the night from Amiens and made good,
>   At their glad cost, the breach that perilled all.
>
> Then they returned to their desired land—
>   The kindly cities and plains where they were bred—
> Having revealed their nation in earth's sight

> So long as sacrifice and honour stand,
> And their own sun at the hushed hour shall light
>   The shrine of these their dead.

Notwithstanding some commonplace touches I find this greatly moving. Like "Recessional," it is public without presumption. It reveals a marked change from the language of that poem; and the change is not entirely for the better: "made good, / At their glad cost, the breach that perilled all" is antique writing, as it means to be, but close to Macaulay's imitation of the antique. Yet the phrase "nurtured by accepted peace" is both fine and modern in its understatement, and there are many such phrases in the poem.

Recall that the year is 1934. We can easily forget what it means for an inquisitive mind to remain in the world so long. Kipling, I believe, when he wrote this ode, had been reading the later Yeats—"because of certain men," "Because of horsemen, gathered apart and hid," "Half earth had learned to speak of it with fear," "Which shall outlive Troy's tale when Time is old." And curiously, the style of "Coole Park and Ballylee" and "Nineteen Hundred and Nineteen" proves at home in the texture of these lines. This is the sort of thing about which the history of poetry can say only that it ought not to happen. It can be explained, however, by an appeal to the history of rhetoric. Kipling and Yeats in their different ways were both of the school of Burke. More particularly, they were distrustful of political reasoners, and sympathized with a social order whose claims they had imagined from within. Defenses of an establishment tend to be a matter of reflex. But neither Kipling's nor Yeats's was: their attachments, being in some measure late-found, were deliberate rather than merely habitual. As Yeats's career was haunted by his discovery of loyal patronage among an aristocracy who were supposed not to exist any longer, so Kipling's was haunted by memories of the Indian Mutiny, which, eight years before his birth, had given a terrible actuality to the Law. His story "The Head of the District" makes it clear that he interpreted the episode in the light of a simple moral: such things happen when authority is relaxed. What he witnessed of the Boer War seemed to confirm his fears; he called it "a first-class dress parade for Armageddon."

Since Burke's time the grand style, in poetry as in prose, has been the weapon of an established order that sees itself passing from strength to weakness. In a poem like Kipling's "Ode" the larger elegiac story is presumed. The encouragement that he does take from his subject may be owing to the circumstances of the Australian sacrifice. The more obvious of these he notices in saying that the "certain men" came of a protected people, by their remoteness made safe from all but an abstract threat. But the ode gains its effect as well from the force of something unsaid. That the citizens of "the kindly cities and plains," not kindly themselves but speculators, main-chance men, the exiled of the empire, should have joined cause with *his* dead: this makes the occasion personal to Kipling. A reward of associating these political and familiar sentiments may be traced in the Latinate elegance of the fourth stanza, where the syntactical inversion and inward repetitions announce the very distress that the similes are working to conceal, or hoping anyway to subdue to the order of natural fact: "Thronging as cities throng to watch a game / Or their own herds move southward with the year / Secretly, swiftly, from their ports they came. . . ." The most striking feature of the poem is the scheme of *anacoluthon* with which it ends, or rather fails to find an end except in feeling. The grammar of the last stanza flows into two channels, in one of which "So long as" appears to govern everything after, while in the other "honour stand" completes the sense and the rest is a murmured blessing.

I want now to compare Kipling's eloquence with Burke's; and the most convincing specimen for this purpose is the summing up, in the "Letter to a Noble Lord," of Burke's attack on the French system of things. From a long survey of the enemy, we are brought back to England and her fortifications:

Such are *their* ideas, such *their* religion, and such *their* law. But as to *our* country and *our* race, as long as the well-compacted structure of our Church and State, the sanctuary, the holy of holies of that ancient law, defended by reverence, defended by power, a fortress at once and a temple, shall stand inviolate on the brow of the British Sion,—as long as the British monarchy, not more limited than fenced by the orders of the state, shall, like the proud Keep of Windsor, rising in the majesty of proportion, and girt with the double belt of its kindred and coeval towers, as long as this awful structure shall oversee and guard the subjected land,—so long the mounds and dikes of the low, fat, Bedford level will have nothing to fear from all the pick-axes of all the levellers of France. As long as our sovereign lord the king, and his faithful subjects, the lords and commons of this realm,—the triple cord which no man can break,—the solemn, sworn, constitutional frank-pledge of this nation,—the firm guaranties of each other's being and each other's rights,—the joint and several securities, each in its place and order, for every kind and every quality of property and of dignity,—as long as these endure, so long the Duke of Bedford is safe, and we are all safe together,—the high from the blights of envy and the spoliations of rapacity, the low from the iron hand of oppression and the insolent spurn of contempt. Amen! and so be it! and so it will be,—

    Dum domus Aeneae Capitoli immobile saxum
    Accolet, imperiumque pater Romanus habebit.[7]

Every trick of amplification is employed, and every one serves to advance the argument, so that we feel the passage itself "rise in the majesty of proportion." The main device of balance is a series of pairs: "Church and State," "not more limited than fenced," "oversee and guard," "each other's being and each other's rights," "joint and several securities," "place and order," "the high from the blights of envy" and "the low from the insolent spurn of contempt." And yet this progression is so instinctive, so much a matter of following cues which the writing can hear itself lay down, that "the low, fat, Bedford level" is immediately picked up by the ironic echo of "all the levellers in France." So, again, the three adjectives together prompt "the triple cord which no man can break," and then with our attention fixed a clear Amen: "the solemn, sworn, constitutional frank-pledge of this nation." Kipling, it may be admitted, is too confident with the light arms of the skirmisher ever to attempt a sentence like that.

Nevertheless, his poetry can sustain effects of gentleness and power at once which make the comparison far from absurd. Consider a well-known passage from "The Islanders," written after the withdrawal of English sentiment from the Boer War, and addressed to a people complacently assured of all that guards them.

    Ancient, effortless, ordered, cycle on cycle set,
    Life so long untroubled, that ye who inherit forget
    It was not made with the mountains, it is not one with the deep.
    Men, not gods, devised it. Men, not gods, must keep.
    Men, not children, servants, or kinsfolk called from afar,
    But each man born in the Island broke to the matter of war.
    Soberly and by custom taken and trained for the same,
    Each man born in the Island entered at youth to the game—
    As it were almost cricket, not to be mastered in haste,
    But after trial and labour, by temperance, living chaste.
    As it were almost cricket—as it were even your play,

Weighed and pondered and worshipped, and practiced day and day.
So ye shall bide sure-guarded when the restless lightnings wake
In the womb of the blotting war-cloud, and the pallid nations quake.
So, at the haggard trumpets, instant your soul shall leap
Forthright, accoutred, accepting—alert from the wells of sleep.
So at the threat ye shall summon—so at the need ye shall send
Men, not children or servants, tempered and taught to the end;
Cleansed of servile panic, slow to dread or despise,
Humble because of knowledge, mighty by sacrifice.

Let an ordinary line serve as a test of Kipling's workmanship. "Weighed and pondered and worshipped, and practiced day and day": the single word that might feel like cant is deferred twice, until we know exactly what gravity it had for the author; and, as a grace-note, "from day to day" and "day by day" are elided, with an unhackneyed vigor superior to both. For the rest Kipling's triumph seems complete. Where a phrase like "servile panic," with its faintly Augustan ring, is used at all it is used flexibly, beside a terse anglicism like "cleansed." The metaphor of "the game," on which the drama turns, is brought out by such quiet steps that it seems to have been looked at from all sides, before our assent is requested. "Trained for the game," says Kipling, and then "As it were almost cricket," and again, as we reflect uneasily on the words: "As it were almost cricket—as it were even your play." At the close, war has become one of the things men live for, a thing that has all the seriousness of play.

The tenderness of this passage is unusual for Kipling, in its depth as well as its complication. For his affection is given to a corporate body, as distinct from the individuals who compose it; and yet, the quality of his words suggests a concern with the suffering of individuals. The confusion of feelings is so poignant that one would suppose him to have prepared for "The Islanders" through much of his work in the preceding years. In fact, only months before this poem, Kipling had made a popular success with a poem of almost an opposite tone, "The Absent-minded Beggar."

He chucked his job and joined it—so the job before us all
   Is to help the home that Tommy's left behind him!
Duke's job—cook's job—gardener, baronet, groom,
   Mews or palace or paper shop, there's someone gone away!
Each of 'em doing his country's work
   (and who's to look after the room?)

> Pass the hat for your credit's sake,
>
> > and pay—pay—pay!

Was this meant for the same islanders? Certainly, the moral is altruistic rather than selfish, and so far in keeping with a Burkean high-mindedness. Yet it appeals to, and wants to foster, a native coarseness of temperament, according to which nothing need ever be changed. "Patch up everything you skipped," it seems to say, "but get on just as you are." The words were set to music by Arthur Sullivan.

It takes some ingenuity to trace the work of a single hand in these two poems. The difficulty will be more vivid if I add to the comparison still a third tone, "The odds are on the cheaper man," and a fourth:

> So the more we work and the less we talk the better results
> > we shall get.
> We have had an Imperial lesson. It may make us an
> > Empire yet.

With many other poets, a solution to the puzzle could invoke "the willing suspension of disbelief." This will not do for Kipling. Indeed, it would be truer to speak of an unwilling adoption of beliefs. Kipling's practice therefore sharpens the more general difficulty that I pointed to in his thinking about poetry. His rhetorical versatility makes him, once again, an unlooked-for double of the modernist, by producing the results associated with the ironic doctrine of "the mask." If the Victorian question remains—What was it like to be the author of all Kipling's utterances?—one thing only is plain. His poems offer themselves as *tests of authority:* of the degree of our loyalty to it, of what we feel when we hear its tones and what we feel when we speak them. Such gestures will seem to be implausible except where an author claims his audience's limitations as his own. But that is just what Kipling always does. The chance, however, for a next experiment is left to the author alone, who knows of other audiences and can imagine other gestures.

I prefer "gesture" to its synonyms because it is connected etymologically with "jest"—a word that carries a peculiar importance for Kipling. The easiest text to recall is "Zion":

> The Doorkeepers of Zion,
> > They do not always stand
> In helmet and whole armour,

> With halberds in their hand;
> But, being sure of Zion,
> And all her mysteries
> They rest awhile in Zion,
> Sit down and smile in Zion,
> Ay, even jest in Zion;
> In Zion, at their ease.

The poem—though inscribed "1914–1918"—is among the happiest Kipling ever wrote about warriors. If, in this opening stanza, the word were not "jest" it would have to be "love," for it prefigures a communion in which all may "Sit down and sup in Zion— / Stand up and drink in Zion / Whatever cup in Zion / Is offered to our lips." What made Kipling put this kind of pressure on the word?

According to the *Oxford English Dictionary,* jest, which shares a root (*gesta*) with other words about exploits or doings, itself began by referring to the same class of things. A closely derived meaning was a tale, or narrative of exploits; so that the modern sense we take for granted occurs at a third remove: for us, it denotes the witty, sometimes mocking interruption which splits up the telling of a tale (but which in doing so may offer a fragmentary rival tale). The first citation to place "jest" as a merely antithetical expression—"a thing that is not serious or earnest"—comes from Gay in 1732: "Life is a jest, and all things shew it, / I thought so once, and now I know it." But there, we are still halfway between "Life is a joke" and the older "Life is a tale (told by an idiot)." Cowper takes it a step further, making the newer sense the primary one, but staying alert to the etymology for the sake of a compound that suggests antithetical *wisdom:* "The Scripture was his jest-book, whence he drew / Bon-mots to gall the Christian and the Jew." One may be reminded that Cowper was another party poet, though of a party opposed to Kipling's. At any rate, the 1885 "Prelude" to *Departmental Ditties*—a completely felt poem, written when Kipling was barely twenty—relies on a similar perspective that stops short of irony.

> I have eaten your bread and salt.
> I have drunk your water and wine.
> The deaths ye died I have watched beside,
> And the lives ye led were mine.
>
> Was there aught that I did not share
> In vigil or toil or ease,—

> One joy or woe that I did not know,
>   Dear hearts across the seas?
>
> I have written the tale of our life
>   For a sheltered people's mirth
> In jesting guise—but ye are wise,
>   And ye know what the jest is worth.

Kipling here apologizes for what may seem to need no apology, the sharing of every action and passion with his characters.

But perhaps it is not altogether a sharing. Oscar Wilde said that Kipling was a great poet of vulgarity: "Dickens knew its clothes and its comedy. Mr. Kipling knows its essence and its seriousness."[8] So Kipling may have felt a warrantable anxiety, lest in allowing outsiders to see the clothes of a life he be accused of betraying its essence. To judge by the poem, however, he had a more elusive sense of his role. He tells us only that there is a connection in his writings between a truthful bearing of witness and a watch kept *beside* a subject. He is a jester in that he stands apart from a storyteller who would identify with his hero effortlessly. At the same time, his attitude is only a "jesting guise"—not part of his disposition, but a security without which the tale would stay wrapped in earnest decencies. Kipling does not exempt himself from the jester's unhappy fate as a comic butt: one can see his acceptance of the role in a self-depreciating flippancy which sometimes brings his early poems to a premature close; and, much more, in his self-portrait in *Soldiers Three,* as the journalist whom the men can be easy with and blow the gaff, because they know his place is at the safe edge of things. All these qualifications give "jest" a special strength for the wise, and with the concluding line it turns into another name for truth.

One might say more conditionally that jest is truth, accommodated to an audience with whom the poet's relation is tactical, but ready for another audience with whom his relation may be moral. Good propaganda in Kipling's view—including much of the poetry he would have called great, and the prose he thought greatest, John Bunyan's—must seek to convert the first sort of audience into the second. He does not suppose once the task is accomplished, jest will have become unnecessary; on the contrary only then will it be fully intelligible: having ceased to be entertainment, it emerges as the part of experience that can be borne. In *Something of Myself,* Kipling avoids so exalted a conception of his powers, largely I think from the same modesty that keeps him from an irritable self-regard. Yet he does break with his reticence once, near the end of the book, in the chapter on "Working Tools."

> Let us now consider the Personal Daemon of Aristotle and others, of whom it has been truthfully written, though not published:
> —This is the doom of the Makers—their Daemon lives in their pen.
> If he be absent or sleeping, they are even as other men.
> But if he be utterly present, and they swerve not from his behest,
> The word that he gives shall continue, whether in earnest or jest.
> Most men, and some most unlikely, keep him under an alias which varies with their literary or scientific attainments. Mine came to me early when I sat bewildered among other notions, and said: "Take this and no other." I obeyed and was rewarded. It was a tale . . . called "The Phantom Rickshaw." Some of it was weak, much was bad and out of key; but it was my first serious effort to think in another man's skin.
> After that I learned to lean upon him and recognize the sign of his approach.[9]

To include the word he is willing to pay a visible cost, in the form of the quaint rhyme-word "behest."

But the passage is revealing for another reason as well. More plainly than any earlier moment of Kipling's writing, it declares that a liberty of invention which could be granted by the Daemon alone was to him inseparable from the act of sympathy. And his capacity for that act, the "attempt to think in another man's skin," he connects with the possibility of jest. This seems the place to observe that Kipling elsewhere can be very loosely idiomatic. Though always a careful writer, he is an early modernizer—using "transpire," for example, as an equivalent of "happen," and calling a wild fit of laughter "hysterics." In view of such habits one is all the more impressed by the passages—otherwise quite various in style—where he elects to use an old word in a sense that is fading. At intervals, he does present jest as a simple counter for "joke," and his motives are easy to see. It helps to legitimate the Stalky world—gives a Shakespearean panache to the disgusting adolescent prank. Yet after first noticing the word, I began to read with an eye for it, and an extraordinary number of his uses belong to the sense I have been citing.

Of the many other instances I choose one from *Kim* which echoes the 1885 "Prologue." Kim has already gone to St. Xavier's school, measured himself against the other Anglo-Indian boys for a term, and decided to run away for the summer. He intends to return after vacation; meanwhile, to make the escape he needs a disguise:

> He went out into the warm rain, smiling sinfully, and sought a certain house whose outside he had noted down some time before. . . .
> "Arré! Dost thou know what manner of women we be in this quarter? O shame!"
> "Was I born yesterday?" Kim squatted native fashion on the cushions of that upper room. "A little dye-stuff and three yards of cloth to help out a jest. Is it much to ask?"
> "Who is *she?* Thou art full young, as Sahibs go, for this devilry." [10]

He tells her of an assignation with the daughter of a regimental schoolmaster—a lie based on her mistake—and proposes a disguise as a gardener's boy. The woman then completes the jest she has started: making him up for the role, dabbing his face with brown dye; and, when he complains of being unshaven, granting his wish even though it is not her trade.

> "All this disguise for one evening? Remember, the stuff does not wash away." She shook with laughter till her bracelets and anklets jingled. "But who is to pay me for this? Huneefa herself could not have given thee better stuff."
> "Trust in the Gods, my sister," said Kim gravely, screwing his face round as the stain dried. "Besides, hast thou ever helped to paint a Sahib thus before?"
> "Never indeed. But a jest is not money."
> "It is worth much more."
> "Child, thou art beyond all dispute the most shameless son of Shaitan that I have ever known to take up a poor girl's time with this play, and then to say: 'Is not the jest enough.' Thou will go very far in this world." She gave the dancing girls' salutation in mockery. [11]

The encounter works up to a kind of ingratiation that Kipling was scrupulous to omit from the rest of *Kim.*

Of course any reader will feel charmed: by the boy's confidence, his adroitness and impudence; and by the impression that he is right to show these qualities, for he will go far. But the delighted marveling at "the most shameless son of Shaitan," followed by "the dancing girls' salutation," gives a prominence to the encounter that is in excess of the dramatic motive. The exchange lingers uneasily for another reason too. We have been aware throughout that Kipling *can* think in another man's skin, whether it is Kim or the lama or the British soldiers and missionaries. Now at this turn of the story, when Kim has proved to be adequately white, with the result that the effort to sympathize with him looks less remarkable—just at this point, Kim himself decides to put on another man's skin, literally: he is dyed brown to help him pass. From the perspective of melodrama it might simply appear that he has reverted to an earlier nature. But for Kipling a more solemn change has occurred. It is here for the first time that Kim justifies the affection of his author, by becoming like his author. And the drama is played out exclusively for those who know the code of the jest: "Ye know what it is worth." We are thus asked to share Kipling's own pleasure in his disguise as the wayward boy—a boy of secret good parentage, gifted with the impulsive sympathies of the author, who can compass all humanity by his sport. The recognition takes place through Kim's connivance yet without his knowledge, and therefore without spoiling him. I do not think it quite comes off: it has an air of wheedling with the reader behind the hero's back. Nevertheless, the scene gives a clue to the pathos Kipling invested in a book that modern critics have ranked highest among his works.

In his 1906 speech at the Royal Academy dinner, Kipling described the artist as the "masterless man," and this may be taken equally as a description of Kim. He is still a boy, just on his way to manhood, but, one feels, unmastered and certain to remain so. As one looks back at the story, however, he takes on a slightly different aspect. He is a serviceable boy, fond of obeying many masters provided his duty is also sport. Colonel Creighton (master of the "game"), the lama and Mahbub Ali (mentors of spiritual life and commerce respectively), all praise him in the style of Prospero's compliments to Ariel: "Bravely done!" Their words suit a character whose service is never in question. Doubtless to say this of Kim is not quite just—nothing one can say of him is—but the reason is not the subtlety of his moral life, but rather a confusion in Kipling's sense of him. Kim descends from a pair of nearly antithetical characters, Tom Sawyer and Huck Finn. The plot of the novel, indeed, is modeled on that of *Huckleberry Finn*—the lama is Nigger Jim—and it faithfully repeats the Tom Sawyer ending of *Huckleberry Finn,* with its elaborate practical jokes. But, partly because of this resemblance, I believe there is a promise in *Kim* that is not kept. We are led to expect that Kim will resemble Huck in the depth of his judgments of the grown-up world around him. But whereas for Huck the judgments come from himself and have a cost, for Kim they are one stage of a game whose rules he wants to learn in full. Some of his judgments do carry moral weight; but they always have a grown-up behind them. When he calls Mr. Bennett a fool, he is reporting the lama's opinion; when he puts paid to the spies, he does it on instruction from Huree Babu; when he thinks that the talkative widow of the Hill Rajah is a tedious old proser, he follows a pattern of healthy revolt prescribed for boys by civilization. Even his escape from school is esteemed harmless by the usually suspicious Mahbub Ali: it is "the pony breaking out to play polo." Like Tom, and unlike Huck Finn, Kim breaks out of one game in order to play another.

Kim is therefore profoundly congenial with society just where Huck is dangerous to it; and though both novels deal with a rite of passage, *Huckleberry Finn* alone questions the authority that may control such a ritual: it affords neither a single pervasive tone, nor a decisive incident, to assure at last the worth of the game. In *Kim* by contrast, we are given the tone so steadily that we lose all concern for the incident, and are not disappointed when it fails to occur with much force. From a distance, the plot appears to require the coordination of two quests: one for a total knowledge of the codes of white India, the other for an unqualified acceptance of the vision of old India. But these quests are discrete from each other. The first begins with a memory planted in Kim at infancy, which fortune brings back when he can use it to join the game; the second he himself begins voluntarily, from an inward conviction of the lama's uniqueness; and the two coincide during the lama's pilgrimage in the Himalayas, where wisdom and counterintelligence may be pursued together. The moment of triumph for the game-quest is the moment of defeat, hence of humility and the passage to true vision, for the lama's quest to be released from the wheel of things.

Let us try putting this another way. A jest (the trick that baffles the spies by coaxing their wicked designs into the open) leads to a truth (the lama's discovery of the connection between wickedness, self, and the desire for revenge). On this view the jest that gives the story its final turn is a trial of both of the authorities that have set the plot in motion: the English police (who were right to entrust a delicate business to a novice) and the lama's faith (which lives up to its claim of dwelling apart from the world's business). The result is that both authorities are confirmed. We never learn to which of them Kim owes his first loyalty. But their coincidence is so lucky that it seems mean-spirited to doubt he can satisfy both. Notice, however, that the jest is made anonymously. Kim works under cover in the last part of the story, his new identity guarded by his old friends the lama and Huree Babu, just as earlier he was protected by the dancing girl's makeup. These are the only circumstances in which he can be sure of testing his powers without constraint. By now, the analogy between Kim and his maker ought to be clear. They are the hidden agents of a legitimate authority; and in its service they control, by feigning, all the personae of the life they witness. One might variously describe what they achieve by the sum of their inventions. A fair name for it, which Kipling himself was happy with, is empire.

Kipling's bias seems an unlikely one for a free mind to adopt. But, as one reads him, it feels consistent with his best qualities, among them an individual sense of duty and of compassion. His strengths are troubling because we have forgotten what imperialism could mean as an ideal. In his time it was not simply, what it has become simply, the exploitation for profit of a weaker people by a stronger one. A great power, now, in Africa or Latin America, means itinerant officers of multinational corporations, who supervise the projects of their company and think of the native population as either helpful or obstructive. Or else, it means the special forces of an interested government, who serve as advisers to a friendly militia and encounter the native population as either subordinates or suspects. India gave Kipling a more complicated set of relations. It was possible in his time to associate imperialism with duty, with the long habitation of colonial and native races in a single region, and with a sort of knowledge that comes of responsibility. One may honor above Kipling those who saw that the oppressions of the imperial system made it finally wicked; but Kipling's was a position that could still be maintained without meanness and without self-deception.

The ideal was seldom realized even then. To speak of it eulogistically, however, did not seem merely delusive, any more than it did at the end of the eighteenth century. Here again Burke is an important figure. When he led the prosecution of Warren Hastings, the chief agent of the East India Company, he argued that money itself was the corrupter of empire. The articles of impeachment against Hastings, accordingly, charged him not with failing to show a large profit, but with insulting human nature by the establishment of power for the sake of profits. To gain his private ends, Hastings made a routine practice of bribery, extortion, and the petty stratagems of plunder: wherever he went to work, in the name of his company, he presided over the displacement of the local authorities and the eradication of the native culture. These Burke understood as abuses and for these Hastings was tried by the united lords and commons of England. A similar feeling for the morality of conquest became Kipling's natural inheritance, and may be traced not only in the teachings of his poems but in their incidental assumptions. They are expert in the implicit ways of giving a lesson half-learnt already. And so, very deftly, they call to mind the things that do not need to be taught.

As evidence of all the variety that the empire contains and ought to preserve, Kipling offers the many voices of his poetry. Their having been collected under a name, "Kipling," points to the vulgarity and the mystery of his calling, which turn out to be the same thing. Poetry since 1915 or so has not wished to be vulgar in his way. Yet Kipling's interest in empire seems to me another feature that marks him as a disturbing counterpart of the modernists, and not their antithesis. Modernism, too, was enthralled by the idea of empire, even if this was admitted in any number of sublimated versions, as the task of "saving civilization." That slogan, as Lucy McDiarmid has shown, appeared regularly in the postwar writings of Yeats and Eliot.[12] Civilization meant above all the intuition of a past which ought to shape the present: an artist might invent, but always at the bidding of larger forces, compared to which his identity was nothing. To renew our awareness of his fate, he was even advised deliberately to hold himself at a distance. All this bears a contingent likeness to Kipling's practice, as the taboos of one culture may in principle repeat those of another, in spite of every disparity in the customs of marriage, worship, and feeding the dead. The great difference that remains between Kipling and his successors has commonly been put down to the weaker gifts or the slighter seriousness of Kipling. My quotations all along have aimed at showing that this estimate is false. Rather, Kipling and the modernists addressed different habits of mind in their readers. The modernists won the battle. In time, people who knew how to read poetry stopped being people who knew how to read Kipling.

There is a quality of style by which a poet reveals that every word has been sounded to accord with his temperament. The audience of modern poetry may be defined as readers who have learned to listen for this—to hear a cadence, and know they hear the values that make it one poet's alone. Before the twentieth century, this was a property of certain poets, without respect to rank. Milton has it (not Shakespeare). Dryden has less of it than Pope, and Blake less than Coleridge.

But modernism treated the presence of the quality as an index of poetic worth, and indeed as the defining trait of poetry as such. By this measure Yeats succeeds often; Eliot, often in his early work; and Kipling, at every phase of his career, fails utterly: he was toiling up the wrong path to art. Yet what modernism has taught us to care for need not be supposed a mark of a great soul. What is at stake is two attitudes toward speech, both of which are compatible with poetry, and both of which cannot exist in the same person at once. Yeats when he writes, "I have passed with a nod of the head / Or polite meaningless words," Eliot when he writes "The conscience of a blackened street / Impatient to assume the world," do not display finer sensibilities than Kipling. But they somehow evoke a reserve that he lacks. For, with a tact he could not possibly have admired, they imply an attitude of listening.

Eliot's terms of victory required him to say that poetry was naturally superior to rhetoric. The truth in his remark is that irony—an irony cleared of doctrine and emphasis—has proved easier to manage than jest. But there is a related contest from which I believe Kipling emerges more favorably. He cherished an ambition to recover the human types, from the high to the low, the refined to the grotesque and the fluent to the stammering, all with an ease which appeared to have passed away from poetry after Browning. Some such ambition may be granted also to the critic who wrote essays, close together, on Lancelot Andrewes and Marie Lloyd: but we read these, and they are meant to be read, as a wishful declaration of hopeless aims. Kipling, on the other hand, sat down and wrote "Sestina of the Tramp-Royal":

> It's like a book, I think, this bloomin' world,
> Which you can read and care for just so long,
> But presently you feel that you will die
> Unless you get the page you're readin' done,
> An' turn another—likely not so good;
> But what you're after is to turn 'em all.

He is the poet, and almost the *man* of all who ever lived, to have made a sestina of the end-words "long," "done," "world," "die," "good," "all."

Sometimes, as here, the possibilities that Kipling opens do belong to the common sentiments, and in that case a dramatic speaker detached from the author can explain them adequately. The larger possibilities of invention which concern him as well emerge only if one reflects on more than a poem or a story at a time. I have in mind everything that is suggested by a remark he makes at the end of "False Dawn." The story tells of a handsome young man who falls in love with the plainer of two English sisters in India. He accompanies both of them on a picnic excursion, and, in the confused darkness of a sandstorm, declares his love mistakenly to the prettier one; watches her become for some minutes the happiest girl on earth; but sends a male accomplice to retrieve the other sister, who has run out into the storm to console her grief. The story is told by the accomplice—anyone who knows Kipling can guess this—yet at the end it varies the sensational device that says, "The rest of what passed there cannot be told." We are informed instead: "There is a woman's version of this story, but it will never be written." It is odd how long one thinks about that; and it seems a good clue to Kipling's genius. For him, the reality of the other version, though it never can be told, is always what the jest was worth.

11

Edward Thomas and Modernism

IN ANY DISCUSSION of modern poetry Edward Thomas is apt to be praised in a subordinate clause; if the speaker has mastered the tone of patronage appropriate to a survey, the clause may well be: "though an interesting secondary figure, Thomas. . . ." *Interesting* in this case admits the integrity of a style which, though never consciously modernist, still does not feel archaic sixty years later. In America Thomas is of course mentioned now and then in connection with Frost; but his poems are not read; few scholars of poetry could give the titles of five of them. In England, where both the poems and "writings on the English countryside" are more familiar, Thomas is seen as expressing unassimilable tendencies. Critics in search of his tradition have placed him with Clare and Crabbe for the poetry, and with Richard Jefferies and W. H. Hudson for the prose; Thomas is accordingly cherished as a writer of insular concerns, who worked in a genre now all the more appealing for being almost extinct. Different as the results are, Thomas has been poorly served by his reputation in both countries. The truth is that one cannot read widely in his work, including the criticism, reviews, and sketches of daily life, without growing convinced of his importance in the early history of modernism. He not only pointed the way for others, he himself exemplified the value of pursuing it. A great part of the change of mood, with the testing of a new eloquence, which is commonly associated with Yeats, Eliot, and Pound, he helped to create. His manner was calmer than theirs but not less decisive.

Edna Longley's anthology of Thomas's prose, *A Language Not to Be Betrayed*, reprints many of the articles he wrote after 1902 for the *Daily*

Chronicle, where he took Lionel Johnson's place as regular reviewer.[1] Here he soon established a continuity between Johnson and himself by an unstinting admiration for Hardy's poems: "The moan of his verse rouses an echo that is as brave as a trumpet." Here too, he considered volumes by Frost, Pound, de la Mare, and the lesser Georgians, as they first appeared. These reviews, with their incidental statements of creed, are not otherwise available in permanent form, and so in one respect the anthology is a meticulous work of restoration. But the editor's feeling for what is essential in Thomas, in a discussion of Keats's odes or of prose writers like Borrow and Cobbett with whom he felt an affinity, comprehends all his more substantial writings as well; and with twenty years' labor in prose so finely represented, it will no longer be plausible to regard Thomas as a man whose moment arrived quite suddenly with the war and passed as suddenly. Indeed, Edna Longley's selections after 1913 suggest that for Thomas the war was simply a large public event in which he could not help being interested, because it happened while he was alive. But he never saw it more grandly than that. He wrote frank descriptions of the patriotic mood, of which he was critical, as a native may be critical; and when he came to write the poem that begins, "This is no case of petty right and wrong," he justified his decision to enlist by the sentiment of a place and not a generation: it was a confession of his attachment to home in the largest sense. Soldiers mattered to Thomas, hardly in a personal way, as part of the humanity he counted as his audience, and therefore part of his subject beyond war. He cared, not so much for writers who contributed to a public record, as for those who were or might become individual voices, and in the end he aimed to be known as such a voice. I will be quoting disproportionately from Thomas's criticism because it seems to me the least understood area of his achievement; but for readers who know his poetry, a tone it shares with the criticism may be worth keeping in mind from the start. In both, a certain reticence guards his stronger sentiments, and at the same time announces them more firmly than any imaginable emphasis. The result is a kind of writing in which sincerity becomes a well-defined term of praise.

The advance signaled by the criticism of T. E. Hulme, and of Eliot and Pound when they wrote as his disciples, might be reduced to a single perception. These critics saw that the language of the third and fourth generations of romantic poets had been refined beyond the service of a living speech: by the twentieth century, it had become a machine for poem-making. Much of their polemic was anticipated in Ruskin's criticism of the pathetic fallacy, and yet the new school had the wit to make theirs a battle not merely of practices but of personalities. Swinburne was only one, though perhaps the typical, object of routine derision, and it may seem in retrospect that the profuse monotony of his eloquence fostered bad habits of dismissal in those who had tired of it. Still, Hulme, Eliot, and Pound were admired by their contemporaries for the simple daring of having sought to dislodge a great reputation of the 1880s and 1890s, a name sacred to *The Education of Henry Adams*. The spirit of exclusion, which served at first to weaken the shadow of those decades, was eventually carried backward into the nineteenth century; and a sustained movement of intellectual history, in which poetry had been among the larger powers, was dismissed as the consequence of a wrong turn—with what success may be judged by Pound's triumphant allusions to the bankrupt firm of "Kelly, Sheats & Co." At this point Hulme and the others lose credit with us, now that their daring has ceased to be appreciable; yet the only alternative to faith in the modernist rewriting of history has often seemed to be an imputation of roughly the same blindness to all the more original minds of the period. In the name of a tolerant historicism, one may reason that some things are invisible to those who invent, and who are as happy to believe lies as they are to tell them if it means more life for themselves. But, after all, an intolerant historicism is more interesting, and the very existence of a critic like Thomas helps to justify it. In his observations on the language of poetry he looks forward to most of the better-known modernist strictures without their anti-romantic bias, and his polemic is much finer in its gradations.

It begins in his reviews of contemporary critics but emerges as a consistent argument where one might expect it, in *Algernon Charles Swinburne* (1912), with remarks like this: "Other poets tend towards a grace and glory of words as of human speech perfected and made divine, Swinburne towards a musical jargon that includes human snatches, but is not and never could be speech." [2] By the time he started rereading Swinburne, Thomas had already proposed to himself two maxims: that poetry is what cannot be translated, and that it ought to be at least as well written as prose. The book is a closely illustrated attempt to persuade his readers of the soundness of both. One can see them working together when Thomas observes of some characteristic lines that they "can be translated into prose, and have possibly been translated out of it—not into poetry." But he points out, as a more pervasive fault in Swinburne, a defect of imagination which cannot be blamed on the diction of an age or a century:

> He can astonish and melt but seldom thrill, and when he does it is not by any felicity of as it were God-given inevitable words. He has to depend on sound and an atmosphere of words which is now and then concentrated and crystallized into an intensity of effect which is almost magical, perhaps never quite magical.[3]

Throughout the book Thomas is disposed to recognize the many poems in which Swinburne's ends claim only as much as his means respect, above all "The Forsaken Garden" and "Ave Atque Vale." But the concern with expressive "magic" reveals Thomas's deeper allegiance to Shelley, of whose prophecy he treats Swinburne as an imperfectly satisfying fulfillment. The poetry is deficient not because it is sensational, or republican, or subjective in a style neither hard nor dry, but because the poet has used words as counters, even if not as counters of sense. In a passage of delicate irony, we are invited to accept Swinburne's lack of valor with words as a cause also of the charm by which he subdues them without protest.

> Perhaps the greatest of his triumphs is in keeping up a stately solemn play of words not unrelated to the object suggested by his title and commencement but more closely related to rhymes, and yet in the end giving a compact and powerful impression. The play of words often on the very marge of nonsense has acted as an incantation, partly by pure force of cadence and kiss of rhymes, partly by the accumulative force of words in the right key though otherwise lightly used.[4]

When he looked at Swinburne lowering his immense press of words onto a half-formed intuition of a subject, Thomas did not say, "This is wrong because some way back the history of poetry went wrong." It was a matter of individual strengths and weaknesses. Thus he supposed that Tennyson no less than Swinburne, though more quietly with his "voluptuous avoidance of excess," had failed to make any but the "entirely personal impression, far different from Wordsworth's, which made of nature a neighbour commonwealth to our own." Yet from the poetry of his youth Thomas turned not to the sixteenth century but back to the first generation of romantics. In this he resembled Yeats, and the parallel is worth drawing out for contrast.

Symbolism gave Yeats a name for the elements of romantic practice that he wished to recover, together with a ready-made fellowship of collaborators. But it was Pater's prose that had shown him how the symbolic ramifications of an image could be almost infinite and yet be controlled by the forethought of the writer. A "marmoreal muse" left with each of the words of a Paterian sentence some reminiscence of the pains that had gone to form them. To Yeats this was treating words the opposite of lightly. Thomas, however, when he read even the paragraphs of exposition in Pater's lectures, was impressed by a finish like Swinburne's. His objection to such writing was that it could not serve naturally as discourse: in Pater's biographical sketches, there would be times when it aimed to do so and could not, because its success had placed it at too secure a distance from conversational disciplines. *Walter Pater* (1913) isolates many sentences like the following, for an exquisiteness that has pared away any suggestion of purpose: "And who that has rested a hand on the glittering silex of a vineyard slope in August, where the pale globes of sweetness are lying, does not feel this?" Here, says Thomas, "The words 'pale globes of sweetness' remind us that grapes are pale, globular, and sweet; they do not vividly suggest or represent grapes, but rather the mind of a man who has pondered the subject of the relation between things and words, and has come to no inspiring conclusion."[5]

Thomas sees a connection between such traits of style and the special conditions of Pater's solitude. A professor and official mentor to the young, his sense of duty is visible in the mostly somber, but at times arbitrarily heightened, coloring of his style. He writes like a man who must be sure every moment of "professing frankly"—that is, with careful ingenuousness and a careful decorum.

> The most and the greatest of man's powers are as yet little known to him, and are scarcely more under his control than the weather: he cannot keep a shop without trusting somewhat to his unknown powers, nor can he write books except such as are no books. It appears to have been Pater's chief fault, or the cause of his faults, that he trusted those powers too little. The alternative supposition is that he did not carry his self-conscious labours far enough. On almost every page of his writing words are to be seen sticking out, like the raisins that will get burnt on an ill-made cake. It is clear that they have been carefully chosen as the right and effective words, but they stick out because the labour of composition has become so self-conscious and mechanical that cohesion and perfect consistency are impossible. The words have only an isolated value;

they are labels; they are shorthand: they are anything but living and social words.[6]

Clearly as Pater may have displayed his convictions, a tutorial relation to his listeners bound him to write English as if it were a dead language. That his words are not fine enough is a criticism Thomas does not make. Rather, he argues, words used for their "living and social" value feel plain to the writer in that they feel inevitable. This effortless authority was the single grace of style denied to Pater.

Yet living and social words alone have the effect of somehow modifying the reader's imagination. They can do so because they seem to have claimed the writer's recognition intimately from his life, temperament, and circumstances, and because they command in turn the reader's own recognition as something more than the name of an object: something his life, temperament, and circumstances have to translate. A word of this sort is always mysterious to the reader to the extent that it was familiar to the writer, and nothing is gained by calling it either literal or figurative. Thomas writes of its effect in one of his happiest statements of vocation, "The Word";[7] the poem describes a spring sound which "Though 'tis an empty thingless name" the poet cannot forget, since

> Spring after Spring
> Some thrushes learn to say it as they sing.
> There is always one at midday saying it clear
> And tart—the name, only the name I hear.

Frost gave a lovely echo of this in "The Oven Bird"; but, of the birds which these poems offer as figures of poetic speech, Thomas's is the less flatly anti-rhetorical: its song is closer to the "tone of meaning" Frost speaks of in another sonnet. The reader who does not know how much a tone can mean will misremember the poem's title as "The Thrush," and that is part of the poem's teaching. Such a reader thinks the word's work is done when the associated object has appeared. But for Thomas the wonder of "the word" poetry can discover or revive is that it makes all substitutions a matter of question-begging:

> This name suddenly is cried out to me
> From somewhere in the bushes by a bird
> Over and over again, a pure thrush word.

It is not quite the same as a pure thrush's word; indeed, the poem suggests a definition of a poet as someone for whom words and objects have mingled inseparably. By listening for the word a writer joins his names with ours; and we go on reading him because his society affords as much hope of renewal as a season.

Yeats for a time considered the Image a fair exchange for words like this, and he would likely have approved, for he sometimes imitated in principle, the passage about grapes which Thomas quotes as stilted. Imagism in general codified the practice of isolating such passages as the essence of poetry. I think Thomas would have been inclined to reject the movement on the ground that it was doctrinally unequipped to notice the poetry of "No motion but the moving tide, a breeze / Of merely silent Nature's breathing life," poetry not written and not to be valued as naturalistic transcription. But here his graver opinions can only be surmised: all his criticism of the Imagists he contracted into a joke, with the suggestion that the movement's real source lay less in classical authors than in classical editions. "The chief influence appears to have been the ordinary prose translation of the classics—in short, the crib. Burlesqued this had been already by Mr. A. E. Housman and others. The Imagist poets must have the credit of being the first to go to it for serious inspiration."[8]

Imagism and Symbolism as Thomas understands them have much in common: by both movements poetry is identified not with the animating passion of words but with the ideal distillation they achieve on the page. Some such effect was Yeats's design too when he broke the *as*-clauses of Pater's Mona Lisa into separate lines of free verse. The editor's creation of discretely vivid pictures, out of a purposeful series interlinked in prose, made symbolic images of what earlier readers had encountered as allegory. The referent of each clause was expected in consequence to emerge reliably line by line. But why should the symbolist concern himself with reference at all? "It is a little unkind to words," writes Thomas, "to suppose that they can be bounded by their meaning, but apparently the symbolist must insist that his words are not only not so bounded, but have a further significance which is quite precise; otherwise there were no difference between the old and the new." The old reader whom Thomas has in mind did not assume that words were bounded by their meanings, but rather that everyone interpreted them from a modest consensus about kinds of meaning, after which everyone built for himself and within his imaginative powers. The symbolist on the contrary grants an independence to words which they already enjoy, and then returns to guide their interpretation with a new control. Thomas cites as an example Yeats's conscientious notes to *The Wind among the Reeds,* for the help they bring to the poem entitled "Mongan laments the Change that has come upon him and his Beloved." Perhaps "a day will come when the force of Mr. Yeats's genius will have added to common culture the special knowledge through which alone the poem is intelligible. At present [its language] is dead or merely private, and the note, so far from helping the poem, attracts attention exclusively to itself." The poem most fortunate from the symbolist point of view is most opaque to the common culture of meaning.

Poetic language in Thomas's view is everything that may disclose a mind in motion, or a mind occupied with what most concerns it.

> In the mainly instinctive use of [language] the words will all support one another, and, if the writing is good, the result of this support is that each word is living its intensest life. . . . Whatever be the subject, the poem must not depend for its main effect upon anything outside itself except the humanity of the reader.[9]

One may read these sentences, along with Thomas's more straight-forward acts of homage to Wordsworth, as a record of how much survived in him of the spirit of the Preface to *Lyrical Ballads,* in spite of the many features of its program he seems to have discarded. There is no claim for purity of diction, only for dramatic propriety. There is none either for the repose of large feelings in rural places, and the poet's difference from other men is no longer measured by degrees of imagination. The difference now comes from an understanding of the conditions of language which the poet alone employs actively and continuously. He is one more person who knows English words. And yet, by picking out an emphasis among the words we use, he touches our habits of thinking and feeling. This he does in a way so commonplace as to be unmeasurable, and in this sense the language of poets is the second nature of all of us.

According to high-modernist precept, a modern style requires, apart from imponderables like genius, the omission of certain untimely artifices. Syntactical inversions are among these, as well as words of quaint pedigree, "casement" for window or "lamp" for star; but if one looks for tokens of this sort in Thomas's poetry, he will seem far from sufficiently modern. He appears never to have developed a simple distaste for inversions, and his poems are unsuperstitiously free even with Miltonic orderings of adjective-noun-adjective ("stony square unlit")

or, by extension, adverb-verb-adverb ("wisely reiterating endlessly").
These were conscious practices, and not the lapses of an unguarded
mood; for Thomas supposed that being modern was a matter of escaping the belief that there was one preeminently poetic attitude. Some
of his changes of heart about other poets can be traced to his refusal to
be charmed when an attitude that once seemed natural became a self-
regarding manner. A 1912 review of Rupert Brooke's *Poems* is quick to
detect the process well advanced by then in the work of a youthful
poet:

> He writes of Helen, of London, of afternoon tea, of sleeping out, of
> seasickness. He experiments in choriambics. He is full of revolt, con-
> tempt, self-contempt, and yet of arrogance too. He reveals chiefly what
> he desires to be and to be thought. Now and then he gives himself away,
> as when, in three poems close together, he speaks of the scent of warm
> clover. Copies should be bought by everyone over forty who has never
> been under forty. [10]

There is nothing to prevent a poet of whatever age from addressing the
characteristic emotions of readers under forty and producing poems as
lasting as Housman's. But a poet like Brooke, with his pet words and
scenes, wrote partly from sheer irritability at those whom he did not
care to have as readers. Thomas replies by advising them to use the
book as a kind of instruction manual on how to *become* Brooke's readers:
the understatement here, which turns an ordinary offense into a splendid curiosity, is a critical tactic both rarer than irony and more versa-
tile. Thomas shows the same tact for managing imperfect sympathies
in his reviews of Ezra Pound.

As a fashioner of dramatic speech, Pound had gone further than
anyone of the age except Yeats in his plays, and Thomas's first impulse
as a reviewer was to report the cheering news. Of *Personae* he writes in
1909: "Carelessness of sweet sound and of all the old tricks makes Mr.
Pound's book rather prickly to handle at first. It was practically nothing but this prickliness that incited us to read the book through a
second time. We read it a third time . . . because it was good the
second." [11] Pound's approximation of personality by an unconnected
series of negative gestures would later dictate the structure of "Hugh
Selwyn Mauberley," with its undertone of self-congratulation, its overtones of revolt, contempt, self-contempt, and the ad hoc satire of its
portraits giving an appearance of consistency to the whole. Even at
this early stage, however, Thomas was annoyed by the caginess of a

poet who never materialized among his own personae. The steady vehemence of some poems made the unsteady shifts of voice all the more
troubling. But in 1909 Thomas preferred to think that "the disdain is
the other side of a powerful love for something else."

Yet he came back to *Personae* in a second review, and added several
qualifications withheld from the first. "Let us straightway acknowledge the faults; the signs of conflict; the old and foreign words and old
spellings that stand doubtless for much that the ordinary reader is not
privileged to detect; the tricky use of inverted commas; the rhythms
at one time so free as not to be distinguishable at first from prose, at
another time so stiff that 'evanescent' becomes 'evan'scent'; the gobbets
of Browningesque." Innovation, in which Pound's work is certainly
rich, does not impress Thomas as a sign of genuine invention. He had
said earlier, in a neutral tone, that Pound seemed to have "practically
no extravagance." As he followed Pound's career this began to emerge
as a defect. For without natural extravagance, Pound was forced to rely
on an unlimited number of mannerisms. And a poet who says of all
his devices, "these are provisionally mine and yet not me," may end in
a condition of moral weightlessness. Thomas saw this as a danger for
Pound, and in a review of *Exultations* later the same year he delivered
his warning straightforwardly.

> When he writes in the first person he is so obscure as to give some
> excuse for finding him incapable of self-expression. And both in per-
> sonal and detached poems he is, as a rule, so pestered with possible ways
> of saying a thing that at present we must be content to pronounce his
> condition still interesting—perhaps promising—certainly distressing.
> If he is not careful he will take to meaning what he says instead of saying
> what he means. [12]

The reader of our age, who has lived after the first decade of cantos,
the tracts against usury, the broadcasts for Mussolini, the harangue of
Pound's speeches and the harangue of his silence, will be equipped to
appreciate the depth of the critic who in 1909 found little gravity in a
mind so "pestered with possible ways of saying a thing."

Nor can it be objected that Thomas had really failed to comprehend
the modernist idea of masks—that he cherished an anachronistic fondness for personality-as-such. He knew the idea very well, not as a
modern discovery but from its sources in Keats, and he observed in
praise of de la Mare that though his "personal quality is intense and
consistent . . . it has no obvious egotism, no significant first person

singular, no confession, defiance, lament, or hinted mystery. Mr. de la Mare's work is, in fact, the perfection of personality, and in an impersonal way, without deliberation or obtrusiveness." In the end he saw de la Mare as a personal poet without egotism, and Pound as an egotist without personality, or with one that "rises to the appearance of being positive only by contradiction." His comments on de la Mare bring to mind Eliot's observation a few years later in "Tradition and the Individual Talent," that the aim of poetry is a continual extinction of personality, though only those who have it know what it means to escape from it. If Thomas made his remark more in passing, this was because he took it to express an elementary truth. Poetry since Wordsworth had been the projection of a few intense personal interests as "a neighbour commonwealth to our own." The reader feels at home there because his interests, and for that matter his intellectual activity, are not different in kind from the writer's.

I suspect that what first drew Thomas to the poetry of Frost was its explicit concern with reading. "This," he began his review of *North of Boston*, "is one of the most revolutionary books of modern times, but one of the least aggressive." The language "is free from the poetical words and forms that are the chief material of secondary poets"—here he seems to be thinking of the Georgian movement as a general tendency. As for the rhythms, they avoid "not only the old-fashioned pomp and sweetness, but the later fashion also of discord and fuss"— here unquestionably he has Pound still in view. The sentences that follow are worth pausing over:

> Almost all these poems are beautiful. They depend not at all on objects commonly admitted to be beautiful. Neither have they merely a homely beauty, but are often grand, sometimes magical. Many, if not most, of the separate lines and separate sentences are plain and, in themselves, nothing. But they are bound together and made elements of beauty by a calm eagerness of emotion.[13]

When one considers the range of Frost's tones, from poems like "The Vantage Point" to poems occasional and even ceremonial, like "The Master Speed," that phrase of Thomas's about "a calm eagerness of emotion" seems marvelously precise. But as with *Personae*, he reviewed *North of Boston* more than once, and here again the second article repeats hardly anything from the first. A passage, however, which Thomas does return to is the conclusion of "The Wood-Pile": "I thought that only / Someone who lived in turning to fresh tasks /

Could so forget his handiwork. . . ." One may recall the self-forgetting that Thomas had missed in Pater, and these lines were probably in his mind when he summed up his estimate of Frost:

> Mr. Frost has, in fact, gone back, as Whitman and as Wordsworth went back, through the paraphernalia of poetry into poetry again. With a confidence like genius, he has trusted his conviction that a man will not easily write better than he speaks when some matter has touched him deeply, and he has turned it over until he has no doubt what it means to him, when he has no purpose to serve beyond expressing it, when he has no audience to be bullied or flattered, when he is free, and speech takes one form and no other. [14]

"With a confidence like genius" expresses a great deal that is finely and not obviously true about Frost's character as a poet. It does not pamper the author's self-esteem, but says: this poetry has the kind of intimacy we are used to seeing earned by genius alone; yet it is remarkable for a *conscious* self-trust which genius has not often been known to display; indeed it steals a march on our deliberations over merit. The most impressive fact about Thomas's advocacy of Frost, as even a brief excerpt shows, is the decency of its reticence. By its refusal of hyperbole, of historical comparisons that merely flatter, of the invention of a new category in which the poet because he stands alone will stand highest, it leaves the reader to think further for himself.

About the time Thomas was writing these reviews, Frost was telling friends he had invented a theory of "sentence sounds" which Thomas would some day expound in an article. As it happened Thomas knew better than to call it a theory or attribute it to Frost. He quotes the good terse phrases, "Pressed into service means pressed out of shape" and "Three foggy mornings and one rainy day / Will rot the best birch fence a man can build," but he gives them not as instances of a language now forgotten except by Frost, but to remind us that this is the healthy employment of English words in common exchange. Before he saw *North of Boston* Thomas had written: "Men understand now the impossibility of speaking aloud all that is within them, and if they do not speak it, they cannot write as they speak. The most they can do is to write as they would speak in a less solitary world." Frost's sentence sounds made the world less solitary. But their importance for all writing had been a leading emphasis of Thomas's criticism for a decade before he met Frost. He would I think have been willing to accept a generous definition of poetry as anything that created such sounds by design. The point, at any rate, is that between Frost and Thomas the friendship that grew was reciprocal, and included critical thinking no less than poetic practice. Of the temperamental differences that seem to have kept them interested in each other, the most vivid evidence is Thomas's reaction to "The Road Not Taken." The poem, as is now generally known, was meant by Frost as a gentle reproof of Thomas's study of self-regret. Yet Thomas failed to see that there was mockery in it: he liked it simply as a Shelleyan poem by Frost and was struck by the pathos of "I shall be telling this with a sigh." When Frost protested against the misreading, Thomas pronounced himself content with the poem as he had loved it first, and ready to forgive but not credit Frost's insistence on a contrary intention. One might turn this into a parable for interpreters, with the moral, "Parody no Excuse for Eloquence."

The story is immediately helpful for what it shows of the more trusting mood in which Thomas as a poet is likely to manage a subject he shares with Frost. He makes a softer approach to the emotions of a poem, or is longer in testing their resonance. The effect in either case is of words used not lightly but seldom quite as emphatically as they are by Frost. The quick pace varied by fluent metrical deviations has its part too in the reader's sense of a decisive voice telling of things not yet decided. Frost conveys the opposite impression, even where his words are most tentative, his step most held by voluntary pauses. He wrote "Spring Pools" with the confidence Thomas knew how to praise as an unconfiding strength, and one wants it nearby to compare with "Tall Nettles," a poem by Thomas similar in theme and movement.

> Tall nettles cover up, as they have done
> These many springs, the rusty harrow, the plough
> Long worn out, and the roller made of stone:
> Only the elm butt tops the nettles now.
>
> This corner of the farmyard I like most:
> As well as any bloom upon a flower
> I like the dust on the nettles, never lost
> Except to prove the sweetness of a shower.

The grammatical complication of the first line and a half is like that of "These pools that, though in forests, still reflect / The total sky"—yet here it brings to the utterance an air of leisure that Frost excludes from the start. This feeling in Thomas, of having always time enough to voice the human sense of a thing, is a poetic trait one has to go a long way back to match, possibly as far back as Cowper. It is what allows him to introduce himself into the second stanza so quietly that we do not notice the change. Whereas the "I" of Frost's poem is all the more powerfully present for being withheld: "These trees that have it in their pent-up buds / To darken nature and be summer woods, / Let them think twice." The reflections Thomas cares for are not displaced to the landscape but claimed by the speaker in an unexceptional way: his pair of imperfect rhymes, and his eye for "the nettles" in the seventh line, though they cost him an extra syllable, are proof against any charge of obliqueness or cunning. Of the two poems Thomas's is the more modest, and yet it requires no less tact of the reader than Frost's. "Only the elm butt tops the nettles now" is as measured in its bluntness as "These flowery waters and these watery flowers" is measured in its grace.

Thomas's description of Frost as "one of the least aggressive poets" is a curious and revealing testimony to set alongside the anecdotes about Frost at other periods and in other companies. But if one reads these poets together for any length of time one may feel that Thomas after all was describing himself. What is sometimes vulnerable in his poems—to the point of stopping them short of a promised expression—is the poet's conviction of an infinite debt to a nature that was here before him. In *A Literary Pilgrim in England* (1917) the debt was recorded in other writers' names, the study's premise being that imagined landscapes are finer when their prototypes can be traced in nature. It is a scholarly book and a beautiful one, but it goes to extremes: Shelley's childhood haunts are combed for possible clues to "Alastor"; and Thomas suspects that the "deep romantic chasm" of "Kubla Khan" connects it, though tenuously, with the neighborhood of Somerset. He was able to contemplate a nature altogether prior to man and greater by itself, as others have only pretended to contemplate it. So in reading him, and especially his early prose, one now and then enters a realm of primary natural sensibility, without selfish thoughts or fears, which regards nature unaccompanied, not as a nightmare of the earth closing like a dent in dough, but as what "I like most." The result from a human point of view is oddly unreviving. A wise passiveness rewards him with intervals of simple repose; yet these intervals have their own nightmares of listlessness. And Thomas is committed to record in words whole passages of time in which neither mood has quite settled, when he stays "listening, lying in wait / For what I should, yet never can, remember"—and still more often, the sense of revelations that have passed as if in his absence, when he was offered "truths I had not dreamed, / And have forgotten since their beauty passed." These last are not Wordsworthian epiphanies of "A motion and a spirit that impels / All thinking things, all objects of all thought," but rather ecstasies of the knowledge of intellectual beauty, in a severer tradition: "Sudden, thy shadow fell on me." When he writes of such moments, Thomas as a rule communicates less than he wishes. No reader will challenge the testimony unless from a dogmatic contempt for some part of experience itself. But, with Thomas, the report that he has been changed by what happened remains only a report. He is writing in an elegiac mode without any representation of *that time* from which the singer has fallen away. The poems therefore that continue long in this mode, from Thomas's identification with a power beside which he himself is nothing, mark a limit of the uses of sincerity.

His great poems also describe a situation of listening or lying in wait, though in many instances they follow the action to a farther stage, when the revelation has come, or when its results are connected with the fate of other men by the poet's conversion to social speech. I will be discussing "Liberty," "I never saw that land before," and "The Owl," with parts of some others, and it is worth stressing that these are composed in the same register as the slighter pieces; what sets them apart, along with "Rain," "Roads," "The Gallows," and "Lights Out," is the ease and distinctness with which they figure the poet himself. Thomas speaks in one poem of his interest in "the ghost / That in the echo lives and with the echo dies," and it has to be said that his poems harbor their echoes with as little worry as any written in this century. The poet's affinities are understood to be a large part of his personal identity: he discloses them with the pride of memory rather than of possession, and quotations are never used as a signal. Since Thomas wrote all his poems in the last three years of his life, the Keatsian echoes of "Liberty" in particular have a special weight with the reader.

> The last light has gone out of the world, except
> This moonlight lying on the grass like frost
> Beyond the brink of the tall elm's shadow.
> It is as if everything else had slept
> Many an age, unforgotten and lost—
> The men that were, the things done, long ago,
> All I have thought; and but the moon and I

Live yet and here stand idle over a grave
Where all is buried. Both have liberty
To dream what we could do if we were free
To do some thing we had desired long,
The moon and I. There's none less free than who
Does nothing and has nothing else to do,
Being free only for what is not to his mind,
And nothing is to his mind. If every hour
Like this one passing that I have spent among
The wiser others when I have forgot
To wonder whether I was free or not,
Were piled before me, and not lost behind,
And I could take and carry them away
I should be rich; or if I had the power
To wipe out every one and not again
Regret, I should be rich to be so poor.
And yet I still am half in love with pain,
With what is imperfect, with both tears and mirth,
With things that have an end, with life and earth,
And this moon that leaves me dark within the door.

It is a poem of intense consciousness, with the check of irony in the halts and false drifts of its many double negatives. "Unforgotten" in the fifth line for example, and "what is not to his mind" in the fourteenth, resist comprehension even after several readings, and half-sentences are in places so loaded with doubt that any affirmation they end in seems intransitive. Yet for all that, it survives as a poem of hope—one of the few such poems by anyone that do not fake a victory—and its success is probably owing to the invention of the moon as a companion. Here one sees the consolation Thomas's naturalism could bring when its subject was not nature. The moon is a circle of light, barely personified, yet for him this little is enough. He speaks from an indecision that to other minds would appear as acedia, but with no prospect of advancing he is cheerful to a degree, for his dread vanishes at the thought of "The moon and I." By remaining in the door, he commits himself neither to suffering nor patience but to a state in which everything once experienced will be known without exemption. Thus the entire poem protracts a mood Keats reserved for the penultimate stanzas of the "Ode to a Nightingale." The *mirth-earth* rhyme belongs to Keats only less notably than "I still am half in love with pain": Thomas, however, had used the rhyme elsewhere with such a range of effects that it joins his melody almost as a personal refrain. As a whole the poem feels composed in a single breath. Its uninterrupted lyrical phrases, "Beyond the brink of the tall elm's shadow" and the last line most prominently, break free for only as long as the conditional cast of other phrases permits. Yet it is modern in effect for no technical reason, but because its doubts, connected alike with the poet's circumstances and his period, have refused admittance to a phrase like "pleasant pain." What may be most unusual about "Liberty," and this links it with Owen's "Strange Meeting," is the clarity with which the poet's sense of his vocation pledges him to a life of *thoughts*.

There are poems in which Thomas comes to the brink of self-pity, and one test of his mastery is our certainty that the risk has never been accidental. He writes in his letters of being afflicted with a self-consciousness as far beyond mere selfishness as selfishness is beyond sympathy. This was a subject for poetry. So an autumn poem that begins conventionally, "Gone, gone again / May, June, July," recalls other autumns and alludes to them in a phrase of extraordinary vehemence, as a time before "the war began / To turn young men to dung." Only with this do we realize Thomas's thoughts of autumn have been thoughts of himself; this, and the image of a house, "Outmoded, dignified, / Dark and untenanted":

> I am something like that;
> Only I am not dead,
> Still breathing and interested
> In the house that is not dark:—
>
> I am something like that:
> Not one pane to reflect the sun,
> For the schoolboys to throw at—
> They have broken every one.

In a poem as elusive as this (it is called "Blenheim Oranges"), with as solemn a progression as this has, the view of himself makes a delicately controlled ending. "I am something like that" seems the farthest reach of eloquence that his circumstances will allow. As for the poem's originality with a landscape so traditional, the last line is the only one that would have been recognized as poetry a generation earlier.

Extravagance here is a matter of surprise. The house, as a feature of the setting, is withheld until the middle of the poem; the poet is compared to it only at the very end; and the oranges we were shown at first, lying fallen in the autumn rains, are touched in retrospect by the poignance of these things. But Thomas is remarkable for surprise of another sort in poems more predictably organized. "Celandine" recounts a story that reminds one in most details of "Surprised by Joy." In that story the poet turns to share a pleasure, and realizes that the person he would have shared it with is gone forever. Yet as the poem begins Thomas has been tranquilly resigned to his loss, until "I saw the sun on the celandines lie / Redoubled, and she stood up like a flame, / A living thing," and the natural vision enchants him. By this confusion he is enticed to pick the flowers, and the reminiscence of death, which he feels in his own gesture, breaks the spell a second time.

> But this was a dream: the flowers were not true,
> Until I stooped to pluck from the grass there
> One of five petals and I smelt the juice
> Which made me sigh, remembering she was no more,
> Gone like a never perfectly recalled air.

A visible object both represents the woman he loved and consoles the loss of her: the transition is hardly announced, and yet we share its feeling. Thomas seems to have believed more effortlessly than Wordsworth that death and life inhabit each other through the intercessions of memory and imagination, and the belief gives his last line a quality remote from anything one may have expected of an elegy.

The untitled poem that begins "I never saw that land before" describes a comparable episode of second sight, with objects more nearly consequential for the poet himself. A landscape of great beauty, one of many others as the poet walked in the country, comes back to him in memory with all its constituents, "The cattle, the grass, the bare ash trees, / The chickens from the farmsteads, all / Elm-hidden, and the tributaries / Descending at equal interval," made keener by "the breeze / That hinted all and nothing spoke"—and he recognizes too late that this place possessed him even before he saw it.

> I neither expected anything
> Nor yet remembered: but some goal
> I touched then; and if I could sing
> What would not even whisper my soul
> As I went on my journeying,
>
> I should use, as the trees and birds did,
> A language not to be betrayed;
> And what was hid should still be hid

Excepting from those like me made
Who answer when such whispers bid.

"A language not to be betrayed" is a language that both ought not to be betrayed and that cannot be. But this central phrase holds another secret. For "betrayed" has two, almost antithetical, senses, and may suggest *revealed* as much as *given away*. The poem in fact protects the very meanings it affects to disclose.

All this, which baffles a reader or at least halts his progress, affords Thomas himself perfect satisfaction. He has composed a scene of self-discovery, and in such scenes cause and effect—voice and inspiration, the poet and the situation with which his poetry is associated—cannot be extricated from each other: if they could, we would know just what to make of the words, and they would cease to be poetry. The poem does not say and we cannot tell whether Thomas only gives the response to "such whispers," or has provoked their "bidding" by his own act of memory. The last stanza of Hart Crane's "Voyages" is so close to the last stanza of Thomas's poem that it seems a natural part of any commentary.

The imaged Word, it is, that holds
Hushed willows anchored in its glow.
It is the unbetrayable reply
Whose accent no farewell can know. [15]

The syntax of the final line repeats the strangeness of Thomas's "whisper my soul," where the soul may be either giving or receiving. Here the ambiguity of cause and effect, or finder and found, makes two readings equally inevitable: an accent (poetic Word) that can know no farewell because it stays forever; and a farewell (elegiac landscape) that can know no accent because it is imaged only by the Word. There is also the same near-pun on "betray." Crane in his letters mentions Thomas as one of the few modern poets he has read with interest, and this passage feels like one result of his reading.

Such uncanny recognitions by the poet of the place-meant-for-him-alone are interesting to all who believe poetry is the most important fact about the world. But few can hold steadily to that belief, and everything Thomas says about language seems intended to convince us that the poet's situation is *less* special than we ordinarily suppose. Why then should we grant the significance he claims to the search for "a language not to be betrayed"? An answer in keeping with his criticism would be that to grant it, we have to think of the poet as nothing more special than a representative of a community of speech, who sometimes recovers a knowledge others repress in order to live. They forget, and he sometimes remembers with a shock, how far we are modified by what we have made, and how far therefore we are at once servants and masters of language. This sort of knowledge is possible to someone for whom words are always both figurative and literal, as they were for Thomas in "The Word," and to someone aware of precisely what is to be defended and what may be betrayed, as Thomas was aware in his writings on Swinburne, Pater, Pound, and Frost. To read "I never saw that land before" with this in mind is of course to read parabolically. But Thomas warns us he is speaking in parable when he refers to those outside, to whom the poet's task must remain unknown: what was hid will still be hid from them.

The gravity with which Thomas accepts his vocation makes him the most satisfying English poet to carry the intelligence of romanticism into the modern age. In a sentence of prose that recalls the "Defence of Poetry," he speaks of his writing as a pursuit "not of wisdom, but of one whom to pursue is never to capture," an Other he may glimpse but not name. It was a generous credo, and he followed it where it led. Often he described what he pursued as a spirit of place, or as a lover. But increasingly in his last years, Thomas seems to have meant by "the other" (as he called it once in a poem of that title), the interests of other men and women. For this reason "The Owl" may make the fittest conclusion to a summary essay.

> Downhill I came, hungry, and yet not starved;
> Cold, yet had heat within me that was proof
> Against the North wind; tired, yet so that rest
> Had seemed the sweetest thing under a roof.
>
> Then at an inn I had food, fire, and rest,
> Knowing how hungry, cold, and tired was I.
> All of the night was quite barred out except
> An owl's cry, a most melancholy cry
>
> Shaken out long and clear upon the hill,
> No merry note, nor cause of merriment,
> But one telling me plain what I escaped
> And others could not, that night, as in I went.
>
> And salted was my food, and my repose,
> Salted and sobered, too, by the bird's voice

> Speaking for all who lay under the stars,
> Soldiers and poor, unable to rejoice.

A very unaccustomed weight falls on the plain phrase "And others could not," and on the plain word "unable." The gesture of sympathy that opens up after the owl's cry has been heard is larger than in "This is no case of petty right and wrong." Yet the unobtrusiveness of the confession ("and sobered, too") serves as assurance that the poet's words are a bearing of witness, and not a declaration of the aim to do so. It is impossible to read "The Owl" for its place in Thomas's career without thinking of the poetry he might have written after the war in a style like this, "Shaken out long and clear upon the hill." The future of any career that was cut short is, of course, an idle problem and usually explored in idleness. But in Thomas's case the speculation can have a more specific character. He was the poet of the early moderns who gave some promise of including those unable to rejoice in the words of poetry, and making its words again available to them. He was not likely to succeed altogether, any more than Wordsworth did, but he would not have reversed direction and accused history itself of betrayal. What we made of it always depended for him on how soberly we came to know ourselves in our repose.

12

The Sense of Vocation in Frost and Stevens

THE FOLLOWING NOTES on two modern poems were prompted by some reservations about the recent criticism of Wordsworth. That criticism agrees on the importance of "the image," and shows in detail how the image is fitted to the particular occasions of "the crisis poem."[1] I want to acknowledge these ideas at the outset because I too will be relying on them. But the image has come to stand for two different things: first, a picture which has enduring worth for the poet because it is a fact; and second, an imagining that began as such a picture, has been revolved in the mind, and is prized as a thing of the mind. These two sorts of image are related through the change in meaning by which the first brought forth the second, and we now read Wordsworth with the second ascendant, the first being understood as a distant part of its genealogy. My reservation is that the fact-image had a moral significance for aesthetics which the mind-image alone can never have. It signaled a connection between the poet and other men; and this was true, no matter what the poet's relation to the object that yielded the image, whether he disturbed its perfect repose, or sent it wandering, or found himself strangely invigorated beside it; whereas for us, the connection has become less and less interesting. We are concerned instead with what the image helps the poet to do for himself.

This was perhaps inevitable in an age dominated by Yeats, with his thoroughly inward sense of vocation. For us the image has been purged of fact and the crisis poem released from its connection with other men. But Wordsworth himself wished for no such release. He tried to think of poetry in conjunction with other human pursuits, and of the poet as both minister and witness to the needs of others. His eventual failure to meet the conditions of his double office, "by words, / Which speak of nothing more than what we are"—a failure by degrees, of which he left evidence of his own recognition by degrees—produced the poems which at once lament the withdrawal this implies within his vocation, and celebrate the survival of his gift in some form. Wordsworth regarded such poems as a personal response to a personal disappointment. They nevertheless became a pattern to his successors, and one reason why they should have done so is obvious. Wordsworth was the first lyric allegorist of the poetic career. He set the terms in which the whole subject of vocation presents itself to any modern poet. Yet the modern poet as a rule has conceived no Wordsworthian ambitions for the humanizing influence of poetry, and without these nothing compels him to repeat Wordsworth's lament. Looking back at "Tintern Abbey," "Resolution and Independence," the "Ode to Duty" and Immortality Ode, and "Elegiac Stanzas" on Peele Castle, he may feel a good deal less reluctant than Wordsworth to assert that the poet's sympathy with others is really a bondage.

While alluding to Wordsworth, his successors have thus been able to treat solely as a poetic gain what he described in some measure as a human loss. It will be plain by now that the poem I have most in view is "Resolution and Independence." From its plot the later poet has usually had to abstract a few bold features: what is left out, except in attenuated hints, is the poet's continuing relation to something other than his own mastery. Here, modern commentators on Wordsworth have been guided by modern poetry, in a way that is seldom acknowledged. For those who discuss the poetic crisis solely in poetic terms are interpreting Wordsworth in line with what his successors have made of him. On literary-historical grounds one may want to retard this process; it makes Wordsworth's period too neatly continuous with ours. But I believe that more than literary history is at stake. The modern understanding of Wordsworth has fostered great poems, and much thoughtful criticism, but the damage has been great also. What I have to say about two specimens of the Wordsworth tradition is mainly intended to recall the undertone of regret with which an early critic and successor first pronounced him the poet of the egotistical sublime.

Frost's "Two Tramps in Mud Time" and Stevens's "The Course of a

Particular" show these two poets about as remote from each other as they ever get, in the entire range of their practice, and between the poems themselves no affinity will be claimed, other than their shared descent from "Resolution and Independence." Let me begin by rehearsing in the simplest terms the Wordsworthian situation that all three poems ask us to contemplate. In an unpromising landscape, lit by a change of weather from stormy to fair—a happy change, which nevertheless reminds us of the vicissitudes of all outer and inner weather— a poet filled with unsettling thoughts about his vocation is suddenly brought face to face with a common laborer, or one who suffers the common fate of men and not the uncommon fate of poets. Already I must qualify this, because the poems make the scene visible in different degrees, and the second figure is less clearly realized as we move from Wordsworth to Frost to Stevens. At every step of the way he becomes more strictly a creature of figuration. Indeed, Frost puts his tramps into the title partly to call attention to their absence from the poem, while Stevens reduces the figure to a thing heard but never seen, and that in a negative clause: the "human cry" is one of the things that "the cry of leaves" is not.

But to return to the meeting of poet and laborer: the important distinction between them seems to be that the laborer has an immediate result to show for his work—a pile of so much wood, a gathering of so many leeches—whereas the poet has none. The poet may be haunted by what he knows of the waste of powers, his own and those of his brother poets, yet he has a place of work to call his own. The laborer, on the other hand, is at home in no place; he may live in constant fear of adversity, yet somehow his spirit remains untroubled. The special nature of the poet's labor apparently needs to be explained, and even justified: this is what the Poem of Resolution and Independence must do, touched all the while by a suspicion that the making of more poems will depend on its success.

Since the link with "Resolution and Independence" will be clear to many readers of "The Course of a Particular," I will give more sustained attention to "Two Tramps in Mud Time." It may help at first to think of Frost's poem as a kind of riddle. At some level he knew all along that he was occupied with another version of Wordsworth's poem, but part of his "fooling" with the reader was to withhold his definitive clue until the middle of the poem, when many other pieces had fallen into place. It comes in the fourth stanza, with the unexpected appearance of a bluebird:

> A bluebird comes tenderly up to alight
> And turns to the wind to unruffle a plume,
> His song so pitched as not to excite
> A single flower as yet to bloom.[2]

To the question, Why this, in a poem about tramps? the answer is that the bird, along with the topic it introduces, is entirely within its rights by authority of the jay, the magpie, the hare, and the "plashy earth" of the misted sunny moor that occupy the opening stanzas of "Resolution and Independence." It is of the essence of both poems that they should work hard to separate landscape from the scene of labor proper: the pleasures of landscape will belong to the poet alone, and be felt at the intervals of his self-questioning; to the figure who confronts the poet, on the other hand, landscape hardly exists; it thus works its way through the poem as a double counterpoint, always present, but vividly present only to the poet, and much of the time not even to him.

Looking back, one discovers an earlier touch of craft relevant to the allusion. This is the anomalous line—pentameter to vary a tetrameter base, at the end of the third stanza—which makes for the look and feel of the Spenserian stanza one associates with "Resolution and Independence":

> The sun was warm but the wind was chill.
> You know how it is with an April day
> When the sun is out and the wind is still,
> You're one month on in the middle of May.
> But if you so much as dare to speak,
> A cloud comes over the sunlit arch,
> A wind comes off a frozen peak,
> And you're two months back in the middle of March.

The last line, it could be argued, is only a crowded tetrameter, but I would maintain that it is still an alexandrine to the eye, and so far part of the "in and outdoor schooling" Frost's readers are advised to have.

Two further clues are at once subtler and more persuasive. First, the Wordsworthian sentiment of Frost's confession—"That day, giving a loose to my soul, / I spent on the unimportant wood"—with which one connects such moments as the "sweet mood" mentioned in "Nutting," when "The heart luxuriates with indifferent things, / Wasting its kindliness on stocks and stones." And then, the emergence of a second figure from a ground of undifferentiated matter, as from a sedimentary deposit: Frost's two strangers coming "Out of the mud" bring to mind that other stranger whom we first glimpse "As a huge stone is sometimes seen to lie / Couched on the bald top of an eminence," and later, "Like a sea-beast crawled forth."

With these parallels established, one is surprised at a difference that remains. Frost gets through his poem effortlessly, and *without* the tramps. He can do so because in this version of Wordsworth's poem, Frost himself is poet and laborer at once. Imagine now a somewhat modified plot for "Resolution and Independence." Wordsworth looks at the shifting weather, thinks to himself—What a splendid day for a walk!—takes up his staff and sallies out on a leech-gathering expedition, feeling solid as a rock. On his way he meets an old man, the oldest he ever saw, whose life seems to have been lived on the boundaries of misery, and who offers to do the leech-gathering for him. "He wants my job for pay," Wordsworth mutters, and though he admits that this man's claim to the work outweighs his own, he keeps on with it anyway, exhilarated by thoughts of the different virtues of his two adopted vocations, and how they grow richer by being united. This, with the necessary changes, is Frost's story:

> Nothing on either side was said.
> They knew they had but to stay their stay
> And all their logic would fill my head:
> As that I had no right to play
> With what was another man's work for gain.
> My right might be love but theirs was need.
> And where the two exist in twain
> Theirs was the better right—agreed.
>
> But yield who will to their separation,
> My object in living is to unite
> My avocation and my vocation
> As my two eyes make one in sight.

What a peculiar and original story it is, once we hear "Resolution and Independence" as part of the context Frost evokes. Notice, above all, how completely the sentiment has been altered in the parting gesture, from a widening of sympathy brought on by the recognition of human endurance, to what looks like a rejection of sympathy and charity alike. And yet this cannot be the whole story, if only because we cannot make it tally with the swell and uplift of Frost's concluding lines. Frost has an early poem, also about an experience of charity denied, a poem very roughly parallel to "Two Tramps in Mud Time," called "Love and a Question." There a bridegroom on his wedding night finds a stranger at the door, and though willing to give him a dole of bread and a purse, refuses him shelter for the night: the desire aglow in the "bridal house" is too precious for sharing. In that poem too we have the dismissal of the wanderer, and the moralized closing stanza by Frost, but in a situation more congenial to his point of view. "Love and a Question" is a charming poem. "Two Tramps in Mud Time" is not, nor does it mean to be. Its effect is to limit and qualify the humanizing effect of Wordsworth's poem, and in doing so it involves Frost in a curious drama of self-exposure, of a kind that few poets of his cunning would have wished to trace beyond the first hesitant steps.

Still, one may be mystified by the high spirits Frost discovers at the end, and by the triumphal cadence that goes with them:

> Only where love and need are one,
> And the work is play for mortal stakes,
> Is the deed ever really done
> For Heaven and the future's sakes.

I think Frost got this tone from Arnold, who was always among his favorite poets. One poem of Arnold's, "Palladium," he seems to have returned to again and again: the soul to the body is as the Palladium, "high 'mid rock and wood," to the soldiers fighting on the battlefield below; so long as it stands, Troy cannot fall; and, with the soul and body it cannot be wholly otherwise. Frost had this in his ear when he wrote "The Trial by Existence" for *A Boy's Will,* and it was with him again for "Two Tramps in Mud Time." I quote the final stanzas of "Palladium" in which Arnold imagines the earthly battles renewed:

> Then we shall rust in shade, or shine in strife,
> And fluctuate 'twixt blind hopes and blind despairs,
> And fancy that we put forth all our life,
> And never know how with the soul it fares.
>
> Still doth the soul, from its lone fastness high,
> Upon our life a ruling effluence send;
> And when it fails, fight as we will, we die,
> And while it lasts, we cannot wholly end.[3]

This need not have appealed to Frost strictly for the poetry, for there was something else, in the cultural predicament of both men, which made him recognize Arnold as a natural ally. Arnold, to himself, was a spirit wandering between two worlds, between, among other things, the world of romanticism, which he conscientiously but never very cheerfully cast into the outer darkness, and the world of utilitarianism, which he could never love or accept. The result for his poetry was that sense of being embattled but deprived of an aim which makes even the end of "Palladium" sound oddly unhappy, for so happy a conceit. Frost, it seems to me, was attracted to the *soldiering* rhetoric because, though from different historical causes, he had the same sense of being embattled without having an enemy properly in sight. The dimensions of the conflict may be suggested by two facts: that Frost was a product of nineteenth-century New England, and that "Two Tramps in Mud Time" is a poem of the New Deal. In the thirties, Richard Poirier writes,

> Frost began to suspect that the metaphors, including that of *laissez-faire,* which governed his thinking and his poetry were being substantially displaced within the national consciousness by two others. On the one hand, there were metaphors of "wasteland," or apocalyptic disillusion, against which individual resistance was presumably useless; and on the other, the metaphor of "planning," of the New Deal, of provision, which, as Frost saw it, was designed to relieve the individual of responsibility for his own fate.
>
> That was the essential problem, and measured against it Frost's lapses of taste, his occasional paranoiac inaccuracies, and his petty complaints should be treated as inessential.[4]

Without treating "Two Tramps in Mud Time" as a lapse of taste, one may regard it as a striking instance of Frost's predicament. He has to be both poet and laborer to make the point about his independence; he has to begin with Wordsworth's argument, because Wordsworth's is the great poem in English about the poetic consciousness and its sustaining need of sympathy. The comparison with Wordsworth makes Frost seem colder, as all refusal seems colder than indifference, but he will deal with it how he can, for he is determined to write the poem. Poetry and sympathy are just the matters about which Frost wants to tell us something shocking. "My vocation *and* avocation: let others find theirs if they can; the best help I can give is to tell them so."

Certainly the allusion is a remarkable piece of daring, and could only have been risked by a great poet at the height of his self-confidence. It is that; and yet, in almost any reader's first response to the poem, one impression remains fixed: that Frost has not finally earned his eloquence, that his triumph is a little hollow. The impression remains I think because we have never been shown the distance between Frost's vocation and his avocation, and hence between his nature and that of the tramps. When we see Wordsworth and the leech-gatherer together, we learn to our amazement what different beings they are. Frost too wants to make us feel this, so long as we say afterwards, "But he contains the two tramps; they don't contain him." But we do not say this, because the whole poem has been tipped off balance by a touch of bad faith. At the bottom of it, Poirier believes, is a distrust of poetry. I agree but would add: a distrust of being seen to be a poet. The poem lets us see the two tramps, and a man who we know is a poet because he writes poems, this one among them. But Frost-as-poet is not, so to speak, figured into the poem. To have done so would have been to take on the privilege but also the vulnerability of the poet's situation, and the ambivalence that they imply when taken together. It would not have meant going over to Wordsworth's side of the question of sympathy, even if we could be sure just what that means in a poem like "Resolution and Independence."[5] But the stark improbables of the scene with its two figures, the strange out-feeling that passes from poet to laborer, and the "help and stay secure" or stay against confusion which the poet gets in return: these were the things Frost had to confront. His poem had to be much longer than it is, simply to accommodate the full view of the question to which he pledged himself by alluding to Wordsworth. But he escapes by a trick of foreshortening, in the last stanza, of which the tenor is self-sacrifice, and the vehicle sacrifice of others.

By a full view I mean the dialectic to which we feel Wordsworth has committed himself when he writes:

> My whole life I have lived in pleasant thought,
> As if life's business were a summer mood;
> As if all needful things would come unsought
> To genial faith, still rich in genial good;
> But how can He expect that others should
> Build for him, sow for him, and at his call
> Love him, who for himself will take no heed at all?[6]

There Wordsworth steps out of a race humming with labor and purpose, as a special self. After that there was no turning back. Frost, perhaps from an outsize respect for the rhetorical leverage afforded by the style of the ordinary man, never does step forward. Yet he is writing a kind of poem in which this reticence must be fatal. The poet and laborer may indeed be the same person: but we need to see the poet. Frost's reluctance to come to grips with both vocations—a reluctance that really makes us wonder, which is his vocation? which his avocation?—left its stamp on the rousing last stanza. It is a fine enough sort of eloquence that Frost treats us to, a sort that, like Arnold's, can come of an evasion, and cheer us for a while. But it is not quite in earnest. "Two Tramps in Mud Time," could he have gone the whole length and realized the poem that he projected in the shape of an allusion, would have justified Frost's own metaphors of self-reliance more directly than anything else he wrote.

In contrast "The Course of a Particular" may seem to require no supplement at all to assist our understanding.

> Today the leaves cry, hanging on branches swept by wind,
> Yet the nothingness of winter becomes a little less.
> It is still full of icy shades and shapen snow.
>
> The leaves cry . . . One holds off and merely hears the cry.
> It is a busy cry, concerning someone else.
> And though one says that one is part of everything,
>
> There is a conflict, there is a resistance involved;
> And being part is an exertion that declines:
> One feels the life of that which gives life as it is.
>
> The leaves cry. It is not a cry of divine attention,
> Nor the smoke-drift of puffed-out heroes, nor human cry.
> It is the cry of leaves that do not transcend themselves,
>
> In the absence of fantasia, without meaning more
> Than they are in the final finding of the ear, in the thing
> Itself, until, at last, the cry concerns no one at all.

No gloss is needed beyond the assurance that when Stevens writes, "And being part is an exertion that declines," he is making a distant reply to Whitman, whom he had once pictured as the prophet of poetry and life, with his beard of fire, his staff a leaping flame, "singing and chanting the things that are part of him." Besides, so far as the poem refers us to any earlier utterance, it may seem enough to recall another of Stevens's poems, "The Snow Man," and "the misery in the sound of the wind, / In the sound of a few leaves," the words that mark the opening chapter of his lifelong effort to subdue the "Ode to the

West Wind" to the beauty of innuendoes.[7] The snow man must have been cold a long time not to be moved by the pathos of this particular. In "The Course of a Particular" on the contrary, one "holds off and merely hears" the sound: the poet *is* cold, and no longer part of everything; and the exertion once implied by hearing the human appeal in the sound has now declined. One has grown at last severe enough to be unconcerned, to live "in the absence of fantasia."

The poem's immense dignity and power have much to do with the weight it carries in every feature, the deliberation with which it declares by every step of its forward motion that it is the work of a very old man. In what it asserts, however, this poem is as shocking as "Two Tramps in Mud Time," and as firmly antithetical to the "distress" of the Wordsworthian encounter. So I can offer one strong reason for considering "The Course of a Particular" with Wordsworth instead of Shelley in the background. It is, that while Stevens's largest piece of furniture is evidently Shelley's fiction of the leaves, his motive seems to be Wordsworthian. Again, such constituents as will serve have been abstracted from "Resolution and Independence." The poet, as poet, is brought face to face with life, as life, which—like the man half-rock, half-man, on the lonely moor—goes on without him, in a way that is chastening to regard. Stevens tells us that he can no longer be moved by the particular that has been his, the cry; but still, *that it merely is* appears to be a necessary condition for his poetry: it is the sign of a larger endurance that implies endurance for himself.

As an interpretation of Wordsworth "The Course of a Particular" is reductive but far from absurd. We know that Wordsworth, in composing "Resolution and Independence," originally wrote a substantial monologue for the leech-gatherer; in revising, his aim was to reduce this second human figure to the last bareness of mere being; and he told Sara Hutchinson, who could not see the point of the poem, that his concern had never been with anything about the man but, as it were, simply *that* the man: "What is brought forward? 'A lonely place, a Pond,' 'by which an old man *was,* far from all house or home'—not stood, not sat, but *was.*"[8] Stevens's poem contains a line that corresponds perfectly to the reading of Wordsworth sanctioned here by Wordsworth himself: "One feels the life of that which gives life as it is." The title, "The Course of a Particular," I take to mean that the sense of one's own engagement with being has run its course throughout one's life: memories of a thing, and the present consciousness of it, have become a spot of time purged of all inessentials; until at last the thing stands "in the most naked simplicity possible," to adapt another phrase of Wordsworth's from the same letter to Sara Hutchinson.[9] The sound concerns no one at all, and yet it still is, and poetry still gets written. Stevens, it is true, had looked forward to this sense of the life of poetry as early as "The Snow Man." But that was a very programmatic poem, and reads comparatively like a manifesto. By the time he wrote, "One feels the life of that which gives life as it is," Stevens knew that he had grown cold enough, without ever ceasing to think of the particular and its wanderings. His composure had become a full fact.

But does not Stevens in his own way suppress one element of his work as a revisionist? The suppression is of course less imposing than Frost's, it has no broad consequences for the shape of the poem, we are made to feel throughout that Stevens has spent a long time working at poetry. Nevertheless there is something—a deflection, a refinement—which by softening the harsher contrasts of the Wordsworth plot, prevents us from seeing clearly what Stevens has done with it, and so works out as irony. I am thinking of the phrase, "One holds off and merely hears the cry." Now, in common speech, one usually holds off from something one will come back to: "No, I want to hold off the parties until I get to know that crowd better." But Stevens does not have it in mind ever to come back to the cry, except as it echoes in the ear. Once gone, it is gone forever. This is in fact an extreme instance of litotes, close in spirit to the withheld denouements which had been proved on the pulses of Stevens's generation by its leading writer of prose: "Well, you better not think about it."[10] Its value for the poem is to make us worry less scrupulously about the closure of all relations effected by Stevens's detachment. We cease to be troubled by it, for it seems in this light a familiar and honorable sort of patience, born of its share of sympathy and of suffering. The poem can imply all this while saying only, with complete honesty, "I have heard the cry; it ran its course; I need it no more." The understatement thus becomes an apology because we are meant to reflect on Stevens's career, and to remember how often, long after "The Snow Man," he had charted the particular's bearings: in "Sad Strains of a Gay Waltz," and "Mozart, 1935" ("The snow is falling / And the streets are full of cries"); in "Like Decorations in a Nigger Cemetery," the coda to "Notes toward a Supreme Fiction," and "Esthétique du Mal" ("Pain is human. . . . This is a part of the sublime / From which we shrink"). My impression is that the earlier poems or passages are far steadier in tone than the later ones. Stevens would have had reasons of craft as well as temperament for telling us in an ambiguous phrase that his holding-off would be extended indefinitely.

Some differences of concern that separate Frost and Stevens in much of their work ought to emerge from comparing the stances they adopt to "Resolution and Independence." What both try is to internalize the Wordsworthian encounter with the second figure. Frost all but eliminates the figure in favor of the poet, and at the same time he eliminates the pathos of the poetic vocation itself. This last is the only thing Stevens finds interesting, but he has the advantage that it is the only thing he pretends to find interesting. "Resolution and Independence" addresses itself to the continuity of poetry for the poet, and the justification of poetry to the world. Of those concerns Stevens has to do mainly with the first, the question of continuity, and Frost mainly with the second, the question of justification: the division is writ large throughout their careers. And yet, Wordsworth's comprehensiveness in this respect goes a very small way toward explaining the stature of "Resolution and Independence." He schools our admiration for the poem not only by his movement from one concern to the other, but equally by the way he discloses himself in the process of movement:

> The old Man still stood talking by my side;
> But now his voice to me was like a stream
> Scarce heard; nor word from word could I divide;
> And the whole body of the Man did seem
> Like one whom I had met with in a dream;
> Or like a man from some far region sent,
> To give me human strength, by apt admonishment.

The poem moves from justification to continuity, and Wordsworth displaces the leech-gatherer's admonishment with his own "killing thoughts." The familiarity of the stream-as-eloquence topic makes the work of the transition almost inaudible. Yet Wordsworth marks for us each distinct moment of the fade-out and usurpation. In the first line the leech-gatherer is wholly present; in the second he is absorbed into the metonymy of voice; from this follows the metaphor of the stream; and finally the vision. It is here that the comparison with Frost and Stevens becomes most telling. For Frost allows his tramps to lapse from the poem unaccountably. And Stevens begins "The Course of a

Particular" at a point near the end of the fade-out: what he hears is only voice, unembodied; and to judge by this poem, one would say that in the past it had concerned him only as *materia poetica.*

Yet elsewhere in his poetry Stevens allows for a more generous response. In "Notes toward a Supreme Fiction," for example, he uses "image" in a sense entirely consistent with Wordsworth's decision to retain the leech-gatherer as a distinct presence: "the difficultest rigor is forthwith, / On the image of what we see, to catch from that / Irrational moment its unreasoning." About the sort of figure that this effort preserves he says, "These are not things transformed. / Yet we are shaken by them as if they were." So too has the leech-gatherer remained untransformed, to repeat his answer when Wordsworth renews his question. Repetition is here the brute circumstance that discloses all the intractability of being. The leech-gatherer is *there.* Only later, as an after-image, when Wordsworth imagines him in his mind's eye still wandering about the lonely moor, does he begin to be transformed by the mind.[11] But this final movement of Wordsworth's imagination gives no more promise of a self-sufficient triumph than does the hope he confides to Dorothy at the end of "Tintern Abbey," that he may read his former pleasures in the shooting lights of her eyes. It is an uneasy compensation, and he risks turning the leech-gatherer, like Dorothy, into a machine that can be dismissed once it has served its purpose. Since he knows the risk, "there is a struggle, there is a resistance involved," a scruple about his actual relation to the leech-gatherer, and about the cost of making him only a thing of the mind's eye. He neither has nor cares to have the pride that Frost and Stevens exhibit in overcoming that resistance.

Now and then in these pages I have used the word "sympathy," always with some hesitation. I am aware how far the criticism of Wordsworth in our time has been associated with a rejection of Arnoldian ideas about him, and with this rejection I agree wholeheartedly. Wordsworth does not seem to me the poet "Of joy in widest commonalty spread." Nor do I believe that it was a joy of communion which passed between Wordsworth and the leech-gatherer, in either direction. Sympathy may therefore be a misleading word for what I mean; "acknowledgment" or "recognition" might be better. But I have stayed with it because its very etymology includes what is central to my argument: a feeling that touches some second figure, and that could not come into being without it. Granted Wordsworth puts such figures to a use which even a liberalism more modest than Arnold's can never endorse. A comment like A. D. Nuttall's on "The Old Cumberland Beggar" suggests in addition that the poems in which he does so are more closely related to "Resolution and Independence" than one cares to remember:

> There is a moralising argument and I had better confess at once that I find it repellent. It turns on an inversion of the normal order of ethical discourse. Instead of saying that charity is good because it relieves distress, Wordsworth is virtually saying that distress is good because it provides stimulus and scope for charity. Thus a sort of meta-ethical realm is introduced. It is important that men should be happy, but it is far more important that charity should *exist*.[12]

But this takes less from the humanity of the poem than it may seem to do. Wordsworth, even on this view, still keeps the beggar wandering, in the belief that he may some day encounter him again. A search of all Stevens's poetry will produce no such figure. One may, on the other hand, find something resembling him in Frost, but never in a poem where the poet also appears as himself. The great difference between Wordsworth and his modern successors, I have begun to think, lies not so much in "the love of man" as in his simple copresence with another figure, radically unassimilable to himself, and the troubling possibilities that this brings. The egotistical sublime could reach its height when it existed in tension with such possibilities.

13

Some Uses of Biography

OFFICIALLY, CRITICISM HAS NOTHING against biography. Critics sometimes read biographies, and sometimes use them. Yet a prudential concern for boundaries is part of the strength of any discipline, and there is usually a certain pride in the disclaimer that says, "I won't be dealing with biography." Nobody who says this, in fact, can be as sure as he sounds, for a biographical assumption may be implicit in the most abstract critical remark: whether or not we deal with biography, biography may be dealing with us.

The reason critics like to sound assured anyway has to do with a paradox in the history of modern critical theory. The New Critics disdained any inquiry into an author's motives, or weighing of his intentions, as an aid in the interpretation of a work. This followed naturally from their conviction that a text carried in itself everything one needed to interpret it; like all tenable intellectual positions, the New Critical idea of the text was a prejudice well fortified by arguments. The prejudice is no longer widely held, and the arguments are no longer credited by those who can remember them. Today, however, as securely as ever, critics stay clear of the lives of authors. Our habits have outlasted our beliefs.

I want to argue here for a mingling of biography and criticism which follows naturally from a conviction many critics now hold, that nothing in a text or related to a text is intrinsically more significant for interpretation than anything else. On this view the aim of criticism is not truth but persuasion. We select an image, a trope, a gesture, an action apparently self-contained; we explain it by as many reductions, analogies, and revealing anecdotes as the subject will permit and our audience allow; and the result we call an interpretation. Our knowledge of texts thus resembles our knowledge of persons in relying on the same tacit sense of what can properly be said. *You must read more,* or *You must get to know him better,* mark the point at which a discussion of either subject may come to rest. So I know when Stevens writes "oceans in obsidian," he writes it in wonder rather than horror; I know when my neighbor winks, he is not leering but wants help with his shyness. Someone who asks how these impressions can be verified is looking for clues, of a predictable and occasional kind, which texts and people are only equipped to supply arbitrarily and all the time. Any observation we make gains something of its power from our sense of other observations we could have made. It is for this reason that good critics seem to have been in conversation with the author they discuss—seem to know instinctively what he would say or do in any counterfactual situation. When one reads a book like *Milton's God,* criticism seems an effortless reward of biography.

The case for a mutual acknowledgment between these two sorts of writing is even plainer than such illustrations can suggest. Biographies, after all, define the range of plausible interpretations of an author. They do so no matter how thoroughly we try to prevent them, because we read biographies as instructive stories, and cannot help connecting them with the stories we tell about texts. I will be considering three ways this influence has commonly worked, in separate instances: by establishing a consensus about an author's relation to his work, so complete that we are hardly aware of it; by radically altering our picture of an author, and confirming the reputation of his work on a different basis; and by construing an author's work as a transparent apology for his life, with the result that our esteem for the work is diminished and our interest in the life sharpened. This is what happens when we think about lives that have issued in works: none of these instances seems to me especially regrettable, or for that matter especially fortunate. One might sum up the problem unpleasantly by saying that however scrupulous we may be, somehow biography gets in the back door. But we need not regard it as a problem. Instead, that is, of obtaining more sensitive burglar alarms, we can open the front door.

By the last two academic generations, both John Keats and James Joyce have been received as culture-heroes. The term implies a larger and more personal feeling than we grant to others who impress us as "men of very superior make" (to adapt a phrase of A. H. Hallam's). A generous verdict by posterity, to correct the dismissal of contemporaries, is required for such men to emerge as heroes; and by sharing in that verdict, the reader who is called upon to bear witness may come to feel that his admiration too is heroic. W. J. Bate's *John Keats* and Richard Ellmann's *James Joyce* did most to create this sense of the lives of these authors. The books are literary accomplishments of a high order: they tell fascinating stories, at length and without tedium.[1] But it is curious to see how like each other they make Keats and Joyce appear. At a certain distance from the books, one may also reflect that any two authors grow remarkably alike, once the accommodations have been made to fit them for this role.

Keats on the face of it seems an unlikely choice. He died a very young man, with a small body of work to his name. He was a radical in politics and a sensationalist in literature, known and despised by most of the better-known critics of his time, and appreciated by a few others like Hunt and Shelley. Even by them he was cultivated as a special taste. Joyce, on the other hand, cherished from adolescence an avant-garde hatred of the reading public, and the chance of widespread interest in him during his lifetime was therefore not even a live option. Where Keats, having just completed *Lamia,* could declare, "I am certain there is that sort of fire in it which must take hold of people in some way. . . . What they want is a sensation of some sort," Joyce throughout his career was faithful to a Flaubertian ideal which set readers at defiance. He proved this by devoting his final years to a dream narrative that could not be read through by his most loyal admirers. Why should Joyce have been presented as an available hero? Why should Keats have been presented as a hero at all?

For Keats, the outlines of a heroic story were sketched a few years before Bate undertook his work, in Lionel Trilling's essay "The Poet as Hero." Trilling described a character strange to the refined culture of the twentieth century, and invigorating because of his strangeness. Keats's search for truth, his manliness, his gusto for ordinary pleasures, all were seen as affording the modern artist an image of a forgotten but still possible self. But this was barely recognizable as the Keats of the 1820s. Then he had seemed notable for an easy freedom which concealed something of both sensualism and refinement. His supporters and detractors agreed about this; they disagreed only about what to make of it. His major work was *Endymion,* a failure (Croker said) though a noble one (Hunt replied), since it aimed to realize an unmoralized life of the imagination. This Keats, if he was praiseworthy, could not be praised as representative: the tendencies to which he gave a voice were frankly marginal. Still another story about Keats seems to have been current among the aesthetes of the 1890s. They read him as an adventurer, who had dared to live "a life of sensations," and had secreted in art the evidence of his best moments. This was also the Keats of Matthew Arnold, who did seek culture-heroes, but sought them elsewhere. The typical poem for the 1890s was the "Ode on Melancholy":

> She dwells with Beauty—Beauty that must die;
>   And Joy, whose hand is ever at his lips
> Bidding adieu; and aching Pleasure nigh,
>   Turning to poison while the bee-mouth sips.

The character imagined by Trilling and Bate, with his assurance and sanity, was meant to displace the altogether different character, morbid, uncertain, and congenial to decadence, for whom these lines serve as a touchstone. The revision has worked so well that the "Ode on Melancholy" now seems a very odd poem to have been written by John Keats. We favor instead the odes "On a Grecian Urn" and "To Autumn," the two *Hyperions,* and, above all, the letters. The modern Keats is, in short, a successful creation, the most recent of a long line. He bears a closer likeness than one could wish to those marble busts on display in the home of Leigh Hunt, which Keats himself came to detest. But in this as in his other traits, he stands for the hopes of the ascetic ideal to which critics and scholars feel their own lives are dedicated. It is an ideal that must be defeated in life, so that it may be restored and delivered into the custody of the future, which alone can make a unifying gesture of appreciation.

That we have a similar picture of Joyce may still be partly due to the enthusiasm of his first generation of readers. Modernists in the 1930s and 1940s, even if they were academic, felt themselves to be members of the avant-garde, and with some justice. So they launched the advocacy of Joyce with the zeal as well as the protectiveness such an attitude calls for; to win acceptance for him, they translated his genius into a familiar idiom; and that meant turning Joyce into a humanist. No one I think has ever read *Ulysses* without feeling that its author was greatly gifted with sympathy. But humanism evokes a more general virtue, and a harder one to associate with a man as self-alienated as Joyce was from the whole life of society. Nevertheless, this

has remained our only credible version of Joyce: the modernist trick-
ster and sage, who shares a name with Joyce in the writings of Hugh
Kenner, comes from a view of intellectual history so foreshortened that
only specialists can care for him. The details of Ellmann's biography
do not, however, give a sufficient clue to the success of its portrait; the
hero is there in the commentary, but not in the anecdotes, the correspondence, the drafts of poems and stories. Nor are the circumstances
of Joyce's first reception quite a sufficient clue. Something apart from
the life, and beyond the veneration felt for particular works, was
needed to bring forth the figure we admire.

I believe that part of the atmosphere of Joyce's heroism belongs to
another life from a different period. For the Joyce of the twentieth
century is closely based on the Milton of the eighteenth; the extent of
the analogy may be suggested by the passage at the close of Johnson's
Life of Milton:

> From his contemporaries he neither courted nor received support; there
> is in his writings nothing by which the pride of other authors might be
> gratified, or favour gained; no exchange of praise or solicitation of sup-
> port. His great works were performed under discountenance, and in
> blindness, but difficulties vanished at his touch; he was born for what-
> ever is arduous; and his work is not the greatest of heroic poems, only
> because it is not the first.[2]

That is what Ellmann, or any of us if we could write as well as Johnson, would willingly say about Joyce. But again, as with Keats, there
was nothing inevitable in our coming to credit this version of the life.

Joyce was a rebel, who at the age of sixteen could tell his parents,
after they had seen a performance of Sudermann's *Magda:* "The subject
of the play is genius breaking out in the home and against the home.
You needn't have gone to see it. It's going to happen in your own
house." It is true that Milton's rebelliousness, like Joyce's, made him
write often as a satirist; but his most unappeasable savagery was spent
only in propaganda, in the service of a political movement he never
deserted; whereas Joyce's seems to have been a large tributary of his
genius, in the great works themselves. Indeed, it could be argued
plausibly, on the basis of his life and works together, that we ought to
read Joyce as a grave but esoteric satirist and scholastic crank, in the
tradition of Swift, and more specifically the Swift of *A Tale of a Tub.*
Johnson again, in the *Life of Swift,* gives a strong impression of the

character I have in mind, and suggests its compatibility with much that we know about Joyce.

> He is querulous and fastidious, arrogant and malignant; he scarcely speaks of himself but with indignant lamentations, or of others but with insolent superiority when he is gay, and with angry contempt when he is gloomy. . . . The greatest difficulty that occurs in analysing his character, is to discover by what depravity of intellect he took delight in revolving ideas from which almost every other mind shrinks with disgust.[3]

With a milder emphasis the same question might be asked about Joyce. Though Ellmann nowhere attempts an answer, his awareness of the difficulty may account for the defensive tone of his apology for Leopold Bloom: "Unimpressive as Bloom may seem in so many ways, unworthy to catch marlin or countesses with Hemingway's characters, or to sop up guilt with Faulkner's, or to sit on committees with C. P. Snow's, Bloom is a humble vessel elected to bear and transmit unimpeached the best qualities of the mind."[4] The subtext for this sentence is, "Let me now say something about Bloom which I am wary of saying about Joyce." The effect is to condemn as probably philistine those who do shrink with disgust either from the author or from his hero.

Yet the judgment pays a high cost for its eloquence. To the reader who knows Hemingway and Faulkner, these summaries of their works are vulgar; and indeed, the summary of Bloom himself is false: one invention of *Ulysses* is that we discover more in Bloom's mind than he can possibly know—"vessel" and "transmit" have to be craftily qualified before we can take them as good advice about how to read the book. Bate, it may be noted in contrast, is always more tactful than this. But his biography too celebrates a man who can transmit unimpeached the best qualities of the mind. "We own the soft impeachment," was the cry of early admirers of Keats, "and love him the better for it." To make an appeal to a less indulgent public, Bate's hero has been almost cleared of his sex; much erudition is devoted to the proof that he could not have been with Mrs. Isabella Jones on a certain night in 1818. My point in looking at casual moves like these is to show that the successful biographies of an age have as much in common as their biographers rather than as little as their heroes.

An image of the artist who struggles nobly, in solitude, on behalf of his civilization: this is what we have come to trust, and our routine judgments help to sustain it. We classify *Ulysses* as an epic, beside Homer, Virgil, and Milton; we rate the letter on Negative Capability above "The Eve of St. Agnes." The code-words employed by early opponents of both writers ("cockney" and "uncouth" for Keats, "atheist" and"obscene" for Joyce) name qualities we can still feel in their work, but to describe these at all we have had to invent a new code-word of our own, "embarrassment." A modern critic who found Keats and Joyce interesting because they transmit something other than the best qualities of the mind would not be expelled from professional societies. He would simply be seen as entering a discussion that does not exist. Of this situation the immediate cause is that criticism has established a certain way of thinking. But a more remote and more powerful cause is that biography has made certain facts unthinkable.

Between 1966 and 1976 Lawrance Thompson published a three-volume life of Robert Frost, the last volume having been completed after Thompson's death by a collaborator, R. H. Winnick.[5] It seems to be generally agreed that this biography is foursquare in its documentary chronicle of selfishness and conniving; but it is sometimes added by friends or acquaintances of the poet that his biographer wrote from a sinister bias. Thompson had motive enough for doing so: a book, contracted for when Frost was in his sixties, had to be deferred indefinitely as Frost survived into his nineties, supplying with each passing year fresh reminders of the unpleasantness of the task. Nobody, however, has shown the work to be inaccurate, and the complaint that it tries too resolutely to unmask its hero betrays a misunderstanding of the nature of biography. Unmasking is a theatrical gesture at home in any moral narrative. And in Frost's case the mask had been imposing: he managed effectively through a long life to present himself as a good-natured teacher of the ways of the heart. By exposing him as an extreme instance of self-reliance in practice, Thompson changed all this. He accomplished what biographers of superior subtlety have often felt restrained from attempting, and what can only be tried with a large subject and unpublished documents. Because of Thompson we now read Frost in a different light, as a writer of a dangerous strength—the way Randall Jarrell's essays had proposed he might be read, though Jarrell lacked a view of Frost's personality to confirm his intuitions. Among the things that have altered as a result are the poems we select for emphasis: "Directive" and "The Trial by Existence," for example, have begun to count more seriously than

"Birches" and "Mending Wall." We may in consequence allow Frost's poems more value than we did before; we certainly describe them in a less hackneyed style: the poet who cheered old readers and bored young ones for decades has ceased to exist outside Louis Untermeyer's anthologies.

Thus, from whatever bias and with whatever degree of crudeness, Thompson gave a more convincing picture of Frost than any that had preceded him, and prepared the way for a criticism more sensitive than he himself was competent to give. Writing several years after the appearance of Thompson's first two volumes, Richard Poirier could interpret "Provide, Provide" as a personal dissent from the literary consensus of the 1930s, which otherwise favored the New Deal. The biography had shown the connection between this poem and Frost's disdain for the organizers of a 1935 strike by the charwomen of Harvard University. I have already sketched these circumstances in Chapters 7 and 12. But Poirier also mentioned a related incident, when, at a poetry reading with Henry Wallace in the audience, Frost summed up the moral of his poem, "Provide! Provide!—or somebody else'll provide for ya!" In this light its shocking last stanza appeared not as an ironic condemnation of the Protestant spirit of commerce, but a piece of advice Frost was urging directly on his readers, from the depth of his own experience. The analysis seems to me persuasive; and Poirier is within his rights in hating Thompson.[6] But without the biography somewhere reliably in the background, he would have had to write a separate book to explain the quality of concern he brought to his reading of Frost.

In the biographies of Keats and Joyce, we were offered an ideal from which many of the gratingly individual features had been trimmed away. Here, on the other hand, we have a full and individual portrait, but one which the biographer himself, who grew up believing a more conventional story about his hero, is unable to put into relation with the poems he must discuss. The result is the division of labor I have illustrated, between biographer and critic. Some such division seems to be characteristic of literary studies wherever the story we believe concerning a life has become strangely individual all at once. The biographer, in cases like this, is unable to imagine how the person whose image he has changed could have written the works he once loved with a simple trust. His reaction is to stare at the works blankly, or rather to look away from them as if they were written by someone else—while the critic who also knows the life, and who can hold two opposed ideas together in his mind, prefers to deal with biographical matters lightly or in passing. We preserve this division even though we have rejected the metaphor that licensed "intrinsic" readings, according to which the poem itself was profound, organized, internal, and the poem's circumstances shallow, unorganized, external. With the metaphor out of the way, unidealizing critics might be expected to become biographers. Their reluctance to do so may owe something to the superstition that narrative writing demands an entirely different sort of talent; it owes more to a natural recalcitrance about ever giving up the intellectual prestige of criticism as a discipline.

I turn now to a case in which a biographer has chosen to exhibit a poet's life in some detail, in the belief that it matters to the poems; found himself baffled by the chronicle that emerged, which spoils his love of both; and ended by reasserting a value for the artist as representative victim, even where life and work confront each other in a stalemate. Ian Hamilton's *Robert Lowell* appeared in 1982, and was reviewed with cautious praise.[7] As the leading English publicist of modern poetry, the successor to A. Alvarez in the late 1960s and early 1970s, Hamilton is equipped to write well about schools and personalities. He does not know quite enough about American poetry to write confidently about an American. Elizabeth Bishop he treats as an interesting secondary figure; his praise of Lowell's early Boston poems as *sui generis* shows that he has not heard of John Brooks Wheelwright; about Allen Tate he knows the pertinent facts but in a sense misses the point. Tate may almost be said to have created Lowell. He gave him not only advice, friendship, and an idea of modernity, but a complete set of mannerisms to study, down to the very inflections of the Agrarian-Eliotic accent which Lowell picked up early and never wore out. Still, this is essentially a Victorian-style Life and Letters, with many of the strengths of its kind, including some excellent letters in the first half. The perplexities it leaves us with belong to the more general puzzle about biography and criticism.

Confessional poetry, because it aims for a flat representation of crisis-moments, has to build a transparent wall between the fictions it employs and the actual persons behind them. In this way it commits itself to a biographical reduction almost before the biographer arrives on the scene; any change in our understanding of the poet will affect our judgment of the poem along predictable lines. A more particular difficulty with Lowell is that he sacrificed his life to his art as much as anyone ever; yet his art has a provisional cast that solicits justification from his life. Hamilton realizes exactly what is at stake and is judicious in his efforts to explain. But I suspect the obstacles are too great to be overcome by any critic who begins by placing value chiefly in the poems. In the nature of Lowell's enterprise, the reader is always going to know too little, and the biographer too much. The only solution, it would seem, is to stop treating a defense of the poems as the main reason for writing a life of the poet. Yet Hamilton, who solves many greater enigmas, is defeated by this simple one. He constantly assumes that when he expounds the genesis of a poem he is vindicating its procedure.

His analysis is largely, almost overwhelmingly, clinical. "'Making sense'" of one of Lowell's poems requires "fitting the poem to what was happening, or had just happened, in Lowell's life." With a more coherent personality than Lowell's, the word *sense* would hardly call for inverted commas; they are used here because Hamilton feels over-informed by comparison with the reader, and at the same time uncertain about how to share the information: so much of Lowell's obscurity comes from gossip or stray associations or the data of psychosis that "making sense" means decoding. Thus, Hamilton discovers that Lowell wove into the texture of "The Mills of the Kavanaughs" some borrowed details from the "intense communications [he was receiving] from his sick, abandoned wife." By juxtaposing these letters with the poem, he gives a more intelligible account of its narrative than any critic before him. "Lowell," he writes, "was not just using poetry in order to recapture the flavor of marital quarrels. He seems genuinely to have been trying to fathom how *he* seemed to his women—to know this, and to judge it. And—being Lowell—to judge it without mercy. The paradox is that although he needed to do this in poetry he could hardly bear to do it in public."[8] Let us note that *public* is a new euphemism for *life*. But if, in fact, Lowell did this in his poetry, there would be no paradox. In "The Mills of the Kavanaughs," however, the judgment is never made, with mercy or without it. As we read the poem we feel acutely Lowell's effort to "fathom how he seemed"; it took the sifting of a biographer to recover both his motive and his emotion. In effect, Hamilton tells us he is reading the poem as successful self-therapy, and the next moment announces that this is the same thing as appreciation.

Of the autobiographical method which Lowell brought to refinement in *Life Studies,* Tate wrote to him:

> By and large, and in the total effect, the poems are composed of un-
> assimilated details, terribly intimate, and coldly noted, which might
> have been transferred from the notes from your autobiography without
> change. . . . Quite bluntly, these details, presented in *causerie* and at
> random, are of interest only to you. They are, of course, of great interest
> to me, because I am one of your oldest friends. But they have no public
> or literary interest.[9]

From the careful poems of the mid-1950s to the careless ones of the
late 1960s, Lowell's method changed in two ways. He revised much
less—or published a draft, and published the revision later. And he
began to incorporate more openly than before the materials of his own
life that seemed unimprovable by invention. This last practice he reduced to a routine of quotation (no sooner lived than written down),
when he published in *The Dolphin* whole stretches of letters written by
his second wife, sometimes altered but no less exposed for that. In the
envoi to the book, Lowell spoke of having

> plotted perhaps too freely with my life,
> not avoiding injury to others,
> not avoiding injury to myself—
> to ask compassion . . . this book, half fiction,
> an eelnet made by man for the eel fighting—
>
> my eyes have seen what my hand did.

Notwithstanding the appearance of a rigorous self-inquest, the third
line sounds like a plea for compassion, and it was doubtless a canny
awareness of the effect that made Lowell balance it with the final line
in his "judging" mood. But there is a moral idiocy in the very idea of
plotting with one's life; and to this Adrienne Rich objected memorably
in a review of the book: "It is presumptuous to balance injury done to
others with injury done to myself . . . [and] the question remains,
after all—to what purpose?" Long before that judgment was in print,
Lowell had been warned by Elizabeth Bishop about the "infinite mis-
chief" of mixing fact with fiction in unknown proportions; her patient
and generous letter contained a single sentence in italics: "*Art just isn't
worth that much.*" It is one clue to Lowell's character, as a poet and as a
man, that he never could understand the force of protests like these.

What did his madness consist of? He himself called it mania, and
at other times enthusiasm. It led him to become "a fire-breathing
Catholic C.O." during the war against Hitler, after several unavailing
attempts to enlist in the armed forces. In 1949, it stimulated him to

campaign furiously for the dismissal of Elizabeth Ames as director of the writers' colony at Yaddo, from an intuition that she was controlled by "sinister forces," that is, by Communists. These were moments of enthusiasm. Yet by association they call into question what had seemed Lowell's most dignified public moment, his refusal to attend President Johnson's White House Festival of the Arts, at the time of our first bombings of Vietnam. As for the mania itself, it went far beyond what is loosely called hypomanic, and by the late 1950s was forcing Lowell to be placed in confinement about once a year. "A violent man," is the phrase repeated by many of Hamilton's witnesses; and the madness was what brought out all his lurking fascination with power. This too, of course, had been manifest since his childhood; it gave him the nickname "Cal," for Caligula. To the end of his life, the infallible sign of a breakdown was his insistence on reading aloud, with more than usual gusto, his favorite passages from *Mein Kampf.*

If genius is an unbroken series of successful gestures, Lowell was never within reach of being a man of genius. But to say so feels wrong; and we get into this sort of trouble because aesthetic and moral thought, working apart from each other, have made us define people more narrowly in theory than we do in our common judgments. Lowell could appear to friends, and to the public at large, in the shape of any of three mutually exclusive selves: (1) the ambassador of culture, "in my Plutarchan bubble," lofty and aloof; (2) the craftsman who had meditated long on art and made it live for others, holding a continuous dialogue with the great dead; (3) the maniac. A curious feature of Lowell's fame is that many persons knew him only as (1) or only as (2); and, knowing each one respectively, were convinced it told the whole story apart from the inaccessible (3). Shortly after reading Hamilton's book, I saw an ITV-London television documentary on Lowell's career. Some important witnesses were absent, but among those interviewed it was plain that Frank Parker, one of Lowell's earliest and closest friends, still remembered and honored (2); while A. Alvarez, a later and less intimate literary friend and ally, considered (1) sufficient for an understanding of this poet. The advantage of Hamilton's book is that he is the first spectator with enough of the life before him to illustrate the strength of all three.

(2) may after all be the Lowell most worth retrieving. Such characters exist as conspicuous energies: they communicate a possibility of feeling, and can seem to enlarge the world. Works may be subordinate to the ends of such a life—they were, with few exceptions, for By-

ron—but even where the works are unread, much can survive without them. In the second decade of the nineteenth century, everybody read *Childe Harold;* by the second decade of the twentieth, everybody had stopped; and yet, somehow we still manage to talk about Byron. It seems to me that Tate may have been right for posterity, though out of step with his contemporaries, when he said Lowell's autobiographical poems had no literary interest. Elsewhere, on occasion, Lowell wrote so powerfully that it is hard to imagine future readers not caring for some poems—"The Drunken Fisherman," "Falling Asleep over the Aeneid," "Skunk Hour," "For the Union Dead," and a few others. But the winnowing here is likely to be pretty thorough. With Hamilton's biography we stand at the beginning of a change of emphasis, as with Thompson's life of Frost; but the literary achievement is less secure in this instance; and for the time being, a persuasive image of a great writer, on the order of Bate's or Ellmann's, does not seem anywhere near ready to emerge.

All this I believe Hamilton saw. Unfortunately he appears to have been frightened by the prospect. In his concluding sentences he is obliged, therefore, to pretend he has written a book he has not written.

> Christopher Ricks quotes words that I myself was privileged to read out at Lowell's memorial evening in New York on September 25, 1977. On Lowell's death, Ricks says, "there came to me the words of Empson on King Lear":
>> The scapegoat who has collected all this wisdom for us is viewed at the end with a sort of hushed envy, not I think really because he has become wise but because the general human desire for experience has been so glutted in him; he has been through everything.
>> We that are young
Shall never see so much, nor live so long. [10]

So he denies the possibility that Lowell might appeal to us as anything other than a great man and heroic artist who endured the worst for the sake of all of us. One cannot help noticing how many times this sentiment had to be mediated before it could reach us from a safe distance: Hamilton on Lowell quotes Ricks quoting Empson on Lear. Even at so many removes, it is wrong for Lowell. Or rather, false to this story about him. In reflecting on Hamilton's book for the past few months, I have tried to account for the consistently depressing effect of reading it from start to finish. Had we been given occasions for sympathy and praise, or for anger and indignation, as we are in *King Lear,* the result would have been different. A picture of conscious suffering, of passion, of experience, is just what the book refuses to yield. Its failure is largely due to Hamilton's determination to write the story of a maker of poems, his disappointment at having found that the story was not there to be told, and his fear that no other story would justify the enterprise to Lowell's readers.

Johnson knew that we care about the lives of artists for any number of reasons, only some of them artistic. And his own practice teaches that the drama of biography and criticism together is the test they offer to our admiration. This seems to me so inescapably the lesson we have to learn from him, in the *Lives* of Milton, Pope, and Swift above all, that I will end with quotations rather than analysis.

> No sooner is [Milton] safe, than he finds himself in danger, *fallen on evil days and evil tongues, and with darkness and with danger compassed round.* . . . Of *evil tongues* for Milton to complain required impudence at least equal to his other *powers;* Milton, whose warmest advocates must allow, that he never spared any asperity of reproach or brutality of insolence.

Of course, Milton's poems bear no provocative relation to his private life. But many of Pope's do. *The Dunciad* was aimed at the reputations of actual persons: when Johnson read it he felt that his task was partly biographical; and for him the tone of apocalyptic satire did not sort well with the victories over rivals which belonged equally to the scheme of the poem.

> Aaron Hill, who was represented as diving for the prize, expostulated with Pope in a manner so much superior to all mean solicitation, that Pope was reduced to sneak and shuffle, sometimes to deny, and sometimes to apologize; he first endeavours to wound, and is then afraid to own that he meant a blow.

But Johnson moves not only, as here, from the work to the life, but almost as often from a trait of the life to a quality of the work:

> To his domestics [Swift] was naturally rough: and a man of a rigorous temper, with that vigilance of minute attention which his works discover, must have been a master that few could bear. That he was disposed to do his servants good, on important occasions, is no great mitigation: benefaction can be but rare, and tyrannic peevishness is perpetual.[11]

Nor does this rob Swift of his well-earned reputation for charity. What it may do is qualify our view of Swift's own view of his humility: "He never thought an Honour done him, / Because a Duke was proud to own him: / Would rather slip aside, and chuse / To talk with Wits in dirty Shoes." Yes, replies Johnson, but the thanks he received from those wits would have been dearly bought. From the perspective of a close reader or textualist, the most unexpected turn in Johnson's remark is the simple phrase, *which his works discover.*

My only practical suggestion, as I hope has been apparent, is that modern critics ought to follow the implications of their skeptical beliefs, and confuse as much as possible the boundaries between criticism and biography. I am not urging a return to Johnson's way of presenting moral judgments. But the reason trying to copy him would be impractical is not that criticism will no longer tolerate our holding an artist answerable for matters beyond his art. It is rather that our morality is less distinct to us than Johnson's was to him: we do not even know what it would feel like to reach conclusions like his about a modern poet. Other judgments come to us more easily—the sort that we make of the people we meet, or that novelists make of the characters they represent—and only institutional habits prevent us from bringing these into criticism. With respect to the old biographical restrictions, we are like people who have lost a superstition and still cling to its observances, knowing that their power is an illusion, but hopeful that a protective magic will continue to guard us so long as we do not surrender them altogether.

14

Why Authors Do Not Create Their Own Worlds

MY SUBJECT IN THIS CHAPTER is a particular habit of thinking about works of art, a habit best captured in phrases like "Every author gives us his own world," or "We read novels because they give us their own world." Many scholars have echoed the sentiment of such phrases, at some time or other, especially when trying to justify the teaching of literature. But I think as a serious account of art the habit is dying out; and I hope to do a small part here to kill it off more quickly. The remarks that follow are not related to the many recent arguments that associate a defense of literature with the reality of possible worlds. Ingenious as such arguments often are, they make no aesthetic claim and have no interest for interpreters. They may vindicate the status of literary conventions, and therefore legitimate them to those who doubt their legitimacy. But people like that are not at home with literature anyway. By contrast, the argument that interests me is used by people who are at home there. They use it to wheedle with likely guests, assuring them, with a glance and a phrase, that the furnishings will be of a very special character.

It is worth asking at the start why the gives-us-its-own-world conceit appears to be peculiarly serviceable in the classroom. And the reason seems to me simple. We resist saying to students that books are imitations of nature, or life, or even a curious substrate of life called reality. At the same time, though we can point to books that have helped to shape our lives, we feel wary about presenting any text as somehow instructive or exemplary, because we know what a silly free-for-all that encourages in discussion. So, sometimes, we end up saying, "The value of a novel (or poem or play or picture) is that it gives you its own world." The brightest students, we may feel, are prepared to concede too much to the world which they call the real world; while we have them, we might as well do what we can to make them feel that its claims do not penetrate everywhere; and we palm off on them this rough-and-ready version of art as heterocosm.

The tactic has some excellent uses. An English journalist who taught in Nigeria told me that he set the following topic to a class of fourteen-year-olds: "Write an essay on the witches in *Macbeth,* trying to imagine what the play would feel like to people who did *not* actually believe in witches." You can see at once how this works. Scotland in the time of Edward the Confessor was in one respect like Nigeria in the early 1960s—the belief in witches was fairly common, so that, as a dramatic assumption, it could be taken for granted. Shakespeare's play was in fact giving these Nigerian students their own world, or something sufficiently like it. They were then invited to trace the consequences for appreciation of looking at the play as it appeared to the English in the early 1960s, who did not hold the appropriate beliefs, were therefore comparatively remote from the world of the play, but nevertheless found reasons for admiring it. One thing the students might learn from this exercise was that works create their own world, and it takes some trouble to enter them. Having deduced as much from the superficially familiar *Macbeth,* they might be in a more tolerant mood for the superficially less familiar *Hamlet.*

But this example is loaded in favor of the work of art giving us its own world. Besides, it is somewhat misleading, in that it makes "awareness of many worlds" imply nothing more than "charitable acts of cultural translation." When used by critics, to justify their interest in a given work, it has an altogether different sound. I do not need to describe the usual tenor of this style of apologetics; it has been done already by P. N. Furbank in *Reflections on the Word "Image."* But let me quote Furbank's polemic at some length. "It is clear," he observes,

> that writers, at present, find it extremely convenient to talk about "worlds". . . . "The impressionists and their world," "the world of that Barrault film *Les Enfants du Paradis,*" "the world of Japanese woodcuts" or "the world of Truman Capote". . . . No-one seems to have much use for these worlds after the moment of their creation. . . . And what they amount to is a deliberate act of laziness. Being unwilling to commit oneself to any noun of definite signification, however vague—even

"spirit" or "ethos" would say too much—one falls back on a word which can be relied on to define nothing whatever and merely appears to draw a circle round the subject. . . . It is a favourite theory of reviewers and literary critics that novelists should create a special fictional "world". . . . Often the theory includes the notion that the world is a novelist's own, a unique one, his particular specialty. . . . The novelist praised in this way is thought to secrete a certain unique colouring, of which he alone has the formula, and to impregnate his fictional "world" with it. . . . Now I will say at once that I think the theory that a novelist should "create his own world" is false. But what I am objecting to is not so much the idea of his creating a world as of its being his own. . . . All the same, when a [critic] says that so-and-so's novel "creates its own world," it is often a genuine reaction. Only he is using the wrong metaphor. What he means is not that the novelist is creating some rival to the real world, but that he is fencing off a part of the real world, with himself inside it, and converting it into a playground where he can erect follies and rearrange Nature as it pleases him. It is very true that some novelists do this; and that is what is wrong with them.[1]

To confirm the truth of these observations, one may recall the titles of three recent, notable, and dissimilar studies of a single author: Humphry House's *The Dickens World,* J. Hillis Miller's *Charles Dickens: The World of his Novels,* and Angus Wilson's *The World of Charles Dickens.*

Indeed, the metaphor of "worlds" is pervasive in academic criticism. Its various presuppositions cover the range from pedagogic aptness to phenomenological completeness—the process, as W. K. Wimsatt put it, "of exposition by shredding or atomization," by which "a fine mist of the mind" of an author may be generated. Of the books named above, only Miller's exemplifies the latter phase of world-realizing. Yet their agreement of emphasis seems to me far from incidental. To suggest the common belief from which they start, I have to quote some familiar sentences—familiar, because we have heard them often elsewhere, if not here—from Maynard Mack's 1952 essay "The World of *Hamlet.*" "Great plays," says Mack, "as we know, do present us with something that can be called a world, a microcosm . . . [though] unlike our own [world] in being perfectly, or almost perfectly, significant and coherent. In a play's world, each part implies the other parts, and each lives, each means, with the life and meaning of the rest."[2] By the end this sounds like a Coleridgean, that is, an idealizing and aesthetic, version of the Renaissance metaphor which figured art as "another nature." But the assurance of Mack's tone, right down to the "as we know," brings us back again to the special situation of a teacher in a classroom.

It is an odd, almost an extravagant, metaphor, to be trusted to explain so much. How did we come to accept it?

The story begins long before Proust, with the symbolist ideas of "correspondence" and "suggestiveness"; more specifically, with the view that any detail of a work may imply the whole in which it participates. Nevertheless I begin with Proust's novel *The Captive* (1923) and its sustained meditation on how the artist makes his own world. The passage has great interest since it shows the metaphor in an early and heroic phase. As it occurs in the story, it also has a kind of personal power which quotations like mine will not convey. To recall the constituents of the scene: the narrator's thoughts are prompted by "a tender phrase, homely and domestic, of the septet" by Vinteuil, at the party Mme Verdurin gives for M. de Charlus. By an association he cannot track, it reminds him of Albertine at home: his only important possession, but one that he is unable to cherish except when he sees her as possibly lost, as something he must return to in order to save. Albertine is the captive of his life, as certain impressions are the captive of his memory. Both have been chosen by an error of the will; and they are linked in his mind by the phrase of Vinteuil. So the association given to the narrator by this composer—the trace of one life printed on another—may be felt to represent a moral about art. It is pledged to the return of things that can be known in experience only as loss.

A further comparison is implied between the contingencies of life and the consolations of art. For an artist's idiosyncrasy (like a character's perversity) makes a signature that cannot be copied: "With other and more profound gifts Vinteuil combined that which few composers, and indeed few painters [such as Elstir] have possessed, of using colours not merely so lasting but so personal that, just as time has been powerless to fade them, so the disciples who imitate him who discovered them, and even the masters who surpass him do not pale their originality." Granted his works are bound to differ greatly from each other:

> And yet these so widely different phrases were composed of the same elements, for just as there was a certain universe, perceptible by us in those fragments scattered here and there, in private houses, in public

galleries, which were Elstir's universe, the universe which he saw, in which he lived, so too the music of Vinteuil extended, note by note, key by key, the unknown colourings of an inestimable, unsuspected universe, made fragmentary by the gaps that occurred between the different occasions of hearing his work performed.[3]

It is, the narrator goes on to say, just at those moments when an artist like Vinteuil questions himself, and tries to renew and change his art, that his essential nature stands revealed: "This song, different from those of other singers, similar to all his own, where had Vinteuil learned, where had he heard it? Each artist seems thus to be the native of an unknown country, which he himself has forgotten, different from that from which will emerge, making for the earth, another great artist."[4] With this last remark Proust announces his faith in the analogy between individual artists and separate worlds.

His analogy is rounded off when the narrator compares the nature of Vinteuil's compositions with that of Elstir's paintings. Till now, the difference between them has been that the narrator shared, as a contemporary of Elstir, the world from which his paintings emerged, whereas Vinteuil's music really did belong to an earlier way of life. Still, their effect is the same:

> The only true voyage of discovery, the only fountain of Eternal Youth, would be not to visit strange lands but to possess other eyes, to behold the universe through the eyes of another, of a hundred others, to behold the hundred universes that each of them beholds, that each of them is; and this we can contrive with an Elstir, with a Vinteuil; with men like these we do really fly from star to star.[5]

This sensation of flight affords an unchallengeable testimony that art "does correspond to some definite spiritual reality," or "is surely symbolical of one." By this, however, the narrator means that the uses of art belong to a self-knowledge that lies *beyond* the bounds of aesthetic competence. Those phrases which accrete, as if by necessity, to the work of a single composer, so that they "are to be found only in his work, and appear constantly in it, where they are the fairies, the dryads, the household gods," have nothing to do with the scenes of aesthetic instruction elsewhere in *A La Recherche du Temps Perdu,* such as those that depict the narrator schooling himself in the craft of the great actress Berma. Rather, they bear the charm of objects sacred to ourselves alone. And in this they resemble "those impressions which at remote intervals I recaptured in my life as starting points, foundation-stones for the construction of a true life."

But one cannot help noticing that genius—like the genie of the *Arabian Nights,* with its "Open Sesame"—works by finding objects of the world itself. Only by making them appear as arbitrarily *ours* does it create *a* world which would otherwise remain unknown. One's movement, in imagination, from the first to the second stage of this process, from selection to transfiguration, is presented as the last reward of a consummated apprenticeship in art, or of a lifelong dedication to connoisseurship. Swann has bequeathed it to the narrator. We are not to imagine the narrator passing it on to a generation of lycée students. For that matter, the one interlude of actual teaching which the novel does give only shows the distance between the narrator, for whom experience and art have separated out in this way, and Albertine, from whom they have not: "This unknown quality of a unique world which no other composer had ever made us see, perhaps it is in this, I said to Albertine, that the most authentic proof of genius consists, even more than in the content of the work itself. 'Even in literature?' Albertine inquired. 'Even in literature.'"[6] *The Captive,* I noted, illustrates a discovery of the metaphor of an artist's world, at a time when that could still evoke a heroic quest for originality. The making, or finding, of an artist's world is here a task which isolates the person who undertakes it. But there remains a vivid sense in which the recovery of Swann's world depends on the narrator, and the recovery of the narrator's world depends on the reader. These links imply a continuity of fate in the world that is common to all of them.

If you were to methodize Proust's invention, the result would sound like this: "The consideration of ulterior ends, whether by the poet in the act of composing or by the reader in the act of experiencing, tends to lower poetic value. It does so because it tends to change the nature of poetry. For its nature is to be not a part, nor yet a copy, of the real world (as we commonly understand that phrase), but to be a world by itself, independent, complete, autonomous."[7] The quotation comes from A. C. Bradley's lecture "Poetry for Poetry's Sake," but I found it in Roger Fry's essay "Some Questions in Esthetics"—written about the time of Proust's novel, and reprinted in 1926, in *Transformations.* It is instructive to see how Bradley works his way to the metaphor by means of an argument against "ulterior ends." To clinch that argument, he did not have to say anything about worlds. All he needed to assert was the propriety of goods that are internal to the practice or experience of an art—as distinct from such external goods as conveying instruction, softening the passions, or furthering a good cause (to stick with Bradley's own examples). Yet his sentences exhibit with unusual clarity the motives by which critics are sometimes led to propose that a work of art is a world by itself.

The uses to which Fry puts the quotation are a different matter entirely. "For poetry," he comments, "in this passage [of Bradley's],"

> we may, I think, substitute the idea of any literature used as pure art. This passage at least suggests to us that the purpose of literature is the creation of structures which have for us the feeling of reality, and that these structures are self-contained, self-sufficing, and not to be valued by their references to what lies outside.[8]

Now Bradley's remarks only related to the criteria by which we were to estimate the formal powers and properties of a work. The comparisons we ought to make, he said, were dictated by something within the work, and by nothing outside it. He did not say, however, that these powers and properties were "self-sufficing," so far as our interest in the work was concerned; or that the work was not to be valued for its relation to anything else in the world, whose ways of naming and believing it partly shared. Of course, we were not to judge art's world-by-itself, morally or practically, with the habits we had learned from the world outside. And we were not to expect the world outside to hang together, or to make sense of itself, as a work of art may do for those who know it well. But that was all Bradley is likely to have meant by his words "independent, complete, autonomous." Fry makes him mean something different, rarer, and harder to defend: that the work of art is wholly unavailable to our ordinary ways of knowing. To judge by the rest of Fry's essay, he needs this special and sequestered understanding of art to make sense of such otherwise improbable entities as "psychological volumes," in which he is on the brink of declaring his credence. For him, the argument about worlds is a necessary step to the claim he will make on behalf of certain phenomena unique to art, and formally significant there, but vacant when judged from any point of view we could adopt in the world.

With Roger Fry, we have almost reached a point where *having a world* becomes the mark of good as opposed to bad art. I want to conclude this survey by looking at passages from two critics, T. S. Eliot and George Orwell, who began writing when some such attitude was already commonplace. Eliot does indeed consider having a world as a sufficient criterion of aesthetic success. He is writing on Kipling in 1919, in the review for the *Athenaeum* that I cited in Chapter 10:

> Swinburne and Mr. Kipling have these and such concepts; some poets, like Shakespeare or Dante or Villon, and some novelists, like Mr. Conrad, have, in contrast to ideas or concepts, points of view, or "worlds"—what are incorrectly called "philosophies." Mr. Conrad is very germane to the question, because he is in many ways the antithesis of Mr. Kipling. He is, for one thing, the antithesis of Empire (as well as of democracy); his characters are the denial of Nation, of Race almost, they are fearfully alone with the Wilderness. Mr. Conrad has no ideas, but he has a point of view, a world; it can hardly be defined, but it pervades his work and is unmistakable. It could not be otherwise. Swinburne's and Mr. Kipling's ideas could be otherwise. Had Mr. Kipling taken Liberty and Swinburne the Empire, the alteration would have been unimportant.[9]

"These and such concepts" is itself a satirical turn of speech, as Eliot hears it: "But this or such was Bleistein's way." If one is familiar with Eliot's personal code, one may feel that the whole argument against Kipling and Swinburne is deducible from that phrase alone. By comparison with the exchangeability of *these and such concepts,* there seems to be something almost palpable about the notion of creating a world.

Even so, one can feel that a romantic prejudice is still at work here: the prejudice against mere ideas, the dead counters of the understanding, which issue only in allegories and abstractions. Against these are arrayed all the richly particular sensations that pervade an artist's *oeuvre* and make his world. But Eliot is uncertain about the metaphor, and he does not present it handily. He has in mind a quality of temperamental consistency, and the vividness that comes of having a point of view; but he implies in passing that he will settle for point-of-view if we prefer it. Anyway, to become Eliot's sort of world-maker, you must commit yourself to (1) a denial of association or solidarity with others, something like the denial of fact and reason in "negative capability"; and (2) a steady portrayal of those who are "fearfully alone," and who therefore represent versions of the modern artist. These are puzzling requirements if one takes them to express a general truth about art. They are less so if one sees them as part of an evolving self-image of modernism, which Eliot was helping to form in just such articles as this. His examples are certainly not credible when looked at in their own right. One might perhaps conceive of Swinburne without Liberty, but only because many specific features of his thought, and not his politics alone, are drowned in the undulations of his rhetoric. That is an effect of the texture of his poems, rather than a consequence of his wrong choice of "concepts" over "a world." With Kipling, the experiment yields an even unhappier outcome. One simply cannot imagine a Kipling who would have been for Liberty and against the Empire. Such a writer would have nothing in common with the expounder of the Law, the Game, and the whole great artifice of human subordination, which exists always and necessarily at the sacrifice of personal liberty.

What Eliot wanted to make plain, I think, was that an artist like Conrad never essentially betrays himself, he cannot be drawn from his task by any gnawing annoyance. Whereas Kipling sometimes does betray himself, and Swinburne sometimes does, and they do it with peculiar facility in their ideas-and-concepts work. To put it like that, however, points no moral at all for aesthetics. It comes to saying that the temperaments of the latter pair are more mixed—more at the mercy of what their public may expect from them—than Conrad's ever could have been. Eliot was looking for a way to declare his affinity with, or maybe his distant admiration of, Conrad's kind of purity: something he would manage elsewhere by his deployment of epigraphs. This should be seen for what it is, namely, a statement of preference and loyalty. It is not a hypothesis that works of art by their nature can prove, much less an axiom against which they can be tested.

In most of Orwell's writing, there is hardly any talk about worlds. Then, suddenly, with "Inside the Whale," there is a great deal of it: from a certain distance, that essay of 1940 appears as a dialogue between "an artist's world" and "conditions in the world." Its occasion, apart from a summing up of the thirties, is a backward look at Henry Miller's novel about "the American Paris" of the twenties. This already involves a specialization of "point of view," since the American Paris was distinct from the Parisian Paris; and what chiefly distinguished it, according to Orwell, was the predominance of artists: "During the boom years, when dollars were plentiful and the exchange value of the franc was low, Paris was invaded by such a swarm of artists, writers, students, dillettanti, sight-seers, debauchees, and plain idlers as the world has probably never seen. In some quarters of the town, the so-called artists must actually have outnumbered the working population—indeed, it has been reckoned that in the late 'twenties there were as many as 30,000 painters in Paris, most of them impostors."[10]

They were all, presumably, carrying about with them their own worlds. But to Orwell they were "hordes of shrieking poseurs" and he says that his initial reaction to Miller was "a refusal to be impressed" by the unprintable words. Nevertheless, he found, both with *Tropic of Cancer* and *Black Spring,* that "the atmosphere of the book . . . seemed to linger in my memory in a peculiar way." We may recall Eliot's curious usage, in which a world, rather than an atmosphere, was said to "pervade" an author's work.

Having started with "atmosphere," Orwell now feels the same need Eliot did to raise the ante slightly:

> Evidently [Miller's] books are of the sort to leave a flavour behind them—books that "create a world of their own," as the saying goes. The books that do this are not necessarily good books, they may be good bad books like *Raffles* or the *Sherlock Holmes* stories, or perverse and morbid books like *Wuthering Heights* or *The House with the Green Shutters.* But now and then there appears a novel which opens up a new world not by revealing what is strange, but by revealing what is familiar.

His leading example is a great, instead of a good-bad book, *Ulysses:* "Here is a whole world of stuff which you supposed to be of its nature incommunicable, and somebody has managed to communicate it. The effect is to break down, at any rate momentarily, the solitude in which the human being lives." [11] Orwell proceeds to identify such books by the sentiment they evoke in the reader: "He wrote this specially for me." That is to say, the solitude is shared. Thus, books like Miller's and, at a greater depth, Joyce's intensify a common sense of the world, and make us feel that something has been noticeably added to it. This, in turn, breaks up the separateness of individual worlds, the sense Eliot had evoked of being fearfully alone. It makes you feel that you "are dealing with the recognizable experiences of human beings."

Why, if his purpose was worldly in this familiar sense, did Orwell choose to speak of worlds in the first place? The answer I believe has to do with the discrete moods of the twenties and thirties. Underlying the essay is a tacit comparison between the aesthetic milieu of Miller's Paris, with its harmless fraudulence, and the political milieu in which Orwell himself was living, with its daily treacheries of party, sect, and person. In this comparison Miller, and his ethic of keeping one's own world, came off rather favorably. Indeed, the whole essay is an ambivalent defense of Miller's quietism, his "completely passive" attitude, the trick of withdrawal that allows his work to appear as all externalities (none of them political). It is in the effort to praise this style of life that Orwell turns to the allegory of Jonah and the whale. There, if anywhere, was an eminent instance of someone inhabiting his own world, but Orwell does not stress this. He is interested rather in the wish to escape from the world: "The historical Jonah, if he can be so-called, was glad enough to escape, but in imagination, in day-dream, countless people have envied him. It is, of course, quite obvious why. The whale's belly is simply a womb big enough for an adult." But this is a *fantastic* existence, and Orwell's admiration for it is equivocal. He means to defend literature against the political claim to a single right view of the world. Miller, he decides, will do as a limiting case, to oppose to the ethic of "Today the struggle." And yet, "there exist 'good' writers whose world-view would in *any* age be recognized as false and silly": Poe, for example, who was "not far from being insane in the literal clinical sense." He does not commend Miller now any more than he would have commended Poe a hundred years before. It is only "symptomatically" that Miller's attitude may be clarifying; for it demonstrates "the *impossibility* of a major literature until the world has shaken itself into its new shape." Notice that Orwell's closing reference is merely to the world. What had looked like a chosen aesthetic premise, very much in line with Fry and Eliot, has turned out to be a terminological vagary, in an analysis of the social history of art. "Inside the Whale" proposes that the creation of a world is the fulfillment of a distinctly minor literature.

My aim in the rest of this chapter will be to continue the work of retraction that Orwell began in 1940.

In class, when the door shuts and the room is sealed tight for discussion, you can easily feel like Jonah. You have entered a middle state, somewhat remote from the world, and the work that goes on there may seem unified from within. This is the state that many students look forward to looking back on, as a time when they knew of other realities. We need a phrase to describe the sensation of living in it, and "the author's own world" is a good candidate. It gives a promise of variety to our conversations, without tempting us into games about the lives of characters outside the story. It does justice to our feeling that there is something cumulative about our knowledge of texts, without warranting a superior dismissal of the innocent remark that sounds right. The author's own world is all there, all available, all together, as, the teacher may imply, ours is not, or as we cannot thoroughly convince ourselves that it is. Our world matters too much for us to suppose that we ought to think about its inward relations to itself; but what luck to be given the chance, twice a week or so, to do this with someone else's world.

Besides, Eliot's remarks on Conrad and Orwell's on Miller, Joyce, and Poe do capture a feeling most readers have shared. In discussing the works of some authors, it seems natural to think of their creations as forming a separate species. To expand the list, we might put Kafka at one extreme, as an author of strange inventions that compel our interest for reasons not plainly connected with our world; and, at the other extreme, Tolstoy, who has impressed critics from Arnold to Leavis as extraordinarily lifelike: as applied to *him,* the defense that he creates his own world would seem beside the point. But what if we complicate the scheme a little? Let us put Jane Austen on the Tolstoy side, as a moderate case of lifelikeness, more mannered than Tolstoy, that is, working with more visible conventions, but still comfortably of our world; and, on the Kafka side, as a moderate case of strangeness, let us put Dickens. Now, if we tried to run through this group, from Tolstoy to Austen to Dickens to Kafka, where would we draw the line and say that *there* the author had begun to give us his or her own world?

It seems to me that if books have mattered to you, then you cannot in fact draw the line at all, because no piece of writing is ever completely strange in the way the author's-world argument requires it to be. Nor does it ever become completely familiar, in the way this argument seems to promise it will do in the long run, when each part implies the others and each lives and means with the life of the rest. Every author who has ever fascinated any reader for any length of time has been read as if his world were ours; read, not with a constant respect for his separate and integral nature as a creator, but with a constant willingness to see that nature dissolve and merge with ours. By Eastern European writers and readers, in the second half of the twentieth century, Kafka's stories are read as representations of the social pathology of everyday life. By American psychoanalytic interpreters, they are read as allegories of narcissism. The moral weight of these interpretations may differ, but the principle of accommodation is the same in both. One reads a story, perhaps as short as this: "As yet the hounds are still playing in the courtyard but their prey will not escape, however fast it may already be charging through the forest." [12] And in reflecting on it one thinks: "It's curious, but that has something to do with our life (though to say how will take some doing)." When we read even Kafka strangely, we do so to find out something strange about the world. This I take to have been Freud's point in his essay on the uncanny: that the uncanny or unhomelike is always canny or homelike somewhere else, and the conditions of that somewhere else always implicate us.

My argument has been derivative. It follows the same line of reasoning that Donald Davidson used to attack the idea of separate and integral conceptual schemes; and the application to worlds was suggested by Richard Rorty's questioning of the Kuhnian notion that scientists in different paradigms actually *see* different worlds. You can get a fair idea of the habits we still have to break from some casual multiple-worldly remarks in Clifford Geertz's "The Way We Think Now," an address to the American Academy of Arts and Sciences first published in 1982, and reprinted in Geertz's *Local Knowledge.* He says there that reflection on "the commensurability of conceptual structures from one discourse community to the next" has led people like Kuhn, Foucault, Nelson Goodman, and himself "more complexly into" what he calls "relativism"; and he sums up the difficulties of such commensurability by observing that "thinking (any thinking: Lord Russell's or Baron Corvo's; Einstein's or some stalking Eskimo's) is to be understood 'ethnographically,' that is, by describing the world in which it makes whatever sense it makes."[13] I am not sure Goodman would accept the description of his outlook as relativist. But, of all the theorists in the group above, he has had the most to say about worlds, and his books help to show what the metaphor of world-making can and cannot explain.

Both in *Ways of Worldmaking* and its predecessor, *Languages of Art,* Goodman's account of the work of art gives precedence to the knowledge of convention and context. In every place where the account seems to me faulty—and they are far between—the problem is traceable to his use of the metaphor as such. For Goodman, the experience of art is a matter of knowing how to read conventions and, accordingly, how to modify expectations, either of a single work or a family of works: it is never entirely clear which, and so it is never clear whether, for example, Goodman would feel most comfortable with "the world of impressionism," "the world of Manet," or "the world of the painting entitled *A Bar at the Folies-Bergère.*" However that may be, we interpret a work, Goodman thinks, in keeping with all we know of its conventions of representation and expression, two things which an author's-world theory has to work hard to keep distinct. It often happens that they are *not* distinct in literature. The third line of *The Waste Land* uses the word *stirring* in a way that can be felt neither as quite representative nor as quite expressive. It picks up expressive hints by association with "memory and desire" (being stirred by a feeling), and representative ones by association with "mixing" (being stirred by a stick). The sense it thus introduces, of a possible swell of emotion and a sudden flattening or reduction, agrees with the shuttling images and ghostly attenuations of the poem throughout, but we can say that without any help from representation or expression. This seems the place to remark that Goodman's hunches about art in general come from painting more than they do from literature. A painting, he says, may represent something like a building, and at the same time express something called sadness. The claim for world-making appears to be that once we know enough conventions, we will be in a position to interpret a work rightly. That means seeing it within its own world or as its own world.

I think the best way to exhibit the disadvantages of world-making is to compare it with the differently shaded metaphor that William James employed in *A Pluralistic Universe,* in giving an account not of art specifically but of all our mental constructions. James's argument has much in common with Goodman's. Both say that the phenomena we confront have no structure of their own, only an infinity of projectable structures. Both admit that we are always emphasizing certain aspects of things at the expense of others, and both see this as a by no means unhappy necessity of thought. I can bring out the difference that remains by noting what disparate responses Goodman and James would have to make to Oscar Wilde's thesis that art reforms nature. The relevant passage is in "The Decay of Lying," where the author's stand-in, Vivian, at the bidding of a Mrs. Arundel, is asked to look outside at the glorious sky—a request sufficient in itself to identify her as "one of those absurdly pretty Philistines." For, asks Wilde, "what was it?" The sky "was simply a very second-rate Turner, a Turner of a bad period, with all the painter's worst faults exaggerated and overemphasized." James, as I understand him, would want to take this literally: it is still a sky, but the existence of Turner has changed its look for all who do know Turner. Whereas Goodman would have to take the statement as saying, very fancifully, that we could, if we chose to, see the world outside right now in a mood we associate with the world of certain paintings by Turner; but in doing so, we would be switching a gear in our minds, and deciding for the moment to treat nature as a canvas. For James as much as for Wilde, however, there was no choice of whether or not to make the switch. The sky at certain moments simply joined its effect with Turner; and at such moments the author of nature seemed to have been influenced by the author of *Rain, Steam, and Speed.* This follows from thinking about plural contributions to a single universe rather than multiple shifts among any number of worlds.

Near the end of *Ways of Worldmaking,* Goodman comes close to offering an explicit defense of his metaphor. "Do a Soutine painting," he inquires, "and a Utrillo drawing, the one in thick impasto and curved lines showing a facade with two twisted windows, the other in straight black lines showing a facade with a door and five windows, represent different buildings or the same building in different ways?"[14] This is the question the metaphor of worlds was designed to split down the middle; and Goodman's answer is that "the question about the Soutine and the Utrillo is much like the question whether a certain mess of molecules and my table are really the same." In short, the paintings belong to different worlds of artistic discourse, just as the two versions of the table belong to different worlds of scientific discourse, but each member of each pair functions very well in its own world. How true is this?

The trouble comes in with the conclusion Goodman wants us to draw: "A Mondrian design is right if projectable to a pattern effective in seeing a world." That sounds as practical-minded as one could wish; but how can we tell where "the pattern effective in seeing" starts and where it stops? Where, that is, ought we to draw the boundaries of the world it makes or locks into? The idea of seeing *a* world feels odd in any case. Maybe that is the way a formalist reader of Mondrian would describe his activity, though even he can justify his results without relying on the metaphor. But does it cease to be *a* world when a viewer knows that the title of the picture is *Broadway Boogie-Woogie?* What, then, if he goes a step further and thinks of the picture in relation to the rhythms of the boogie-woogie; or if he looks down from his skyscraper office at night, and sees a Mondrian of a bad period, with all the painter's worst faults exaggerated and overemphasized? Questions like this reveal some curious alignments. The skeptic Wilde has as much interest in *the* world as a classical critic who believes that art is a mirror of life, while the contextualist Goodman, in his attempt to think consistently with the metaphor of worlds, comes out sounding as uninterested in the world as any nineteenth-century idealist.

But idealists like Shelley gave force to their account of art by an absorbing concern with tradition: every act of seeing took place in relation to other such acts from the past, even if one only regarded these as kindred examples of energy. This sort of concern is absent from Goodman's idea of world-making, and he has nothing to say about tradition, except as one more possibly relevant convention to be learned. The belief that makes his argument go blank at just this point, I suspect, is the same belief that led him to adopt his chosen metaphor from the first. He supposes that our knowledge of art is generated from a sufficient number of repetitions of a single intense act of seeing. Gradually (it stands to reason), we become acquainted with the new object and others of its family, its conventions start to seem natural, and we find our way into its world. But this is not what really happens, except, perhaps, to those who put into practice the "creative writing" theory of literary history. Rather, our knowledge of art is generated by acts of seeing that preceded us into the world, and they are part of what we know. No intense act of seeing repeated often enough will lock us into a world we call Mondrian's or Utrillo's; we know both of them by habit only because we know other painters by habit; and the interpreter who chooses to emphasize certain aspects of their work at the expense of others, is no more inventing a new world from theirs than they were inventing a new one from ours. Of course we can say they are, if we like; but it seems a wrong way of honoring their activity.

Goodman cites as an important distinction between art and science "that earlier theories [in science] but not older works [in art] may be rendered obsolete by later ones"; and he thinks the reason is that in science "the earlier theories, in so far as [they are] sound, are absorbed into and are rederivable from the later while works of art . . . cannot be absorbed into or rederived from others."[15] I guess this seems to me as intuitively false as it seemed to Goodman intuitively true. Intuitively, because it is impossible to know just what one means by absorption and derivation. But if we agree to mean this—that later works in a practical sense *contain* earlier ones (absorb them), and that a well-informed and tactful historian could reconstruct a persuasive chain of earlier works from the evidence of a later one (rederive them)—then this happens all the time in art, and indeed is one strong definition of what interpretation is. If you are interested in poetry, you will see as much of Milton in a great modern poem, as you will of phlogiston in the latest path-breaking article in theoretical physics. There are many differences between art and science but this not one of them.

In the light of the foregoing remarks, I ought now to revise what I said at the start about the Nigerian students reading *Macbeth*. They were asked to imagine what the play would feel like to readers who did not believe in witches, and the moral seemed to be that these students might, by an act of abstraction, realize that one could admire the play without such a belief. Further, in realizing this they would have understood that the function of an author is to give us his own world. But in at least one respect, that was a far-fetched moral to draw from the anecdote. After all, *Macbeth* was easy for these students because they held the relevant beliefs without effort. For them, the work of accommodation—of naturalizing the story to their nature—was as painless as it is for us when we read Tolstoy. The students we have to fit into this anecdote are rather the English and American ones who do not believe in witches and who think they cannot imagine what it would be like to believe in them. "This play gives us its own world": here the sturdy reassurance does not go far enough. If one wants to make the play matter one will have to naturalize, or in this case supernaturalize it, by observing that even English and American readers are acquainted with the feeling that someone has chosen his destiny and been chosen by it. And if we can come up with an example (the recognition, say, that in a great tract of one's personal life, statistics have told one's fortune in advance) we do what we can to illustrate it. So we naturalize, we accommodate, we bring home the uncanny, and make it part of the world. There seems to me nothing trifling or shallow in this sort of translation, and nothing to discourage an interest in the translations that have mattered in the past.

Nelson Goodman associates his own thinking with the larger tendency I began by tracing, in which world-making offered itself as a natural extension of symbolism. By contrast, the thinking I have tried to defend is a natural extension of allegory. Symbolism, which makes many worlds, regards a given work of art as new and timeless. Allegory, which draws connections within the world we have, regards it as new and destined some day to be old.

15

Literature and Theory

THIS CHAPTER WAS ORIGINALLY CALLED "Recent Work in Literary Criticism." But the title felt wrong, and the reasons were easy to assign. The book that interprets the works of an author, the study in practical criticism that is widely read by nonspecialists, has ceased to be a kind of success that commands attention. Such books go on being written and published; but only the specialists know their names. What has replaced them, as the genre that represents the common interests of the discipline, is books on theory. I dislike this tendency, for what seem to me the faults of the intellectual temperament it has fostered: on the one hand, the pretension to social importance of much contemporary literary theory; on the other, its lack of social and historical information or even curiosity. Theory exists now in a protected condition, in comparison with which the situation of literature as well as criticism in the past may look admirably unprotected. Still, it would be pointless to ignore the drift of things. The objects of study are gradually being redefined, both for advanced students of literature and for the students whom they instruct in turn. To isolate a single effect: someone informed by theory, and aiming to write on a certain author or a group of texts, will read more widely than he would have done a decade ago, but also more thinly. If, for example, the result is an article on *Frankenstein,* then Rousseau and Nietzsche may be brought in, together with several current theorists. In the economy of the argument, they displace other works by Mary Shelley and her contemporaries; as, in the thinking and reading that helped to construct the argument, a similar displacement is likely to have occurred. The visible result is a change in the look of interpretations—or interrogations, to use the up-to-date word. A larger and less obvious change has to do with the traits that are looked on as useful in a critic.

Tact was an available name to sum up these traits, but what did it mean? A competence, supported by an instinct. A critic who expected to persuade readers of the sense of an interpretation would show some feeling for the language in which the work was written, for the period in which its author wrote, and for the particular inflections that its style gave to the idiom it inherited and revised. A false hope on which this idea of criticism was premised, but a hope inextricable from the acceptance of literature as an academic subject, was that something as elusive as tact could somehow be taught. It could not be, any more than insight into personal lives can be taught to a psychologist. It ought to be taken to imply, therefore, nothing but a form of practical wisdom, which most critics wished to encourage. By contrast, few critics since the Enlightenment have believed that their efforts converged on a single right interpretation of a text. Their consensus was modeled rather on other sorts of common sense: in the reading of a literary work, there was such a thing as *getting things right.* This was linked with the conventions of making sense that governed more ordinary social practices as well. In literature, however, it related specifically to the practice of honoring the complex over the simple, the worth-rereading over the not-worth-rereading. A clue to what has happened in criticism over the past several years is that every key word in this paragraph would now be challenged by many theorists: "sense," "competence," "instinct," "complexity," "practical wisdom." All these are constructed, the theorist can say, for purposes that theory exists to expose. It might be replied that one such purpose is the creation of works of art. A powerful interpretation like the Orwell-Empson reading of *King Lear*—which says, "If a great man decides to give up everything, he really gives up everything, and that is terrifying"—leads to a powerful work like Kurosawa's *Ran.* Yet the idea of the work of art is not far from becoming just one more of the constructions that theory exists to expose.

People in other academic disciplines often assume that making sense of a literary work and valuing it are activities on approximately the same level. In criticism, they think, it is all a matter of opinion anyway. To forestall this reaction and limit the truth I want to assert, it will help to give an example of what "a competence, supported by an instinct" may mean. In *Day of the Leopards: Essays in Defense of Poems,* W. K. Wimsatt relates the following anecdote:

> There was a student once who wrote a paper saying that a couplet by Alexander Pope, ". . . no Prelate's Lawn with Hair-shirt lined, / Is half so incoherent as my mind" (Epistle I.i.165–66) ought to be read in the light of a couplet in another poem by Pope: "Whose ample Lawns are not asham'd to feed / The milky heifer and deserving steed" (*Moral Essays* IV.185–86). Since I believe in the force of puns and all sorts of other verbal resemblances in poetry, I do not know quite how to formulate the rule of context by which I confidently reject that connection. But I seek first ineluctable confrontations, only later, if at all, rules.[1]

To Wimsatt, lawn (the fabric) simply was not answerable to lawn (the plot of land), notwithstanding their identity as sounds and their possible relationship as signifiers.

A sense of where such confrontations did occur was on this view the only guide one needed to point out the improbability of their occurrence somewhere else. But the sense in question did not apply to verbal resemblances alone. The social judgments which a text presumed, and to which it might allude subtly or openly, also ruled in certain critical statements as interesting, while it ruled out others as spurious. To keep for a moment with Pope: in the line "Or stain her honor, or her new brocade," the rhetorical scheme is *zeugma,* with abstract and concrete nouns sharing a verb. Now, a remark that Pope's uses of this scheme were concentrated disproportionately in his satires on women would be interesting if true; while a remark that, just when he wrote the line, brocade sellers were flourishing in England as never before would be spurious even if true. Whatever the latter might add to the reader's view of the economic arrangements of the time, it would say nothing about what made Pope worth studying as a writer. In the two decades since Wimsatt wrote, however, the criteria he evoked for the pertinence of a statement have partly dropped away from criticism. The questions "How could that matter?" (said of an unjustified turn in an argument) and "But where is it?" (said of a piece of evidence conspicuously overlooked) are asked less often. In their absence a thesis may be advanced with elementary errors that defeat its credibility but do not stop its publication. The interest is taken to lie elsewhere.

Thus a recent article in a respected critical journal proposed that *Jane Eyre* was an imperialist text.[2] The novel, that is, aimed to gain sympathy for a heroine whose passions were in complicity with the dominant prejudices of the age. It is not a startling general argument, and *Jane Eyre* is not the last place one would look for it to be tried. To make the case, Gayatri Spivak recalls the colonial origins of Mr. Rochester's mad wife, Bertha. Jane first sees Bertha Rochester's face reflected in a mirror, and the scene involves a repressed self-recognition. So far, the details and emphasis are familiar. The new element in this reading is the discovery that such a recognition could never be genuine since Jane Eyre herself is among the colonial oppressors. Her attitudes are established in part by an inquiry into her attachment to St. John Rivers, who is taken to represent the worst both of a male-dominated society and of an imperial ethic abroad. But here the *But where is it?* ought to stop one short. For the novel identifies Rivers as belonging to an evangelical sect that fought hard for the abolition of slavery: his parentage, though at a distance, includes men like Zachary Macaulay. If described as imperialist, it ought to be described carefully. Of all this the article says nothing. It is not treated as an irony, or as a complicating fact. Nor is it plain that late notice of the error would be received with much embarrassment by the critic. The standard defense for such an occasion will have been anticipated by people disposed to accept the reading. The aim, after all, was to reproblematize the text, and this meant that the details prized by a historian would yield to the details required by a particular anticolonialist metanarrative.

At what point in arguing against procedures like these does one have to appeal to some version of reality or of objectivity in interpretation? There has been a long line of critics—at least beginning with Hume's essay "Of the Standard of Taste" and Johnson's *Lives* of Swift and Milton—who say that without ever arriving at such a point at all, one may coherently judge interpretations as well as literary works themselves. Emphatically included in their idea of judgment was a belief in the worth of correcting errors. The roots of academic criticism, however, were always in a different tradition, with its beginnings in Coleridge and German idealism. The modern concern with the single right interpretation and the unified text to be right about may be traced largely to Coleridge's belief in the perfect work as a mediatory object between man and God. It was a misfortune, it seems to me, of the theoretical debates of the 1970s that critics who made similar emotional demands of truth were supposed to represent the common wisdom about interpretation; so that if one rejected them, one took oneself to be rejecting something like Hume's conception of taste or Johnson's of original invention, neither of which is committed to an epistemological way of truth. These writers, with Burke, Leigh Hunt, Shaw, and many others after them, are so far from supposing their judgments will lack validity without a diffuse but substantial something called reality to anchor them that they suppose their judgments to be founded on merely the common habits of reading and the long duration of certain opinions which acquire the force of custom. Such critics were not "essentialists" about meaning, and they would not have seen essentialism versus relativism as a choice that confronted anyone. Yet in the debates I mentioned above, one side, particularly in the writings of E. D. Hirsch and Gerald Graff, chose to make the stability of critical judgments depend on the stability of their objects.[3]

The theorist wants, and Hirsch tells him he is right to want, all or nothing: if interpretations do not tend toward truth, then there is no such thing as getting things right. The developments I sketched at the start of this review are symptoms of a very quick passage from all to nothing. The dilemma was taken seriously, I think, because both sides agreed that criticism gave the method for tracing the discoveries of literature itself. The idea of method was the first mistake; the picture of someone following up clues was the second. It would have made better sense to think of criticism as a language for discussing representations of the way people live and think and feel. The language is secondary in that it comes later. But it aims to give fresh interest to a narrative that owes everything to life, as life owes everything to the narratives that put it within our grasp. The idea of criticism as a language, rather than a map to a special province of truth, might well have gained acceptance while the New Critics were still active, had they chosen Wittgenstein rather than Coleridge as their guide. His questions in the *Philosophical Investigations,* on the difficulties of a private language, fall in very well with arguments more familiar to critics, and written about the same time, on the difficulties of reckoning intention as part of meaning: "And how do you know what you are to give yourself an exhibition of before you do it? This *private* exhibition is an illusion." Again, the best aphorisms there are on interpretation itself as a perspective come from the *Investigations:* "What I can see something *as,* is what it can be a picture of." Criticism resembles the making of a picture by seeing something as something else; and the work is the sum of the things that the picture can be of. Wittgenstein defines the interpreted character of a figure, which one may take to stand for a work, by talking of its possible aspects: "The aspects in a change of aspects are those ones which the figure might sometimes have *permanently* in a picture."[4] A critic can say, in short, certain things the picture will *not* be, so long as sight, cognition, the passions and interests of the lookers-on, stay even roughly as they appear to be at present. But this does not limit the ways in which one can see a thing *as*.

Further, Wittgenstein, as much as Hume, urges his readers to think of meaning as intelligible only in the light of habits or a more-than-private history of practices. He remarks in *Zettel* that it is a mistake "to say that there is anything that meaning something consists in." Saying a thing is a way of seeing what you mean; but meaning a thing is not seeing something that you do not say. "Only in the stream of thought and life do words have meaning."[5] In sentences like this and in the promptings, second guesses, and illustrations that enlarge them, Wittgenstein is the theorist who feels closest to the great, non-religious and nonepistemological, critics from the eighteenth century to the present. Academic critics tend in practice to share their bias, and yet with rare exceptions for a critic like Empson or Wimsatt they are not close arguers, or conscious of the beliefs that their arguments presuppose. Faced by a question like "Do you believe in determinacy of meaning?" they sometimes fall back on memories of epistemological arguments, themselves modeled on religious beliefs, which have nothing at all to do with their practices. This may entail at first a ready assent to the sentence "If we know, we must be knowing something"—from which it may falsely be shown to follow that we know things as they are in themselves. I said the New Criticism need not have explicated its leading doctrines with the help of Coleridge; and its emphasis on the unity of texts may be traced to the accident of its early success with short poems. But an older idealism might have been noticed in the deference accorded to "the poem" in certain titles of the period. Its presence was confirmed by the reception of the New Critics themselves, together with modern Coleridgean scholars like M. H. Abrams, as the ground note in most of the standard recent histories of criticism.

The influential attacks on the text-in-itself came not, where they might have been looked for, from social or intellectual historians, but from a tendency within theory, for which the best name anyone yet has offered is "textualism."[6] When Derrida said there was nothing outside the text, he meant there was nothing apparently discrete from the text which its words would assist in keeping so. It took only implication, the play of rhetoric, the return of repressed opposites, to bring it inside. The chapters on Rousseau in *Of Grammatology* and on Plato in *Dissemination* proceed by translating such distinctions as that between voice and writing, or cure and poison, into the undistinguishable doubles they become when the concepts of philosophy are read with the ambivalences language can never exclude.[7] The opponent in these inquiries is every hierarchy of knowledge, whether it is figured as a progress from writing to speech, or from a rhetoric that conceals the forms of justice to a dialectic that reveals it. Because modern philosophy habitually abstracts arguments from the words that make them, and words themselves from the history they were conditioned by, Derrida's writing had a plainer moral for philosophers than for literary critics. His deconstructions came to this: a showing that epistemology only asserts what the language of its asserting must call into question. A recognition of the way that happens might be expected to provoke a close historical study of the languages by which the problems of philosophy are generated from age to age. It has had that effect, in a small degree. But the ambition of Derrida's writing was not confined to a discipline in any case. It suggested that what is called philosophy and what is called literature are not different in kind. When philosophy begins to be read as writing, literature may be read as thinking. The signs of such a response have begun to appear in a few studies of novels as moral philosophy—studies that take their motive from a belief that literature gives a density to examples which argument alone cannot supply.[8] Yet it needs to be added that the use of literary texts as a sort of primary materials for philosophy was not what Derrida had in mind at all: as if novelists wrote to pose a problem ("the acknowledgment of others," for example) which had already been framed by philosophers. Within literature, Derrida's work has encouraged a reading of fictional and nonfictional, literary and philosophical, narrative and argumentative writings under their common aspect as texts. As a result, students of literature are perhaps freer now than at any time since the mid-nineteenth century to read books of several kinds—religious tract, political pamphlet, satire against mankind, essay in aesthetics—without a ranking of kinds and with the hope of attaining a competence for all rather than each.

In a review of Jonathan Culler's *On Deconstruction,* in the course of some extremely sensible comments on the all-or-nothing propensities of literary theorists, John Searle summarized an aim of deconstruction as the removal of metaphor from a marginal to a central position in language.[9] This was a good example of the all-or-nothing propensities of philosophers; and it brought out the persistence of the habits of mind that Derrida opposes. The point of his dealings with metaphor is that *any* rule separating the metaphorical from the literal will dissolve under scrutiny. Neither is central because neither can be prior; as the following illustration may attest: "The eminence was really an eminence when I saw him on the podium." Nobody ought to try to find the metaphor in the last sentence. And yet Shelley's "Defence of Poetry" is rich in suggestions like this concerning metaphor, as are many essays of romantic and modern criticism. What now appears strange in the reception of Derrida's work is that it has been taken generally as saying something shocking about how criticism is done. One strong definition of literary power has always held that it impresses the reader with a specific gravity at every point while leaving its final emphasis unsettled. Doubtless Cleanth Brooks's discussions of irony and Allen Tate's use of the word "tension" were not in this sense deconstructive. But Empson's discussions of complex words certainly were. Among the priorities that deconstruction set out to overturn, the only one that academic criticism had retained was the privilege of the single text to be examined as a unity, together with an unreflecting and incantatory style of speech concerning "the reconciliation of opposites." The former was chiefly a pedagogical convenience, though it may have looked like something larger. The latter was a rhetoric formed by the meeting of two unpleasant scholar's traits, the will-to-tidiness and an affectation of moral concern. Neither of these has vanished but for the moment deconstruction has forced them to seek new disguises.

About the status of Derrida's procedures there was always a puzzle. Was deconstruction a technique proper to the commentator, and necessary as a tactic against the naive constructionism of the author? Or was it something the author's writing practiced for itself, in which case the commentator's only role would be to tease out the language it had been speaking all its life? Derrida's interests did not require him to choose between these descriptions. But his mode of analysis became current in America, and later in Britain, largely through a long essay devoted to his reading of Rousseau, in Paul de Man's *Blindness and Insight*. There de Man appeared to choose the second description. Recounting Derrida's own argument on the metaphysics of presence, which had tracked the privilege of speech (as presence) against writing (as deception) from its prominent use in Lévi-Strauss back to its invention in the anthropology of Rousseau, "Jacques Derrida's Reading of Rousseau" pointed out that this and kindred oppositions were called into doubt in Rousseau's texts themselves. Rather than expose a self-deception, therefore, which literature shared with metaphysics, de Man vindicated literature as a place of self-suspicion that was exemplary for language in general. The same work was carried into de Man's later essays in *Allegories of Reading* and *The Rhetoric of Romanticism;* in the introductory chapter of the former book, on "Semiology and Rhetoric," de Man propounded his thesis unambiguously:

> A literary text simultaneously asserts and denies the authority of its own rhetorical mode, and by reading the text as we did we were only trying to come closer to being as rigorous a reader as the author had to be in order to write the sentence in the first place. Poetic writing is the most advanced and refined mode of deconstruction; it may differ from critical or discursive writing in the economy of its articulation, but not in kind. [10]

It is worth noting that the main points of this assertion—its leveling of text with commentary and its ranking of poetry, in degree, above criticism by virtue of its "rigor" and "economy"—were made with a slightly different emphasis in the opening chapter of Empson's *Seven Types of Ambiguity.* Of ambiguities Empson wrote: "Meanings of this kind, indeed, are conveyed, but they are conveyed much more by poets than by analysts; that is what poets are for, and why they are important"; of the implicit statements of speech and writing he also remarked: "printed commonly differ from spoken ones in being intended for a greater variety of people, and poetical from prose ones in imposing the system of habits they imply more firmly or more quickly." [11] In the same way, Derrida's comments on the assimilability of all language to rhetoric may seem to recall Kenneth Burke's inquiries in the *Grammar* and *Rhetoric* he published in 1945 and 1950. Empson and Burke are the critics of the last generation who wrote with genius and not just a refined competence, and if their limited, but real, affinities with later rhetoricians have been noticed without ever prompting a revival of their work, a reason may be the unchallenged anti–Anglo-Saxon bias which modern theory professes sometimes ironically and sometimes sarcastically.

De Man's most impressive essay for me is "The Rhetoric of Temporality," which has been reprinted in a second edition of *Blindness and*

Insight.[12] It argues that two dogmas have shaped critical thought about the literary object since the early decades of the nineteenth century: the conception of irony as a fixed perspective, and of the symbol as a fusion of image and idea which cannot be found in allegory. Hazlitt, Shelley, Lionel Johnson, Edward Thomas, and a good many others might be cited as critics outside the consensus that de Man writes against, but the people he really has in view are recent and synoptic literary historians: M. H. Abrams, for example, in his discussions of the symbol, and Wayne Booth in his treatment of narrative irony. After one has read this essay, one's sense of the uses of irony can never be quite the same, and there seems to be very little point in ever talking of the symbol again, except for the historical purpose of exhibiting the preoccupations of a school. The essays on romantic authors which de Man wrote soon after, particularly those on Rousseau, Shelley, and "Autobiography as De-Facement," add up to a denial of the consolations of writing. It is always pertinent, Iris Murdoch observed in *The Sovereignty of Good,* to ask of a philosopher, What is he afraid of? De Man in these essays asks the same question of writers, as the makers of inscriptions that are meant at once to outlast and to represent them. "Autobiography as De-Facement" starts from the Proustian datum that a life cannot speak to us as a life until it is inscribed on a monument; and yet the speaking monument is the author who, in order to address us, must imagine himself as already dead. Nor is this stance merely figurative. In writing his life, the author changes it from pure face to defacement, as all monuments are defaced or scarred by their inscriptions. Any testimony from a writer, then, which we receive concerning the writer's life, is a testimony from the point of view of death. Accordingly, the very words that mean to reflect a life must deform it in order to make its story come into existence at all. Once, however, we concede that "autobiography is a defacement of the mind of which it is itself the cause," it follows that "death is a displaced name for a linguistic predicament," for the discovery that autobiography hoped to gain through writing "deprives and disfigures to the precise extent that it restores."[13] Here again, though de Man's text is Wordsworth's *Essays on Epitaphs,* his recognition is familiar above all to readers of Proust. Phrased as a truism, it may be supposed to mean: every book leaves something out. Beneath this nevertheless one may discern the starker claim that there are no true stories.

Thus de Man asks the reader to give up, as the writer's work itself has done, any curriculum by which one could move from allegories of reading to intimations of experience. This is not one of the things that literature does, and to fancy that it can is only to seek a "shelter" (a favorite term of reproach). Two concerns are perhaps separable here. In some of his later essays, de Man wrote of literature as dramatizing fears about the instability of knowledge, which other linguistic practices simply repressed. A possible explanation of the difference, though one not entertained by de Man, was that useless writing can do some things that use-bound writing cannot do. The distinction in any case passed out of sight in other essays, where "an aporia" was asserted "between performative and constative language," and the illustrations were drawn from literary and nonliterary sources indifferently. De Man gave as examples Archie Bunker's sentence "What's the difference?" in reply to a question about two ways of tying his shoes ("Who cares!" but also "Please describe the ways"); and Yeats's line "How can we know the dancer from the dance?" at the end of a great poem ("The dancer and the dance seem almost one" but also "Can we be sure?"). Neither of the examples is convincing to my ear; but any reader can think of his own. This line of argument brought a strong reply to de Man from Stanley Cavell, who recalled that it was precisely to defeat "the idea that constative and performative utterances differ in their responsibilities, or responsiveness, to facts and to distinguish among the ways in which words may have 'effects' or 'forces'" that J. L. Austin wrote in the first place about both sorts of statement. Cavell then offered a counter-illustration: "Someone says that the difference between knives and forks is that you cut with a knife and spear with a fork; a second objects that you can also cut with a fork and speak with a knife; whereupon a third concludes that there is an aporia between knives and forks, that there is no stable distinction we can draw between them."[14] While the applications of this response are local, it shares Wittgenstein's approach to thinking, speaking, and action, the adaptiveness of the needs that one learns and the choices that language makes to the situations they fit. Indeed, the response brings out by contrast one of the intractable elements in de Man's criticism, which one may read for a long time before giving the problem a conscious formulation. He believed, what some philosophers but few critics have believed, that language and, *a fortiori*, literature are games that cannot be played.

An implication of most deconstructionist criticism is that an end of self-deception requires an end of the self. Writing and the self are said, in short, to confirm each other in the illusion that they can transcend the death that is another name for a linguistic predicament—the existence of what is called literature being the chief source of their positive reinforcement. From a critic who works pretty steadily within this train of speculations, Neil Hertz, have come some of the best essays of the past several years on romantic and modern authors; and in the summary chapter of his collection, *The End of the Line,* Hertz affirms his interest in a plot that is common to both the self-portraits of romantic autobiography and the sublime moments of poetry or fiction.[15] Tocqueville's account of the 1848 Paris uprising, Wordsworth's lines on his encounter with the blind beggar in London, Freud's reconstruction of the case history of Dora, all show the self's return to the knowledge it has promised itself, at the sacrifice of the others whose portrayal had justified the making of a narrative. The result, says Hertz (summarizing de Man but also, apparently, himself), is to "leave the field littered with the remains of acts of mutilation," so that the questions that concern an interpreter are: "At the end of the line, who pays? and why?" The end of the line here signifies both a climactic turn in the narrative and a recovery of the affects, powers, and laws of the self which writing threatened first only to sanction later. It is a suggestion of Hertz's criticism, never fully stated, that these self-recognitions coincide with a form of social loss; and it is a suggestion of the sentence quoted above, again not fully stated, that the cost after all may be too high.

What conclusions follow from investigations like these? Sometimes, Hertz believes, political judgments of a sort will materialize in the direction that criticism seems to point, and his juxtaposition of the motifs of political and sexual hysteria in Tocqueville is ingenious but baffling unless such judgments do follow. He sees this difficulty, and goes the length of reprinting, after his essay on 1848, two very acute replies from critics who take him at his word and prod him to say just what the politics of his essay come to. Hertz's defense is curious: "Can political questions be boiled down to a dilemma?" The moments, he goes on to say, "that strike me as most suggestive" in the political writings of Foucault and Derrida

> are precisely those that work to elude symmetrical formulations of this sort. In Foucault these moments are often marked by long lists of plural nouns, which produce the exhilarating sense of just how many factors one must take into account in a particular issue; in Derrida, by the

mullings and backings-and-fillings with which he works his way into a problem, his remarkable ability to both fish *and* cut bait.[16]

Note that these exhilarations bring us no closer than we were at the start to politics, either as a dilemma or as something less simple. Instead we are invited to share the "sense of just how many factors" one theorist asks us to consider, the ambidextrous finesse with which another shows that he is able "to both fish *and* cut bait." The deference to Foucault and Derrida—names brought into the discussion by Hertz's critics, but to which he adds no others—is also curious in the light of the consistent prejudice against psychology in both writers. But I think their authority does in fact have a bearing on the insufficient account of its motives to which criticism in this mode feels bound in principle to stay confined.

The effect is as follows. A promise of social analysis is made, tacitly by the tone itself of the criticism, more overtly by the choice of objects for analysis, yet the argument is foreshortened just at the point where what was promised might be performed. I have only a hunch about why this occurs, and since others have even less I will give it briefly. Deconstruction was a way to upset, from within, a system controlled by certain hierarchies of knowledge, which related in turn to hierarchies of power. Critics aware of what it could do to conventional linguistic arrangements saw how easily it might do something similar to conventional social arrangements. And yet here Foucault, whose *Discipline and Punish* has had a wide vogue in literary studies, proves to be as unrewarding a guide as Derrida. Talking about social arrangements, after all, means talking about the sorts of persons who live in them, and who suffer or profit by them. Talking about persons, however, is prohibited in advance by the exclusion that Foucault and Derrida alike enforce against comparable entities. It is almost like talking about character, almost like talking about the self. Foucault in this respect is all the more discouraging in that he writes from the perspective of a reformer. For the successions of *epistemes,* by which he denotes historical periods, have so total a control of the discourse of any thinker within them that they appear to preclude an account of change. If one reads several consecutive chapters of *The Order of Things,* one gets the impression that an old *episteme* grows dull like an illegible photograph or, to adapt the book's concluding image, grows smooth like a shallow inscription on a soft tablet, until, since of course it cannot remember, language thinks in a new *episteme.* There is no trace of pathos in such an account, and no sympathy with the victims who are described at length, because there is no idea of agency. On premises like these the subtle moralism of the attack on the self in literary theory has consented to build the little that it can.

In an essay of 1971 entitled "Nietzsche, Genealogy, History," Foucault came closer than anywhere else to a lucid statement of a credo. "Nothing," he wrote, "in man—not even his body—is sufficiently stable to serve as the basis for self-recognition or for understanding other men. The traditional devices for constructing a comprehensive view of history and for retracing the past as a patient and continuous development must be systematically dismantled."[17] The other thing besides the body, to which his phrase "nothing in man" referred, was evidently the mind, but here one may recur to Wittgenstein's criticism of all such maps of the alternative: "One of the most dangerous of ideas for a philosopher is, oddly enough, that we think with our ideas in our heads. The idea of thinking as a process in the head, in a completely enclosed space, gives him something occult." This did not affect the usefulness of an idea of thinking or for that matter a history of thoughts. "Only God sees the most secret thoughts. But why should these be all that important? Some are important, not all. And need all human beings count them as important?"[18] Foucault, having replaced God with "Power/Knowledge," replies to the second question with a simple yes. The impossibility of forming a comprehensive view ought therefore to stop us from seeking a view at all. And the lack of a basis, in our heads or bodies, either for self-recognition or for understanding of others, itself decides the next of "the problems that have been posed for human knowledge" by terminating the cause of the last. "Where religions once demanded the sacrifice of bodies, knowledge now calls for experimentation on ourselves, calls us to the sacrifice of the subject of knowledge."[19] Among the many things the word "subject" covers is the self. For genealogy, as Foucault explains it—the suspicious tracing of a descent from the past which replaces history—aims to reveal "the heterogeneous systems which, masked by the self, inhibit the formation of any form of identity."[20] The title and procedure of this essay commit Foucault to nothing more than an exposition of Nietzsche. But it will be granted, I think, by most of his readers that he here attributes to Nietzsche both aims and analyses to which he himself assented.

Notwithstanding Foucault's skepticism about the worth of histories, a question remains whether the "subject of knowledge" need be identical with the self. A version of the self though not of the subject does join one's sense of texts when it is part of their claim to be uniquely interesting. At any rate, Foucault's reading of Nietzsche as his predecessor is a separate matter. A chapter on "Self and Subject in Nietzsche," in Stanley Corngold's *The Fate of the Self*, argues that, however Nietzsche's genealogies may subvert any defense of humanism, they do not end in a rejection of an idea of the self. Or rather, they can be made to do so only in an interpretation that stresses a few passages of *The Will to Power* while excluding all consideration of *Thus Spake Zarathustra*. Corngold regards as peculiarly non-Nietzschean

> the too easy assertion that the self is merely a metaphor, always but a metaphor, always transparent to its own constructedness, always a fiction. . . . This is a view that cannot be lived. To live it is to go mad, so it will come as no surprise that many a professional killing has recently been made by arguing its necessity. It may therefore be helpful to suggest the hold against this unraveling which the memory of other selves offers. It is for us, really, to decide how far we want to let go of the self—our own and others—and to persist in asking: where does the self unravel? In what place, at what time? . . . The madness of *literature* without a self no more exists than does the sanity of a *self* without literature.[21]

That sentences like these should sound unaccustomed now proves that they needed saying. And yet the diagnosis they give of the character of literary theory seems to me incomplete.

Without "living" a view, or going mad in the attempt to live it, one may criticize others for the more tolerable views which alone permit their life and work. The theorist who chooses this perspective comes to look on the author as merely symptomatic of the conditions that determined him—another naive believer in the sublimation of texts from the materials that produced them, whose irony about his own position is less developed than the theorist's. This explains not only the antihumanism of some recent criticism but also a new tone, at once authoritative and clinical, which oddly resembles the tone of the very social-scientific texts that Foucault wrote with the hope of discrediting. Read either as social history or as history of ideas, his writings have tremendous power as an estrangement device; they were not meant to license a project of intellectual surveillance directed, this time, upon the guilty self of the author. But the tendency I am describing, though its vocabulary is largely Foucault's, has another and earlier source in the writings of Althusser. Here in fact one arrives at a part of theory's own genealogy of which few of its practitioners are aware. In the French Communist party in the 1950s, the antihumanism of Althusser was an instrument of discipline with a specific purpose. It was offered as a weapon against the socialist humanism of Eastern European political thinkers, and was found extremely serviceable in justifying the Soviet suppression of the 1956 Hungarian uprising. Beyond that, a vocabulary which incorporated persons only as the bearers of structures became a highly respected, plausible, Western constituent of an apology for the historical necessity of Stalinism.

This is a history that has been recounted in detail by E. P. Thompson in "The Poverty of Theory." Yet it may still be asked why such a theory should find its appeal just now, among advanced students of the humanities in America, who are seldom political enough to be either Stalinist or anti-Stalinist. A short answer is the erosion of secular individualism in general, perhaps the worst intellectual disaster of the 1970s and 1980s. The result owes much to the isolation of radical impulses in the teaching of advocacy subjects like "cultural studies," and much to the connection of individualist rhetoric now with the public-relations genius of the big corporations. Thompson himself sees an additional reason, however, for the appeal of antihumanism in theory: it seems to afford an understanding that is prior and, in consequence, superior to any historical agency. Further, it does so at a time when the distance between intellectuals (who can help to understand the world) and the working classes (for whom, in a pre-Althusserian Marxism, the tasks of understanding it and changing it coincided) has widened to such a point that if it were not a cause of pride it would be a cause of shame. Thompson observes:

> What is so obvious is that this new *elitism* stands as direct successor in the old lineage: Benthamism, Coleridgean "clerisy," Fabianism, and Leavisism of the more arrogant variety. Once again, the intellectuals— a chosen band of these—have been given the task of enlightening the people. Whether Frankfurt School or Althusser, they are marked by their very heavy emphasis upon the ineluctable weight of ideological modes of domination—domination which destroys every space for the initiative or creativity of the mass of people—a domination from which only the enlightened minority of intellectuals can struggle free. . . . It is a sad premise from which Socialist theory should start (all men and women, except for us, are originally stupid) and one which is bound to lead on to pessimistic or authoritarian conclusions. Moreover, it is likely

to reinforce the intellectual's disinclination to extend himself in practical political activity. To be sure, the (ideal) proletariat may, in this or that critical conjuncture, suddenly shift itself, like a geological fault, into a revolutionary posture, when it will be ready to receive the ministrations of Theory. Meanwhile, why bother to try to communicate—to educate, agitate, and organize—since the reason is powerless to penetrate the mists of "ideology"? [22]

In this respect the shift from Althusser to Foucault involves only a change of degree: a still further dimension of pessimism, with a still more attenuated emphasis on class. Together, these combine to make accounts of the domination by a mesh of power and knowledge over authors, readers, books, and the things a book can or cannot represent.

The emergent style has led to some remarkable examples of the inter-disciplinary cross-sterilization of ideas. If I set out tomorrow to con-nect the Victorian decline of satire with the rise of sentimental comedy, the repression of women's sexuality, and the dietary practices which, with many other practices, controlled the arbitrary differences of a social order, I would need perhaps the following bits of evidence: an essay of eighteenth-century criticism which identified the satirical genres with the "acid" style; a textbook of etiquette for young ladies, published between 1830 and 1880, asserting that acidulous foods were particularly improper for persons of the female gender; and a letter from a standard Victorian author (Thackeray, say), with a comment in passing that satires tended to exacerbate rather than comfort people's resentments about their condition, and besides his wife had never en-joyed reading them. Whether these wire-drawn and empirical-looking hints carried conviction or failed to, the article in which I published them would not be attacked on the ground that connections like these could not possibly add up to anything cogent. They are the stuff the practice of theory is made of. Indeed, one's interest or lack of interest in the results is a master-clue to the recent adoption, in discussions of the politics of interpretation, of the wholly misleading political terms of art "left" and "right." To want to make, as Benjamin did in his *Arcades* study, a direct inference from the duty on wine to Baudelaire's "L'Ame du Vin," without adducing any intermediate chain of evi-dence, is a *left* position. To say of such a procedure what Adorno said of an early draft of the study, that it is "located at the crossroads of magic and positivism," is a *right* position.

Adorno's responses to Benjamin remain instructive for another reason. Of the few critical essays that have been read by many people and are still felt to define a period, Benjamin's "The Work of Art in the Age of Mechanical Reproduction" is the most influential, and its conscious and unconscious ambivalences have been repeated again and again by recent critics. Since this has happened, I believe, because its motives are not commonly understood, a short summary of the way they affect the argument may be useful. The essay is divided logically into two parts, even if these do not quite correspond to the sequence of presentation. In part one, Benjamin establishes his conception of the "aura," but relates it to some special orders of circumstance: first, an archaic mode of experience, no longer available after the Enlightenment; second, a mysterious valuation of the work of art, which high capitalism in turn is rendering precarious. It is plain that Benjamin cherishes the aura of the work of art as something distinct both from its text and its reputation. But he sees that the aura is being withdrawn above all by the mass culture of reproduction, in photography and the cinema for example, with the powers of which the masses themselves are in thorough complicity. In part two, Benjamin escapes from the alternative he has pictured as hopeless on both sides by recasting the argument in a gnostic form. He resigns himself to the end of the work of art under the assault of mass reproduction; but he treats the work as an element of created life that must be destroyed for the sake of a blind assertion of freedom. Fortunately, the agents of destruction are the proletariat. So photography and the cinema, which had been his antagonists at the start of the essay, return as his heroes at the finish. They represent the forward striving of the masses (even if not created by the masses), and the change they effect will shatter the powers that have wrecked art (though only by "politicizing" the wreckage). Part one of this argument comes mostly from a reading of Baudelaire, part two mostly from conversations with Brecht; and Adorno denied that in combination they become Marxist when he wrote to Benjamin: "You have swept art out of the corners of its taboos—but it is as though you feared a consequent inrush of barbarism (who could share your fear more than I?) and protected yourself by raising what you fear to a kind of reverse taboo."[23] What Adorno did not foresee what that the same negative taboo—the things-forbidden redefined as things-welcome, for the sake of a revolution outside art—would eventually be cultivated as an aesthetic in itself. The trick is carried off with none of Benjamin's savage irony or regret.

A pertinent and much-discussed example of this tendency is Fredric

Jameson's 1984 *New Left Review* essay, "Postmodernism, or the Cultural Logic of Late Capitalism." In an earlier work, *The Political Unconscious,* Jameson had proposed an analysis of the utopian moment in the capitalist work of art—a category which itself was indebted to Benjamin's use of the "dialectical image," the figure that yields a coalescence of the archaic into the modern. When, in objecting to such terms, Adorno wrote of the dialectical image as regression, he meant that the only form of classlessness it uncovered was "a phantasmagoria of Hell." But the phantasmagoria of late capitalism which Jameson wants to explore for its utopian possibilities is not a moment but the imaginary space of a whole culture. Its lineaments, says Jameson, may be traced in "a new depthlessness, which finds its prolongation both in contemporary 'theory' and in a whole new culture of the image or the simulacrum; a consequent weakening of historicity, both in our relationship to public History and in the new forms of our private temporality."[24] Thus, scanning the contributions of video, television, the urban sprawl of shopping centers and the megalithic hotels that have squatted among the remnants of uprooted neighborhoods, Jameson composes an appreciative montage of what he calls "a new kind of superficiality in the most literal sense [sic]." As a defining trait of postmodernism, this has its avatar in Warhol's Campbell's Soup cans, which, Jameson says with emphasis, "*ought* to be powerful and critical statements." If they are not yet, it is the fault of the critics who have not made them so. Packages, simulacra, or works of commerce like Warhol's adequately represent the feelings of people now—feelings that, Jameson reflects, "it may be better and more accurate to call 'intensities'" since they "are now free-floating and impersonal, and tend to be dominated by a peculiar kind of euphoria."[25] Other features of the postmodernist look are a flat and affectless style of pastiche and "an omnipresent, omnivorous and well-nigh libinidal historicism." To give force to these impressions, Jameson then typifies postmodernism by an amalgam of objects and persons. "Cage, Ashbery, Sollers, Robert Wilson, Ishmael Reed, Michael Snow, Warhol or even Beckett himself" are all on this account postmodernist; so too are De Palma's *Blowout,* Polanski's *Chinatown,* Michael Herr's *Dispatches,* and all of the novels of E. L. Doctorow.

The list betrays a general tastelessness that is in harmony with the essay's ambition to read a culture as a seamless general text. Jameson draws his main exhibit not from literature or the arts but from the economic rescoring of a large city through the building of a gigantic architectural complex, John Portman's Bonaventura Hotel in Los Angeles. There, as in any postmodernist text, the structure induces in the reader a "feeling that emptiness is here absolutely packed, that it is an element within which you yourself are immersed, without any of that distance that formerly enabled the perception of perspective or volume. You are in this hyperspace up to your eyes and your body." Also, for the postmodern *flâneur,* there are escalators: "Here the narrative stroll has been underscored, symbolized, reified, and replaced by a transportation machine which becomes the allegorical signifier of that older promenade we are no longer to conduct on our own." But is not all of this irrelevant to the habits of the crowd in an older narrative, since their successors are excluded in advance by the very placement of the hotel? Instead of allowing such objections to halt the inquiry, Jameson deduces from this "new collective space" as such "a new collective practice, a new mode in which individuals move and congregate, something like the practice of a new and historically original kind of hyper-crowd." His is the sort of analysis that follows from a resolution to "think this development positively *and* negatively all at once; to achieve, in other words, a type of thinking that would be capable of grasping the demonstrably baleful features of capitalism along with its extraordinary and liberating dynamism simultaneously, within a single thought."[26] Jameson associates his strategy here with that of Marx. What Marx did not do, however, was advise his readers to think the negative features of a system positively. At this crossroads of magic and positivism, Marxism has grown indistinguishable from what it contemplates. To judge by the above description of being "immersed . . . up to your eyes and your body" in a space that is "absolutely packed," its aesthetic has likewise come to share certain traits with an aesthetic of fascism. As for the excited account of the vistas, escalators, and other attractions of the place, it is done in a style not far removed from advertising—a special variety of it, for which the French reserve the phrase *pour tromper les clercs.*

Faced with the necessity of immersing oneself in the antihuman junk of capitalist culture, in order to think its destruction in a properly antihuman light, it may seem that a shorter way out lies in simply abolishing the profession of criticism. Leave the reading of old books to evasive or elitist types in the other professions: for those who have seen through them, the best employment of critical skills will be in the making of revolutionary ideology. This is actually the position of Terry Eagleton in *Literary Theory,* a book that in any other period would have found difficulty getting published because of its wholesale inaccuracies. But it has sold well and deserves to be considered here. An anomaly of Eagleton's design is the moralistic, unpragmatic, and academic compulsion to prove that, before the study of literature can be decently terminated, it ought to be shown to have *earned* its death warrant. The story of why it has done so is what interests me in the book—the rest being cribs of other theorists—and it occupies a first chapter on "The Rise of English" as well as a last on "Political Criticism." Eagleton believes that from Arnold on, literary study has been consciously expounded as a tactic, and a most important one, in the ideological defense of the capitalist state. This, and not something more oblique, was Arnold's point in saying that literature could take the place of religion. Eagleton describes the New Critics as disciples of Arnold (which they were not) and imputes to them the view that "the Decline of the West was felt to be avertable by close reading" (which they would have denied). He asserts very frequently that modern critics have deceived their audience by promising that "reading literature did make you a better person." It is questionable whether a single modern critic of any authority has ever held this view, apart perhaps from I. A. Richards in his more waywardly inspirational moments; but Empson, a closer student of his opinions than Eagleton, reports that he thought the only good of reading literature was to teach you how other people lived. Many critics would want to add, if they talked much about these things, that it could also help you to think about life. But they would not claim that it, more than other pursuits, had any marked capacity for prompting the right choices.

If criticism helps to strengthen the apparatus of the state, its practitioners must be conscious of the necessity to promote conservative authors. This Eagleton believes was true of Leavis in particular, of whom he reports that "almost all of [the authors in his canon] were conservatives." Now, among those whom Eagleton names are Blake, Keats, George Eliot, Lawrence, and Bunyan, none of whom could be called conservative on any definition of the word. Yet errors or careless falsehoods of this sort do not matter until they are repeated by others; and what is edifying about Eagleton's perspective is that it shows how extremes meet. The believer in the all-sufficing good of an ideological exposure of the text reaches a tacit accord with the believer in the substantial existence of a meaning of the text in itself. The only difference is that for the former the fixed meaning is political. "Let us imagine," Eagleton invites his readers, "that by dint of some deft archaeological research we discovered a great deal more about what ancient Greek tragedy actually meant to its original audiences, recognized that these concerns were utterly remote from our own, and began to read the plays again in the light of this deepened knowledge. One result might be that we stopped enjoying them." [27] But a first premise of hermeneutics suggests that the result would be less decisive. Situations like this confront us all the time, and we meet them with the principle of charity in translation. [28] We read the work differently, selectively, emphasizing some of its features rather than others—we even, as it may appear to later scholars, misread the work in order to preserve something of it that does interest us. But Eagleton's sole criterion of literary worth does not have to do with reading. It is simply a criterion of political membership and, further back, of political loyalty construed from an inspection of biographical facts. If an author's life shows him to have been radical, then we will learn to read him radically.

By the end of *Literary Theory*, all Eagleton lacked was a utopian moment of his own in literary history, an age of egalitarian discourse to show what literature ever since had fallen away from. In his next book, *The Function of Criticism,* he picked the moment almost at random. It was the 1710s, in the coffeehouses of London, where Addison and Steele wrote their papers: "What is said [in those coffeehouses] derives its legitimacy neither from itself as message nor from the social title of the utterer, but from its conformity as a statement with a certain paradigm of reason inscribed in the very event of saying." [29] Thus an ingratiating blend of Habermas with high common room speculation is offered as a theory of the lost public sphere. Though answerable for none of the details, Eagleton wants to make his story as suggestive as possible, and this requires of course a dating of the fall. To serve the function he summons—the next critic most people can remember after Addison—Johnson. With Johnson, "we are evolving towards just that rift between literary intellectual and social formation out of which a fully specialist criticism will finally emerge." Johnson, as Eagleton argues or, rather, as he wonders if he might not half-commit himself to arguing some day (theory needs a new grammatical *mood* to describe this sort of thought experiment): Johnson is "isolated and abstracted in contrast to the busily empirical Addison." The choice, by the way, of Addison over Steele is merely conventional, since, to anyone who has read them both, it is Steele who seems to have seen or heard or felt the life of the streets and taverns, while Addison kept to his closet and worked out his dicta with an agreeable pedantry. Still, let us take the contrast as it stands. Johnson (the "iso-lated and abstracted"), who equipped his rooms with a small chemical laboratory, spoke of having talked away his life in company, and once carried a prostitute who had collapsed of fatigue a very long walk up Fleet Street on his back. And Addison (the "busily empirical"), who supped and was snug with the great and almost great, never wrote a word without an eye on the Whig ascendancy, and codified the taste of his day without altering it one particle. Which of these looks like the hero of legitimate sociable public reason?

A moral of the foregoing pages may be that bad theory makes bad history. Yet it is the contempt for history among theorists as a rule that has led to the hatching of stories like Eagleton's on a regular basis. His books are forgotten two at a time, almost as fast as he writes them. Meanwhile, they are treated respectfully, since the presence of a Marx-ist whose iconoclasm about literature goes all the way is felt to round out the company at any theory colloquium with pretensions to toler-ance. Earlier, I alluded to Wittgenstein as a counterweight to the phi-losophers most influential in recent theory, and I have to quote here a final passage from *Zettel*:

> What does it mean to say: "But that's no longer the same game!" How do I use this sentence? As information? Well, perhaps to introduce some information in which differences are enumerated and their consequences explained. But also to express that just for that reason I don't join in here, or at any rate take up a different attitude to the game.[30]

I have tried to point out how by gradual adjustments theory has been turning criticism into a game that is no longer recognizably the same. And I have tried to enumerate some of the differences, and to explain some of the consequences. If the description was adequate, my reasons will be plain for concluding, "Here is where I don't join in." A survey like this, however, would seem to me incomplete without some ac-count of a proposition I believe is worth refuting, which many theo-rists either assert or do not want to be seen to challenge. It is, that once we give up the unity or complete intelligibility of the text as an attainable ideal, it makes less difference what texts we choose for anal-ysis; so that the mass-cultural object has an equal claim with the work of art, all other considerations being favorable; and perhaps a better claim, if what interests us is the habits or projectable responses of the largest sheer mass of readers. I want to end by saying how this attitude came about and what may be wrong with it; and, finally, by defending the interpretation of great writing on non-aesthetic grounds.

At first glance, the rhetoric of theory sounds as if it wanted to look at texts the way a physicist looks at elementary particles. If the aim is to account for their behavior, one sample is as good as another. To discriminate at all ("Sorry, this kind isn't worth my trouble") seems therefore not so much retrograde as pointless: if your theory concedes in advance a prejudice against certain objects without yielding a rule to help identify them, it ceases to be a theory and becomes just a disguise for personal judgments, "value judgments." And yet, since judgments come into play however we try to neutralize them—a point that theorists admit without exception—the embarrassment about what to do with them suggests an ambivalence in the theoretical attitude. An ambivalence, rather than a contradiction, because theorists only act as if a concern with judgments would betray the very nature of their work. They do not in fact hold views that would make it a betrayal. Thus a reader-response critic might say consistently with his theory: "Melville's reader is more interesting than G. P. R. James's or even Stowe's: I will show that the responses are options taken at a higher level." A deconstructionist might make a similar move with respect to linguistic figuration, and so on. But this move is not made now, while the opposite one ("And this applies to any text you can think of—defining text as broadly as you like") is made all the time. A reason for the emphasis will appear if we realize that the physicist was only a rough-and-ready analogy. The scientist from whom literary theory has consciously borrowed both a self-image and a rhetoric is the anthropologist. This influence is traceable to Foucault's method as well as his titles; and, in English, to Clifford Geertz, Mary Douglas, and a few others. What does the anthropologist's stance tell us? Above all, that, in seeking to understand a culture, we had better exempt none of its elements from consideration. The most familiar help as much as the least in reconstructing a cultural code. Nor is the case altered when the culture is our own. Our descriptions, if careful, will represent relations and not objects; but we cannot know what texts may end up serving our purpose until the interpretation itself is complete; and it is never complete. Besides, to a modern academic researcher, mass-cultural texts come at once under the headings of the most and the least familiar.

The theoretical geniality toward mass culture is also part of a larger history: it is the last chapter in the convergence of the avant-garde with the academy. The time lag between the advent of the new and its assimilation has grown shorter with every movement since the first appearance of an avant-garde around 1800. For Wordsworth, the period was forty years or so: almost the length of a career. For the younger American painters honored by museum retrospectives in the 1970s, it had shrunk to a little over a decade. What has always been known about high art throughout this period is its equivocal indebtedness to popular culture and mass culture. It draws on these without being subservient to them. Now, by joining, in the name of "intertextuality," the work of art with the product of mass culture, critics level themselves with artists as exponents of the new. The practice has occasionally been employed against the valuations of any possible canon—the canon, it is said, acts in the service of mere ideology. Such arguments carry a persistent appeal even though they risk confusing mass consumption with democratic expression. But I believe that Adorno was right to maintain very steadily that a radical practice of criticism could not retreat from the defense of the work of art. He gave his own justification of "immanent criticism" in an essay on "Cultural Criticism and Society":

> Where [such criticism] finds inadequacies it does not ascribe them hastily to the individual and his psychology, which are merely the facade of the failure, but instead seeks to derive them from the irreconcilability of the object's moments. It pursues the logic of its aporias, the insolubility of the task itself. In such antinomies criticism perceives those of society. A successful work, according to immanent criticism, is not one which resolves objective contradictions in a spurious harmony, but one which expresses the idea of harmony negatively by embodying the contradictions, pure and uncompromised, in its innermost structure. Confronted with this kind of work, the verdict "mere ideology" loses its meaning.[31]

Adorno wrote from the perspective of modernism, and other recent defenses of the modernist work of art, by Harold Rosenberg and Thomas Crow for example, have followed a similar pattern and rejected the interpretation of the mass-cultural object as a text like any other.[32]

In defining the interest and originality of modernist works, all of these critics notice a relation between such qualities and the accepted styles of mass culture. But the relation is not taken to be one of identity or resemblance. In short, they reject the anthropologist's idea of a seamless general text of culture. Their procedure seems to follow from reflection on a part of the critic's work for which the anthropologist cannot serve as a guide. This may be described broadly as the problem of allusion, or the ascription of self-consciousness in reading the motives of representation. Consider the use that art makes of clichés. It is a salient practice of modernist works in particular, and the tact with which a cliché is managed often serves as one index of an artist's temperament. Yet the anthropologist has no interest in this, and no equipment to measure it: from the point of view of the seamless general text, the commonplace, the daily banality, the cliché, and the cliché quoted ironically (let alone the cliché quoted with an unsuccessful attempted irony, as in "Hugh Selwyn Mauberley"), all have the same status. It has lately been claimed that, by interpreting early folk versions of the story of Little Red Ridinghood, we can reconstruct Frenchness.[33] It would be odd to make a similar claim about a modernist work—say, that by interpreting Flaubert's *Dictionary of Received Ideas,* we could reconstruct even a piece of Frenchness, late romantic bourgeois philistine Frenchness. Partly, the trouble is that the work does too much of the reconstruction itself; partly, that it yields information in excess of the attitudes it records. Perhaps this is another way of saying that reading a modernist text is something different from reading a text. For, grant that modernism owes it identity to a conscious relation with mass culture, and it follows that a modernist text knows a mass-cultural text as the latter does not know itself. Even the perspectivism of theory is logical and teachable, almost to the point of transparency, by comparison with the perspectivism of modern painting or poetry.

What is sometimes described as the resistance to theory is nothing but the usual tremors of passage as one professionalist vocabulary displaces another. New textualist methods of reading are pedagogically apt in much the same way that New Critical methods were, and the widening emphasis on theory belongs to a political action confined to the academy and its outworks. This verdict contradicts that of theory on itself, which may be summed up: "Literature dreams; theory knows." That what it knows may be dangerous to the order of things is a surmise undertaken and destined to stay in the register of as-if. States have no objection to theorists until they propose the undoing of existing structures by more than textual means. But to do so means also to step outside theory once and for all. At the same time, literature itself remains manifestly dangerous. Ignored by theory, the works of a Kundera, a Konrad, a Milosz evoke keen interest from the customs agents at any number of borders, and are interdicted as the works of a Derrida or a Jameson are not. This still happens because there was always a volatile element in the very texture of romantic and modernist works, which their appropriation by the academy has caused to pass from view but which is still recognized outside it. By asserting an unstable but strangely renewable connection with the past, they called into question the self-images of the present. And they did so at a time when the latter, either through censorship or the opinion-making efficacy of the media, were beginning to be rationalized under a new political authority.

"Who controls the past controls the future," goes the party slogan of Orwell's *1984*, but it has a corollary: "Who controls the present controls the past." The modern statist wants to control the understanding of the present. Literature and, when it chose to be active, criticism have been among the forces that stood in the way. Like the other slogans of the party, this one was drawn, as Orwell made clear, not only from the standard procedures of totalitarian states but also from emerging tendencies in America and Europe. What Orwell observed both in his novels and in many of his critical essays was that established governments were starting to share certain aims with revolutionary dictatorships. They might see the aims as temporary, while the dictatorships saw them as final, but year by year anyway the damage was being done. The modern state wanted not merely to govern but to control; to control the present it was necessary to control the past; and if that meant obliterating the past, it would not shrink from doing so. Orwell's predecessor as a critic was Edmund Burke, who wrote: "People will not look forward to posterity, who never look backward to their ancestors." But the state has a gaze more flatly purposeful than the writer's. When an Eastern leader cites Tolstoy approvingly, or a Western leader cites Lincoln approvingly, the same thing is happening, and to capture it one needs another phrase of Burke's: "They unplumb the dead for bullets to assassinate the living."

The first mistake of theory has been to suppose that criticism can have a direct relationship with the political control of the present. A second mistake has been to suppose that its main rival is literature. Orwell and Burke together suggest a different idea of what criticism ought to do. It cannot itself attain, or even supply others with tools for attaining, control of the present. But it can insert itself between those who control the present and their wish to control the past. It can, that is, weaken the state's inertia and qualify its authority, by affording a few of its citizens a backward glance which is not the same as the look sanctioned by the state. To the degree that it teaches the differentness of the past, criticism acts on behalf of a future.

I am proposing that for criticism today a consciousness of the past as such performs a critical function. To believe this does not require a faith in the objectivity of interpretation or a prior belief that history is the sum total of positive facts. It presumes only that other times hold other persons in other situations which we may think of as alternative to ours: in some respects better, in some respects worse, in all respects different. And that these materials are not altogether tractable: they will not do everything we want them to. This last is what the modern state most needs to forget. How much so we Americans were shown memorably when a president, on a foreign visit, recalled, and almost succeeded in making us recall, the Second World War as a contest against the Soviet Union in which Americans and Germans fought side by side. I give this last illustration for the same reason that I offered Orwell and Burke as representative critics, because it seems to me that literary criticism, when it matters, is not easily separated from cultural or social criticism. In the past few years, academic critics have seen all at once that they too are engaged in unclassifiable activities, and the recognition has led them to talk vaguely but ominously about power. Much of the talk conceives of power as a synonym for habits, customs, usages, practices of any kind, as if commentaries on texts could help people to live eventually without these things. The idea that they could is nonsense, with a short future in practice. Nevertheless, critics still do make a usable record of the ways people have thought and felt, or might think and feel, outside the mastery of the present. By translating, from a distant or otherwise hidden time, the testamentary parable or the unforeseen inheritance, they interpret for readers the hidden powers of living men and women.

Notes

1. The Invention of Literature

1. Walter Pater, *Appreciations* (London, 1889), pp. 223–224.
2. Friedrich von Schiller, *Naive and Sentimental Poetry,* trans. Julias A. Elias (New York,1966), p. 85.
3. Ibid., p. 100.
4. Ibid., p. 154.
5. René Wellek notices the same coincidence of dates in "Carlyle and German Romanticism," reprinted in *Confrontations* (Princeton, 1965), p. 34.
6. Thomas Carlyle, *Works,* 30 vols. (London, 1896), XXVIII, 1.
7. Ibid., pp. 4–5.
8. Ibid., p. 18.
9. Ibid., pp. 2–3.
10. Ibid., pp. 16–17.
11. Wordsworth and Pater are later versions of the meliorist; Yeats and Walter Benjamin are later versions of the skeptic; and the attitudes are equally marked outside poetry and criticism. Stevens's "Notes toward a Supreme Fiction" (a work of theory in verse without a genre) is unique in the way it attempts to overcome this division, by a skeptical questioning of the imagination that does not come to rest in myth.
12. Besides "Of the Standard of Taste," the relevant texts seem to me "Of Essay Writing" and "Of the Delicacy of Taste and Passion." My general account of Hume is indebted to Annette Baier's in *Postures of the Mind* (Minneapolis, 1985), chaps. 12–13.
13. Quoted in Henry Thomas Lord Cockburn, *Life of Lord Jeffrey,* 2nd ed., 2 vols. (Edinburgh, 1852), II, 406.
14. Leo Tolstoy, *What Is Art?,* trans. Almyer Maude (Library of Liberal Arts edition, New York, 1960), p. 49.
15. Ibid., p. 140.
16. Edward Thomas, *Walter Pater: A Critical Study* (New York, 1913), p. 208.

17. Marianne Moore, "When I Buy Pictures," in *Collected Poems* (New York, 1951), p. 55.

2. *Reflections on the Word* Genius

1. Thomas S. Kuhn, *The Structure of Scientific Revolutions,* 2nd ed. (Chicago, 1970); and "Logic of Discovery or Psychology of Research," in Kuhn, *The Essential Tension* (Chicago, 1977), pp. 266–292.

2. Michel Foucault, *The Archaeology of Knowledge,* trans. A. M. Sheridan Smith (New York, 1972), p. xxii; Stanley Fish, *Is There a Text in This Class?* (Cambridge, Mass., 1980), chaps. 13–16.

3. Edward Young, *Conjectures on Original Composition,* ed. Edith J. Morley (Manchester, 1918), p. 12.

4. Ibid., pp. 17, 20.

5. Quoted from the *Life of Cowley,* in Logan Pearsall Smith, *Words and Idioms* (Boston, 1925), p. 96. This sense may be derived from the *Dictionary* by amalgamating two definitions: "4. Disposition of nature by which any one is qualified for some particular employment," and "2. A man endowed with superiour faculties."

6. William Duff, *Essay on Original Genius* (London, 1767), p. 281.

7. Ibid., p. 33.

8. *Complete Works of William Hazlitt,* ed. P. P. Howe, 21 vols. (London, 1930–1934), VIII, 42.

9. *Shelley's Critical Prose,* ed. Bruce R. McElderry, Jr. (Lincoln, Nebr., 1967), p. 6.

10. See, for example, Owen Barfield, *Poetic Diction,* 3rd ed. (Middletown, Conn., 1973), chaps. 3–4; and Mary Hesse, "The Explanatory Function of Metaphor," in *Revolutions and Reconstructions in the Philosophy of Science* (Bloomington, Ind., 1980), pp. 111–124. Barfield quotes the passage from Shelley but interprets it, in keeping with his own interests, as an incitement to decode metaphors for the sake of confirming our surmises about the past.

11. Hobbes is a theorist of the first sort, Foucault of the second; for a more general comparison of their understandings of sovereignty and discipline, see Michael Walzer, "The Politics of Michel Foucault," *Dissent* 30 (Fall 1983), 481–490.

12. In part because his writings on morals are not read. J. B. Schneewind, *Sidgwick's Ethics and Victorian Moral Philosophy* (Oxford, 1977), chap. 3, brings out Whewell's distinctiveness and has a thorough treatment of his challenge to Utilitarianism.

13. *The Prose Works of William Wordsworth,* ed. W. J. B. Owen and Jane Worthington Smyser, 3 vols. (Oxford, 1974), I, 140.

14. Roger Sharrock, "The Chemist and the Poet: Sir Humphry Davy and the Preface to Lyrical Ballads," *Notes and Records of the Royal Society of London,* 17 (May 1962), 57–76. Sharrock believes, as I do also, that nothing in Coleridge's speculations concerning the sciences could have prepared the way for the remarks in the Preface. He was at times a friend of "men of science" (including Davy), at times a hater of them, but never a reasoner about their moral influence in society.

15. Wordsworth, *Prose Works,* I, 141. The involuntary echo of "sleep no more," from *Macbeth* II.ii.40, is very different in tone from the conspicuous use of that phrase to describe the effects of the French Revolution (1805 *Prelude,* Book 10, line 77).

16. Lawrence Manley's *Convention: 1500–1750* (Cambridge, Mass., 1980) is a thoughtful presentation of this view.

17. William Wordsworth, *Poetical Works,* ed. Thomas Hutchinson, rev. ed., (London, 1936), p. 104.

18. William Whewell, *The Elements of Morality including Polity,* 2 vols. (New York, 1845), I, 215.

19. A relevant text may be found in *The Doctrine of Virtue,* trans. Mary J. Gregor (New York, 1964), p. 113 (Book II, section ii.21), under the general heading "On Man's Duty to Himself to Increase his *Moral* Perfection." Kant there lays it down that "It is man's duty to *strive for* this perfection, but not to *achieve* it (in this life), and his pursuit of perfection, accordingly, is only a continual progress." The pursuit being once undertaken, man's progress may still be weakened by a failure of resolution, together with failures of right action. But Whewell vividly imagines the case in which "malicious acts" themselves insensibly weaken the resolution to practice virtue. I am grateful to Jeffrey Stout for raising the questions that prompted an expansion of this point.

20. For a more sustained reading of the "Ode to Duty," which develops the same contrast between Wordsworth and Kant, see James K. Chandler, *Wordsworth's Second Nature* (Chicago, 1984), pp. 250–252.

21. Schneewind, *Sidgwick's Ethics,* p. 108.

22. William Whewell, *Philosophy of the Inductive Sciences,* 2nd ed., 2 vols. (London, 1847), I, 42.

23. Ibid., II, 52,60.

24. Darwin believed in the doctrine consistently but found a polemical use for it. In *The Origin of Species* he refers to "that old canon in natural history, 'Natura non facit saltum'": one claim he made for evolution was that it vindicated the canon with a more thorough conservatism than its rivals. Between any two creatures A and D, that is, Darwin could picture the transitional gradations B and C, where others only imagined an abyss. By a theory of slight successive variations he was thus able to support the Linnaean motto with evidence rather than faith. My treatment of Darwin owes much to comments by Stan Rachootin on an early draft of this essay.

25. A misleading clue has been Darwin's quotation of Whewell's *Bridgewater Treatise* as an epigraph to *The Origin of Species;* see, for an instance of the emphasis in question, Gertrude Himmelfarb, *Darwin and the Darwinian Revolution* (Garden City, N.Y., 1959).

26. R. G. Collingwood, *The Idea of Nature* (Oxford, 1945), p. 118.

27. William Whewell, *History of the Inductive Sciences,* 2nd ed., 3 vols. (London, 1847), III, 626.

28. Whewell, *Philosophy,* II, 461.

29. William Paley, *Works,* ed. D. S. Wayland, 5 vols. (London, 1837), IV, 1.

30. Charles Darwin, *The Origin of Species,* ed. J. W. Burrow (Harmondsworth, 1968), p. 217. Michael Ghiselin's remarks in *The Triumph of the Darwinian Method* (Berkeley, 1969), p. 54, on the significance of a population ("a group of things which interact with one another") as distinct from a family (a group defined by its traits) help to clarify the motive of this passage.

31. The volute anecdote is related in Neal C. Gillespie, *Charles Darwin and the Prob-*

lem of Creation (Chicago, 1979), p. 42, a book on which I have relied extensively
for its account of Darwin's response to contemporary forms of creationism.

32. George Levine, in "Darwin and the Problem of Authority," *Raritan* 3 (Winter
1984), 30–61, observes that Darwin cared for "change, diversity, growth—for
the world and for the mind: he was interested in keeping intellectual inquiry
alive" (p. 55). It seems to me that Darwin cared for these things in principle, as
many people do. He claimed, however, to have discovered a truth, and did not
like to see it challenged: on any other view, his treatment of Butler, as well as
better-qualified heretics, passes into the realm of mere eccentricity. Gillian Beer,
quoted in the same article, thinks that Darwin's "theory deconstructs any formulation which interprets the world as commensurate with man's understanding
of it" (p. 35). "Deconstruct" is used as a rough synonym for *debunk, disarm,
defuse,* but even so it is not quite appropriate to Darwin. Reading him would be
a queer experience for someone who believed that asparagus was commensurate
with the words "spear-like and nutty-tasting vegetable." Nevertheless, his theory
exists in order to render one sort of knowledge pragmatically available. It is a
lever to move the world.

33. *Works of John Ruskin,* ed. E. T. Cook and Alexander Wedderburn, 39 vols. (London, 1903–1912), XXII, 125.

34. On Galton, see Peter B. Medawar, *The Hope of Progress* (Garden City, N.Y.,
1973), pp. 71–79.

35. Francis Galton, *Hereditary Genius* (London, 1869), p. 343.

36. Samuel Butler, *The Way of All Flesh* (Modern Library edition, New York, 1950),
p. 129.

3. Burke, Wordsworth, and the Defense of History

1. The conception is almost a century too late for Burke; but I do not think the
same is true of a parallel habit of thought concerning morals. The latter relates
to the advantage, over time, of instincts, customs, or conventions which allow
us to survive, as against those which hasten our extinction. The moral observer
is asked to notice the adaptation of mores to "human nature," without the intervention either of principles or of commandments. Such a perspective was available to Burke as a reader of Joseph Butler's *Sermons.* It is pertinent that he also
greatly admired Butler's *Analogy of Religion,* a book he recommended to James
Barry as a nondogmatic cure for religious doubts. Burke and Butler have in
common a sense of the reality of *purposes created by accident.* For them, no dramatic
choice offers itself between revealed purposes (whether in arguments from design
or natural law) and the apparent purposelessness of certain aspects of the natural
record. Butler, with his hostility to "the *a priori* method" and his readiness to
discern pattern in mere continuity, for similar reasons looks ahead to Darwin
also; see James R. Moore, *The Post-Darwinian Controversies* (Cambridge, 1979),
chap. 12.

2. The foregoing summary may be felt to impute to Burke a modern "perspectivism" which could hardly have been his. But his understanding of the contingency
of even the deepest moral beliefs or loyalties can make paragraphs of his writing
sound like Nietzsche's essay *On the Genealogy of Morals.* It is possible to explain

this affinity historically—for instance, by reference to the common background of Machiavelli—and Conor Cruise O'Brien has done it well in *The Suspecting Glance*. But the causes of Burke's perspectivism go back to his own original argument about taste, in which the choice of a common viewpoint is both voluntary and compelled. Thus, in some striking phrases of the *Reflections*, characteristic in their assurance and evasiveness, he speaks of the benefits we derive from "considering our liberties *in the light* of an inheritance"; and again, of the good of our "always acting *as if in the presence* of our canonized forefathers" (emphasis added). His words ask to be held answerable only for an imaginative truth that follows from an act of the will.

3. Edmund Burke, *Correspondence,* ed. Thomas W. Copeland, 10 vols. (Chicago, 1958–1978), VI, 215; and Burke, *Reflections on the Revolution in France,* ed. Conor Cruise O'Brien (Penguin edition, Harmondsworth, 1970), p. 271.

4. Edmund Burke, *Works,* 12 vols. (Boston, 1869), IV, 377.

5. Burke, *Reflections,* p. 212.

6. Burke, *Works,* I, 441.

7. H. N. Brailsford, *Shelley, Godwin, and Their Circle* (London, 1913), p. 20.

8. Burke, *Reflections,* p. 175.

9. Ibid., pp. 119, 140.

10. Ibid., p. 121.

11. On sympathy and convention I here borrow from some remarks by J. B. Schneewind.

12. Early among the many responses to Burke's *Reflections,* Joseph Priestley's *Letters to the Rt. Hon. Edmund Burke* (1791) remarked a paradox in the concern to judge a given order only as relative to a given society. Writes Priestley: "Must every thing once established be, for that reason only, ever maintained?" He wonders at the vicariousness of Burke's feeling for the French church: "You condemn the French National Assembly, for innovating in *their* religion, which is Catholic, as much as you could do the English Parliament, for innovating in *ours,* which is Protestant"; and he makes the logical deduction: "We may therefore presume, that had you lived in Turkey, you would have been a mahometan, and in Tartary, a devout worshipper of the grand lama." Excerpt reprinted in *The Debate on the French Revolution 1789–1800,* ed. Alfred Cobban (London, 1950), pp. 438–440.

13. Burke, *Works,* IV, 55.

14. Burke, *Reflections,* pp. 128–130.

15. Ibid., pp. 297–298.

16. See J. G. A. Pocock, "The Political Economy of Burke's Analysis of the French Revolution," in *Virtue, Commerce, and History* (Cambridge, 1985), pp. 193–212, where Burke is associated with the argument that "commerce . . . was the sole agency capable of refining the passions and polishing the manners" (pp. 195–196); though Pocock also adds the following reservation: "A strictly progressive theory of manners, such as Burke might have derived from his Scottish acquaintances, presented them as arising, and fulfilling the natural sociability of man, only in the course of the commercialization, refinement and diversification of society. . . . [Yet] Burke declared that manners must precede commerce, rather than the other way around" (p. 210).

17. Burke, *Works,* I, 483.

18. Ibid., V, 393.
19. Ibid., IV, 440.
20. Wordsworth, *The Borderers,* ed. Robert Osborn (Ithaca, N.Y., 1982). I prefer Wordsworth's 1842 revision to the early version of 1797–1799, and pick most of my quotations accordingly, though I have kept his early names for the characters. In 1842, Mortimer becomes Marmaduke; Rivers becomes Oswald; Herbert stays Herbert. The later set of names have sometimes, however, been wrongly adduced in a general complaint about Wordsworth's tactlessness at revision. The main point about this change would seem to be that he went from the naming conventions of Shakespeare to those of Walter Scott. It is, whatever one makes of it, an interesting and thoughtful choice.
21. See Donald Davidson, "Hume's Cognitive Theory of Pride," reprinted in *Essays on Actions and Events* (Oxford, 1980), pp. 277–290.
22. Wordsworth, *The Borderers,* p. 67.
23. Ibid., p. 51.
24. On this and the relation between inheritance and sheer repetition, the argument that follows is anticipated in James Chandler, *Wordsworth's Second Nature,* chap. 7.
25. See Chandler, *Wordsworth's Second Nature,* passim; Michael H. Friedman, *The Making of a Tory Humanist* (New York, 1979); Nicholas Roe, *Wordsworth and Coleridge: The Radical Years* (Oxford, 1988).
26. These two distinct characters—the Nietzschean hero of self-overcoming, and the Burkean hero of self-subordination—hardly ever come together in the play. But Rivers's great speech in Act IV, which recounts the story of his life, shows vividly how the latter can give way to the former. His crime, he says, had freed him for lonely wanderings. Then, communing with himself in a stark landscape, he arrived at a different understanding of life:

> When from these forms I turned to contemplate
> The opinions and the uses of the world,
> I seemed a being who had passed alone
> Beyond the visible barriers of the world
> And travelled into things to come.   (IV.ii.1815, 1797 version)

The passing beyond all ordinary beauty in the sublime is felt to parallel the passing beyond a common morality by this kind of hero. He turns from the "forms" he has known till then in the same gesture with which he turns from customary "opinions" and "uses."
27. E. P. Thompson, "The Moral Economy of the English Crowd in the Eighteenth Century," *Past and Present* 50 (February 1971), 76–136.
28. There are other echoes between "Tintern Abbey" and *The Borderers;* most unexpectedly, in Rivers's gaze from a height in Lebanon: "I perceived / What mighty objects do impress their forms / To build up this our intellectual being" (IV.ii.1810, 1797 version)—a strain of associationist eloquence which has been said to require an English setting.
29. Wordsworth, *Prose Works,* I, 228.
30. Alfred Cobban, *Edmund Burke and the Revolt against the Eighteenth Century* (New York, 1929), p. 147, remarks the clear influence of Burke in the *Convention.*

31. David Erdman, "Milton! Thou Shouldst Be Living" (unpublished lecture, 1986).
32. Wordsworth, *Prose Works*, I, 326.
33. Burke, *Works*, V, 398.

4. William Cobbett, Reformer

1. George Spater, *William Cobbett: The Poor Man's Friend*, 2 vols. (Cambridge, 1982).
2. Quoted in Spater, *William Cobbett*, II, 426.
3. William Cobbett, *Rural Rides* (Penguin edition, Harmondsworth, 1967), p. 45.
4. G. K. Chesterton, *William Cobbett* (New York, 1926), pp. 21–22. This book gives a fine general sketch of a Tory radicalism that touched the thinking of Wordsworth and Ruskin as well.
5. Quoted in Spater, *William Cobbett*, II, 455.
6. Cobbett, *Rural Rides*, p. 199.
7. Ibid., p. 260.

5. Keats's Politics

1. John Strachey, *The Coming Struggle for Power* (Modern Library edition, New York, 1935), chap. 11, with the passing remark: "Keats was as typical an Englishman as Wellington" (p. 223).
2. E. P. Thompson, *William Morris: Romantic to Revolutionary*, 2nd ed. (London, 1977). See pp. 10–21 on Keats as "one of the first poets to feel in his own everyday experience the full shock of 'bourgeoisdom and philistinism'" (p. 15).
3. George Bernard Shaw, "Keats," in *The John Keats Memorial Volume* (1921), reprinted in *Bernard Shaw's Nondramatic Literary Criticism*, ed. Stanley Weintraub (Lincoln, Nebr., 1972), p. 134.
4. Quoted in Donald Davie, *Purity of Diction in English Verse*, 2nd ed. (London, 1967), p. 172.
5. *Keats: The Critical Heritage*, ed. G. M. Matthews (New York, 1971), p. 109.
6. *The Poems of John Keats*, ed. Jack Stillinger (Cambridge, Mass., 1978).
7. *The Letters of John Keats*, ed. Hyder E. Rollins, 2 vols. (Cambridge, Mass., 1958), II, 176.
8. Ibid., 180.
9. *Poetical Works of Leigh Hunt*, ed. H. S. Milford (London, 1923), p. 244.
10. *Edinburgh Review*, January 1830, p. 565.
11. Keats, *Letters*, I, 397–398.
12. Karl Marx, *Capital*, trans. Samuel Moore and Edward Aveling (New York, 1906), pp. 184–185.
13. Keats, *Letters*, I, 207.
14. Tilottama Rajan, *Dark Interpreter: The Discourse of Romanticism* (Ithaca, N.Y., 1980), chap. 4; Thomas Reed, "Keats and the Politics of Poetry" (Ph.D. diss., Princeton University, 1985).
15. Hunt, *Poetical Works*, p. 313.
16. Hazlitt, *Complete Works*, XII, 122.
17. Keats, *Letters*, II, 193–194.

18. Ibid., I, 281–282.

19. T. W. Adorno, *Aesthetic Theory*, trans. C. Lenhardt (London, 1984), p. 369.

6. *The Genealogy of Disinterestedness*

1. Matthew Arnold, *Prose Works*, ed. R. H. Super, 11 vols. (Ann Arbor, Mich., 1961–1977), III, 265. I take the phrase "normal science" from Kuhn's *Structure of Scientific Revolutions* and use it as he uses it there: to denote a way of thinking proper to a time of reasonable stability, when intellectual workers engage in "problem-solving" with a consensus as to methods as well as aims. Arnold's most vivid feeling about modern culture, the motive of his most impassioned writing, was that revolutions in taste were succeeding each other too quickly. Work in the arts was now almost wholly directed to a mood of crisis rather than normality. He proposed as a solution that we retrieve the norms by an act of faith. In practice, his own faith supports his irony, and leads to the tactical judgment that if we give the emerging genres an old name we can ignore them. Hence, for example, his allusion to the novel as the "domestic epic." This wish to find a remedy for crisis in some stable genre—a category for which the romantic lyric, the realistic novel, the dramatic monologue, somehow will not do—accounts I think for the tone of sincere indifference (occasionally broken by a compelled attention), with which Arnold was able to treat every great contemporary from Emerson to Tolstoy.

2. Hazlitt, *Complete Works*, V, 69.

3. Ibid., XVII, 296.

4. On the good reasons for rejecting this assumption, see Frederick A. Pottle, *The Idiom of Poetry* (Ithaca, N.Y., 1946), chaps. 1–3. With the doctrine of unvariable uses and habits Arnold also accepts—though he does not strictly require—a doctrine of epistemological immediacy or transparency. This comes out in his theory of translation, especially in a passage like the following from "On Translating Homer": "Chapman translates his object into Elizabethan, as Pope translates it into the Augustan of Queen Anne; both convey it to us through a medium. Homer, on the other hand, sees his object and conveys it to us immediately."

    Arnold's thinking here brings him closer to, say, Dryden's than his dismissal of "an age of prose" might suggest. Compare the remarks on Shakespeare in the "Essay of Dramatic Poesy": "All the images of nature were still present to him, and he drew them, not laboriously, but luckily. . . . He needed not the spectacles of books to read nature; he looked inwards, and found her there." On the uses of such metaphors in the moral sciences generally, see Richard Rorty, *Philosophy and the Mirror of Nature* (Princeton, 1979), Parts I and II.

5. Arnold, *Prose Works*, IX, 206–207.

6. Walter Pater, *Works*, 9 vols. (London, 1900–1901), I, vii.

7. David Hume, *A Treatise of Human Nature*, ed. L. A. Selby-Bigge (London, 1888), I.4.vii, p. 269; though he frequently gives the predicament a less dramatic shading, as in the following comments from a letter to Hugh Blair: "No man can have any other experience but his own. The experience of others becomes

his only by the credit which he gives to their testimony; which proceeds from his own experience of human nature." Solipsism on this view is one, emphatic, way of stating the limitation of all our knowledge, once we have granted a perspectivist idea of knowledge. As a "problem" it has no place in any dispute concerning idealism versus realism or subjectivity versus objectivity.

8. Pater, *Works,* I, 220.
9. Ibid., pp. 236–237.
10. Ibid., pp. 237–238.
11. Ibid., pp. 238–239.
12. Leigh Hunt, *Imagination and Fancy* (London, 1883), p. 2.
13. Oscar Wilde, "The Critic as Artist," in *The Artist as Critic,* ed. Richard Ellmann (New York, 1969), pp. 368–369.
14. Ibid., p. 312.
15. Thomas, *Walter Pater,* p. 108.
16. Wilde, *Artist as Critic,* p. 339.
17. Ibid., p. 392.
18. Ibid., p. 393.
19. Hazlitt, *Complete Works,* XII, 10–11.
20. Pater, *Works,* V, 23–24.
21. Wilde, *Artist as Critic,* pp. 382–383.

7. Emerson and the Ode to W. H. Channing

1. Quoted in *Selections from Ralph Waldo Emerson,* ed. Stephen E. Whicher (Boston, 1957), p. 505.
2. *Journals of Ralph Waldo Emerson,* ed. Edward Waldo Emerson and Waldo Emerson Forbes, 10 vols. (Cambridge, Mass., 1909–1914), VII, 219.
3. Ibid., p. 223.
4. Ibid., p. 26.
5. Emerson, *Works,* 12 vols. (Cambridge, Mass., 1903–1904), I, 12–13.
6. Emerson, *Journals,* VII, 67, 39.
7. Ibid., pp. 125–126.

8. Literary Radicalism in America

1. O. W. Firkins, *Ralph Waldo Emerson* (Boston, 1915), pp. 169–170.
2. *The Dial* I (July 1840), 2–3.
3. Emerson, *Journals,* VII, 441.
4. *Margaret Fuller: American Romantic,* ed. Perry Miller (Garden City, N.Y., 1963), p. 259.
5. Emerson, *Works,* II, 286.
6. Van Wyck Brooks, *Three Essays on America* (New York, 1934), pp. 64–65.
7. Randolph Bourne, *War and the Intellectuals: Collected Essays 1915–19,* ed. Carl Resek (New York, 1964), pp. 60–61.
8. Ibid., p. 12.
9. Brooks, *Three Essays,* p. 139.
10. T. J. Clark coined the phrase "Eliotic Trotskyism," in "Clement Greenberg's

Theory of Art"; see *The Politics of Interpretation*, ed. W. J. T. Mitchell (Chicago, 1983), pp. 203–220.

11. Clement Greenberg, "Avant-Garde and Kitsch," reprinted in *Art and Culture* (Boston, 1965), p. 14.

12. Emerson, "The Poet," in *Works*, III, 16.

13. John Ashbery, "The Invisible Avant-Garde," in *Avant-Garde Art*, ed. Thomas B. Hess and John Ashbery (New York, 1968), pp. 183–184.

9. *A Simple Separate Person*

1. Walt Whitman, *Notebooks and Unpublished Prose Manuscripts*, ed. Edward Grier, 6 vols. (New York, 1984); *Complete Poetry and Collected Prose* (Library of America, New York, 1981).

2. Whitman, *Notebooks*, I, 77.

3. Whitman, *Complete Poetry and Prose*, pp. 1313–14.

4. D. H. Lawrence, *Studies in Classic American Literature* (New York, 1961), pp. 171–172.

5. Paul Zweig, *Walt Whitman: The Making of the Poet* (New York, 1984).

6. Whitman, *Notebooks*, I, 385.

7. Whitman, *Complete Poetry and Prose*, pp. 892–893.

8. Whitman, *Notebooks*, II, 881.

10. *Kipling's Jest*

1. *Rudyard Kipling's Verse*, Definitive Edition (Garden City, N.Y., 1945).

2. T. S. Eliot, "Kipling Redivivus," reprinted in *Kipling: The Critical Heritage*, ed. R. Lancelyn Green (London, 1971), p. 324.

3. Ibid.

4. Rudyard Kipling, *Works*, 36 vols. (New York, 1934), XXXVI, 71.

5. Lionel Johnson, *Reviews and Critical Papers*, ed. Robert Shafer (New York, 1921), p. 31.

6. Ibid., p. 37.

7. Burke, *Works*, V, 210–211.

8. Oscar Wilde, "The Critic as Artist," in *The Artist as Critic*, ed. Richard Ellmann, p. 402.

9. Kipling, *Works*, XXXVI, 200–201.

10. *Kim*, chap. 7, in *Works*, XVI, 206.

11. Ibid., p. 207.

12. Lucy McDiarmid, *Saving Civilization: Yeats, Eliot, and Auden between the Wars* (Cambridge, 1984).

11. *Edward Thomas and Modernism*

1. *A Language Not to Be Betrayed: Selected Prose of Edward Thomas*, ed. Edna Longley (New York, 1981).

2. Ibid., p. 47.

3. Ibid., p. 44.

4. Ibid.
5. Thomas, *Walter Pater,* p. 124.
6. Ibid., p. 213.
7. Edward Thomas, *Collected Poems* (London, 1961).
8. *A Language Not to Be Betrayed,* p. 124.
9. Ibid., p. 55.
10. Ibid., p. 108.
11. Ibid., p. 116.
12. Ibid., p. 121.
13. Ibid., p. 126.
14. Ibid., p. 128.
15. Hart Crane, *Complete Poems and Selected Letters and Prose,* ed. Brom Weber (New York, 1966).

12. *The Sense of Vocation in Frost and Stevens*

1. See Frank Kermode, *Romantic Image* (London, 1957), chap. 1; and Harold Bloom, *The Ringers in the Tower* (Chicago, 1971), pp. 323–337.
2. *The Poetry of Robert Frost,* ed. Edward Connery Latham (New York, 1969).
3. *The Poetical Works of Matthew Arnold* (London, 1942).
4. Richard Poirier, *Robert Frost: The Work of Knowing* (New York, 1978), pp. 230–231.
5. My aim is to observe the sort of caution that David Ferry argued for in *The Limits of Mortality* (Middletown, Conn., 1959); especially in his remarks on the "uncouth shape" somewhat akin to the leech-gatherer, who crosses Wordsworth's path in Book IV of *The Prelude:* "His lack of feeling about his own experience . . . may be what should be learned from him. This is a figure as close to the border of death as possible, and as far as can be from involvement in 'the ordinary interests of man.' Yet he is an image of that mankind which the love of nature leads us to love" (p. 142).
6. Wordsworth, *Poetical Works,* ed. Thomas Hutchinson.
7. I have drawn here upon the discussion of Stevens and the pathetic fallacy in Harold Bloom's *Wallace Stevens: The Poems of Our Climate* (Ithaca, N.Y., 1977), pp. 54–63, 354–359. But I prefer not to confine the reference of the "particular" to "the fiction of the leaves" (p. 354).
8. Letter to Sara Hutchinson, 14 June 1802, in *Early Letters of William and Dorothy Wordsworth,* ed. Ernest de Selincourt (Oxford, 1935), p. 306.
9. Ibid.
10. Last line of "The Killers." Stevens's description of Hemingway is pertinent: "Obviously he is a poet and I should say, offhand, the most significant of living poets, so far as the subject of EXTRAORDINARY ACTUALITY is concerned." The words come from a letter to Henry Church, 2 July 1942, in *Letters of Wallace Stevens,* ed. Holly Stevens (New York, 1970), pp. 411–412.
11. See Geoffrey Hartman, *Wordsworth's Poetry* (New Haven, 1964), pp. 269–271, where the after-image is defined as "a re-cognition that leads to recognition." This seems to me to involve a fully Yeatsian use of the image. It implies a method of internalization, a recognition-scene projected in the mind, and a therapeutic

outcome, about all of which Wordsworth is more skeptical than the epigram requires him to be. A true adept of the after-image should be able to report moments when for "twenty minutes more or less / It seemed, so great my happiness, / That I was blessed and could bless." Eventually he may plot such moments in advance. But Wordsworth is always startled by the gift of self-blessing, and never glances at his watch.

12. A. D. Nuttall, *A Common Sky: Philosophy and the Literary Imagination* (London, 1974), p. 131. Whetever the propriety of this judgment, Nuttall reads the poem as Frost is likely to have read it.

13. Some Uses of Biography

1. Walter Jackson Bate, *John Keats* (Cambridge, Mass., 1963); Richard Ellmann, *James Joyce* (New York, 1959).
2. Samuel Johnson, *The Lives of the Most Eminent English Poets,* English Classics edition, 3 vols. (London, 1896), I, 134–135.
3. Ibid., III, 32.
4. Ellmann, *James Joyce,* p. 3.
5. Lawrance Thompson, *Robert Frost: The Early Years* (New York, 1966); *Robert Frost: The Years of Triumph* (New York, 1970); Lawrance Thompson and R. H. Winnick, *Robert Frost: The Later Years* (New York, 1976).
6. See Poirier, *Robert Frost,* passim.
7. Ian Hamilton, *Robert Lowell* (New York, 1982).
8. Ibid., p. 184.
9. Quoted in Hamilton, *Robert Lowell,* p. 237.
10. Ibid., p. 474.
11. Johnson, *Lives,* I, 100; III, 82; III, 29.

14. Why Authors Do Not Create Their Own Worlds

1. P. N. Furbank, *Reflections on the Word "Image"* (London, 1970), pp. 116–122.
2. Maynard Mack, "The World of *Hamlet,*" *Yale Review* 41 (1952), reprinted in *Hamlet* (Signet edition, New York, 1963), p. 234.
3. Marcel Proust, *The Captive,* trans. C. K. Scott Moncrieff (Modern Library edition, New York, 1929), pp. 344–345.
4. Ibid., p. 347.
5. Ibid., pp. 348–349.
6. Ibid., p. 512.
7. Quoted in Roger Fry, *Transformations* (London, 1926), p. 8.
8. Ibid.
9. Eliot, *Kipling: The Critical Heritage,* p. 324.
10. George Orwell, *Collected Essays, Journalism and Letters,* ed. Sonia Orwell and Ian Angus, 4 vols. (New York, 1968), I, 493.
11. Ibid., p. 495.
12. Franz Kafka, *The Great Wall of China,* trans. Willa and Edwin Muir (New York, 1946), p. 170.
13. Clifford Geertz, *Local Knowledge* (New York, 1983), p. 152. For some difficulties

of seeing anything simply in its own conceptual or linguistic world, see Donald Davidson, "On the Very Idea of a Conceptual Scheme," reprinted in *Inquiries into Truth and Interpretation* (Oxford, 1983), pp. 183–198; and Rorty, *Philosophy and the Mirror of Nature,* chap. 7.

14. Nelson Goodman, *Ways of Worldmaking* (Indianapolis, 1978), p. 132.
15. Ibid., p. 140.

15. *Literature and Theory*

1. W. K. Wimsatt, *Day of the Leopards* (New Haven, 1976), pp. 196–197.
2. Gayatri Chakravorti Spivak, "Three Women's Texts and a Critique of Imperialism," *Critical Inquiry* 12 (Autumn 1985), 243–261.
3. See E. D. Hirsch, Jr., *Validity in Interpretation* (New Haven, 1967) and Gerald Graff, *Literature against Itself* (Chicago, 1979). A good exposition of Hirsch's views, with a polemic against them, may be found in David Couzens Hoy, *The Critical Circle* (Berkeley, 1977), chap. 1.
4. Ludwig Wittgenstein, *Philosophical Investigations,* trans. G. E. M. Anscombe, 3rd ed. (New York, 1968), pp. 103, 201.
5. Wittgenstein, *Zettel* (Berkeley, 1970), p. 31.
6. See Richard Rorty, *Consequences of Pragmatism* (Minneapolis, 1982), chap. 8. I have profited from the remarks on Derrida in chapter 6 as well, and in the same author's "Deconstruction and Circumvention," *Critical Inquiry* 11 (Autumn 1984), 1–23. My reservations about the idea of a "general text" appear later in this chapter.
7. The afterword to William James's essay "On Some Hegelisms" in *The Will to Believe* (New York, 1897) includes some notations on the circumstances of his temporary conversion to the Hegelian philosophy, under the effects of nitrous-oxide gas. They give a strong emphasis to the coincidence of sameness with difference: "Strife presupposes something to be striven about; and in this common topic, the same for both parties, the differences merge. . . . *Yes* and *no* agree at least in being assertions," and so on. The leading vehicle for his conversion, as James describes it, was *puns,* and he gives as a specimen "What's a mistake but a kind of take?" James sums up his feelings throughout the episode: "It is impossible to convey an idea of the torrential character of the identification of opposites as it streams through the mind in this experience" (p. 295).
8. See, for example, Martha Nussbaum, "Flawed Crystals: James's *The Golden Bowl* and Literature as Moral Philosophy," *New Literary History* 15 (Autumn 1983), 25–50, a study of the novel's characters as responsible moral thinkers. One would not quite guess from this account that they are interested in money and power.
9. John Searle, "The Word Turned Upside Down," *New York Review of Books,* October 27, 1983, pp. 74–79. A more accurate skeptical estimate of the claims by theorists to do without an idea of making sense is Hilary Putnam, "The Craving for Objectivity," *New Literary History* 15 (Winter 1984), 229–239. I have borrowed in this essay something of Putnam's emphasis on the worth of trying to "get things right."
10. Paul de Man, *Allegories of Reading* (New Haven, 1979), p. 17.
11. William Empson, *Seven Types of Ambiguity,* 2nd ed. (London, 1947), p. 4.

12. Paul de Man, *Blindness and Insight: Essays in the Rhetoric of Contemporary Criticism,* 2nd ed. (Minneapolis, 1983).

13. De Man, *The Rhetoric of Romanticism* (New York, 1984), p. 81.

14. Stanley Cavell, *Themes Out of School* (San Francisco, 1984), p. 42.

15. Neil Hertz, *The End of the Line: Essays on Psychoanalysis and the Sublime* (New York, 1985).

16. Ibid., p. 208.

17. Michel Foucault, *Language, Counter-Memory, Practice,* ed. Donald F. Bouchard (Ithaca, N.Y., 1977), p. 153.

18. Wittgenstein, *Zettel,* p. 98.

19. Foucault, *Language,* p. 163.

20. Ibid., p. 162.

21. Stanley Corngold, *The Fate of the Self: German Writers and French Theory* (New York, 1985), p. 12; on Nietzsche, see chaps. 3 and 4, passim. Richard Poirier gives a related account of an ambivalence between the Nietzsche-Foucault hostility to the self and the status they share as authors with signatures and styles, in "Writing Off the Self," *Raritan* 1 (Summer 1981), 106–133. Both Nietzsche and Foucault afford "an occasion," Poirier writes, "for participating in the only momentarily exhilarating and cleansing imagination of self-eradication. Indeed, the excess of rhetorical power and the lack of caution which makes it so enlivening, on occasion, to read Foucault, and especially Nietzsche, is at the same time the most telling evidence that each is aware of the resistance in language itself to any persuasive argument for self-obliteration. It is in the nature of writing that whatever Foucault and Nietzsche say will be taken as metaphor and subjected to its constraints. They know this" (p. 118).

22. E. P. Thompson, *The Poverty of Theory and Other Essays* (New York, 1978), pp. 185–186.

23. "Letters to Walter Benjamin," in Ernst Bloch et al., *Aesthetics and Politics* (London, 1977), p. 123.

24. Fredric Jameson, "Postmodernism," *New Left Review,* July–August 1984, p. 58.

25. Ibid., p. 64.

26. Ibid., p. 86.

27. Terry Eagleton, *Literary Theory: An Introduction* (Minneapolis, 1983), p. 12.

28. On the principle of charity, see Davidson, "On the Very Idea of a Conceptual Scheme"; and W. V. O. Quine, *Word and Object* (Cambridge, Mass., 1964), chap. 2. Roughly, the principle holds that in moving from one language to another, we accommodate as many of its unfamiliar properties as we can to our familiar ways of understanding. Given, therefore, a choice between treating a piece of language as utterly opaque and treating it as intelligible, we make the necessary adjustments of our general view to bring about the latter outcome. Interpretation has a comparable principle of charity, in keeping with which a reader, when shown a difficult passage or work by a great author, tries before losing patience to work out how the author may have been making an unexpected sort of sense.

29. Eagleton, *The Function of Criticism* (London, 1984), p. 15.

30. Wittgenstein, *Zettel,* p. 60.

31. Theodor W. Adorno, *Prisms,* trans. Samuel and Sherry Weber (Cambridge,

Mass., 1981), p. 32. The letters to Benjamin cited above also contain a defense of the work of art: "The reification of a great work of art is not just loss, any more than the reification of the cinema is all loss. It would be bourgeois reaction to negate the reification of the cinema in the name of the ego, and it would border on anarchism to revoke the reification of a great work of art in the spirit of immediate use-values" (p. 123). On Adorno's "logic of aporias," see his *Aesthetic Theory*, trans. G. Lenhardt, chap. 12.

32. Harold Rosenberg, "Art and Its Double," in *Artworks and Packages* (New York, 1971), describes the mutual influence of the arts and the media as continuous throughout the modern period, but with the arts now on the brink of vanishing into the media. Thomas Crow, "Modernism and Mass Culture in the Visual Arts," in *Modernism and Modernity*, ed. Benjamin H. D. Buchloh, Serge Guilbaut, and David Solkin (Nova Scotia, 1983), pp. 215–264, sees the exchange as repeating a single pattern: "the appropriation of oppositional practices upward, the return of evacuated cultural goods downward."

33. See Robert Darnton, "Peasants Tell Tales: The Meaning of Mother Goose," in *The Great Cat Massacre* (New York, 1984).

Acknowledgments

FOR PERMISSION to reprint essays that have appeared elsewhere, in a few cases under different titles, I thank the editors of the following journals: "Reflections on the Word *Genius*," *New Literary History*, Autumn 1985; "William Cobbett, Reformer," *The New Republic*, December 13, 1982; "Keats's Politics," *Studies in Romanticism*, Summer 1986; "The Genealogy of Disinterestedness," *Raritan*, Spring 1982; "Emerson and the Ode to W. H. Channing," *The Hudson Review*, Summer 1980; "Literary Radicalism in America," *Dissent*, Winter 1985; "A Simple Separate Person," *The Times Literary Supplement*, March 21, 1986; "Kipling's Jest," *Grand Street*, Winter 1985; "Edward Thomas and Modernism," *Raritan*, Summer 1983; "The Sense of Vocation in Frost and Stevens," *Studies in Romanticism*, Spring 1982; "Some Uses of Biography," *The Yale Review*, Winter 1984; "Why Authors Do Not Create Their Own Worlds," *Salmagundi*, Fall 1988; "Literature and Theory," *Social Research*, Autumn 1986.

Grateful acknowledgment is also made to the following for permission to reprint previously published material:

Henry Holt and Company, and Jonathan Cape Limited: excerpts from *The Poetry of Robert Frost*, edited by Edward Connery Lathem. Copyright 1923, 1928, © 1969 by Holt, Rinehart and Winston. Copyright 1942, 1951, © 1956 by Robert Frost. Copyright © 1970 by Lesley Frost Ballantine. Reprinted by permission of Henry Holt and Company, and of Jonathan Cape Limited and the Estate of Robert Frost.

Alfred A. Knopf, Inc., and Faber and Faber Ltd.: "The Course of a Particular" by Wallace Stevens. Copyright 1957 by Elsie Stevens and Holly Stevens. Reprinted from *Opus Posthumous* by Wallace Stevens, by permission of Alfred A. Knopf, Inc., and of Faber and Faber, Ltd.

Farrar, Straus & Giroux, Inc., and Faber and Faber Ltd.: excerpt from "Dolphin" from *The Dolphin* by Robert Lowell. Copyright © 1973 by Robert Lowell. Reprinted by permission of Farrar, Straus and Giroux, Inc., and of Faber and Faber Ltd.

For permission to quote poems by Edward Thomas, thanks are due to Mrs. Myfanwy Thomas, to Oxford University Press, and to Faber and Faber Ltd.

"Reflections on the Word *Genius*" was originally read at a conference on Philosophy of Science and Literary Theory, at the University of Virginia, April 1984, organized by Richard Rorty and E. D. Hirsch. "Burke, Wordsworth, and the Defense of History" was given as a paper for discussion to the graduate seminar on History and Literature at the University of Chicago, May 1988. It has benefited from the comments of James Chandler, Elizabeth Helsinger, and the other participants in that group, as it did earlier from many conversations with Jeffrey Stout. In the last stages of preparing the manuscript, Georgann Witte's reponses to several chapters led me to remove some passages and to clarify others; Mary Ellen Geer, the manuscript editor, was steady and unsparing in every phase of our work; and Andrew Elfenbein read the proofs with an intelligence that helped as much by adding detail as by subtracting error. I am grateful to the John Simon Guggenheim Memorial Foundation for a fellowship which enabled me to write part of the book, and to Lindsay Waters of Harvard University Press, whose encouragement and sound advice were a help from start to finish.

Index

Webster and, 138; other references, 158, 159, 165–166
WORKS: "American Scholar, The," 148; "Each and All," 143; "Experience," 143; "Merlin," 133, 150; "Monadnoc," 139; *Nature,* 137–138, 140–142; "Ode to W. H. Channing," 133–144; "Over-Soul, The," 152
Empson, William, 233, 244, 265, 271, 272, 284
Enlightenment: Carlyle an opponent of, 7–9; challenged from within by Burke, 43–46; destroyer of the aura, 281; Keats's adherence to, 103; naturalized conception of knowledge, 23, 265
Epstein, Joseph, 156
Erdman, David, 75

Ferry, David, 303n5
Firkins, O. W., 147
Fish, Stanley, 21–22
Flaubert, Gustave, 289
Foucault, Michel: antihumanist, 279–280; intellectual historian, 275–277; on *epistemes,* 21–22, 276–277; self and subject, 277–278, 306n21; use of metaphor, 26, 294n11
Fox, Charles James, 63
French Revolution: Burke's reaction to, 46, 48, 53, 54–55, 57; Cobbett's changing view of, 89, 91; Keats on, 103; Windham on, 82
Freud, Sigmund, 259, 275
Friedman, Michael, 63
Frost, Robert: biography, 238–240; poems reviewed by Edward Thomas, 207–208; self-reliance, 222–224, 239
WORKS: "Love and a Question," 223; "Oven Bird, The," 202; "Provide, Provide," 144, 239; "Road Not Taken, The," 209; "Spring Pools," 209–210; "Two Tramps in Mud Time," 219–226; "Wood-Pile, The," 17–19, 207–208

Fry, Roger, 253, 257
Fuller, Margaret, 148, 150, 151–152
Furbank, P. N., 248

Galton, Francis, 40–42
Gay, John, 187
Geertz, Clifford, 259
Ghiselin, Michael, 295n30
Gillespie, Neal, 295n31
Goethe, Johann Wolfgang von, 2, 115
Goodman, Nelson: on world-making, 259–263
Greenberg, Clement, 157–158
Gross, John, 12

Hallam, A. H., 234
Hamilton, Ian, 241–242, 243–245
Hardy, Thomas, 198
Hartman, Geoffrey, 303–304n11
Hazlitt, William: Cobbett's character described by, 83, 90; critical idiom compared with Pater and Wilde, 128–131; elective affinity, 119; genius defined by, 24–25; historical critic, 113–114; impression, 124, 129–130; individual taste, 10–12; interest, 106–110, 118; Napoleon the "one alternative" for, 101; prose, 107, 129; skepticism regarding genre, 113; sympathy, 107, 120; worldly objects, 113
Hemingway, Ernest, 303n10
Hertz, Neil, 275–276
Hesse, Mary, 294n10
Hirsch, E. D., 268
Historicism: in Burke, 44–46, 53–56; in Wordsworth, 26–27; revision of Enlightenment naturalism, 20–21; tolerant and intolerant, 199; with no hands, 280
Hobbes, Thomas, 50–51, 294n11
Homer, 116
Hopkins, Gerard Manley, 94
Howells, W. D., 156
Hoy, David, 305n3